GIVE ME LIBERTY, NOT MARXISM

LTC ROBERT L. MAGINNIS

Author of *Collision Course* and *Deeper State*

DEFENDER

CRANE, MO

Give Me Liberty, Not Marxism: Globalists' Transformation of America and the Coming One-World Government

By LTC Robert L Maginnis

All rights reserved. Published 2021. Printed in the United States of America.

ISBN: 9781948014465

A CIP catalog record of this book is available from the Library of Congress.

Cover illustration and design by Jeffrey Mardis.

All Scripture quotations from the King James Version unless otherwise noted.

Dedicated to those Christians over the past century who resisted Marxism in places like the former Soviet Union and the current communist China, to win their freedom and stand firm for their faith in a religiously hostile, totalitarian environment.

Acknowledgments

I gratefully acknowledge …

My wife, Jan, is a godly woman who is my counselor and constant companion along life's journey. She encourages me and, best, prays for me every day, for which I'm eternally grateful.

Don Mercer, a fellow soldier and Christian brother, provided wise counsel and great edits to this, my eighth book. I treasure his advice, especially regarding the challenging issues related to Marxism because of his firsthand knowledge gained while serving as a US military attaché in the former Soviet Union and as a Russia specialist for the US Army, Pentagon, and at the Central Intelligence Agency.

Every writing project begins with a seed of an idea but matures thanks to the Lord's guidance, which ultimately shapes the outcome to fit His purposes.

Robert Lee Maginnis
Woodbridge, Virginia

Contents

Section III
What Does a Marxist Great Reset Mean for America?

Section IV
How Marxists Take Over the World, and What Follows

Preface

An American-style Marxist revolution picked up momentum with former Vice President Joseph Biden's 2020 presidential election victory, and now with his cabal of co-conspirators, he is in the process of remaking America alongside his globalist allies, who together just might doom this country to historic oblivion. Could this be the catalyst that explains the absence of America in biblical end-times prophecy and ushers in the biblically anticipated one-world government?

Give Me Liberty, Not Marxism examines the evidence for this possible outcome by providing an objective review of the histories of past Marxist regimes, accounts that are juxtaposed with the political proposals of those who, such as Mr. Biden, seek a global "Great Reset" that produces a radically different America that becomes subordinate to a godless, totalitarian one-world government that might be ruled by the communists in Beijing.

Specifically, section I in three chapters provides a primer on the "isms" that dominated the 2020 election's political discourse—capitalism, Marxism, socialism, communism, and progressivism—and how each rose to prominence in America and their contribution to the ongoing cultural revolution testing America's foundation.

Section II in five chapters identifies co-conspirators (the Democratic Party, the Communist Chinese Party, our leftist public education establishment, America's mainstream media, Satan and his army of demons, secret societies, and a host of Marxist-inspired ground troops like Antifa) who fuel the current Marxist-inspired American revolution and how they are each contributing to redefining this country in preparation for a coming one-world government and likely the prophetic end times.

Section III in three chapters demonstrates how these co-conspirators are changing America's civil liberties and key institutions like family and faith in preparation for this country becoming a member state in a future one-world government ruled by a Marxist and globalist elite.

Section IV in two chapters addresses the Marxist-inspired global Great Reset, which parallels many markers associated with the biblical end times and concludes with a description of the coming pre-Rapture life and how Christians can prepare for such a tragic future.

Give Me Liberty, Not Marxism charts a fictional and destructive American journey into the future that reflects on real history, Marxist ideology, and end-times prophecy. How will this journey end? Is Mr. Biden and his cabal of co-conspirators leading America to end-times irrelevancy and along a glide path to forming a one-world totalitarian government? Is America one of the ten horns (end-times nations) mentioned in Revelation 17:12 to become subordinate to that one-world government? Perhaps neither outcome will happen, but at this point, that's the story being created across Washington and among the globalists elite.

What's clear is that America will never be the same again unless true patriots rise to put people who love our Constitution back in Washington's seats of power and this country turns its heart and soul back to God!

Section I

Modern Marxist Revolution
Comes to America

America faces perhaps the most serious threat ever to its freedom. It's a threat that comes from within (with outside encouragement) and is present with our key leaders, starting with President Joe Biden, a weak, manipulatable man who came to the White House through hook and crook, and who now could be the instrument to usher in a dangerous, lasting ideological shift in this country.

US Senator John Kennedy (R-LA) said it best on Fox News that Mr. Biden and his leftist allies "will run America like they run Chicago," a frightening reference to that troubled city known for leftist, corrupt politicians, oppressive anti-freedom policies, a poorly managed infrastructure, high taxes, and extraordinarily high levels of violence. That's a Marxist-style and radically different type of governing and social environment compared to where America began.[1]

America from its founding was a land of opportunity where citizens thrived because they enjoyed the freedom to prosper. That outcome was embedded in our system of government with first principles that included equality, liberty, and limited government. America became the envy of the world because she reflected Christian values like charity and protecting the disadvantaged, and its form of government gave us a system of wise checks and balances to mitigate against man's many flaws.

All that is changing, thanks to leftists—arguably the Marxists—now creeping into positions of power, which includes Mr. Biden and his phalanx of administration appointees and a host of elitist supporters.

Mr. Biden brought to the Oval Office a team that represents leftist ideologies, and with the help of the left-leaning (socialists, progressives) in both the US House of Representatives and Senate, they will ride atop a true revolution that aims to change America's foundation and culture forever.

The first chapter in this section is a primer on the isms that dominated the 2020 election political discourse—capitalism, Marxism, socialism, communism, and progressivism. Understanding these ideologies is key to understanding what is happening to America and is the material addressed throughout the balance of *Give Me Liberty, Not Marxism.*

The second chapter shows how and why Marxism and its byproducts—socialism, communism, and progressivism—rose to prominence in America. Their goal is to transform the nation into something its founders would not recognize.

The third chapter demonstrates that the isms created a cultural revolution that is severely testing America's foundation.

1

Understanding the Isms
of Contemporary American
Political Discourse

The election of Joe Biden to the American presidency was accompanied by the banter of a number of ideological terms used in a variety of derogatory or supportive ways. We must define those terms, their origins, and their consequences to establish a starting point for this volume.

These descriptive isms were used as both nouns and adjectives in the 2020 political discourse—capitalism, Marxism, communism, socialism, and progressivism—but too few Americans really understand the differences, much less the background and implications of each, especially from a Christian worldview perspective.

For most people, these isms became throw-away labels meant as adjectives modifying personalities (e.g., "She's a socialist," or "He's a progressive") and ideas more often than not used in a derogatory fashion. Certainly in 2020, the political class at all levels used these isms to describe political philosophies and political figures or movements either to gain support or scandalize their opponents. However, these terms have serious meanings and implications for America's future, as well as for other societies that may embrace them either as the basis for governance or for influencing their way of life.

For me, an evangelical Christian, I will define and describe each of these isms from my biblical worldview perspective. That's where I begin this volume, and these definitions and my Christian perspective will guide the development of their impact for the American experiment going forward into the middle of the twenty-first century and especially the immediate dangers posed by the Biden administration that may embrace or excuse the most dangerous of these isms.

CAPITALISM

Now you know my credo: Free-market capitalism is the best path to prosperity. And let me add to that from our Founding Fathers: Our Creator endowed us with the inalienable rights to life, liberty, and the pursuit of happiness. In other words, freedom.[2]

—Lawrence Kudlow, director of the
National Economic Council

We begin with perhaps the most commonly understood ism associated with the American experience: capitalism. It might surprise the reader to know that many Americans are ignorant concerning capitalism and many prefer alternatives like socialism.

A 2019 Pew Research poll found that 39 percent of Americans have both a positive view of capitalism and a negative view of socialism, "a quarter have positive views of both terms and 17% express negative opinions about both. Another 16% have a positive opinion of socialism and a negative opinion of capitalism."[3]

While two-thirds (65 percent) of Americans have a positive view of capitalism, they demonstrate a lack of understanding of the system. One middle-aged man spoke truth to Pew by paraphrasing a famous quote attributed to the World War II-era British Prime Minister Winston Churchill: "Capitalism is the worst way to set up a society, except for all the other ways…. Free markets allow for more innovative solutions and for more people to succeed."[4] That man was the exception, however.

Criticism of capitalism among those polled included the allegation that it creates an unfair economic structure, whereby only a few benefit from the system. Others claim capitalism "has an exploitative and corrupt nature, often hurting either people or the environment." And yet others (8 percent), according to Pew, mentioned that "corporations and wealthy people undermine the democratic process by having too much power in political matters. And 4% of those with a negative view say that capitalism can work, but to do so it needs better oversight and regulation."[5]

What is capitalism? It is the engine (economic system) that made and keeps America prosperous. I also believe it is the best economic system known to man and closest to the biblical prescription for mankind. In other words, I begin this volume with a description of the biblical "right way" to understand how wealth and means for creating wealth are controlled and owned. Capitalism is the vehicle that fuels free enterprise, allowing individuals to operate businesses with minimal government interference, but the state does have a role enforcing laws that protect property rights and maintaining a stable currency.

David Landes, an economic historian and nonbeliever, explained that religion provided the engine behind the West's great economic success. Specifically, Landes said the Judeo-Christian religions provided the individual with the "joy in discovery" granted by the Creator; acknowledged the value God attaches to hard and good manual work; subordinates nature to the will of man without reservation; prescribes linear time, which can result in progress for one's efforts; and grants respect for the market.[6]

Capitalism—the essence of what Landes described above—came

about thanks to the Roman Catholic Church in the Middle Ages, according to historian Randall Collins. The Church found the correct mixture of rule of law and bureaucracy to resolve economic disputes, the specialization of labor and investment, and allowed for the accumulation of wealth empowered by the individual's zest for enterprise and wealth creation.[7]

Capitalism really began to fully blossom under the tutelage of the Catholic Church at the advent of the Industrial Revolution, which together transformed the world of enterprise. That marvelous marriage—Church and Industrial Revolution—sparked competition and created markets for products like mechanical clocks, grist mills, ship rudders, and eyeglasses, and the production of iron and much more came to fruition thanks to human innovation and the engine of capitalism.

The coincidence of invention and the steady hand of the dominant, bureaucratic rule of law by the Catholic Church, which owned at the time nearly a third of all Europe, provided the environment for capitalism to flourish. The Church administered its resources via Church-based bureaucracies of arbitrators, negotiators, judges, and a common law that impacted every aspect of life to include the economy, known in Latin as the *jus canonicum*, or canon law.[8]

The Order of Cistercians, a Catholic religious order of monks and nuns, gave capitalism the spark to encourage entrepreneurs. The Cistercians created a system of cost accounting, practiced the reinvestment of their profits back into their businesses, and moved capital among their various businesses to optimize their return and even cut their losses in order to pursue better investment opportunities. In fact, the Cistercians came to dominate iron production in France; as historian Randall Collins wrote, they were the first founders of "the Protestant ethic without Protestantism."[9]

The Catholic Church also brought "spontaneous order" to the emergent markets, explained Friedrich August von Hayek, one of the most influential economists and social theorists of the twentieth century. This was necessary because it gave way to predictable economic activity, a necessity for markets to develop. That concept of stability, thanks to economic rules, meant that if France needs wool, "prosperity can accrue to the English sheepherder who first increases his flock, systematizes his fleecers and combers, and improves the efficiency of his shipments," according to Michael Novak, writing for the Acton Institute.[10]

The evidence is undeniable: The Catholic Church played a critical role in the creation and success of capitalism, especially in the Western world. However, the Church helping to create capitalism as an economic system does not necessarily mean that capitalism, per se, has a biblical endorsement. After all, economics influences many of our life choices, and those decisions should be governed for the Christian by a biblical worldview.

It is true that the Bible nowhere mentions capitalism, but it does address characteristics and behaviors that are consistent with biblical principles. For example, the book of Proverbs deals extensively with economic matters and attitudes toward acquiring and handling wealth (e.g., Proverbs 10:15; 11:28; 14:20; 18:11; 19:4; 28:11).

The Bible acknowledges the worth and dignity of every individual in the eyes of God. Capitalism as an economic model affords each person the best opportunity (dignity) to succeed subject to their talents, skills, intelligence, and effort applied. That doesn't mean it promises equal outcomes, but it does offer equal opportunity and encourage hard work.

There are numerous Scripture passages that address man's sin nature, which provides caution to believers when applied to their economic realm. For example, God grants humans the right to own property, and, as Genesis 1:28 states, the right to exercise dominion over the earth. That translates to property ownership and the opportunity to use it as one sees fit, such as exchanging it for other goods and services—evidence of a free market.[11]

The Bible calls us to be good stewards of our property. After all, God committed the world's resources to humanity (Genesis 1:28–29). Obviously, capitalism grants to men, who are made in the image of God, the opportunity to be good stewards of those God-given resources, which allows them to exercise their judgment to grow His property, albeit honestly. Yes, that outcome is evidence of exercising self-interest, which is supported by New Testament obligations to be accountable for ourselves and our actions (e.g., Matthew 12:36; Romans 14:12; 1 Corinthians 4:2).

We are also instructed to exercise wise stewardship within the free market, but that opportunity risks the emergence of sinful behaviors, such as laziness and neglect. That is why biblically we are each held accountable for our own productivity.[12]

Capitalism also embraces the scriptural principles of equality and liberty, which influence our treatment of others (e.g., Galatians 3:28–29; Acts 2:1–47). Liberty is a key biblical principle that must not be flaunted, as warned about in verses like Romans 14:22 (CSB): "Whatever you believe about these things, keep between yourself and God."

Individually, each person enjoys the freedom to use his or her talents and gifts through entrepreneurial efforts, thanks to capitalistic economies and without government interference. Success is more often than not a product of personal effort.

Admittedly, modern capitalism has its flaws, which are mostly attributable to the sinful nature of man. Specifically, sometimes government interferes in the marketplace by granting exclusive rights to certain entities, thus creating unfair monopolies. There are also instances of people in positions of power who use their stature for improper gain. That's a sin in God's Word, such as in Ephesians 6:9 (NASB): "And masters, do the same things to them, and give up threatening, knowing that both their Master and yours is in heaven, and there is no partiality with Him."

The Bible calls on believers to be generous, especially to the less fortunate. This issue comes up most often when considering the human flaw of greed (Jeremiah 17:9), which is often highlighted by critics, and especially when Christians appear to be greedy, thus spoiling their witness. What's not disputed in the free-market, capitalistic system or by the Bible is that some people use capitalism to satisfy their lust for greater wealth, but that's a moral issue, not the fault of the system. What's true, however, is that capitalism grants both the moral and immoral person equal opportunity.[13]

Finally, Christian charity is the opposite of greed and is encouraged for believers. The biblical concept of charity is infused in capitalism by what Dante Alighieri describes in his narrative poem the *Divine Comedy* as *caritas*, "The love that moves the sun and all the starts." *Caritas* is the glue that holds families and nations together and promotes honesty and mutual respect, which are biblical concepts and key ingredients in a functioning capitalistic economy.[14]

Also, there's nothing biblically wrong with exercising self-interest, which is starkly different from being selfish. An adult with a family to feed exercises self-interest by earning wages in a capitalistic system to support his/her family.

In conclusion, capitalism is successful because, when properly implemented, it employs the principles of liberty, equality, and numerous biblical values. Admittedly, it is abused by man's sinfulness, which is a human, not a system, flaw. What's clear—and will become more evident as we review the other economic-related isms—is that capitalism is the superior system from biblical, productivity, and sociological perspectives.

MARXISM

My object in life is to dethrone God and destroy capitalism.[15]
— Karl Marx, author of *Das Kapital*

Black Lives Matter (BLM) is a Marxist movement, according to Carol Swain, a Black conservative and former professor at Vanderbilt and Princeton universities. Ms. Swain said, "Now, the founders of Black Lives Matter, they've come out as Marxists."[16]

Patrisse Cullors, one of the three cofounders of BLM, said in a 2015 interview, "We do have an ideological frame. Myself and Alicia, in particular, are trained organizers; we are trained Marxists. We are super-versed on, sort of, ideological theories. And I think what we really try to do is build a movement that could be utilized by many, many Black folks."[17]

Black Lives Matter is known for race-based violence and alignment with the Democratic Party's radical leftist agenda. But what is Marxism if these radicals are "trained Marxists"? BLM is not the garden-variety Marxism, as I'll explain below. No, it's neo-Marxism that redefines today's fight to incorporate biological sex, race, ethnicity, and much more.

These neo-Marxists distort original Marxism to mean most everything and reduce it to a war between "oppressors" versus the "oppressed." The BLM neo-Marxists target "oppressors" for punishment. But it's important to realize, as we explore Marxism below, that not everyone who claims to be a Marxist is true to Marx's original intent, which is radical enough.

What is classical Marxism? It is a political philosophy developed by Karl Heidrich Marx, a nineteenth-century German philosopher, economist, historian, sociologist, political theorist, journalist, and socialist revolutionary. Marx's philosophy focuses on class struggle to ensure an equal distribution of wealth for all citizens and illustrates the inequality created by the ruling class in a capitalistic system that historically oppresses the lower (working) classes, thus triggering social revolution that creates a classless society, where there is no private property and every citizen gives selflessly to the good of all persons. This ideal model is variously called socialism (communism) or progressivism, examples of Marxism explored in this chapter.

Marx's theory is perhaps best known for its sharp critique of capitalism, which claims that workers in a capitalist system are little more than a commodity, "labor power." This economic clash, which is set forth in Marx's 1859 book, *Das Kapital*, creates a conflict between the proletariat (workers who transform raw commodities into goods) and the bourgeoisie (owners of the means of production), which has a "built-in" inequality. The bourgeoisie, with the help of government, according to Marx, employ social institutions against the proletariat. Marx argues in his writings that capitalism creates an unfair imbalance between the bourgeoisie and the workers whom they exploit for gain, and those inherent inequalities and exploitative relations ultimately lead to revolution that abolishes capitalism and reconstructs society into a socialist form of government.

Of course, Marxism addresses more than just the inequalities between the proletariat and the bourgeoisie. It is a comprehensive ideology—some call it a religion—that expresses a broad worldview about most aspects of ordinary life and society that are contrary to a Christian, biblical worldview.

Marxist Worldview

Summit Ministries, a Christian organization, provided a thumbnail sketch of the Marxist worldview across major categories, which are summarized and elaborated on by me below.[18]

First, Karl Marx was a devout atheist from the time he was in college. In 1844, he wrote, "The abolition of religion as the illusory happiness of the people is required for their real happiness. Religion is the sigh of the oppressed creature, the heart of a heartless world, and the soul of soulless conditions. It is the opium of the people." He also said religion is a "spiritual booze," and that putting his atheism into practice meant a "forcible overthrow of all existing social conditions," which included economic structures like capitalism, but Marx makes government his god—the provider, sustainer, protector, and lawgiver. Meanwhile, atheistic aspects of Marxism became a trademark of communist regimes like the old Soviet Union and the present-day Peoples Republic of China, which is known for the persecution of religious Muslims (especially Uighurs in the western province of Xinjiang) and Christians alike.

Second, Marxist philosophy is known as dialectical materialism, which is another name for naturalism. The concept says there are polar opposite states of being—one is the thesis and the other the antithesis, which inevitably clash. That struggle produces a new thesis (way things are), which eventually clashes with a new antithesis. This is an evolutionary process, a series of steps not that different from Charles Darwin's theory of evolution (spontaneous generation): inorganic substances evolve into life; single-celled life becomes animals and then humans.

Third, Marxist ethics or proletariat morality means that whatever advances the working class is good and, by association, whatever hinders that progress is morally evil. The logic of extension of class morality is evidenced by communist China's former leader Mao Zedong, who committed mass murder of perhaps forty million people who allegedly opposed the advances of the working class.

Fourth, Marxist psychology leaves no room for the spiritual dimension, because all behavior is purely based on the material. He argues that human behavior is the result of purely material reasons, physical makeup (genetics), and outside environmental influences. He argues that our brain is programmed to react a certain way, and our socialization (education, background, etc.) causes us, like Pavlov's dog, to respond to outside stimuli.

Fifth, a classless society is Marx's vision for sociology whereby everyone is the owner and employee; there are no class distinctions. That means there is no need for government or outside influencers, because the owner/employee will always act responsibly. Translation: The working class' (proletariat's) sovereignty is the rule in Marx's world, a view traced to his concept of private property (Marxist law). The basis for this law is to protect social or state property that advances socialism and evolution. Once socialism is victorious, explains Marx, then the working class will realize its communist paradise, and law is no longer needed.

Sixth, a communist world government is Marx's ultimate political vision. He believed the working class will rise up, overthrow the bourgeois oppression to seize power, and establish a worldwide "dictatorship." That is the next evolutionary step to world government, and once bourgeois ideology is vanquished and all traces of capitalism are history, then a communist society exists—a utopia on earth.

Seventh, Marx believes economics determines the nature of all legal, social, and political institutions. He blames social problems on imperfections in the modes of production, and over time evolution makes things better—slavery became feudalism, which gave way to capitalism, which will become socialism and eventually communism. The final step in his economic determinism view is a socialist society where there is no private property, whereby man is oppressed by his fellow being, which leads to a classless society, communism (the highest economic state).

Marxism: The Religion

It is important to put Marx's rejection of the existence of God into proper perspective. Marxism seeks to replace all religions with itself, and a major fault with his theory is that Marx believed in the perfectibility of man while rejecting the perfect God.

Although Marxism rejects the existence of God and labels religion as an "opium," Marxism is a true religion to its followers. Consider Marx's background and perhaps come to appreciate how he substituted his Marxist religion for Christianity.

Karl Marx was born to a Prussian attorney who converted to Christianity in order to practice law. Marx's father introduced Karl to the greats—gods at the time—Frederick the Great; the Prussian state and Enlightenment thinkers like John Locke, who saw human nature as a blank page; and Jean-Jacques Rousseau, who wrote, "We do not know what our nature permits us to be."[19]

Marx's Christian background was thanks to religious training in the Prussian school system, which he abandoned once at the University of Bonn, and after that at the University of Berlin, where he joined the "Young Hegelians (German: *Junghegelianer*)," a group of German intellectuals who reacted to the writings of Georg Wilhelm Friedrich Hegel, the father of progressivism.

Marx wrote in his PhD dissertation at the University of Jena (Thuringia, Germany) his view of the deities: "In truth, I hate all gods."

He continued, "I shall never exchange my fetters for slavish servility." Marx spent his life arguing against the existence of the God of the Bible and in fact he sought in his work to create an entirely new religion based circumspectly on a mirror image of Christianity.[20]

"Marxism retains all the major structural and emotional factors of biblical religion in a secularized form," wrote Boston College philosopher Peter Kreeft. "Marx, like Moses, is the prophet who leads the new Chosen People, the proletariat, out of the slavery of capitalism into the Promised Land of communism across the Red Sea of bloody worldwide revolution and through the wilderness of temporary, dedicated suffering for the party, the new priesthood."[21]

Ulster University economist Esmond Birnie shared that view. "The deep structure of Marxism parallels that of Christianity," he said. "It has a 'fall' event—the concentration of ownership of property in the hands of the capitalists—and a 'chosen people,' the proletarians—as well as a coming 'day of judgment,' when capitalism is replaced by the classless society."[22]

Marx essentially displaced Christianity with an alternative faith, Marxism, which at its core rejects God but is very much a religion. As one author states, it replaces monotheism with mono-statism, whereby all authority rests with state government. In fact, Pavel Hanes, an associate theology professor at the University of Matej Bel in Slovakia, wrote: "Marx himself insisted that an atheistic state predicted in his philosophy would be a perfect realization of the essence of Christianity."[23]

Professor Hanes' "essence of Christianity" view is shared by German philosopher Karl Löwith, who believed that "Marx's historical materialism is a secularized version of Christian teleology" (the explanation of phenomena by the purpose they serve rather than by postulated causes), according to Bryan S. Turner, a British and Australian sociologist. Löwith wrote Turner that he "treats Marx's philosophy of history as a global vision that depends fundamentally on the Christian scheme of eschatology, the doctrine of the Last Days and the Restoration of man to Grace."[24]

Marxism and Christianity do not mix, however. Marxism never works. The Marxist-inspired brutality realized in communist governance is a human tragedy. Even the late Martin Luther King Jr. addressed the issue in a 1953 sermon: "Communism and Christianity are at the bottom incompatible," he said. "One cannot be a true Christian and a true Communist simultaneously.... They represent diametrically opposed ways of looking at the world and transforming the world. We must try to understand Communism, but never can we accept it and be true Christians."[25]

Marxist-inspired communism has a documented history of failure, with many anecdotal testimonies. Laura M. Nicolae, who fled communist Romania, wrote about communism in her former homeland:

> Communism cannot be separated from oppression; in fact, it depends upon it. In the communist society, the collective is supreme. Personal autonomy is nonexistent. Human beings are simply cogs in a machine tasked with producing utopia; they have no value of their own. Thankfully, we serve a God whose valuation of those he has made in his own image led him to send his Son to take the penalty for our sins as he hung on a cross. The God-man Jesus of Nazareth came gladly to save us and sent his Spirit to live within us. This is transformation. This is the beginning of a whole new humanity and a whole new world.[26]

Differences between Marxism and Christianity

The Bible doesn't use guilt as a weapon. Marxism and especially the neo-Marxists use collective guilt as a weapon, a significant contradiction with Christianity. Neo-Marxists like BLM claim that all white people bear the guilt of past slave owners, and if Caucasians remain silent, they are accused of violence.

Marxism uses a broad brush to accuse large segments of society with guilt, such as Marxist BLM supporters who say white people bear the guilt of sins committed by former slave owners. Yet Christianity holds that we are accountable to God alone for our sins.

No Scripture passages tell Christians to cast guilt on entire people groups; rather, the sins of a nation are God's to address, not fellow humans. This view is expressed in Ezekiel 18:20 (NIV): "The one who sins is the one who will die. The child will not share the guilt of the parent, nor will the parent share the guilt of the child. The righteousness of the righteous will be credited to them, and the wickedness of the wicked will be charged against them."

God deals with humans on a personal level. We become Christians by asking Jesus to save us, forgive us of our sin, and become Lord of our lives. Issues of guilt were addressed at Calvary, and no ideology or group can replace the ultimate forgiveness that Christ grants believers.

The Bible endorses the ownership of private property. Earlier, I established that Marxists embrace a materialistic worldview. Simply, the concept is that when a society shares everything in common, life becomes a utopia, according to Marx. However, the abolishing of private property runs contrary to the teachings in the Bible, such as the injunction in Deuteronomy 5:19 (ESV), which commands, "And you shall not steal." Stealing presumes private property ownership. Further, 2 Thessalonians 3:10 presents the requirement that people must be willing to work to eat; once again, there is no entitlement to another's property without labor in exchange. Even Jesus' parable of the bags of gold (Matthew 25:14–30) becomes non sequitur as an application where there is no private property.

Marxism claims that man will reach the point where he is solely satisfied with possessions, and God becomes irrelevant. However, common sense and decades of observing human behavior demonstrate that wealth in itself breeds sin, not satisfaction. The fact is that numerous verses in Scripture illustrate the spiritual nature of mankind (e.g., Job 32:8; Ecclesiastes 12:7; Proverbs 20:27; Romans 8:16).

Marxism is the source of much sin. After all, classical and especially neo-Marxists like those in the BLM movement are filled with anger and resentment. Instead of demonstrating the virtues of peace, love, and thankfulness, they tend to be violent and coveters, demonstrating sins that are specifically condemned in the Scriptures. For example, Exodus 20:17 says we must not covet our neighbor's possessions, and in the New Testament, we are encouraged to be content "in every situation" (Philippians 4:11–13).

The Bible focuses on spiritual things. A major distinction between Marxism and Christianity is the different views of material and spiritual matters. Marxism focuses on man's physical (material) needs, while Christianity, as Jesus explained in Matthew 6:26, 33 (NIV) focuses on the spiritual: "do not worry about your life, what you will eat or drink; or about your body, what you will wear. Is not life more than food, and the body more than clothes? …But seek first [God's] kingdom and his righteousness."

Marxism promotes division, not equality. Marxism is divisive. For example, "group identity" is everything to neo-Marxists like supporters of the BLM. By contrast, America's founders fought the British to create a level ground that promoted the first principle of equality. Further, for the Christian, Christ erased all cultural and ethnic/racial barriers to God. The Apostle Paul wrote in Galatians 3:28–29 (NLT): "There is no longer Jew or Gentile, slave or free, male and female. For you are all one in Christ Jesus. And now that you belong to Christ, you are the true children of Abraham. You are his heirs, and God's promise to Abraham belongs to you."

Karl Marx, as explained earlier, discriminated against all people of faith. He called for the abolition of religion and as noted earlier, he compared it to opium (an intoxicating drug). He also claimed, "My object in life is to dethrone God." And that view of religion is evident even today where Marxism prevails: Christians are oppressed.

In conclusion, Marxism is an anti-Christian theory that rejects biblical freedom and personal responsibility. Besides, it sets itself up as a religion exclusively focused on the unrealistic vision of an earthly utopia and the perfectibility of mankind. It has never attained—nor ever will attain—its utopian goal because of its view of man. Efforts to follow Marx's prescription in places like the old Soviet Union will always result in massive suffering at the hands of dictatorial governments.

SOCIALISM

The American people will never knowingly adopt socialism. But, under the name of "liberalism," they will adopt every fragment of the socialist program, until one day America will be a socialist nation, without knowing how it happened.[27]
　　　　　—Norman Thomas, six-time presidential candidate
　　　　　　　　　　　　for the Socialist Party of America

The 2020 election was a petri dish for socialism, and it came up short. A post-election analysis by US Representative Abigail Spanberger (D-VA) found that Democrats shouldn't say the word "socialism" "ever again." Why? It was a major political loser in the 2020 election cycle, according to Spanberger—which, evidence suggests, was one of the reasons Joe Biden lost in Florida and was a major disappointment for so-called Democratic socialists like Senators Elizabeth Warren (D-MA) and Bernie Sanders (I-VT), who celebrated their socialist credentials during the campaign and promised more of the same for America's future.[28]

Bernie Sanders explained his perspective for his beloved socialism. He said, "To me, democratic socialism means democracy."[29] But to conservatives like former President Ronald Reagan, "Socialism only works in two places: heaven where they don't need it and hell where they already have it."[30]

Most every astute American knows that socialism earned considerable press during the 2020 election cycle, but according to veteran pollster George Barna, that support didn't come from many Christians. He found that 98 percent of Americans who support socialism reject the biblical worldview. "The 2020 election is not about personalities, parties, or even politics," Barna explained. "It is an election to determine the dominant worldview of America."[31]

What is socialism? It is the realization of the social and economic theory attributed to Karl Marx that embraces state ownership of all property and the means of production. This idea of sharing of wealth in society theoretically results in a classless society where everyone is equal and the distribution of the means production is the chief characteristic. Not surprisingly, it is in direct opposition to capitalism.

Socialism depends on Marx's wrongheaded assumption about life based on the Hegelian dialectic, which is explained in the earlier section on Marxism—thesis, antithesis, synthesis—which is a social evolutionary theory much like Charles Darwin's evolution of the species. The problem for Marx and socialism in particular is that, with hundreds of years of empirical evidence, it is capitalism, not socialism, that works. Economist Paul Samuelson observed, "As a prophet Marx was colossally unlucky and his system [socialism] colossally unuseful."[32]

Socialism is not just "unuseful," as Samuelson wrote, but it is dangerous, because it leads to big government, and, as F. A. Hayek, a twentieth-century British-Australian philosopher, observed, centralized and big-government planning inevitably leads to dictatorship. A simple study of socialist leadership over the past century conclusively demonstrates that such leftist authorities promise freedom but end up delivering only misery and tyranny.

The evidence is conclusive: Socialism is an abject failure across time and continents, from the Marxism-Leninism in Soviet Union and Maoism in China to so-called democratic-socialism in Sweden and national socialism in Nazi Germany. Across time, socialists who survived have been forced to consistently compromise Marx's original vision by embracing aspects of capitalism such as economic zones and foreign investment, to name just a couple.

The best-known socialist experiment, the Soviet Union, couldn't be saved by Mikhail Gorbachev, who tried *perestroika* ("restructuring") and *glasnost* ("openness"). Those efforts ended with the lowering of the Soviet hammer and sickle (the Soviet Union's national flag) for the last time on Christmas Day 1991. Much the same outcome happened in communist China in the late 1970s, when Deng Xiaoping compromised Maoist ideas of socialism to accept more capitalist ways, such as enterprise and foreign investment. Unfortunately, the communist Chinese were sufficiently flexible to adjust their adherence to Marxism in order to maintain control of that nation unlike their communist Russian peers.

Socialism also long ago failed in America when Robert Owen (1771–1858), an English philanthropist, invested much of his fortune in the experimental socialist community at New Harmony, Indiana. That nineteenth-century experiment lasted about two years before Owen returned to London.[33]

Unfortunately, empty socialist promises still inspire people today in spite of a record of total failure across the globe. Specifically, socialism manifests itself in some Western countries where there is increased reliance on big government, centralized programs such as universal healthcare, and massive social welfare programs. These policies are key to modern socialism, which advances the view that communal sharing helps society prosper.

Perhaps it isn't surprising that some socialist ideas regarding healthcare, climate change, free education, and government assistance for the needy all poll well today, especially among American Millennials (born 1981–1996), who tend to favor socialism thanks to sympathetic mainstream media reporting and the influence of the public educational establishment that more often than not advocates for leftist philosophies. By contrast, older-schooled Baby Boomers (born 1946–1964) tend to favor capitalism, a result of their histories—and, not surprisingly, these Americans are often labeled by Millennials as indifferent to the needs of the common man for their opposition to socialist ideas.

Those differences in view across the generations beg the question: Just what makes someone embrace socialism? Perhaps part of the attraction is a result of personality or youthful idealism. After all, some young people who favor socialism tend to be very personable themselves and feel good about sharing and collaboration, as opposed to being competitive. They tend to believe the greatest good comes from self-sacrifice for the common good, and they aspire to redistribute resources until everyone is equal, a reflection of Marx's well-known exhortation: "From each according to his ability, to each according to his needs."[34]

Our public educational establishment tends to endorse socialism as well. After all, who hasn't heard true accounts of the socialist-leaning teacher, school administrator, and/or coach who promotes equal outcomes for all the children on sports teams? They don't keep score and they don't like labels like "winner" or "loser." That's why every member of the team gets a participation trophy at the end of the season—because it's all about everyone feeling equal, no matter one's talents and contributions.

At the aggregate economic level, the socialist is passionate about the equal distribution of financial resources, and he/she becomes quite upset when there are disparities in society whereby some people are obviously very wealthy while others live a meager existence. The socialist expects the strong arm of government to rectify those disparities and is upset when that doesn't happen.

The extreme version of socialism is communism, which is profiled in the next section of this chapter. However, for now, consider that these people, according to one author, are an exaggerated version of the socialist person profiled above, but with a vengeance. The communist's psychological profile is best described by terms like defeatism, deceptive hypocrisy, low self-esteem, and the tendency to be delusional about their theoretical notion of equality.[35]

These psychological characteristics are on full display most every day in the halls of the US Congress. Leading socialist activists like US House of Representatives Congresswoman Alexandra Ocasio-Cortez (D-NY), a member of the Democratic Socialists of America (DSA), earns considerable attention and support, especially among socialist-leaning younger Americans. She calls for government ownership of industries such as railroads and coal mines, and would "democratize" private businesses to give the workers total control, a Marxist idea. Not surprisingly, the DSA national steering committee called for the "democratization of all areas of life, including but not limited to the economy."[36]

Even though socialism may still not be an integral part of the Democratic Party's public platform, some of those closely associated with the party, like Senator Sanders, a hard-core socialist, pushes the party to implement socialist policies—albeit gradually—and, like what Norman Thomas, a former presidential candidate with the Socialist Party of America, said, they will press that agenda as they did with Joe Biden "until one day America will be a socialist nation, without knowing how it happened."[37]

Socialism's Worldview

Below is socialism's worldview followed immediately by a biblical perspective of this ism.

First, socialism is an expression of Marxism, a belief that the material universe is all that exists—or, said otherwise, it is an atheistic belief system. It places total trust in the evolution of man to create a utopia, and holds that, once we die, there is no afterlife.

Christianity was a favorite target of Marx because of its concept of a fixed human nature. Marx's disciples, especially Vladimir Lenin (1870–1924), waged a campaign of terror against Christian churches in Russia, where he executed priests and violated nuns. For socialists like Lenin, these horrors were a necessary part of the Marxist-inspired and necessary class warfare.

Second, socialism, in spite of protests from its proponents, is a kind of faith system, like most religions. Like all religions, socialism answers three key questions about ultimate reality, the nature of mankind, and what can man achieve in this life. The socialist worships his/her god—Marxist socialism.

Third, the socialist is totally focused on human existence. That doesn't mean those socialists who have a faith in God don't perhaps embrace aspects of true socialism, but it is an issue they must somehow hybridize.

Fourth, socialists believe in the evolution of man from the animal species, and their focus is on human life in this world. There is no hereafter, says the socialist. Therefore, they exclusively focus on the survival of the human race and do whatever is necessary to ensure that the species thrives.

Fifth, socialism embraces moral relativism because it doesn't believe in absolute moral laws that transcend mankind (God). However, socialists do recognize the need for moral rules to prevent chaos; these rules are imposed by their political masters.

Sixth, socialism advocates central control of the economy with the goal of equity across the entire population. That means the government is expected to take resources from those who earn it and give it to others who need it. They do this by creating a centralized authority that plans the production and distribution of all products and services.

Seventh, socialists accept centralized political control in order to enforce equity across society, which translates into the need for a ruling class to make and enforce the rules. The end result in every case of socialism is that the ruling class becomes some form of dictatorship, with all power vested in a single political party or a strong-man dictator like China's President Xi Jinping and the ruling Chinese Communist Party.

The consequences of socialism are tragic. There are millions of people living today who can testify to the ravages of socialist tyrants like those in China. Obedience to the will of the party is expected; there is no alternative.

The American author Richard N. Wright (1908–1960) wrote the following about socialist tyranny: "At that [socialist] meeting I learned that when a man was informed of the wish of the Party he submitted, even though he knew with all the strength of his brain that the wish was not a wise one, was one that would ultimately harm the Party's interests."[38]

French Nobel laureate André Gide spoke bluntly after visiting the

Soviet Union: "I doubt whether in any country in the world—not even in Hitler's Germany—have the mind and spirit ever been less free, more bent, more terrorized and indeed vassalized—than in the Soviet Union." Gide said that "the Soviet Union has deceived our fondest hopes and shown us tragically in what treacherous quicksand an honest revolution can founder."[39]

Even the American journalist Louis Fisher, who once boasted of the Soviet Union's advances, provided a stark picture of that regime: "Ubiquitous fear, amply justified by terror, had killed revolt, silenced protest, and destroyed civil courage. In place of idealism, cynical safety-first. In place of dedication, pursuit of personal aggrandizement. In place of living spirit, dead conformism, bureaucratic formalism, and the parrotism of false clichés."[40]

Eighth, socialism is not biblical, but is a Marxist method of execution, and it runs contrary to Bible teachings. Consider key areas where socialism and Christianity diverge, in spite of the fact that, according to a George Barna poll, many Americans think Jesus was a socialist (24 percent) as opposed to a capitalist (14 percent).[41]

Socialism: Antithetical to Christian Teachings

Socialism focuses on an earthly (material) heaven and rejects a spiritual heaven. Further, it defines salvation in terms of material goals rather than the biblical teaching of a spiritual salvation. It assumes that sinful man can overcome the effects of sin through social engineering.[42]

Socialism's materialistic worldview contradicts biblical Christianity, which teaches that man's problems are mostly spiritual. The cause of man's suffering is his sin, and his salvation is found only in Christ, who came to earth to die for mankind's sin.

Socialism also distributes resources without regard to need and effort. After all, Marx said, "From each according to his ability, to each according to his needs."[43]

That means the socialist punishes those who excel in industry and rewards those who don't necessarily contribute to the common welfare by working hard. By contrast, the Bible states that anyone who refuses to work ought not eat (2 Thessalonians 3:10).

Translation: Socialism approves of stealing from the more prosperous (hard-working) and then turns over resources (wealth) to the less fortunate. Famously, former president Barack Obama expressed that socialist view to a young girl: "We've got to make sure that people who have more money help the people who have less money. If you had a whole pizza, and your friend had no pizza, would you give him a slice?"[44]

Obama evidently endorses the forced redistribution of wealth—a socialist, not a biblical, value. After all, as illustrated above, socialists don't believe in private property. By contrast, the Bible calls on Christians to protect private ownership while encouraging believers to share their resources with the less well-to-do as God's Spirit directs.

Socialism also creates class warfare by blaming the wealthy for all problems. Socialist Senator Bernie Sanders illustrates the point: "Let us wage a moral and political war against the billionaires and corporate leaders on Wall Street and elsewhere, whose policies and greed are destroying the middle class of America."[45] That view is contrary to Scripture verses such as Proverbs 14:31 (NIV), which states, "Whoever oppresses the poor shows contempt for his maker," but socialists like Sanders condemn the wealthy as a class and encourage revolution to overthrow them, what Hillary Clinton called "toppling" the top 1 percent of Americans.[46]

Socialists like Sanders and evidently Clinton misunderstand that the wealthy are not stealing from others, but create products and jobs for the broader population. Further, Scripture does not demand the transfer of money from the wealthy, but it teaches us not to covet (Exodus 20:17) and to be content in all circumstances (Philippians 4:11–13).

Socialists are not pro-marriage and family. Marx's coauthor of *The Communist Manifesto* (1848), Friedrich Engels, proposed that the government strive for a future whereby "the single-family ceases to be the economic unit of society. Private housekeeping is transformed into a social industry. The care and education of the children becomes a public affair."[47]

Sanders said much the same. He called for a "revolution" in child-care, beginning with all six-week-old children.[48] Further, he's a proponent of so-called gay marriage as a means, perhaps, to destroy traditional Christian marriage.[49]

In conclusion, socialism has a violent, bloody history and offers no hope for humanity either in this life or the next.

As a final nail in the socialists' coffin, we see in *The Black Book of Communism* (1999) that there have been at least one hundred million victims of socialism (communism). That volume documents that every Marxist socialist regime to date exclusively existed thanks to the muzzle of a gun and forced labor camps—no exceptions, from Cambodia's Pol Pot to China's Mao Zedong and to the present socialist regime in Venezuela.

Let there be no doubt that socialism is a religion itself grounded in political tyranny where its god (big government) fails, its theory (Marxism) never works, and its social structure/political system always destroys the lives of the people it is set up to support.

COMMUNISM

There is no difference between communism and socialism, except in the means of achieving the same ultimate end: communism proposes to enslave men by force, socialism—by vote. It is merely the difference between murder and suicide.[50]

—Ayn Rand, twentieth-century Russian-American writer and philosopher

Many people use the terms "Marxism," "socialism," and "communism" interchangeably, perhaps because they mistakenly believe they are the same philosophies. It is true that these philosophies are related, and in fact Marxism provides the foundation for the economic and political philosophies of both socialism and communism.

A major distinction between socialism and communism is the necessity for the public to own all property and means of production and services. The centralization of ownership gives everyone a chance to develop their very best, or so the theory contends.

Karl Marx believed there is a natural progression from socialism to communism. The first step is for the proletariat (the workers) to push the bourgeoisie (the wealthy owners) out (translation: "kill them"), then society would evolve into a classless utopia without a government, a concept found in Marx and Friedrich Engels' book, *The Communist Manifesto*. That text states:

> [Communists] are, on the one hand, practically, the most advanced and resolute section of the working-class parties of every country, that section which pushes forward all others; on the other hand, theoretically, they have over the great mass of the proletariat the advantage of clearly understanding the line of march, the conditions, and the ultimate general results of the proletarian movement.[51]

Communism is the extreme version of socialism, which, like the original ideology, Marxism, is atheistic to its core. Invariably, socialism given license eventually morphs into communism marked by tyranny, suffering, and death.

The biblical differences noted earlier between socialism and Christianity also apply to Marxist communism, but on steroids. History exposes the bloody path of communism's march through Russia, China, Venezuela, and elsewhere. Fundamentally, that toll is the result of communism's stark failure to recognize a higher moral authority; without a constraining god, even mass murder is permissible as the means to pursue the communist's utopian social goal.

Unfortunately, there are some rather naïve people who believe communism is in fact somewhat acceptable. They express that view by offering a sympathetic portrayal of communist ideology and try to reconcile it with Christianity. One such person is Dean Dettloff, who wrote in *America*, a Jesuit magazine, an article, "The Catholic Case for Communism," that attempted to reconcile the similarities of communism and the Catholic Church's teaching.

Mr. Dettloff compares the communist view about the class struggle with that of the Catholic Church. "For communists, global inequality and the abuse of workers at highly profitable corporations are not the result only of unkind employers or unfair labor regulations," he writes. "They are symptoms of a specific way of organizing wealth, one that did not exist at the creation of the world and one that represents part of a 'culture of death,' to borrow a familiar phrase."[52]

Further, "Although the Catholic Church officially teaches that private property is a natural right, this teaching also comes with the proviso that private property is always subordinate to the common good," wrote Dettloff.[53]

Long ago, comparisons like that above between communism and Christianity were condemned, however. Paul Kengor, the author of *The Devil and Karl Marx* (2020), wrote: "In 1846, Pope Pius IX released *Qui pluribus*, [an encyclical subtitled 'On Faith and Religion'], affirming that communism is 'absolutely contrary to the natural law itself' and if adopted would 'utterly destroy the rights, property, and possessions of all men, and even society itself.' In 1849, one year after the [*The Communist*] *Manifesto* was published, Pius IX issued the encyclical, *Nostis Et Nobiscum*, which referred to both socialism and communism as 'wicked theories,' 'perverted theories,' and 'pernicious fictions.'"[54]

Communism and religion (especially Christianity) are incompatible, as history demonstrates. That's because communist tyrants refuse to share their authority over the people and all social institutions with any other group, especially the Christian God. This all-encompassing authoritarian focus explains why the Soviet Union, the world's best-known communist regime failed, a surprise to many.

At the beginning of 1991, the year the Soviet Union collapsed, it was the largest country in the world (one-sixth of the earth's land surface), with 290 million people. It had tens of thousands of nuclear weapons and a massive military presence that extended deep into Europe. But it failed because of many flaws directly attributable to its Marxist foundation.

First, the Soviet Union collapsed because politically it didn't have the tools to right its failing economy. Mikhail Gorbachev became the secretary of the Communist Party in 1985 and quickly tried to jump-start his flagging economy. That failed, so he instituted policies of openness (*glasnost*) and restructuring (*perestroika*). Gorbachev's openness created a groundswell of criticism for the entire Soviet apparatus. That restructuring welcomed the lifting of Soviet-era price controls, but the overseeing of those controls was left to the well-embedded Soviet bureaucracy, who vigorously resisted the new approach—which resulted in its failure, because the corrupt bureaucrats didn't benefit directly.[55]

Second, as late as 1990, the Soviet economy was the world's second largest, even though it suffered from major shortages of consumer goods. That explains the Soviet Union's massive black-market economy that perhaps accounted for at least 10 percent of the country's gross domestic product (GDP). Besides, economic stagnation at the time crippled the nation, which was exacerbated by the government's mismanaged fiscal policy (a Marxist economy) and accompanied by a sharp drop in the price of oil, the country's prime source of foreign currency.[56]

Third, the Kremlin accelerated its defense spending in response to President Ronald Reagan's announced Strategic Defense Initiative, an ambitious project to construct a space-based, anti-missile system dubbed "Star Wars." That 1983 announcement shocked the Kremlin and pushed it to invest more in defense the nation could ill afford. At the time, the military budget already consumed somewhere between 10 and 20 percent of GDP, which ignored the other critical needs of the nation; quickly, the fiscal weight of new defense spending became an unsustainable drain on the country's dwindling resources.[57]

Fourth, Gorbachev's *glasnost* awakened Soviet citizens to just how bad things were at home in comparison with the West. That openness brought new ideas and experiences to a Soviet citizenry accustomed to bland food, shabby clothes, and hopeless lives. Meanwhile, Russians began to explore, thanks to *glasnost*, ideas about democratization and experimented with Western-style food and other imported goods. Quickly the population became disillusioned, mostly disgusted with the country's endemic corruption and poor quality of life.[58]

Aleksandr Yakovlev, Gorbachev's adviser, described the problem: "The main issue today is not only economy," he said. "This is only the side of the process. The heart of the matter is in the political system... and its relation to man." That was the legacy of Marx's idea about socialism, its view about the nature of man and the state's role and its objection to religion, a source of hope for a desperate people.[59]

Finally, the Soviet Union was humbled by its nuclear industry. Throughout the Cold War (1947–1991), the world teetered on the edge of mutual nuclear destruction, but it took the implosion of a civilian nuclear reactor, the Chernobyl power plant in Ukraine, to expose the world to Russia's serious shortfalls. That disaster released more than four hundred times the amount of radioactive fallout as the atomic bomb dropped on Hiroshima (Japan), but communist officials in Moscow at the time suppressed the truth about the disaster.[60]

The Kremlin responded to the unprecedented catastrophe using the same approach it always employed when faced with a serious problem: it lied. After all, the entire Soviet society was based on so many lies that no one knew the real truth, and thus that flaw characteristically hobbled most decision-making. Meanwhile, Western media and governments accused Moscow of "malicious lies" for what the Kremlin characterized as a "misfortune." As a direct result of Moscow's lies about the reactor incident, much of the world quickly lost all trust in the Soviet's account, and, according to Gorbachev, who marked the anniversary of the disaster decades later, the regime's misinformation campaign "was perhaps the real cause of the collapse of the Soviet Union five years later."[61]

In conclusion, what's clear is that communism is the most extreme version of socialism. The demise of the Soviet Union demonstrates that view in terms of its economic and political failures, especially in terms of the trust it squandered with its citizens and much of the world.

PROGRESSIVISM

Progressivism is the cancer in America and it is eating our Constitution, and it was designed to eat the Constitution, to progress past the Constitution.[62]
—Glenn Beck, American political commentator

Contemporary progressivism is the new communism with a twist. It is a social and political movement that promotes unreason and irrationality through the guise of various social justice causes.

Progressivism didn't start out that way, however. In fact, it had many redeeming qualities in the late nineteenth and early twentieth centuries. Progressive ideology at its origin was about making use of or being interested in new ideas, findings, or opportunities. It was, as I explain in *Progressive Evil* (Defender, 2019), "about the advancement and adoption of social reform for the amelioration of society's ills. Progressives through the ages have come from all backgrounds, claiming they promote freedom of the individual to compete in fair conditions while championing the progress and improvement of society." That has all changed.

Modern American progressives flushed out the good from the original movement and embraced a Marxist approach to changing society not that different from past communists. Much like the old Marxists, who gave the task of leading a revolution to overthrow the capitalists to revolutionaries, today's revolutionaries are progressive politicians, social justice reformers, and civil rights warriors who permeate our media, government, education establishments, and workplaces.

Their goal, like the old Marxists, is to set things right through social change in order to create a more just society by advancing equality between men and women, immigrants and citizens, people of color, heterosexuals and homosexuals, the disabled and able-bodied, and more. These postmodern progressives share a vision of a society free of all the modern social isms—sexism, nativism, racism, heterosexism and other so-called perceived communal injustices.

The individual's ability is not a discriminator for the progressive, which is also an aspect of Marxist theory. For the progressive like the Marxist communist and the socialist, private property ought to become taboo in favor of state-controlled resources.

A key aspect of postmodern progressivism is the use of the central, big government to force these changes. Progressives need government to advance civil rights laws and a living minimum wage, to provide housing, to provide guaranteed income, and much more. After all, for the progressive, big government is the blunt instrument that advances equality for all citizens and ultimately leads to utopia.

It's not surprising that postmodern progressives are truly intolerant when it comes to conservative views. They reject our constitutional safeguards (rights)—the right to exercise free speech, freedom of religion, and the right to bear arms—which explains their efforts to rewrite our Constitution in order to grow the government's control over every aspect of life, from healthcare to managing our economy.

They also, in the name of social justice, favor radical directives that put women in frontline ground combat and require public schools to allow K–12 transgender students to use the bathroom or locker room of their choice.

Progressives want to subordinate our national sovereignty to leftist supranational bodies like the United Nations and welcome the introduction of Islamic law (sharia) into our communities, which is contrary to our Constitution, and they also welcome oversight from international tribunals (courts) at the expense of our own sovereign judiciary. Then there is the matter of welcoming a flood of illegal immigrants, and they expect the US to embrace global strategies to address issues like climate change.

How do progressives intend to reach these lofty outcomes? As I said earlier, much like socialist and communist revolutionaries who replaced the so-called oppressive class (the bourgeoisie), progressives intend for the heavy hand of government to create overseers (bureaucrats) who inevitably become corrupt and eventually morph into little tyrants and dictators. Also, they enlist the support of nongovernment radicals like those in BLM and Antifa (the so-called left-wing, political-movement anti-fascists) to do their bidding.

We shouldn't expect postmodern progressives to be any better than communists at restraining the tendency to embrace tyranny, because they suffer from the same ideological deficiencies. For example, communist and progressive ideals of equality aren't realistic, because they ignore the true, sinful nature of mankind. After all, fallen man is competitive by nature, and he will never settle on being an equal among his peers. Rather, he will always strive to improve his lot first, whereby the stronger man always subjugates the weaker—the ingredients of dictatorships.

Just like the communists who built their utopian "proletarian state" in the former Soviet Union through a corrupted bureaucratic class that denied basic freedoms, the social justice progressives today will use the strong arm of big government to enforce affirmative action that tolerates certain types of racism and allows so-called gay liberation activists to trample the rights of Christians.

You see, progressive politics ultimately divides people through identity politics and results in intergroup conflicts across various religions, races, sexual orientations, and economic groups.

Postmodern progressivism is also as anti-biblical as its other fellow isms—Marxism, socialism, and communism. It hates the True God and His followers. It will do everything the other isms endorse that advances an anti-religion future, and it especially targets Christians, who are harbingers of ill content for the dedicated progressive.

In conclusion, postmodern progressives are nothing like their forefathers who sought change to improve their lives. Rather, they are dead set on weakening our constitutional rights—speech, faith, bearing arms—to fit their radical Marxist ideology. They seek to destroy our key institutions—family and faith—to fit their social justice agenda, and ultimately, they will lead this country to ruin, much like the former Soviet tyrants did to communist Russia.

CONCLUSION

This chapter is a primer that sets the stage for the balance of *Give Me Liberty, Not Marxism*. It provides a summary of the isms used across the culture, especially within America's contemporary political discourse. Too few Americans really understand the distinctives of each ism—capitalism, Marxism, socialism, communism, and progressivism—their relationship with one another, and particularly their perspectives about Christianity.

In the next chapter, I will demonstrate the significant influence of these isms for America's future and how these ideological concepts became a major influence within the Democratic Party and specifically within the Biden administration.

Marxist Isms Come to and Remain in America

The isms spawned by Marxism are growing in popularity among Americans, as demonstrated by a host of national surveys. That begs the question: What fueled this rise? The short answer to the question is that a number of key institutions were taken captive by Marxist radicals, and now they advance these ideologies.

ISMS GROWING IN POPULARITY

Socialism is a philosophy of failure, the creed of ignorance, and the gospel of envy, its inherent virtue is the equal sharing of misery.[63]

—Winston Churchill, former British prime minister

There is a shift in America toward favorability for the isms, especially socialism and progressivism, but it has not as yet reached a simple majority. However, the size of that cohort will change as the younger, more isms-supporting generations, age and their attitudes continue to shift the general population to the left.

Evidently, the lapse of decades makes a big difference in American adults' view about socialism in particular. A 1942 Roper/Fortune survey found that 25 percent of Americans at the time considered socialism a good thing, compared with 43 percent in 2019.[64] The fact that a quarter of Americans favored socialism at the height of World War II, when we were fighting Germany's National Socialists (Nazis), is a rather troubling finding.

It is also noteworthy that Americans' definition of socialism has changed over the intervening decades. Today, Americans associate socialism with social equality in places like Sweden, while only 17 percent correctly associate it with the degree of government control over the means of production—much less the broader implications of the ideology outlined in the previous chapter.[65]

Those polls that compare views fifty years apart also measured Americans' outlook about the future of democratic, communistic, and socialistic governments during the future fifty years. When one juxtaposes the responses in 1949 with those in 2019, we find an expectation that there will be more socialist (fourteen versus twenty-nine) nations in the next fifty years, significantly fewer democratic (seventy-two versus fifty-seven) nations, and slightly fewer communist (nine versus six) nations.[66]

Today (2021), Americans who favor socialism tend to fall into two camps: self-identified Democrats and the young. A national poll hosted by NPR/PBS *NewsHour* found that approval of socialism declines as age rises. In 2020, 38 percent of Gen Z (born 1996–2015) and Millennial (born 1981–1996) respondents had a favorable view of socialism, and perhaps not surprisingly, so did half of all Democrats and two-thirds of all self-identified progressives.[67]

An early 2020 poll asked voters to judge a statement about socialism, which demonstrated a clear ideological divide in the country. The statement read: "The country would be better off if our political and economic systems were more socialist, including taxing the wealthy more to pay for social programs, nationalizing health care so that it's government-run and redistributing wealth." Not surprisingly, four in five self-identified "strong Democrats" from all age cohorts agreed with the statement, while Republicans strongly disagreed (83 percent).[68]

That poll question came about in the wake of a 2020 debate prompted by President Trump's statement at his State of the Union, "America will never be a socialist country."[69] Not everyone agreed. Overwhelmingly, 77 percent of self-identified Democrats told a pollster they believe the country would be "better off" under a socialist leader, and overall, four in ten Americans accept some form of socialism or socialist policies.[70]

Those are disturbing figures, and either these people really don't understand the consequences of socialistic policies or they are truly radically inspired to ruin this country. Groups like the Victims of Communism Memorial Foundation (VOC) are particularly concerned about the drift of the isms among Americans.

A 2020 poll by the internationally recognized research and data firm YouGov explored the popularity of the isms for the Victims of Communism (VOC) Memorial Foundation. That poll, which sampled 2,100 representative US respondents ages sixteen and older, found that one in three (37 percent) has a favorable view of Karl Marx's seminal work, *The Communist Manifesto*. It's not clear, however, what those respondents knew about the work, much less about the bloody, oppressive history of Marxism and its offspring, communism.

The VOC called out the survey's disturbing findings about communism. The foundation's press release states that communism is a threat to liberty, especially religious liberty. It cited the story of Father Tomislav Kolakovic, who escaped Nazi Croatia to land in Soviet Czechoslovakia. The priest quickly recognized the communist threat and established a secret church in his new home to prepare the believers there for the rising communist oppression by hosting mock interrogations and surveillance tactics training.[71]

The VOC report included many troubling findings about American views associated with Marxism, communism, and socialism. Those findings include:[72]

- Over a quarter of Americans (26%) support the gradual elimination of the capitalist system in favor of a more socialist system with a surge in support among younger generations (31% of Gen Z and 35% of Millennials).

- 18% of Gen Z and 13% of Millennials think communism is a fairer system than capitalism and deserves consideration in America.

- 30% of Gen Z has a favorable view of Marxism, up 6% from 2019, compared to 27% of Millennials, down 9% from 2019.

- Over one-third of Americans (39%) are likely to support a member of the Democratic Socialist party for office with greater support among younger generations (51% of Gen Z and 44% of Millennials). 16% of Gen Z and Millennials are likely to support a member of the Communist Party for office.

- 63% of Gen Z and Millennials (compared to 95% of the Silent Generation), believe the Declaration of Independence better guarantees freedom and inequality over the Communist Manifesto, a 6% increase for Millennials from 2019.

- One-third of Americans (33%) believe Donald Trump is the biggest threat to world peace over Xi Jinping [China], Kim Jong-un [North Korea], Nicolás Maduro [Venezuela], and Vladimir Putin [Russia], a 6% increase from 2019.

- 32% of Americans think that Donald Trump is responsible for the deaths of more people than Kim Jong-un.

- Nearly two-thirds (64%) of Americans say they are unaware that the Chinese Communist Party is responsible for more deaths than Nazi Germany.

- 47% of Americans believe Xi Jinping of China is more responsible for COVID-19 becoming a pandemic than Donald Trump; however, a higher proportion of Gen Z believes that Donald Trump is more responsible (39%).
- Over a quarter (26%) of Americans think climate change is the number one threat to national security over the rise of the People's Republic of China or Russian expansionism. The greatest concern for climate change is seen among younger generations (38% of Gen Z and 30% of Millennials).
- Over half of Gen Z (51%) think that America is a racist nation with a long history of discrimination.
- Only 44% of Gen Z thinks that the American flag most accurately represents freedom.
- Americans increasingly distrust the government to take care of their interests, with 87% saying they trust themselves over the government and their community (a 7% increase from 2019). This is especially the case in younger generations, with only 6% of Gen Z and 5% of Millennials trusting the government to take care of their interests, down 8% and 11% from 2019, respectively.
- 12% of Gen Z and 10% of Millennials think society would be better off if all private property was abolished and held by the government.
- 53% of Americans think a good government should favor the freedom of its citizens over the safety of its citizens.

Progressivism wasn't included in the VOC report, but it is quite similar to socialism and is growing in popularity among Americans. The ideas behind progressivism come from Marxist socialism, and, ultimately, they share the same goal of improving the lot of the worker at the expense of the corporate establishment and intend to use the arm of government to make that happen and destroy capitalism in the process.

It should concern every capitalist and democracy-loving American that the number of self-identified progressives in the US House of Representative is now nearly one quarter of that body.[73] In fact, in 2020, progressives took home more victories to begin solidifying their base in Congress. However, they didn't win all their races, which they blamed in part on Republicans who correctly identified them with other, less-popular socialists. After all, according to the Democrat socialist from New York, US Representative Alexandria Ocasio-Cortez, "These [Republican efforts to align progressives with socialism and their related policies] were largely slogans or they were demands from activist groups," such as calls to defund the police. The congresswoman, a member of the Democratic Socialists of America, complained that "Republicans levied very effective rhetorical attacks against our party" by linking Democrats like her with the more radical socialist issues. However, some progressive issues earn significant support even among Republicans.[74]

The significant and growing presence of self-identified progressives in Congress is a testimony to the popularity of progressive policies across the electorate. A 2019 CNBC All-American Economic survey found that progressive policies "are bread and butter kitchen table issues that families are dealing with if you're making less than $75,000 and I think that's contributing to the fairly high Republican support numbers," according to Micah Roberts with Public Opinion Strategies. His firm surveyed the American people regarding leading progressive issues and found significant support for a federal requirement that employers provide paid maternity leave (84 percent), increased federal funding for childcare (75 percent), increasing the federal minimum wage to $15 (60 percent), tuition-free state and public colleges (57 percent), Medicare for All (54 percent), and a universal basic income (28 percent).[75]

In conclusion, numerous national polls demonstrate the American people in large and growing numbers are supportive of the isms—even the most harmful, like socialism and Marxist communism. Many Americans may not realize the connection among the isms and that radical applications of these isms across the span of a couple hundred years has produced some very terrifying outcomes.

WHAT FUELED THE RISE?

The previous section of this chapter demonstrated through public opinion polls that the Marxist-inspired isms have growing support among Americans. The question this section addresses is: What prompted that support?

Marxism's Rise in America

There are some devout Marxists in America, as indicated above based on polling, but most Americans influenced by Marxism aren't even aware of their manipulated state because they are hoodwinked by the present cultural revolution. Marxism's influence is rising in America on the crest of a cultural revolution that is part violent and part ideological, but leaves on this nation a clear Marxist fingerprint.

Long ago, Americans gave a home to Karl Marx's destructive ideology within our educational establishment, the mainstream media, Hollywood, some corporations, our arts and science communities, within many churches, and among the political class—especially the Democratic Party.

The root of that insurgency was mostly nonviolent and came to roost thanks to Marx's "dialectical materialism," a concept developed in the first chapter that creates social division. I explained in the earlier chapter that Marx, like his ideological mentors, Georg Wilhelm Friedrich Hegel, a nineteenth-century German philosopher, and Charles Darwin, a nineteenth-century British naturalist, disallowed all things spiritual and focused exclusively on "materialism" and the idea of evolution, mankind's alleged progress to perfection.[76]

Cultural Marxism is the perversion of the original ideology that contemporary American radicals use in the revolution now impacting this country. Simply, and I repeat from earlier, cultural Marxism is the social and political phenomenon that promotes unreason and irrationality through the guise of various social justice causes.

Cultural Marxism walks through three stages of a deconstructionist revolution across American society: dehumanizing persons, demoralizing relationships, and decivilizing institutions. Each stage is played out by the various agents of change fueling this revolution.

These contemporary Marxists are quite skilled at dehumanizing persons, a clear anti-biblical concept. We see this evident vis-à-vis identity politics—racism, sexism, and group victimhood. This process hurts culture, demoralizes relationships, and destroys social trust as it did in the big American city riots of 2020.

The Marxist emphasizes the material and ignores the spiritual component of humans, especially moral rights and wrongs. To the current flock of cultural Marxists, we humans are no more than pieces of flesh without purpose other than to sustain this earthly existence, doing only that which feels best for the majority. The values America once represented—family, faith, and freedom—are gone, and in their place, Marxists litter our ideological landscape with nihilism ("a viewpoint that traditional values and beliefs are unfounded and that existence is senseless and useless").[77]

The institutions that formed America's foundation are mostly gone. After all, institutions like the family and the church are based on relationships, understandings, and covenants that, in a dialectical, materialistic world, mean nothing, because civilization itself and truth are gone, thanks to Marxism. So, the Marxist decivilizes our critical institutions

Another perspective is shared by John Andrews, a former president of the Colorado Senate and vice president of Colorado Christian University. He explained that with life devalued vis-à-vis the deconstruction of America, a concept he attributes to George Orwell's anti-Marxist book, *Animal Farm*, there is a place where some animals like Napoleon the pig (a character in that book) are more equal than others.[78]

The Marxist concept that some animals (humans) are more equal than others, according to Andrews, is part of the deconstructive effort of the neo-Marxist Black Lives Matter (BLM) movement now tearing at our culture. BLM's founders are identified in the first chapter as proudly stating, "We're trained Marxists." Indeed. Their goal is to destroy our culture, decivilize our communities, and start a race war.

Unfortunately, too many Americans turn a deaf ear to these Marxist deconstruction efforts, which are evidence of pure evil. We must not as, Mr. Andrews wrote, chalk all our current turmoil up to wokeness and cancel culture or to the crazy machinations of the left like BLM. It's more, and this spate of violence and fascism won't end well if Marxism continues to fester within America and ultimately metastasizes across this nation.

Another view of the ongoing Marxist revolution playing out across America comes from Scott McKay, the publisher of Hayride, a website that offers news and commentary on Louisiana and national politics. Mr. McKay wrote a fascinating article for the *American Spector*, "The Four Stages of Marxist Takeover: The Accuracy of Yuri Bezmenov." That article explains that in 2020, America was at a revolutionary moment, a Marxist revolution mostly about disinformation. The revolution, McKay explains, is sponsored by intellectuals like billionaire George Soros who are pouring money into the destruction of America.[79]

Those Marxist intellectuals behind the American revolution recruited and helped install Joe Biden in the presidency to become a tool for advancing their transformation of America. After all, these conspirators believe that Mr. Biden is beneficial to them because he is manipulatable due to his clear deficiency of mental function and evidently given his diminished scruples vis-à-vis his alleged corrupt role with his seriously compromised son, Hunter Biden, known for financially leveraging his father's political position during the Obama administration. The taint of corruption from Hunter's dealings suggests that President Biden is possibly devoid of principle, a seriously compromised soul sitting in the Oval Office.

Mr. McKay makes the case that President Biden will be a weak and manipulatable leader much like the former Russian politician, Alexander Kerensky, who served as a vessel (translation: "useful idiot") for communist dictator Vladimir Lenin in the 1917 Russian revolutionary period. Kerensky was set up to be useful for the revolutionary cause and then was quickly removed so the real power brokers could step into the gap.[80]

The Marxist revolutionaries who set up Mr. Biden, much like those who used Kerensky as a temporary proxy, also hosted a low-grade kinetic revolution to complement their disinformation campaign. The most visible players of this second army of the revolution in the US are leftist groups like BLM, whose leaders openly acknowledge their Marxist training and their co-revolutionary partner, Antifa, whose members employ clear Marxist street tactics.

The disinformation part to this loosely coordinated revolution has recruits in legitimate public offices. Specifically, these disinformation insurgents are socialists like Congresswomen Alexandria Ocasio-Cortez, Ilhan Omar (D-MN), and Ayanna Pressley (D-MA). They and their allies have ideological tentacles reaching back to the Marxist Frankfurt School,[81] which helped create critical race theory ("a theoretical framework in the social sciences that examines society and culture as they relate to categorizations of race, law, and power") and intersectionalism to attack American institutions and culture. ("Intersectionality," according to Merriam-Webster, is "the complex, cumulative way in which the effects of multiple forms of discrimination [such as racism, sexism, and classism] combine, overlap, or intersect especially in the experiences of marginalized individuals or groups.")[82]

SOVIET TEMPLATE TO DESTROY FREE SOCIETIES:
ANOTHER PERSPECTIVE

This phalanx of Marxist revolutionaries and its team of useful idiots borrowed a template for taking down America from former communist Soviets. Likely, they aren't aware of the master plan that a Soviet defector and former KGB (Комитет государственной безопасности, Committee for State Security member) operative named Yuri Bezmenov shared in a 1984 interview. That doesn't matter because their masters know the plan well.[83]

Mr. Bezmenov was a KGB agent working as a propagandist before defecting to Canada. His interview outlined the Soviet's process (template) for bringing about the collapse of a free society and a Marxist takeover.

The Soviet template wasn't a top secret stored in a vault in the Kremlin. No, it was very much an open secret plan, but too often ignored, especially in the West. In fact, Nikita Khrushchev, who ran the Soviet Union from 1958 to 1964, was quite open in predicting the destruction of the United States and furthermore said it would happen in the way that every free society eventually collapses—internally and in accordance with the Soviet template.

"We will take America without firing a shot," Khrushchev said. "We do not have to invade the U.S. We will destroy you from within."[83]

I put Khrushchev's quote (above) at the top of the cover of my 2019 book, *Progressive Evil*, because I believe progressives like Marxists seek to destroy the America I love and remake it into something akin to a socialist, communist state. That conclusion remains my view and is relevant to the other isms as well. They share the goal of fulfilling Khrushchev's promise of remaking America into an impotent socialist, communist state controlled by amoral wealthy elites who seek to overthrow America from the inside out by redefining our rights, our institutions, and our ideals.

Khrushchev knew at the time how to do what he threatened would happen using a system of Marxist indoctrination that had already worked in numerous countries during the twentieth century. All of those countries came to embrace communism thanks to the infiltration of Marxist revolutionaries and the fulfillment of the KGB's transforming template.

Mr. Bezmenov knew about the template not just from his own experience but also from his father, who was a high-ranking Soviet military official also trained as a KGB operative and who applied the revolutionary template in India and in various countries in the Warsaw Pact (Eastern European) community of nations.

Fortunately, the KGB's template failed in America, at least until now. Scott McKay attributes the Soviets' failure to effectively apply the template to the United States to President Ronald Reagan, who led this country to a Cold War victory over the Soviet Union before the template took root. It never happened, because Reagan understood Marxism and communism and had the vision to apply pressure on the Soviets that resulted in the regime's collapse, something explained in the first chapter of this volume.[84]

President Reagan warned at the time of the Soviets' collapse that future generations of Americans must not rest on their laurels regarding freedom. He explained that our freedom is never more than a generation from extinction and cautioned us not to become complacent and forget about the ideological threat posed by the isms, especially communism. Unfortunately, many of America's younger generations today don't understand the Marxist, communist threat and how insidious it was during the Cold War and remains today, playing itself out before our eyes through the mechanism of cultural revolution.

Mr. Bezmenov detailed in his 1984 interview the four-stage Soviet template his father used to destroy free Eastern European societies. Unfortunately, aspects of these stages are being played out in the US today.

Step One – The first stage of the Soviet template is demoralization, which Mr. Bezmenov saw in the radicalization of America's educational institutions during the anti-Vietnam war era of the 1960s and early 1970s. Evidently, according to Bezmenov, the radicals who took control of America's educational institutions at that time intended to discard traditional Judeo-Christian morality, classical education, and American patriotism. Unfortunately, as we reflect on that time, that's exactly what happened. Today, America's leftist-leaning public educational establishment has successfully drained away most past appreciation for our rich history, especially the common sense of patriotism and understanding of basic civics.[85]

Long ago, America's public education establishment aligned itself with other cultural Marxist elites in our leftist media, particularly the entertainment media (Hollywood), which became dead set on turning America's youth against this country. The result of this neo-Marxist propaganda spewed across America was demoralization, the belief among our youth that their civilization was lost and, as Mr. McCay illustrated, "Why do you think ordinary white people are so willing to apologize for the sins of their ancestors and to confess to being racist without even knowing it?"

Step Two – The second stage of the Soviet template is to destroy a free society through destabilization. Mr. Bezmenov explains that this step is the "rapid decline in the structure of a society—its economy, its military, its international relations." This should sound familiar to anyone who lived through the year 2020 in America. After all, many state governors, especially Democrats, mandated COVID-19 shutdowns that shuttered much of America's economy in spite of contradictory medical facts. Meanwhile, many of those same, hysteria-mongering leftists sought to destabilize America by piling on every aspect of society to rob the population of all hope. Even the leftists in Congress ratcheted up their dire rhetoric, and then there was an outbreak of disorder in America's streets that triggered widespread insecurity.[86]

Remember the outrage you likely felt when first you heard the story of Mark McCloskey, the St. Louis attorney who stood outside his home armed with an AR-15 and with his pistol-waving wife at his side? They stood there watching as BLM trespassers broke down their private community gate and stormed their private housing area while shouting threats of murder and arson. Meanwhile, Mr. McCloskey told Fox News that local police refused to protect them, as did private security firms that encouraged them to flee the violent mob.

Scenes of destabilization like what the McCloskeys experienced in St. Louis were too common throughout much of the 2020 summer months in mostly Democrat-controlled cities like Seattle, Portland, New York, Chicago, and Minneapolis. The Marxists' second stage had its intended effect of robbing Americans like the McCloskeys of their sense of stability.

Step Three – The third stage of the Soviet template is crisis, which builds on the previous stages. The election year 2020 had one national crisis after the other, beginning in January with only the third presidential impeachment in American history, a constitutional crisis totally manufactured by radical Democrats. When impeachment failed to remove Mr. Trump due to a lack of evidence, that crisis was quickly followed by China's Wuhan-launched COVID-19 crisis, which created widespread panic, shuttered much of our economy, and ultimately silenced the US for months. Then, just as the nation was flattening the virus' infection curve, another crisis erupted: the George Floyd riots.[87]

Mr. Floyd was a convicted felon who was drunk on an illicit drug (fentanyl) at the time of his arrest when he was accidently killed by a police officer. Quickly, Marxists used that incident to justify violent protests, riots, looting, and arson that destroyed many blocks of major American cities. Also, leftists—all Democrats, holding offices from mayor to Congress at the time—used that crisis to pile on more issues by calling for Marxist changes like defunding the police, because, as the radicals explained, law enforcement discriminated against people of color and, besides, society no longer needs policing, or so complained the looney left and their mainstream media mouthpieces.

Step Four – The fourth and final stage of the Soviets' template to destroy free societies is normalization, or establishing a "new normal." This happens when the dust of all the instability and crises settles and people naively accept all the changes that took place during the instability—restrictions on their freedoms, a depressed economy, mandated behavior regarding health precautions like wearing protective face masks, and much more—all the savage changes introduced allegedly to fight the virus and address social-justice issues imposed by dictatorial, fascist-acting Democrat governors and leftist mayors.[88]

Finally, after the four stages of the Soviet's template had their way with the people, in November 2020, America elected a new president— or that's what the mainstream media announced. We may never know whether fraud tipped the election balance scales, as many Trump supporters firmly believe. Mr. Biden, a man known for his mental incapacitation, was elected and could eventually be removed by his behind-the-veil puppet masters citing the Twenty-fifth Amendment, which deals with issues related to presidential succession and disability, much like Lenin removed Kerensky. In Biden's place, America might find the died-in-the-wool, Marxist-inspired Vice President Kamala Harris, some unelected autocrat, or someone even worse, such as the third person in line for the presidency, Speaker of the House Nancy Pelosi.

In conclusion, the Marxist revolution that engulfed America years ago and accelerated in 2020 may continue for some time yet. Meanwhile, the transformation of American society to embrace Marxism thanks to the Soviet template is real, and it is here to stay.

Socialism's Rise in America

The Marxist-inspired cultural revolution described above aims to subvert our institutions and replace them with a state-based alternative unlike any previously known in America. Polls cited earlier in this chapter indicate that a significant percentage of young Americans have surrendered to the lure of the siren call of Marx's socialism, perhaps thanks to their mushy-headed, public, leftist education that favors an expanded welfare state, rigid anti-capitalist oversight of the private sector, and the heavy hand of government righting past wrongs on race, gender, and their sky-is-falling view of past environmental injustices.

Of course, there is nothing democratic about this revolution, and many of America's young enthusiasts for socialism are driving policies even farther left, and they expect Congress and the Biden administration to embrace their radical agenda; evidently, if the president's executive orders are any indication, that's exactly what is happening.

This cadre of modern American socialists embraces a notional utopian, Marxist expectation of progression for humans to perfection, which they believe can only happen where there is fairness, freedom, and full employment for life. Predictably, these modern, naïve socialists are well indoctrinated, because they believe that outcome only happens in a country graced with universal income, improved working conditions, and, of course, unionized employment enforced by a domineering big government that prevents industry from exploiting the workers. Translated into Marxian terms: The proletariat crushes the bourgeoisie.

Any American with two days in business understands that this socialist vision is a pack of lies—a pig with lipstick—because big government translates into the polar opposite of utopia. It means micromanagement by a legion of unelected bureaucrats, which bans individualism (entrepreneurship) and discourages innovation. And, like in the former Soviet Union, it festers with crony capitalism and a black market, and tramples on our Bill of Rights.

This socialist vision can't exist without first removing the old foundation, which is just what the cultural revolution intends to do. But the evisceration of our once-solid foundation started years ago and only now is beginning to show signs of success.

Socialism's Growing Popularity among Young Adults

Why has socialism become so popular? Certainly, the polling suggests socialism's rise is significant and, according to a YouGov poll, almost three quarters (70 percent) of Millennials and nearly two-thirds of Gen-Zs (64 percent) would vote for a socialist.[90]

There are a number of reasons socialism is growing in popularity, especially among our younger generations.

Capitalism Is Leaving Many Young Adults Behind

Capitalism isn't working for many young Americans; at least that's the way it's performing at this time.

That may explain why many young people are flocking to socialism. Evidently, as one young adult told the *Atlantic*: "There is a growing sense that the system is broken."[91]

A similar view about socialism's popularity is expressed by Joel Mathis, a freelance writer for the *Week*. He surmised that capitalism is perceived to be broken because it isn't improving American lives, which is prompting young people to look for better alternatives.[92]

Mr. Mathis dug deeper to suggest that our national leaders are setting up the country for a massive economic crisis that will land on the shoulders of the next generation. He cautions that the coming economic meltdown could lead to another great recession, which he attributes to loosening requirements for big banks, the ease with which banks grant high-risk loans, and a variety of other debt-producing actions—not to mention the massive spending surge thanks to COVID-19 relief.

On the minds of many young adults is the skyrocketing cost of college, which is especially burdensome, and evidence that the system isn't working for them. After all, ever-escalating college expenses are discouraging many young people about greedy capitalist universities. The facts about the costs for a higher education are sobering for many young Americans, chiefly when it comes to paying off that debt. Almost 70 percent of college students take out loans and graduate with an average debt of $29,900, and another 14 percent of their parents are left with an average of $37,200 in federal parent loans as well. The national impact is significant. Americans owe more than $1.64 trillion in student loan debt, across 45 million borrowers.[93]

No wonder socialists like Vermont Senator Bernie Sanders tap into that debt-related angst by promising young voters free college tuition or student-loan forgiveness. Alternatively, if big government abandoned the federal-grant and student-loan business, then colleges would be forced to price themselves at a level that applicants could afford or get out of the education-for-profit business altogether.

The fact is that many young people entering the job market are burdened with a discouraging load of student debt. That pinch on their monthly income causes them to look around and quickly conclude that capitalists rigged the economic game against them by creating a system that "lets money, property, power, and opportunity accumulate mostly at the very top of the food chain." This view is backed by big government action to spend large amounts of taxpayer money, thus adding to the national debt, which these already-discouraged young adults will face in the future.[94]

Growing government debt convinces many young adults that the system is indeed broken. Consider examples over the past decade whereby multiple administrations both Democrat and Republican threw trillions of taxpayer dollars at problems, thus adding to the national debt. In 2008, Congress passed and President George W. Bush signed the Emergency Economic Stabilization Act, which was designed to prevent the collapse of the US financial system. That act authorized the secretary of the Treasury to purchase up to $700 billion in mortgage-backed securities and other troubled assets from the country's banks.[95]

The following year, the newly elected President Barack Obama signed a stimulus package, the American Recovery and Investment Act of 2009, a $787 billion consortium of thousands of federal tax reductions and expenditures on infrastructure, education, healthcare, energy, and much more. It was allegedly intended to jumpstart the US economy out of recession.[96]

More recently, and thanks to the COVID-19 pandemic, Congress and the Trump administration launched a series of stimulus programs, adding trillions more to the national debt. At the end of 2020, the US national debt stood at $28 trillion, with annual tax receipts at maybe $4 trillion.[97]

Little wonder young Americans are frustrated with American capitalism and are looking for an alternative to the broken system's status quo. That view may explain why socialists like Senator Sanders are so popular when they talk about school-debt forgiveness, guaranteed healthcare for all, and higher taxes for the wealthy. Many young adults understandably conclude that since capitalism isn't working, then socialism ought to be tried.

LEFTISTS' PUBLIC EDUCATION ESTABLISHMENT

Perhaps the biggest factor contributing to the popularity of socialism is our public-school system. Today's young people enter the workforce believing in so-called democratic socialism and have no memory or understanding of the long, bloody history of destructive socialism. For many of these young people, socialism is fed by ignorance of the past, which is similar to the statement: It's "like seeing a group of people singing along to a song when they don't understand the lyrics."[98]

Our public education establishment fails the next generation by not teaching the importance of free markets and the destructiveness of socialism across the world and time. In fact, what modern teachers too often instruct is contempt for capitalism and a left-leaning, pro-Marxist, socialist worldview.

Why are many public educators so biased against capitalism and in favor of Marxist ideology? Because many teachers bring their biases and viewpoints into the classroom, and, not surprising to any alert parent, these government-paid educators are typically leftists, and there is proof.

We know that the number of supporters of socialism among the young is directly related to their level of education, which suggests that the longer one remains in the academy, the more likely he/she is to embrace socialist views. A 2015 poll supports that conclusion. It found that while almost half (48 percent) of high school graduates support socialism, almost two-thirds (62 percent) of college graduates are supportive, and worse, more than three in four (78 percent) of post-graduate-degreed young people favor socialism.[99]

Evidently, there is a lot of groupthink and indoctrination taking place at American universities, which is attributable to a predominantly leftist staff at those institutions. Specifically, the evidence of left-leaning faculties is documented as well. A 2018 National Association of Scholars' report confirms that nearly four in five (78.2 percent) of the academic departments of sixty-six top-ranked liberal arts colleges in the US had "either zero Republicans, or so few as to make no difference."[100]

No wonder young Americans favor socialism; they know nothing about free-market ideas and everything about socialism, thanks to their overwhelmingly leftist, often socialist-favoring professors.

SOCIALISM-FAVORING YOUNG ADULTS ARE WOKE ON HISTORY

It shouldn't surprise us that most young adults fail to understand essential aspects of American history and the world history on socialism. Evidently, the understanding of socialism among early-twenty-first-century, young Americans has nothing to do with tyrants like Stalin and Mao and mostly has to do with the *kumbaya* lifestyle commonly attributable to "socialist" Sweden and Norway.

Yes, ignorance of history and civics (the study of the rights and duties of citizenship), much less the true history of socialism, is bliss for many young Americans. A 2018 study by the Woodrow Wilson National Fellowship Foundation found that only one in three Americans (36 percent) can pass a US citizenship test with a "passing" score being only 60 percent. Just 13 percent knew when the US Constitution was ratified (1788), and almost two-thirds (60 percent) didn't know America's World War II enemies (Germany and Japan). Almost as many (57 percent) didn't know how many justices serve on our Supreme Court (nine). [101]

That poll validates the failure of our educational establishment to teach the simplest facts about American history and civics. However, evidently not all Americans are uneducated about our history. The oldest people in the survey (sixty-five years and older) did the best (74 percent), while those under the age of forty-five managed only a 19 percent passing rate. [102]

Other surveys that test American knowledge of history found much the same outcome. Apparently, too few Americans know even the basic facts about our more than 240 years as a nation, and that's especially true about civics. For example, one survey found less than a quarter (23 percent) of college seniors in the nation's top universities know who wrote the US Constitution (James Madison Jr. [1751–1836] was the principal author of the US Constitution). [103]

It shouldn't be surprising, given the dearth of understanding about American history and civics among young Americans, that they know even less about the tragic history of socialism. The same *US News* survey that gave us the dismal report above also asked Americans about the authorship of the statement, "From each according to his ability; to each according to his needs." As noted earlier, that's a famous statement taken from Karl Marx's *Communist Manifesto*, but, perhaps not surprisingly, many American college seniors had no clue while some attributed it to Thomas Paine, George Washington, and Barack Obama. Meanwhile, when young Americans were asked about their support for a government-managed economy (socialism), they overwhelmingly favor a free-market system (74 percent), while a quarter (28 percent) have a positive view of a socialist economy.[104]

It is shocking, given the favorable view of socialism among so many young Americans, that, evidently, they don't even know the ugly history associated with past socialist regimes. That's because woke history is becoming the norm, such as the text *A People's History of the United States* by Howard Zinn, a socialist political scientist who ignores the unsavory facts about past socialistic regimes, which explains why in part many young people hate America and prefer a socialist country.

Mr. Zinn (1922–2010) chaired the history and social sciences departments at Spelmann College (Atlanta, Georgia) and taught political science at Boston University. Mary Grabar exposed Zinn's revisionist history in her 2019 book, *Debunking Howard Zinn* (Regnery). Some of Zinn's revisionism is outlined below.[105]

- America discoverer Christopher Columbus? A genocidal maniac, driven by lust for gold and murder. Zinn juxtaposed passages from Columbus' diaries to construct outright lies about him.
- The English settlers at Jamestown, Virginia, and Plymouth, Massachusetts? Perpetrators of "genocide."
- America's founders? Greedy exploiters who fought a revolution not for liberty but for their own class-driven acquisition of wealth and power.
- The United States in World War II? No better than Hitler's Germany or Japan. In fact, America fought only because our

"main interest was not stopping Fascism but advancing the
imperial interests of the United States."

- The Marshall Plan, in which the United States spent billions
  restoring war-torn Europe? The real purpose was "to creat[e]
  a network of American corporate control over the globe."
- America's internment of Japanese-Americans during the
  war? No different from Hitler's extermination camps, in
  which six million Jews were systematically murdered.
- North Vietnamese Communist leader Ho Chi Minh? A
  people's leader and liberator.

Washington Times columnist Robert Knight elaborated on Ms.
Grabar's critique of Professor Zinn. Evidently, Zinn wrote everything
from the perspective of Marxist class warfare and routinely omitted key
facts such as mass murder. Zinn, perhaps not surprisingly, was a member
of Soviet front groups and even helped found the socialist New Party
and the Student Nonviolent Coordinating Committee, a communist
group that undermined the National Association for the Advancement
of Colored People.[106]

Ms. Grabar argues that Zinn produced fake history which "did
everything—misrepresented sources, omitted critical information, falsified evidence, and plagiarized...he wrote a 'people's' history, telling
the bottom-up story of neglected and forgotten men and women. The
problem is that he falsified American history to promote Communist
revolution. ...all the while denying that he was a Communist."[107]

The expression "ignorance is bliss" comes to mind when considering
the general lack of knowledge among most Americans when it comes
to truth about socialism. We can blame our educational establishment,
radical authors like Professor Zinn, and neglectful parents of today's
young adults for such widespread ignorance and for allowing fake history to fill the heads of our youth.

In conclusion, socialism is gaining popularity because of three factors: woke history, a leftist educational establishment, and out-of-control

federal spending that leaves the next generation a mountain of debt and totally discouraged about their chances of living the American dream.

Communism's Rise in America

America has a long and not-so-glorious history with communists that is picking up momentum now, decades after the demise of the former Soviet Union.

Likely, the leftist-leaning American education establishment and many similarly ideologically inclined historians overlook America's communist history. That's why it is instructive and worth a refresher before describing the ongoing ideological renewal of communism in this country.

At the end of World War I, Russia's October Revolution (1917) sparked the rise of two US communist parties, the Communist Party of America (CPA), which had a significant Russian influence, and the Communist Labor Party of America (CLP).[108] Then, in 1922, the CPA merged with the United Communist Party, an offshoot of a faction of the CPA that joined with the CLP, to create a new party, the Workers Party of America (WPA). By 1929, yet another party, the Communist Party of the United States of America (CPUSA), emerged from the remnants of these predecessors.[109]

The CPUSA formed a trade-union arm, the Trade Union Educational League, much like the American Federation of Labor (AFL). Evidently, orders from Moscow led to the CPUSA refocusing from trade-union members to minority groups such as unskilled immigrants, African Americans, and female workers under the name Trade Union Unity League. That platform became the mechanism for the CPUSA to train its organizers, who joined the national Congress of Industrial Organizations (CIO) unions.[110]

America's Great Depression (1929–1939) gave the CPUSA some leverage, because it used that economic implosion to enlist members from among America's unemployed, and by the late 1930s, it had earned considerable national influence. In fact, the party grew to eighty-two thousand strong by the fall of 1938 and reached a pinnacle of one hundred thousand members in the summer of 1939.[111] Meanwhile, some CPUSA members became major voices in multiple CIO unions, especially in New York City, the epicenter of communist activity in America mostly working on housing disputes and employed by CPUSA candidates for elected city council seats.[112]

Meanwhile, as Germany's Adolf Hitler gained influence in Europe, the CPUSA enhanced its prestige by embracing antifascism here at home. In the mid-1930s, the Communist Parties, both here and abroad, responded to the Spanish Civil War (1936–1939) by supporting the democratically elected Spanish Republic against the fascists by organizing International Brigades of fighters like America's Abraham Lincoln Battalion that provided services such as medical, propaganda, and fundraising. The communists used attractive and misleading names like the Abraham Lincoln Battalion for their units to conceal the communist character of their efforts and make it appear as if these efforts were part of a "campaign on behalf of progressive democracy."[113]

Garnering American support for communist Russia accelerated in June 1941 once the Nazis invaded the Soviet Union, which prompted the pro-Soviet CPUSA to form a Democratic Front, a new win-the-war organization with a strategy that earned considerable American support and sympathy. By 1943, the CPUSA morphed into the Communist Political Association and grew throughout the balance of the Second World War period.[114]

PRESIDENT HOOVER'S HOBSON'S CHOICE

Some Americans looked behind the curtain of the public persona of the CPUSA to expose the treachery of the communists as Europe boiled over with fighting. On June 29, 1941, former President of the United States Herbert Hoover addressed the American people regarding the question of whether the US should join the war raging in Europe.[115] He indicated that, when it comes to the war, America faced a Hobson's choice, "the necessity of accepting one of two or more equally objectionable alterna-tives."[116] America had a choice to either align with the communist Rus-sians or the Nazi Germans; Hoover recommended remaining neutral.

In his speech, the former president identified reasons being bantered about Washington at the time to justify America going to war. Those arguments included the inevitability of Germany's Hitler intending to attack America; the belief that freedom requires the destruction of totali-tarian ideologies; the assertion that America cannot live in the same world with dictatorships; and the fact that it was time for the US to impose permanent peace on the world (a one-world government alternative).[117]

Mr. Hoover didn't favor any of these justifications. Rather, he cau-tioned against joining forces with Stalin's militant communist conspir-acy because it was against the whole democratic ideals of the world. He reminded the American people that four American presidents and four secretaries of state starting with President Woodrow Wilson had already refused to lift a finger to do anything about Soviet Russia's totalitarian actions. After all, Hoover reminded his audience, Soviet Russia was "one of the bloodiest tyrannies and terrors ever erected in history. It destroyed every semblance of human rights and human liberty; it is a militant destroyer of the worship of God. It brutally executes millions of inno-cent people without the semblance of justice. It has enslaved the rest. Moreover, it has violated every international covenant; it has carried on a world conspiracy against all democracy, including the United States."[118]

Hoover strengthened his case for refusing to align with Stalin's Rus-sia when he explained why Moscow couldn't be trusted. He said:

When Russia was recognized by the United States in 1933, the Soviets entered into a solemn agreement that they would refrain from any propaganda, any organization or in any way whatso-ever to injure the tranquility, prosperity, order or security in any part of the United States. It failed to uphold that agreement.[119]

Seven years later, the [Martin] Dies [US House of Represen-tatives] committee reported unanimously and specifically that

the Communist party in the United States is a Moscow conspiracy, masked as a political party; that its activities constitute a violation of the treaty of recognition; that under instructions from
Moscow the Communists had violated the law of the United
States; that throughout the entire time they had been supplied
with funds from Moscow for activities against the American
people and the American government. The Dies committee
only confirmed what most Americans already know. Is the word
of Stalin any better than the word of Hitler?[120]

President Hoover continued his argument that Stalin wasn't to be
trusted:

On August 22, 1939, Stalin entered into an agreement with
Hitler through which there should be joint onslaught on the
democracies of the world. Nine days later Stalin attacked the
Poles jointly with Hitler and destroyed the freedom of a great
and democratic people. Fourteen days later Stalin destroyed
the independence of democratic Latvia, Lithuania and Estonia.
Ninety days later on came the unprovoked attack by Russia on
democratic Finland. Is that not aggression and is not every case
a hideous violation of treaties and international law?[121]

Stalin has taken advantage of the very freedoms of democracy
to destroy them with the most potent Fifth Column in all
history. He contributed to the destruction of France. He has
daily implanted class hate in America and a stealthy war against
our institutions.[122]

Former President Hoover knew about Hitler's "hideous record of
brutality, of aggression and as a destroyer of democracies." He enumerated examples of Hitler's atrocities and then asked regarding the communists, "Does America feel quite right about aiding Stalin to hold his
enslavement of them? That is where power politics has carried us. No

doubt we will make good our promise to aid Russia. But the ideological war to bring the four freedoms to the world died spiritually when we made that promise.[123]

"If we go further and join the war and we win, then we have won for Stalin the grip of Communism on Russia and more opportunity for it to extend in the world. We should at least cease to tell our sons that they would be giving their lives to restore democracy and freedom to the world."[124]

Hoover concluded that to align American ideals alongside Stalin would be as great a violation of everything American as to align her with Hitler, the Hobson's choice that faced then President Franklin D. Roosevelt.

The truth about Stalin's murderous ways was known by many like Hoover. Historian John Lewis Gaddis outlined the communist's toll: "The number of deaths resulting from Stalin's policies before World War II…was between 17 and 22 million," many times the toll attributed to Hitler.[125]

It wasn't just siding with either fascism or communism that bothered Hoover, however. He was concerned about communism's influence in America as well. He knew that on October 10, 1933, President Roosevelt dispatched a message to President Mikhail Ivanovich Kalinin of the Soviet All-Union Central Executive Committee asking the Soviet leader to send an envoy to Washington to negotiate an official relationship. About that time, President Roosevelt released CPUSA leader Earl R. Browder (1891–1973) from prison to promote "national unity" between American communists and the general public.[126]

Mr. Browder was the leader of the CPUSA during the 1930s and the first half of the 1940s. He served as the secret intermediary in the US for Soviet intelligence leading up to World War II. In early 1940, Browder was convicted on two counts of passport fraud and sentenced to four years in prison, and he was serving that sentence when President Roosevelt, as indicated above, released him as a gesture towards wartime unity.[127]

Evidently, it was President Roosevelt alone who decided that communist Stalin was a better war partner than the Nazi Hitler. In August 1938, Congressman Martin Dies (D-TX), chairman of the House Committee on Un-American Activities, opened a hearing with the statement that President Roosevelt had called him (Dies) and said, "You know, all this business about investigating communists is a serious mistake." Roosevelt, according to Dies, said he didn't want the communists investigated, and he insisted that the committee focus exclusively on the Nazis.[128]

Three years later, Dies had yet another conversation with Roosevelt (December 1941). At that time, Dies informed the president that "the Communists were using those 2,000 persons inside this Government and they were stealing everything in the world they wanted and had access to."[129]

The cadre of communists within the US government at the time were in senior positions in offices such as labor and atomic energy, in military research labs, in the Office of Strategic Services (a wartime intelligence agency and predecessor to the Central Intelligence Agency), and in various executive branches. Additionally, there were a variety of communist front organizations, such as those outlined above, that reached deep into American political activities, civil rights, the educational institutions, the arts, science, and even religious organizations.[130]

Communists were also quite influential among the Democratic Party's elite. A Mr. Sidney Hillman, who was born in Russia and a member of the Communist Party, led a US political action committee in the 1940s. Hillman was particularly influential—so much so that President Roosevelt, at the time of the 1944 Democratic National Convention, insisted that his choice of vice president be cleared "with Sidney."[131]

It was obvious to many Washington political observers at the time and not a few historians over the intervening decades that President Roosevelt was dismissive of the communist threat. In fact, he accused Congressman Dies of seeing "a red under your bed every night." Meanwhile, former President Hoover was very suspicious of President Roosevelt's sympathies for the Soviets given the evident open door he granted the communist regime by recognizing Moscow and allowing so many "communist infiltrators" into the American government.[132]

Soon after President Roosevelt's death (April 12, 1945), the American public's tolerance for the Soviets and the CPUSA rapidly diminished. Edward P. Thompson (1924–1993), a British historian, wrote at the time that the causes of "peace" and "freedom" broke as the Soviets claimed "peace" after the Second War while the Americans claimed "freedom." In fact, by 1948, the CPUSA believed the US was preparing for war with the Soviet Union just as many Americans concluded that communism was the biggest threat to world freedom.[133]

Talk of a cold war occupied the minds of many Americans in the late 1940s. Some argued that Americans must "live in crisis—prepared for war." That's when the US government began to discredit the Soviet's faux "peace offensive." The communists' "peace" argument fell apart thanks to the 1948 presidential election when they—i.e., CPUSA—supported Henry Wallace's failed third-party candidacy for the presidential campaign that evolved around the issue of what to do about the Soviet Union. President Harry Truman's winning campaign spelled the end to communist influence and the beginning of the Cold War.[134]

The national decision to engage in that war got a major boost in 1949, which some historians called the "year of shocks." First, the Soviets exploded an atomic device and then, just as important, China fell into communist hands. Meanwhile, at home, Alger Hiss' communist spy trial created significant paranoia about espionage in the United States.[135]

COMMUNISM'S COLD WAR-ERA "SECRET SPEECH"

President Roosevelt's open-handed approach with communism and General Secretary Stalin quickly soured after World War II with the onset of the Cold War (1947). During this period, beginning with President Harry Truman's tenure (1945–1953) and becoming full-blown during President Dwight Eisenhower's terms (1953–1961), America experienced an understandable rise in anti-Soviet (communism) sentiment, and the CPUSA was attacked, particularly with the rise of McCarthyism in the early 1950s.

US Senator Joseph McCarthy (R-WI) led investigations and hearings during the 1950s to expose the communist infiltration of the US government, something that was dismissed by President Roosevelt but investigated thanks to Congressman Dies' efforts. Soon the term "McCarthyism" became a byname for defamation of the Wisconsin senator's character and his alleged communist conspiracies. However, by the mid-1950s, public opinion began to radically change as more Americans became aware of Moscow's moral misadventures.[136]

In 1956, the Soviets invaded Hungary, exposing Moscow's true agenda in the post-World War II era, and then there was the revelation of Joseph Stalin's crimes in Nikita Khrushchev's "secret speech" to the Twentieth-Century Soviet Party Congress.

Late in the evening of February 24, 1956, the first secretary of the Communist Party of the Soviet Union, Mr. Khrushchev, delivered a four-hour long report to the Twentieth Party Congress. The speech was a devastating report that exposed the mechanism of terror and system of arbitrary rule under the regime's communist icon, Secretary Stalin.[137]

Chairman Khrushchev referenced dozens of documents in his delivery to reveal the brutal character of Stalin's terror. One document that the chairman read from was a letter written by Robert I. Eikhe (1890–1940), a former member of the Soviet Politburo, who joined the Bolsheviks in 1905 and who said his spine was broken by his interrogator.[138]

The backstory of this incident is rather telling about the nature of the communist regime at the time. In 1929, Mr. Eikhe, who was a trusted supporter of Stalin, was appointed to become the First Secretary of the Siberian territorial Communist Party, and a member of the Central Committee of the Communist Party. However, in April 1938, he was arrested and brutally tortured until he confessed to counterrevolutionary crimes, which he later retracted. However, Stalin rejected the Eikhe's retraction, and then he was once again beaten, his eye gouged out just before he was executed. Such was the behavior of regime surrogates who fell from grace. [139]

Mr. Khrushchev's speech eviscerated the communists' myth of Stalin, who consistently used criminal acts such as that against Eikhe, as well as assassination, mass deportations, the falsification of history; all these acts were done to feed Stalin's "cult of personality." Chairman Khrushchev portrayed Stalin as a bloodthirsty criminal responsible for systematic and psychological terror.

The speech leaked first as a summary, but then the entire text circulated among the communists worldwide. Khrushchev's words destroyed the mystical aura around Stalin like the "explosion of a neutron bomb." [140]

The ensuing Cold War (1947–1991) reduced the CPUSA's public influence, and the party's membership waned. Going forward, a few communists held leadership positions in a number of anti-Vietnam war organizations in the 1960s and '70s, but their influence in America compared with the 1930s through the mid '50s became quite insignificant.

COMMUNISM'S AMERICAN COMEBACK

The numbers of self-identified communists may be small, yet, according to polling, more than one in three Millennials (36 percent) approves of communism. Further, there is a growing element of those in this country who evidence ideas and activities that are quite reminiscent of past communist actions. Besides, and never forget, the most populated country in the world today is run by a communist regime, and arguably America and the Chinese communists are global adversaries. After all, China behaves like an American enemy with its incessant hacking of American computer networks, its frequent confrontations with the US militarily across much of the world, the havoc it plays with international markets, and much more. For these and other reasons, I argue in my 2018 book, *Alliance of Evil*, that the US is engaged in a new cold war with the communist Chinese, and that regime's actions play an undermining supportive role inside America as well. [141]

Events of the last few years in the US reflect communist tactics seen elsewhere for many decades. Does any alert American today really believe that the events leading up to the corruption-tainted 2020 election were purely random events and without outside influence? What's the probability that the following events were purely organic coincidences: Russiagate (the Democrats' three-year effort to steal the outcome of the 2016 election); America's third and fourth impeachment of a president over a telephone call to congratulate the Ukrainian president on a reelection victory and the allegation that Mr. Trump inspired the assault on Capitol Hill on January 6, 2021; the Wuhan COVID-19 plague hysteria with the associated analog of the 1929 Depression (the economic shutdown); and the pogroms (riots) of the summer of 2020?

No, these events are the result of a confluence of forces that include communist China collaborating with a fifth column inside the United States—the Democratic Party and other players. These forces, to be addressed in greater detail in chapter 3 of this volume and especially in section II, hosted actions designed to transform America. These forces may not have closely collaborated their actions, but the outcome is still the same—a weakened and vulnerable US.

Further, nothing about the Democratic Party's 2020 platform was Americana. It was right out of the playbook of Vladimir Lenin, who in 1917 also proposed the dissolution of police, six months before the 1917 communist revolution in Russia. Economically, the plan was to bring America to her knees thanks to COVID-19 and the whole violent campaign that removed many historic statues was an old Stalinist tactic to erase history.

Yes, the communists are back in force. The old Soviet Union may be gone and in its place are the Chinese communists and their allies on the left using disinformation, social justice, corrupted actions, and violence where appropriate (BLM and the militant wing of the Democratic Party—Antifa).

In 2020, America experienced a communist-inspired series of events meant to transform our republic. These radicals are making gains, albeit somewhat inconsistently and uncoordinated, but gaining momentum.

What's not in dispute is the ideological inspiration has clear communist fingerprints.

Progressivism's Rise in America

America has a growing population of so-called progressives, who occupy positions of influence across our government, our media, the private corporate sector, the educational establishment, and among a growing segment of the voting population. They are a force to be reckoned with and have a long history in the United States.

Progressivism demonstrated its influence during the so-called Progressive Era (1890–1920), when the movement influenced government to provide workers' rights and constrain industrialists who took advantage of the labor force. However, in time, progressives showed their dark, evil side as they became self-absorbed, arrogant, and clearly anti-Christian.

Progressivism has a troubled history. In Europe, progressivism seeded the evil of Nazism, the eugenics movement (forced sterilization), and racial discrimination. More recently, here in America, it fueled the morally bankrupt sexual revolution that includes the #MeToo movement and radical feminism. They are Marxist in their savage lust for destroying the remaining vestiges of American goodness.

My 2019 book, *Progressive Evil*, examines the movement's assault on America. I demonstrate in that book the progressives' dead-set aim to weaken our constitutional rights and destroy America's key institutions. They tend to use fascistic actions to end American exceptionalism by redefining our cultural ideals such as individuality and patriotism.

My research for this book led me to Brad Watson, a lawyer and member of the West Coast Straussian school of political thought, and the author of *Progressivism: The Strange History of a Radical Idea* (Notre Dame, 2020). Watson is also a professor of politics at St. Vincent College in Latrobe, Pennsylvania, and his book provides some unique perspective not just on the progressive ideology and its origins, but on what progressives intend for the future. In fact, Watson writes that "progressivism…is at war with much more than the American constitutional tradition: it is at war with the idea of original sin, and therefore [against]… permanent limits on political power. It is at war with human nature."[142]

Professor Watson defines progressivism as "the idea that the principled American constitutionalism of fixed natural rights and limited and dispersed powers has to be overturned and replaced by an organic evolutionary model of the Constitution that facilitates the authority of experts dedicated to the expansion of the public sphere, the expansion of political control and especially at the national level."[143]

Progressivism's ideological origin is traceable to a couple strains of thought, according to Watson. First, it is a combination of social Darwinism, which insists that "evolution, change, growth, is always and everywhere good, a sign of strength." Second, progressivism embraces "stasis, or fixity, including the fixity of the founders' natural rights constitution will get in the way of necessarily organic evolutionary growth."[144]

That milieu of strains of thought is overlaid, according to Watson, with the unique American philosophy of pragmatism. That mix indicates that "anything that gets in the way of constant experimentation [progression]…[which] the fixed [American] constitution does" is dangerous.[145]

Professor Watson also argues that American progressives embrace much of German idealism, "a kind of worship of the state, the confidence that history is moving toward a concentrated, rational state and we shouldn't get in the way of that inexorable political movement." Of course, as Watson rightly explains, these things "cut against the old founders' constitution view that certain things [like God-given natural rights] are fixed."[146]

Professor Watson identifies a number of progressive views that are quite evident today. Progressives favor experts over the consent of the informed citizen. That's where social Darwinism, pragmatism, and German ideals brew a "potent intellectual cocktail which morphs into, by the early 20th century, into what we have come to see as intellectual progressivism…the father of modern liberalism, new deal liberalism, great society liberalism." Arguably, if you are familiar with the concept of the "deep state," this potent progressive cocktail is part of the bureaucratic (elitist) swamp in Washington.

Professor Watson elaborates on a number of issues worth highlighting for Christians and orthodox American patriots. He explains that nineteenth-century American Christians worked in league with progressives on a variety of causes such as child labor laws. However, unlike traditional Christians concerned with individual sin and salvation, progressive believers morphed into a form of social Christianity. Although this group long ago lost all connection to their Christian roots, today they demonstrate a self-righteousness about their progressive causes that links them to their earlier, more explicit Christian forebearers.

He continued to explain that the metamorphosis of early Christian progressives laid the foundation for today's explicitly secular, "very self-righteous elite progressivism." In fact, contemporary progressive theorists believe one acquires material and spiritual fulfillment through "the good graces of the state."[147] Of course, for the biblical Christian, that view is heresy, thus the believers' rub with the modern idolatrous progressive movement.

Former President Obama, a progressive, demonstrated this view in a 2012 speech to supporters in Roanoke, Virginia. In that speech, Mr. Obama suggested that business owners owe their success to government investment in infrastructure when he declared, "If you're got a business, you didn't build that."[148]

In spite of its elitist persona, "progressivism is kind of hollowed out," Watson concludes. It comes across "as a warm and fuzzy social movement to improve whatever labor laws, factory conditions, things the progressives were concerned about. What it doesn't come across as is a coherent intellectual movement that is so fundamentally hostile to the notion of a fixed constitution, fundamentally hostile to the founders' constitution."[149]

Self-identifying as a progressive has become rather vogue, especially among America's political elite, said the professor. He pointed out that former Secretary of State Hillary Clinton proudly said, "I'm not a liberal. I'm a progressive." The progressive genre that Clinton and others like her espouse includes a "living Constitution," which breathes and changes with the progressive elites' nuanced, leftist proclivities.[150]

This new left, neo progressive came to contemporary attention in the 1960s, and they were operating, according to Watson, "in neo or fuzzy Marxist categories" claiming progressivism was somehow part of America's historical tradition. In fact, Watson explained, "their sort of more Marxist analysis simply said that progressives were only trying to grease the wheels of capitalism."[151]

One can see Marxist ideology fueling some of the progressive concepts explained by Professor Watson. He indicates that, for the progressive, "all aspects of the state really should be understood to be the means to human welfare and…all aspects of moral and theological thought direct themselves to the immediacies of the here and now [Marxist materialism]."[152]

For the progressive, the "purposes of government come to be seen in very broad terms," explained Watson. Therefore, "any notion of natural rights or fixed rights [like our Bill of Rights], including property rights, have to be done away with. Natural rights are seen as less natural, less fixed. Less protective of the irreducible spheres of human thought and activity, certainly than would have been acceptable to America's founders." Further, for the progressive, one gets "material and spiritual fulfillment through the good graces of the state." That view leads to the logical conclusion that "an organic whole which makes us whole, which solves all human problems in the here and now" is the progressive's ultimate goal. And the "only things that are measurable and manipulable by the [progressive] experts are things that the state controls," thus economic data generated by state officials replaces theological teachings, which diminishes the Church.[153]

The founders' constitution and traditional Christianity, according to progressives, gets in the way of necessary cultural reformation as well.

Progressives push cultural radicalism as the evolutionary next stage for society. That explains why they put "so much effort," according to Watson, to "destabilize, trying to undermine people's confidence in their political institutions, trying simply to dismiss the founders."[154]

Today, progressive Christians say, "You have to reconfigure old Christian categories, else be deemed a racist or a sexist or a homophobe." That's an out-with-the-old-and-in-with-the-new view, which explains much of the radicalism among progressives today.[155]

Progressivism is as radical as Marxism, socialism, and communism—only a bit "soft and fuzzy," as the good professor explains. It is the face of the modern Democratic Party and plays a significant role in Congress and with President Biden's administration, but beware, much like the other isms, it has a radical bite.

CONCLUSION

This chapter begins by citing national polls that demonstrate growing ideological support for the isms among Americans. Clearly, I demonstrate in this chapter that support for the isms today is aggressive, especially for the more radical versions, and it is showing no evidence of decline.

At this point, most of the contemporary ism support is found for socialism and progressivism. These supporters, who tend to be young and "well-educated," believe that they have already won most Americans over to their persuasion. After all, in 2020, they won the presidency and will use their new influence to transform America to better fit their radical vision.

This cohort of radical ism supporters are in league with key adversaries like the communist Chinese government, and they have a host of domestic supporters that includes much of the mainstream news media, the entertainment media and Hollywood elite, the social media giants at Facebook and Twitter, some of our biggest foundations, virtually the entire public education establishment, most major sporting franchises, and, of course, the Democratic Party aligned with a host of supporting ism political parties. This cadre of ism supporters is the topic of chapter 4, but before launching into the particulars of those entities, we must address the question: Is America really in a cultural revolution that poses a host of ism agents against traditional values, principles, and our Constitution?

Yes, the left's ism-supporting movement believes the future is theirs, and they will aggressively use their newfound power to push for their radical ideologically focused agenda and pressing for that outcome includes a revolution.

3

America's Marxist Revolution

Revolutions are the locomotives of history.[156]

—Karl Marx

Iknow many readers are still skeptics about the reality of an American Marxist revolution. Convincing you, or at least planting enough doubt about that possibility, is the purpose of this chapter. Be skeptical but open-minded, understand the obvious signs, and accept that Marxist ideology may be discredited, but it is not dead as a worldview among many in the American intelligentsia, the education establishment, some media, and even the halls of government.

We began this journey in the first chapter, which identified the primary ideological isms that comprise much of America's current political discourse—capitalism, Marxism, socialism, communism, and progressivism. That primer was followed by an explanation of just how—aside from capitalism—those isms burrowed their way into America's social and political conscience. This chapter picks up on that logic flow to demonstrate that, in fact, America is in the middle of a cultural revolution pressing her to embrace Marxist-inspired isms that will severely test our foundation. Yes, communism, socialism, and progressivism are Marxist in doctrine, and for my purposes here they are much the same.

What's not disputed by many observers is that a cultural revolution is tearing at the seams of America. It is fueled by Marxism and advanced by a diversity of players who attack across numerous venues. Although these entities may not coordinate their actions directly, they more often than not share a common goal—the radical transformation of America.

NOT ALL REVOLUTIONS ARE THE SAME

"Revolution" is a Latin term for "a turnaround," a sudden change in political power that occurs when a citizenry rejects either the form or substance of a nation's institutions through a variety of mechanisms—nonviolent and violent—which results in major changes in culture, economy, and/or government.

The world has known many revolutions across time, to include one that led to the creation of the United States through the American Revolutionary War (1775–1783). In fact, there are numerous different typologies of revolutions, such as political, Marxist (socialist or communist), those known by their form (rural or urban), and others.

Contemporary America is facing a revolution much like other major powers have across history. Our revolution is hosted by mostly domestic players and, as a result, America is showing real signs of fading in its wake. Today, the US is crippled in part due to mostly internal rebellious actions: graft, corruption, and political opponents or their proxies who act (burn, loot, riot, kill) violently in our streets while the political class is intimidated into non-action by leftists.[157]

Similarly, other great countries and empires faced revolution and some even collapsed under the pressure. Centuries ago, Rome's Julius Caesar announced the end of his republic thanks to revolution—*alea iacta est* "the die is cast"—because of challenges on many fronts: an ineffective army, poor health of the population, waning economic strength, failing leadership, political turbulence, religious disruptions, and mostly ineffective government. The same may well be true for modern America today, thanks to the avatar of modern evil, Karl Marx. His ideology has for some time dug its claws deep into America, and after decades of investment, significant changes are coming fast.[158]

IDEOLOGICAL MUTANTS OF MARXISM IN AMERICA

To be sure, classical Marxism as described in the last chapter is seriously flawed, a historic failure, but there are ideological mutants that retain elements of Marx's core precepts and are quite evident in America today. Those include a number of systems spawned by Marx's teachings that include critical race theory, the Frankfurt School, liberation theology, critical theology, Maoism, and many more. This diverse list, all these mutants, share the same poisoned, Marxist root.[159]

Like it or not, these mutants have considerable influence today, such as critical race theory (CRT), which is taught in many American universities as well as espoused even within our federal government as so-called sensitivity training. In 2020, President Trump ended the promotion of CRT, a blatant form of Marxist indoctrination among our federal workforce.

Consider a definition for CRT that is so popular today with the left and prevalent in so many American venues. It "is a modern approach to social change, developed from the broader critical theory, which developed out of Marxism. Critical race theory approaches issues such as justice, racism, and inequality, with a specific intent of reforming or reshaping society. In practice, this is applied almost exclusively to the United States."[160]

CRT is grounded in several revealing assumptions:[161]

- American government, law, culture, and society are inherently and inescapably racist.
- Everyone, even those without racist views, perpetuates racism by supporting those structures.

- The personal perception of the oppressed—their "narrative"— outweighs the actions or intents of others.
- Oppressed groups will never overcome disadvantages until the racist structures are replaced.
- Oppressor race or class groups never change out of altruism; they only change for self-benefit.
- Application of laws and fundamental rights should be different based on the race or class group of the individual(s) involved.

Thus, CRT claims that every aspect of American society is racist, and minority groups will never gain equal status without reform. It often poses as the solution for issues like white supremacy, but essentially gives license to oppress certain groups. Further, CRT is aligned with Marxism, communism, socialism, progressivism, intersectionality, and social justice.

The effect CRT and other Marxist-inspired theories have had on America has reached a critical point, which puts this country in revolution.

BACKGROUND OF AMERICA'S MARXIST REVOLUTION

America is experiencing an unconventional revolution compared with some past rebellions. Nonetheless, the transformation is very real. On one side pressing the revolutionary turmoil are a host of players: many Democratic Party political operatives who embrace anti-constitutional isms (Marxism, socialism, communism, and progressivism) and other political parties such as the Communist Party USA, most of the mainstream media, many giant left-leaning corporations, virtually all of the social media firms like Facebook and Twitter, the public education establishment, a variety of proxy warrior groups like BLM and Antifa, and the leftist deep staters. On the other side are Trump supporters (evangelical

Christians, nationalists, patriots, the silent majority), desperately cling-
ing to our Constitution and the promises of American founders like
Benjamin Franklin (1706–1790), who, when asked as he exited Philadelphia's Constitution Hall in 1787, "Well, doctor, what have we got—a
republic or a monarchy?" responded, "A republic, if you can keep it."[162]

Never in the life of this country except perhaps the Civil War era
(1861–1865) has this republic been more in jeopardy of imploding.
After all, the anti-American forces are showing their true colors, especially since the 2016 presidential election, when those conspirators self-
identified as the "resistance," waging guerrilla warfare against President
Trump, his administration, and his voters. The "resistance" picked up
the sword of revolution that started decades ago and made it center
stage with the concocted "Russian collusion" hoax, then the Ukrainian
impeachment, and a long list of other nonviolent and violent assaults
on the republic that ended with the corruption-plagued election of Mr.
Biden.

Why did these Marxists go so public with their revolution? They
were responding to Mr. Trump's vigorous campaign to drain the Washington swamp of the "resistance," which included Obama holdovers,
fake-news outlets, and saboteurs like former Federal Bureau of Investigation's former director, James Comey. They saw the possibility of their
blood in the water and had to strike, wasting no more time to finish the
job begun decades ago of radically transforming America.

You see that for much of the past two-plus centuries, the United
States of America was the world's shining light on the hill replete with
enviable freedoms. However, now for decades, that lighthouse of freedom has lost much of its luster, because Marxists long ago infiltrated and
burrowed themselves into America's fabric. Yes, this country is racing to
the brink of a communist abyss, falling victim to a totalitarian ideology,
and too few Americans really even know just how far the nation has
sunk.

The revolution until recently was rather subtle, and many of the
Marxist warriors came from overseas—Western European leftist enclaves

like the Frankfurt School and current and former communist regimes like China and the Soviet Union. The infiltration and revolution happened slowly at first and mostly beyond notice as the French poet Charles Baudelaire wrote: "*La plus belle des ruses du diable est de vous persuader qu'il n'existe pas*," translated: "The devil's finest trick is to persuade you that he does not exist." The Marxist revolution—the devil—started out of the spotlight, which explains why most Americans remain in denial.

The revolution dates back a hundred years. You read in the last chapter about the communist infiltration of America beginning with the early twentieth century and the surge in influence for socialist comrades and their progressive allies, especially during the Second World War. More recently, other infiltrators have raised their voices; some camouflaged behind obfuscated titles and front organizations are now beginning to show their true colors, albeit while denying they ever want to mimic Stalinist Russian or Chinese communist takeover models, yet their actions here at home say otherwise.

AMERICAN REVOLUTION PUSHED BY CHINESE COMMUNISTS

There is reason for the general lack of alarm about the Marxist revolution among many Americans. Simply, they naively thought communism died with the fall of the Berlin Wall in 1989, which was quickly followed by the demise of Moscow's red legions in the former Soviet Union. No, the ideology never died, and today it continues to thrive under the Five Star Red Flag of communist China, the world's most populous nation and leading economy. The faithful among the Communist Party in Beijing lick their chops for world domination and are taking measures to realize that goal at every turn.

Communist China's leader, Xi Jinping, long ago set as a national goal becoming the global hegemon by 2049. However, it must first diminish the United States economically and militarily to reach that goal, and so far, it's making progress. In fact, as I demonstrate in my 2018 book, *Alliance of Evil*, communist China is very much engaged in a new, non-kinetic cold war with the US on four decisive fronts—economic, cyber, ideological, and security/technological.

That new cold war is very mature and is getting worse for the US by the day, and it is having a significant impact, especially here at home. FBI director Christopher Wary claims the agency has approaching three thousand open counterintelligence investigations related to Chinese actions against American interests. Part of those cases were related to Beijing's efforts to undercut the Trump administration, which made his reelection bid a cause *celebre* for the communist tyrants.

On other fronts and in 2020, former Secretary of State Mike Pompeo labeled the Communist Chinese Party the "central threat of our times," and he indicated that, at the time, the Trump administration was vigorously pursuing an effort to rid the US of China's communist influence in this country. Little wonder, as I'll explain in the next section of this book, the communist leadership in Beijing pulled out all stops to end the Trump presidency and then welcomed the far more compliant Biden administration.

MARXIST TRANSFORMATION OF FREE SOCIETY

Those pressing this revolution from abroad like the Chinese have a significant advantage, because most Americans don't understand Marxism and its perversions, like the communist dictatorships in places like China and North Korea. But the American version of Marxism presented a faux face from the start, one that was "soft and fuzzy," much as Professor Watson explained about progressivism in the previous chapter. At the start of the revolution, communist agents coddled free citizens—specifically malleable, idealistic youth—with promises, then employed nonconfrontational means to find loopholes in the nation's legal and political systems in order to create the ways to influence our future.

These "Marxist democrats" (a real oxymoron) always hide their true intent. After all, that's the game plan. Never forget what Soviet communist dictator Vladimir Lenin confirmed about the isms: "The goal of socialism [also progressivism] is communism." And in free societies like America, the introduction of socialist, progressive ideas that once take hold rapidly consume the people's freedoms and give birth to communist totalitarianism with all its brutality.[163]

The communist template for taking over free states like the US was outlined in the previous chapter—a long, four-stage process that leaves citizens numb, oblivious to the changes happening all about them, and then they finally become accustomed to the new normal. By that time, it's too late to turn back. So, eventually and inevitably, once socialism gains a foothold, it morphs into full-blown communism as the elite strip away all rights and replace the government with authoritarianism, dictatorial tyranny.

This transformation to socialism and then to communism eventually drags all of society with its institutions—family, education, religion, economy, government—into the gutter of life, which is littered with the worst of mankind, because they are flushed through political correctness, the tool of the left, and all moral discernment disappears at the state's command. It creates a whole new, ugly world.

Early on in the Marxist revolution, the leaders target the religious communities to marginalize them, because they alone are the true conscience of the broader society. Eventually, as Marx said, "My object in life is to dethrone God," which means the shuttering of places of worship and the denial of believers' religious freedom, resulting in the faithful either taking their faith underground like the house churches in present-day China or embracing a God-free life. For the communist state, there is room for only one god, and that is big government.[164]

So, Marxism teaches people to embrace atheism and materialism and abandon God. That means Marxist elites invert good and evil across all spheres of life and turn ethics on its head, casting righteousness as wickedness, which becomes a reality in the schoolhouse and across all sectors of society as well. We've seen this firsthand in America with the perversion of most everything once sacred.

These purveyors of moral distortion are making progress across America's cultural landscape thanks to our compliant public education establishment. Many public-school teachers pump our next generation with atheistic and anti-traditionalist curricula that fosters a consciousness that will eventually overpower the remaining traditionalist teaching. That influence shows up most clearly in the popularity of the isms among our youth outlined in the previous chapter.

There is no more place for traditionalists—read "conservatives" and "people of faith"—in a communist regime. They are removed—murdered or tucked away in gulags—leaving the balance of the compliant citizens to participate in the revolution. After all, Marxists understand the process of indoctrination and the necessity to remove the traditionalists by nurturing what the Chinese communists call "wolf cubs," youth who are indoctrinated and grow up to do the communists' bidding to advance the revolution, even if that means turning into the state minders their traditionalist parents or neighbors in the name of the cultural revolution. Such thinking has already started here.

Vermont's governor asked teachers to question their students about their 2020 Thanksgiving gatherings, and if they participated in "multi-family" events, "the kids will be forced into quarantine." Governor Phil Scott tweeted that the Vermont Agency of Education would "direct schools to ask students or parents if they were part of multi-family gatherings and if the answer is yes, they'll need to go remote for 14 days or 7 days and a [COVID] test."[165]

Evidently, the compliant education establishment and many citizens across the general public are willing partners helping these Marxist-like officials win over their population. Another major benefactor for the revolution is the mass media, which is recruited either through the outright purchase of those outlets to create state-based biased reporting, or through the regime taking total control by fiat. The result is predictable: All truthful reporting is trashed, and fake news and state propaganda prevail.

Apparently, the left's capture of both education and the media is having the intended impact in America. Polling cited earlier finds that America's youth are already very supportive of the isms, and that bias fuels street unrest that attacks our heritage (tearing down historical markers and monuments) and destroys city blocks in the name of social justice.

Of course, most of the mainstream media embrace leftist ideologies and even defend the communist Chinese, who encourage such kinetic actions like rioting in the name of the peoples' (Marx's proletariat) revolution. I'll address that issue in the next section of this book.

The history of past revolutions also demonstrates that Marxist movements always leverage economic unrest—and, when possible, pandemics like COVID-19—to build up their influence and overthrow existing social order. We examined that revolutionary template for free societies in the previous chapter and arguably are seeing evidence of that today in America.

Another tool in the Marxists' bag of tricks to turn a society its way is to promise free healthcare and education, which, as we've seen, is especially popular among the younger American generations. It was the trademark of the popular socialist Vermont Senator Sanders during his last two presidential bids.

Further, inducing compliance with state directives is a necessary prerequisite to a complete takeover by communist tyrants. They are making good progress on that front as well. In 2020, American compliance management started to show promise beginning with the COVID-19 pandemic, which gave state and local leaders the opportunity to test their leverage to order without statutory authority all citizens to shelter in place, wear masks, report on their neighbors, close their small businesses (even if it meant certain bankruptcy), and depend on big government for handouts. Perhaps surprisingly, many Americans once known for their independence fell in line like nonthinking munchkins, those natives of the fictional Munchkin Country in the *Oz* books by American author L. Frank Baum.

Yes, the fingerprints of a Marxist revolution abound across most American institutions. But nothing is as compelling as firsthand examples of the impact of Marxism from real people.

REVOLUTION THROUGH THE
EYES OF EXPERIENCE

The subversion of America by Marxism is subtle and started a long time ago. There is nothing like hearing the testimony of someone who has lived through a communist revolution to cement in our minds the threat facing America today.

A decade ago, Curtis Bowers, a film producer, made a documentary, *Agenda: Grinding America Down*, which details how communism corrupts American institutions and subverts it from within. The communist strategy outlined in *Agenda* is to divide Americans against one another.[166]

Bowers explains that America's current political moment evidences all the tentacles of a true Marxist revolution. "For many years," Mr. Bowers said, "it's [the communist agenda in America] been more of a behind the scenes, subtle thing in the background, but now it's on our streets." The communist strategy became crystal clear to Mr. Bowers decades ago, however.[167]

In 1992, Mr. Bowers attended a meeting "as a favor to a gentleman that had been studying communism his whole life and [had] written many books on it. And he knew he couldn't go to the meeting. He said they'll know who I am. So, would you go and just hear what they're having to say? Again, people need to remember that in 1989 the Berlin Wall had come down, and then in December of 1991, the Soviet Union had dissolved. Now this is six months later, the summer of 1992."[168]

Mr. Bowers attended the meeting for the Communist Party USA (CPUSA) as a favor. He was shocked by the audience. The auditorium was packed with about 1,400 people, all ranging in age from fifty to seventy years old, well-dressed in suits and carrying briefcases.[169]

The speakers at the CPUSA meeting "clearly talked about how they wanted to finish the US off from within. [That's a reminder of what Soviet Chairman Nikita Khrushchev said in 1956, 'We will destroy you from within.'] They've been working to undermine our families and our business structure and our morality for a long time. But they said, 'We need to really step that up now even more.' They acknowledged they were disappointed that the Soviet Union had to back down from the world revolution as far as militarily and things." He recalled a statement spoken from the podium: "Now we just need to continue what we've been doing at a more serious level through education, media, and entertainment." According to Mr. Bowers, the CPUSA members intended to influence the next generation of Americans to favor communism and wanted their members to "come alongside them in their movements to try to slowly take us [the US] down from within."[170]

At the time of the CPUSA meeting, Mr. Bowers admitted his doubts. He acknowledged to have wondered: "Is this thing for real?" He said that he had bought into the deception, like most Americans, that communism died when President Reagan won the Cold War.[171]

Then he indicated that the CPUSA speakers were passionate, much like "a pastor at a church pounding the pulpit." One speaker, according to Bowers, said: "It's [the American system] the most evil system that has ever been devised." Mr. Bowers offered that he "left [the conference] thinking these people are from another planet.... There's no way they will succeed with their plans. That's what I thought back then, about 30 years ago." That was in 1992, but then things began to change before Mr. Bowers' very eyes.[172]

By 2008, Mr. Bowers was a state representative in Idaho and he began to see legislation that triggered his memory of the CPUSA meeting decades prior. He was considering environmental legislation that crossed his desk. The proposed legislation did nothing to help the environment, but would destroy businesses. Then he recalled, "That's what they [the CPUSA speakers] had said back in 1992 as the way they were going to take down the free enterprise [capitalist] system. They said they were going to get behind the environmental movement and use it to create so much regulation and red tape, that it would be hard for a business to survive."[173]

Then Mr. Bowers reflected on the 1958 book, *The Naked Communist*, by Cleon Skousen, a former FBI agent who describes a very specific agenda for transforming society into the communist image. He called out goal seventeen of forty-five presented in the book: "Get control of the schools. Use them to transmit socialist propaganda. Get control of teachers' associations [unions]. Put the party line in textbooks."[174]

That goal, as many of the others, are mostly accomplished today, according to Bowers. After all, opinion polling addressed in the previous chapter demonstrates that significant parts of America's young generation support socialism, and many endorse communism as well. Mr. Bowers alleged, "They've been brainwashed to think that they're [socialism and communism are] good."[175]

Mr. Bowers indicated that at the 1992 meeting, the goal of getting control of the schools was addressed. The communists said: "We're going to use them as transmission belts for socialism to teach socialist ideas and philosophies and make them sound like they're just and right and true and be focused on that."[176]

The communists also intend to eliminate free speech using what Bowers called political correctness, "which is just cultural Marxism. It was the Frankfurt School, which was a Marxist group that came up with that whole idea of making certain things off limits." Further, Bowers explained, "They always come up with some reason why you can't have free speech. In doing so you're not allowed to ever tell the other side of the story."[177]

Mr. Bowers researched the Frankfurt School, and especially Herbert Marcuse for his film, *Agenda*. He explained that a group of intellectuals from that school were brought to America in the 1930s because of the pending war (World War II). "They were Marxist and communist. John Dewey, who is the father of modern [American] public education, is the one that brought them over to America and dropped them down at a lot of our top universities," Bowers said.[178]

One of Dewey's recruits from the Frankfurt School was Willi Mün-zenberg. He outlined their goals for America: "We're going to make the West so corrupt; it stinks. We're going to rock them from within, and we're going to teach immorality to the young people. We're going to try to push pornography and we're going to try to increase alcoholism."[179]

Mr. Bowers said these Marxist transplants intended, as outlined above, to harness the media and education "to change the culture through capturing those institutions." One of the slogans attributed to this group, said Bowers, was "Make love, not war." The intent of such a slogan was to subtly break down traditions, "and then setting the stage to present something new to the young people. They have done so much damage in Hollywood and in the educational system. That's why they've both changed so much."[180]

Mr. Bowers interviewed Agustin Blazquez, a Cuban filmmaker and a staunch anti-communist, for the film *Agenda*. Mr. Blazquez spoke of the type of idealism and the deception associated with the communist revolution in his former homeland.

"A lot of the propaganda I'm hearing in America right now sounds exactly what Castro was doing back then," Mr. Blazquez told Bowers. At that time, according to Blazquez, the communists spoke of justice, equality, and being fair. However, it was all deception.[181]

"We knew it was really bad one night when we were watching the television station, and we saw our uncle go before a firing squad on the evening news," Blazquez explained. At that point, he realized things had changed, because at first the communists were all nice and democratic—that is, until they controlled everything. Then "they cracked down."[182]

The communist crackdown came quickly, and the impact was felt by everyone. One day, Blazquez's father came home from working at their sugar plantation, which at the time was one of the largest in Cuba. His father was obviously depressed, which prompted his wife to ask, "What's wrong, what's wrong?" He finally said, "We have nothing. They've taken everything. They just took the sugar plantation. I'm just working for them now out in the fields cutting the sugarcane."[183]

Communism is also a system that depends on fear, explained Blazquez. He told about the time he was walking down the street when, all of a sudden, he "was thrown in the back of a police car and taken to prison." He spent an entire day behind bars, where he was abused and then released. Rhetorically, Blazquez asked, "Why did they do that?" He said, "So I would be in such fear of them, I would always obey them. They do it to everybody, periodically. You didn't do anything wrong; you were just there. That's when I knew I had to leave, I was scared to leave my home most of the time, unless I had to."[184]

"Communism and socialism lead to that [use of fear to control the population]," Bowers observed. He indicated that most people don't understand the ism-fear association. That's because "socialism doesn't work. As it starts to [inevitably] collapse, the people in power are not going to lose their power. So that's when the guns come out." That only happens when "they have the levers of control. It's hard to go from free enterprise to communism, because the people still own all the wealth and the power of the money-making things. That's a hard transition, you've got to go into socialism first." That explains what's happening in America today—socialism, progressivism is touted, and then behind the veil is communism waiting to pounce.[185]

The communist system depends on compliance and fear, as Mr. Blazquez explained above. Further, so are informants, a foreign concept for Americans who never lived in a communist country. A portrayal of the informant system was captured in the film *The Lives of Others*. The story line is about a Stasi agent, former East German secret police, and the nature of life "in a society where everyone is informing on everybody else."[186] (For a time, Vladamir Putin, Russia's current president and a former Russian KGB officer, was stationed in East Germany advising the Stasi.)

One significant account of informants from the communist era in Poland was especially sobering. Evidently, Polish people were stunned by what they discovered after the fall of the Iron Curtain, and the Stasi's archives were opened to the public. Those records showed how parish priests informed on those who opened their hearts at confession, and even some husbands had informed on their wives.[187]

Mr. Bowers indicates that informing becomes a necessary part of every communist system. "That concept is the final level of division where you've even broken down every family to where individual people that can't even talk to each other," he says. "The same thing is going on right now with all these movements [in America] to try to divide us from each other, to make us think we're all against each other and to make people discontented and fearful of each other. That is all Marx's strategy."[188]

That strategy has come to roost in America. Informing on others sounds similar to how some American state and local officials recruited citizens to snitch on their friends and neighbors during the COVID-19 pandemic. Politicians across America asked the citizenry to tell authorities after spying on their neighbors about not complying with mask mandates and gathering restrictions. Sounds to me as if many Americans are ready for a Marxist regime such as in New York City.

In New York City, Mayor Bill de Blasio told citizens to tell on others by snapping smartphone photos of social-distancing violations and texting them to the police, and the mayor promised that "enforcement will come." He continued, "When you see a crowd, when you see a line that's not distanced, when you see a supermarket that's too crowded—anything—you can report it right away so we can get help there to fix the problem."[189]

Virginia's Governor Ralph Northam (Democrat) encouraged citizens to inform against small businesses for violating his coronavirus restrictions. The leftist governor said Virginia residents can report violations to his executive orders on face-mask use and social distancing via a portal on the state health department's website. Northam is the same official who admitted to wearing either blackface or a Ku Klux Klan robe while in medical school, and in May 2020 was caught mingling and taking selfies with supporters without a face mask in Virginia Beach just after announcing his order to wear face masks in public areas.[190]

Yes, Marxists must divide and then conquer, Bowers said. America's cohesiveness in the past made a Marxist revolution impossible until recently. To be successful, the Marxist knows he must divide us "with the rich against the poor, the blacks against the whites, and the young against the old." Doesn't that sound much like race-baiting (thanks to critical race theory) and the promotion of class divisions so evident across America in 2020?

CONCLUSION

For decades, the Marxists have worked to fashion the US into a new land. That effort got into full gear with the arrival of the Frankfurt School Marxist philosophers who spread across America's academe and Hollywood, and then quickly sought to undermine every legal and social institution. It immediately became clear that what the old Soviets failed to accomplish economically and militarily in the twentieth century, cultural Marxism and its cabal of collaborators are getting done today, first subtly through the education establishment and now very publicly on the streets of America.

The cultural revolution is having a significant impact on this country, and in fact we've arrived at the moment in the revolution where dramatic changes are taking place at lightning speed. Unfortunately, all the entities pushing the revolution know the momentum is on their side, and they are pressing to accelerate change before the silent majority wakes up to what is happening.

The next section of *Give Me Liberty, Not Marxism* identifies that disjointed cabal of radical Marxist-inspired groups and their partners fueling America's Marxist revolution.

Section II

Cabal of Marxist-Inspired Entities Fueling the Revolution and Their Means

I'm not a conspiracy theorist—I'm a conspiracy analyst.[191]
—Gore Vidal, a twentieth-century American
writer and intellectual

Revolutions require supporters, and this section in five chapters identifies some of the co-conspirators fueling the rebellion and links them to Marxism and the mechanisms they use to fulfill their draconian ambition to transform America.

To begin this section, we need to establish the context. Consider the period following the election of President Trump (2016) up through the 2020 presidential election, which highlights some of the characteristics of the revolution tearing at America's foundation and identifies many of the Marxist-inspired co-conspirators. Further, the evidence indicates that the revolution's intent was never to just remove Mr. Trump, but to radically alter America going forward.

A revealing and significant warning of the Marxist-inspired revolution's sophistication came from the 2020 Democratic Party's presidential candidate himself. Before the election, Mr. Biden famously bragged that his party's elite created the "most extensive and inclusive voter fraud organization in the history of American politics." This was a rare admission of illegal behavior, but likely a true statement from the then-presidential aspirant known for stepping on his tongue. But was this statement distorted by his political opposition?[192]

Snopes.com called foul regarding the Biden voter fraud statement, which was picked up and blasted across social media by the Republicans. The "footage of Biden's statement was not digitally altered, but it was stripped from its original context," observed Snopes, a group that claims "when misinformation obscures the truth...Snopes' fact-checking and original, investigative reporting lights the way to evidence-based and contextualized analysis." In the case of Mr. Biden's voter fraud statement, Snopes argues that he "did not 'admit' to perpetrating voter fraud, but rather was referring to his campaign's efforts to protect the ballots of voters from what they presented as voter intimidation and false claims of voter fraud."[193]

Whether Mr. Biden's statement was taken out of context, as Snopes claims, or he characteristically misspoke revealing a voter corruption scheme, what's true is that his cabal of political operatives (advisors) and fellow revolutionary co-conspirators started decades ago preparing for the opportunity to remake America to fit their radical vision. Yes, their planned remaking of America made significant advances, especially during the tenure of President Barack Obama, a member of that radical progressive cabal who used his eight years in the Oval Office to advance the transformation of America. Recall that Mr. Obama famously boasted, "I've got a pen, and I've got a phone," which he used to trash our government's constitutional checks and balances with executive orders that helped pave the way for a progressive, neo-Marxist remaking of America.[194]

Mr. Obama incrementally changed America with his leftist actions, but it wasn't until Donald Trump threatened to upend the left's decades of transformative accomplishments that the radicalized Democratic Party urgently called out the big guns to protect their gains. Their 911-like call to their troops marshaled the left's phalanx of deep-state operatives, who then desperately pulled out all stops to lay siege to the "Orange Man" from Manhattan, a derogatory reference to Mr. Trump, who has orange-like colored hair. They weren't going to let Mr. Trump reverse their years of progress at remaking America, which included recruiting most of the mainstream media to their radical cause, wrestling control of the public education establishment that brainwashed American children to leftist ideology, and soft-pedaled acceptance of radical change among the gull-ible electorate, which made them naively woke and created a true deep state of faithful, ideological-warrior bureaucrats embedded through-out our federal government. The leftists' vision for a new, transformed America was becoming a reality—that is, until Mr. Trump came on the scene and threatened to expose and eliminate their gains in the name of "Making America Great Again."

Even before Mr. Trump took office in January 2017, the leftist swamp attacked his transition team. The swamp's first victim was retired US Army Lieutenant General Michael Flynn, Mr. Trump's national security advisor. Flynn was quickly removed early in the administration based on rumors and innuendo in part shouted by conspiring swamp creatures at the Federal Bureau of Investigation. Why? General Flynn knew the Washington quagmire, and those deep-state, Democratic Party creatures were fearful of the administration's promise to clean up Washington. After all, Flynn was a true intelligence community insider who could help the new president maneuver around and through the deep state's numerous roadblocks. Meanwhile, then presidential candidate Hillary Clinton's fake dossier, a completely false anti-Trump campaign weapon, was used by anti-Trump media, the deep-state brigade, and Democratic Party operatives in Congress to advance the anti-Trump Russian collu-sion hoax, which they claimed was intended to protect our democracy.

We all know that story, which burdened the administration for three plus years. Deep-state miscreants, like the FBI's counterintelligence agent Peter Paul Strzok II, and some of his colleagues, like his alleged lover, Lisa Page, a Justice Department attorney, convinced the attorney general to appoint Robert Mueller, a former FBI director, as a special prosecutor to pursue Mr. Trump's alleged Russian collusion. Mr. Mueller's all-consuming probe ended up exonerating Mr. Trump at a cost to the taxpayers of $32 million. Simultaneous to the Mueller investigation, others, like US House of Representatives Speaker Nancy Pelosi (D-CA) and Representative Adam Schiff (D-CA), chairman of the House Intelligence Committee, piled on the faux Russian collusion charge both in the media and with totally partisan House hearings. In time, however, the Russia fiasco died due to a lack of substance, but quickly Ms. Pelosi and her allies jumped on Mr. Trump's congratulatory telephone call with the newly elected Ukrainian president to allege an impeachment-worthy offense. That effort also failed when the US Senate's impeachment trial found the evidence insufficient to satisfy the constitutionally required standard of high crimes and misdemeanors.[195]

At every turn, a host of co-conspirators (the Democratic Party, the deep state, the mainstream media, and the cabal of outside, deep-pocketed globalist influencers like billionaire George Soros) tried to trash Mr. Trump and his threatening, pro-America agenda. The last opportunity to turn back Mr. Trump was the 2020 presidential election: prevent his reelection. Fortuitously for the Democrats, the communist Chinese came to the rescue with the best gift of all—the Wuhan coronavirus pandemic. The virus quickly shuttered Mr. Trump's robust economy, and the pandemic became Mr. Biden's path to victory.

That brought us to the 2020 election and the *coup d'état* that landed the cognitively challenged, seventy-eight-year-old Mr. Biden in the Oval Office, the Democrats' third major and only successful full-court press to remove Mr. Trump. Had he gained another term as president, the left's transformative revolution would certainly be on life support. After all, had he been reelected, Mr. Trump intended to finish filling the federal courts with constitutionally conservative judges/justices, ridding Washington of more deep-state swamp creatures, and he was on a campaign to snuff out the flow of illegal immigrants who feed the Democratic Party's voter rolls intended to guarantee their eternal power in Washington.

Two failed *coup d'états* made the left's third attempt to oust Trump literally a must-win. They launched their assault, using every hook and crook imaginable to remove him from office and to finally gain a choke-hold on America's government. At that moment, a phalanx of radical Democratic Party co-conspirators became hell-bent on never again relinquishing power to the likes of President Trump by promising their supporters and naïve, gullible American voters to stack the Supreme Court to act as a super legislature that endorses leftist ideas and installing new states to the Union (Washington, DC, and Puerto Rico) to build their bench of new liberal Democrat senators guaranteeing their permanent power in Washington's swamp.

Now that the left's 2020 power grab succeeded, their Marxist-like revolution is beginning to bear fruit. They are using their new grip on power to reverse everything Mr. Trump accomplished and to remake America into a twenty-first-century Marxist heaven for their ideological globalist partners both here at home and abroad. That effort began early in the Biden administration with an avalanche of executive orders reversing much of the good done by President Trump's administration, far more executive orders early in the administration than the previous five presidents together.

As a last effort to attack and ruin Mr. Trump's future, Ms. Pelosi rushed through the House's second impeachment vote against Mr. Trump based on allegations he fostered the January 6, 2021, riot on Capitol Hill. However, after Mr. Biden took office, Ms. Pelosi sent the impeachment papers to the US Senate for a trial, but at least the vast majority of the Senate Republicans found no constitutional grounds to remove a president who had already left that office.

What I provide above is a glimpse, a snapshot of some of the evidence of a true revolution with many conspirators. This section of *Give Me Liberty, Not Marxism* will expose eight co-conspirators with Marxist connections or leanings that have collaborated on their plans to remove Mr. Trump and then to continue their march to transform America: The Democratic Party and Marxist-supporting political parties; foreign entities, especially communist China; the leftist education establishment; Satan and his demonic army; secret societies; street radicals; mainstream media; and the Washington deep state. Each grouping has some voice in the current radicalization of America.

This revolution is real, and God-fearing patriots must stand up against these radicals and push them and their Marxist ideas into the dust bin of history or America is toast.

4

Democratic Party
Plenty of Marxists and
Marxist-Inspired Political Support

The Democratic Party is infiltrated by Marxists who are using the party to achieve their goals; and these Marxists support the party of Franklin D. Roosevelt and Lyndon B. Johnson only because at present there is no better alternative to tap into America's future.

What's not in doubt is that Marxism (a euphemism for communism, socialism, and progressivism) is playing a significant role in the Democratic Party—and, frankly, few Americans understand how this happened and the Marxists' radical influence for the country.

MARXISM INSIDE THE DEMOCRATIC PARTY

President Trump often said during the 2020 campaign that the country would face communism under a Joe Biden presidency. At a rally in Dayton, Ohio, Mr. Trump said, "The choice in November is going to be very simple. There's never been a time where there's such a difference.

One is probably communism…they keep saying socialism, I think they've gone over that one. That one's passed already."[196]

Throughout the 2020 campaign, Mr. Trump charged that the Democratic Party was in the grip of "radicals" such as the self-described democratic socialist, Senator Sanders, and New York Congressional Representative Alexandria Ocasio-Cortez. They are a "bunch of communists," the president said. Then he painted Mr. Biden as "too scared to stand up to the radical left of his own party."[197]

There is truth to Mr. Trump's allegations in terms of the positions taken by mainstream Democrats and some of their party members across America.

During the campaign, Joe Biden deflected questions about his party's push for socialism. At a town hall meeting, Mr. Biden rhetorically asked: "Do I look like a socialist?" He continued: "Look, I'm the guy that ran against the socialist," but Mr. Biden never gave a straightforward answer to whether or not his party was pushing socialism.[198]

All doubt went out the window when the 2020 Democratic Party platform was released, however. It was filled to the brim with progressive (socialist) policies thanks to a joint effort between former Vice President Biden and Senator Sanders to unify Democrats around Mr. Biden's candidacy with a 110-page progressive policy wish list. Once Biden secured the nomination, he drew heavily from the Unity Task Force document that sealed a support deal with the socialist senator.

Senator Sanders was quite pleased with the document and told NPR, "On issue after issue, whether it was education, the economy, health care, climate, immigration, criminal justice, I think there was significant movement on the part of the Biden campaign."[199]

Evidently, Mr. Biden went all in for Sanders' Marxist agenda. "I don't think you could find any issue that we couldn't find an agreeable resolution on, that everybody in the room said, 'That will work,'" said Jared Bernstein, Biden's former economic adviser in the Obama administration and a Unity Task Force member. "I don't think you could find anything in there that he won't want to take a very close look at."[200]

The Democratic Party's platform basically cemented the socialist takeover of the party when it adopted such positions as calls for reversing President Trump's tax cuts, embraced former President Obama's so-called Jobs Act (that never passed Congress), called for the takeover of healthcare by supporting Medicare-for-All, embraced radical gun control to include banning the sale of guns and ammunition online, and returning to the flawed Iranian nuclear deal.[201]

The Democratic Party's National Convention (August 17–20, 2020) put its new and radical face on full display as well. The convention hosted anti-Semite Linda Sarsour, a progressive activist and member of the Democratic Socialists of America, who said the Democratic Party "is absolutely our party." Another Democratic National Convention (DNC) panelist announced the party's radical stance on key issues, saying, "We're talking about abolishing the police, we're talking about abolishing ICE [US Immigration and Customs Enforcement], we're talking about abolishing prisons."[202]

Senator Sanders virtually addressed the DNC, bragging that his socialist ideas are now "mainstream" in Biden's Democratic Party, while another speaker said the Green New Deal was needed to further the "destruction" of capitalism. And a pastor who spoke at the convention said America "'may well go to hell' if we don't have open borders."[203]

Then candidate Biden's own words put him in Sanders' socialist camp. He pledged, should he be elected, to be the most "progressive of any Democrat running," a statement that no doubt pleased Sanders. Mr. Biden quickly established a task force with Sanders' campaign to give prominent position to socialist issues.[204]

Among those issues, Biden promised a $2 trillion climate plan to achieve net-zero emissions, and said there would be no place for fossil fuels, including coal and fracking, in his administration. He pledged, "We would make sure it's eliminated."[205]

Former Vice President Biden promised tax hikes raising the corporate tax rate to 28 percent, which will be higher than Canada (15 percent) and communist China (25 percent). Meanwhile, his campaign's spending proposals totaled up to more than $6.3 trillion, far outpacing the revenue to be earned via his proposed tax hikes. The totals for his promised spending plan included a climate plan ($2 trillion), universal childcare and in-home elder care ($775 billion), Obamacare expansion ($750 billion), a housing plan ($640 billion), an infrastructure plan ($1.3 trillion), and his preschool and K–12 education plan ($850 billion).[206]

It's obvious that Mr. Biden went full socialist to gain the left's support for his campaign, and it doesn't matter whether he believes in these issues or not. He committed to them, and the leftists like Sanders will hold him to those promises that garnered the left's support to land Biden in the Oval Office.

President Biden sold his soul to get votes, and now we must all live with the consequences.

Biden and the Radicals around Him

Aesop (620–564 BCE), a Greek storyteller and author of *Aesop's Fables*, said: "A man is known by the company he keeps."[207] That applies to the running mate a presidential candidate selects. Mr. Biden selected US Senator Kamala Harris (California) for his vice-presidential running mate, a woman with a very long history marked by associations with ultra-leftists and some communists. Further, Ms. Harris' policy preferences speak volumes about her leftist governing ideology. As a sitting US senator from California, she backed the $93 trillion Green New Deal; in 2015, she lobbied for President Obama's Iran nuclear deal as "our best option;" embraced the $600 billion "College for All" proposal; supported massive tax increases like socialist Representative Ocasio-Cortez's proposed 70 percent tax rate; favored Senator Sanders' government takeover of healthcare; favored repeal of the criminal statute that makes illegal border crossings a criminal offense; wants to reexamine the role of ICE, saying she would "probably think about starting [it] from scratch," and comparing it to the Ku Klux Klan; and supported the decision to make San Francisco a sanctuary city; as well as promoted many other radical policy positions.[208]

President Trump said Ms. Harris is left of Bernie Sanders, a "communist." There is compelling evidence that Mr. Trump's assessment is correct. Miss Harris was raised by hard-core leftists (two Stanford professors) who were active in the Berkeley-based Afro-American Association known for supporting Fidel Castro and Che Guevara, an Argentine Marxist revolutionary and leader of liberation movements. Two members of the Berkeley-based group were Huey Newton and Bobby Seale, better known for founding the Black Panther Party in 1966. That group embraced a Maoist philosophy, which served as the template for the creation of the Marxist Black Lives Matter movement.[209]

Fresh out of Howard University (Washington, DC), Kamala Harris returned home to the San Francisco Bay Area to pursue a legal career. It wasn't long before the thirty-year-old Harris became involved in a romantic relationship with the then sixty-year-old Willie Brown, who became the mayor of San Francisco. Brown opened many doors for Harris, including positions on well-paying boards, and he was instrumental to launching her on a political career.

At the time, Mr. Brown enjoyed the political support of the Communist Party USA, and as a gesture of appreciation he openly cosponsored a Communist Party fundraiser (People's Weekly World Gala Banquet, Berkley Marina, September 26, 1999) while still serving as mayor. Further, Mayor Brown was publicly identified as a friend of communist Chinese dictator President Jiang Zemin.[210]

In 2012, President Jiang stopped in the Bay Area because "he's an old friend of Mayor Brown," said Wang Ling, a representative at San Francisco's Chinese Consulate. "You know Mayor Brown has been (on trade missions) to China three times, and each time he's met with President Jiang. So, they have a very good relationship."[211]

Mayor Brown gave Ms. Harris a political start that launched her to other relationships with radicals. When she was the San Francisco district attorney, Ms. Harris mentored Lateefah Simon, an activist at the time serving on the board of the Oakland-based Youth Empowerment Center. All board members of that organization at the time were associated with the Maoist communist group Standing Together to Organize a Revolutionary Movement (STORM). Today, Ms. Simon is friends with Black Lives Matter founder Alicia Garza, an admitted Marxist.[212]

Evidently, associations with known communists run in the Harris family. After all, Maya Harris, Kamala's sister, was an activist during her time at Stanford University, where she befriended Steve Philips, a leading Marxist-Leninist on campus associated with the pro-China group League of Revolutionary Struggle. In 2012, Mr. Phillips, who apparently never lost his leftist views, explained those positions in his Political Intelligence blog.

He wrote:

> First, let me make clear that I come out of the Left. I've studied Marx, Mao, and Lenin. In college, I organized solidarity efforts for freedom struggles in South Africa and Nicaragua, and I palled around with folks who considered themselves communists and revolutionaries (the non-violent type), and I did my research paper on the Black Panther Party.[213]

Ms. Harris' 2020 campaign chief of staff was Karine Jean-Pierre, someone with political campaign experience who had been a lecturer at Columbia University, a former spokeswoman for MoveOn (a progressive public-policy advocacy group), and active with the New York-based Haiti Support Network. That group was closely aligned with the pro-China/North Korea Workers World Party, and Ms. Jean-Pierre supported Jean-Bertrand Aristide, the leftist former president of Haiti.[214]

Ms. Jean-Pierre, who supports boycotting Israel, is President Biden's principal deputy press secretary. She is the author of a 2019 op-ed that blamed the American Israel Public Affairs Committee for the Trump administration's withdrawal from the Iran nuclear deal and accused that group of Islamophobic views.[215]

Doug Emhoff, Harris' husband, works for the law firm DLA Piper, a multinational law firm in more than forty countries with revenues of

$2.48 billion (2014), which has decades of experience in China support-ing the "China Investment Services' branch." According to the National Pulse, DLA Piper's China practice employs "a host of former Chinese communist party officials." It gets worse.

The *National Pulse* wrote in September 2020:[216]

> Ernest Yang, who serves as the firm's [DLA Piper] Head of Liti-gation & Regulatory department and Co-Head of International Arbitration, was appointed to the Chinese People's Political Con-sultative Conference (CPPCC) in 2013. The CPPCC serves as the top advisory board for the Chinese Communist Party, and Yang was promoted to the body's Standing Committee in 2019.
>
> Jessica Zhao, a Senior Advisor, served as the Deputy Secretary General of the CHINA International Economic and Trade Arbitration Commission (CIETAC), a government-owned body established by the Chinese Communist Party in 1956. It was developed under the auspices of the CHINA Council for the Promotion of International Trade, "a governmental body for the furtherance of Chinese trade promotion."

These associations—a husband with a law firm with Chinese communist clients, a campaign chief of staff intimate with the radical MoveOn, a sister close to a known Marxist and more—would disqualify Ms. Harris from securing a United States government security clearance. However, that's a moot point, because she was elected to be a heartbeat away from becoming the nation's commander-in-chief.

None of this should surprise anyone. After all, as a senator, Ms. Harris, according to the nonpartisan GovTrack, was the most left-wing senator—even to the left of Bernie Sanders. So, it shouldn't alarm any-one when, just before Election Day 2020, Ms. Harris showed her Marx-ist colors when she addressed the difference between "equality" and "equity," and then concluded as any good Marxist would that "equitable treatment means we all end up at the same place."[217]

"So, there's a big difference between equality and equity," Harris posted on her Twitter account. "Equality suggests 'Oh everyone should get the same amount.' The problem with that, not everybody's starting out from the same place. So, if we're all getting the same amount, but you started out back there and I started out over here—we could get the same amount, but you're still going to be that far back behind me."[218]

She continued, "It's about giving people the resources and the support they need so that everyone can be on equal footing and then compete on equal footing."

The fact is that "equity" happens when government uses its power to disadvantage one group over another in order to reach a desired outcome. That "sounds just like Karl Marx," US Representative Liz Cheney (R-WY) said. "A century of history has shown where that path leads. We all embrace equal opportunity, but government-enforced equality of outcomes is Marxist," she insists.[219]

Both President Biden and Vice President Harris have plenty of radical ideas, acquaintances, and fellow travelers in the Democratic Party—most favor using big government to realize "equity." One of the best-known and up-and-coming leaders of that concept is Congresswoman Alexandria Ocasio-Cortez, who was hailed as "the future" of the Democratic Party by DNC chair Tom Perez. She is a member of the Democratic Socialists of America, a Marxist group profiled previously that believes in the "abolition of capitalism" and "that the government should 'democratize' private businesses i.e., force owners to give workers control of them."[220]

No doubt the Biden administration will fill itself with known and secret radicals, many with true leftist (Marxist) credentials for future policy work and not that different from the progressive/socialist cabal now in the House of Representatives. Time will tell just how radical they are and how quickly these people will push our government—and, by association, this country—into the socialist camp or worse.

It's bad enough that the Democratic Party is overflowing with leftists and Marxist sympathizers. Many similarly minded radicals outside the party see the Democratic Party as a great vehicle to advance their agenda.

Marxists Hiding inside Democratic Party Ranks

All across this country, Communist Party USA (CPUSA) members and other like-minded radical groups seek to increase their influence by enlisting with the Democratic Party. These communists and ism cousins work in Democrat campaigns, hold Democratic Party leadership positions, and even run for public office on the Democratic Party ticket while hiding their true ideological beliefs.

Some of these radicals push their leftist policies while inside the Democratic Party, making it hard to distinguish between the communist, socialist, progressive, and Democratic Party programs. The worst offenders are true wolves in sheep clothing because they hold public office while pretending to be Democrats.

There are numerous examples of these faux Democrats across the country. Much of the following material comes from the work of Trevor Loudon, an author and filmmaker who has spent more than thirty years researching radical left and Marxist groups.

Patrick Morales, an Arizona Communist Party ally on the Tempe Elementary School Governing Board, ran for that state's House of Representatives as a Democrat. In Texas, Communist Party member Penny Morales Shaw ran for the Texas House as a Democrat as well.[221]

CPUSA political action committee chair Joelle Fishman referenced the two (Morales and Shaw) by name in a report to the party:

> Our concept of the revolutionary process and building broad unity against the right and for people's needs is more relevant than ever, as is the importance of a larger Communist Party.... In Texas we had five candidates in the primaries who got a quarter million votes for US Senate and plans to run again. In the general election Penny Morales Shaw ran for county commissioner in a Republican area and got 45% of the vote in a great campaign with union support. In Arizona, in addition to races at every level, in Tempe Patrick Morales came in first for re-election to the School Board.[222]

The policy similarities between communists and Democrats may not be all that different, which might explain the communists' election success. For example, communists in Tucson and Phoenix focus on protecting illegal immigration (a Democratic Party issue), and they are quite effective. Communists helped elect Tucson's US Congressman Raúl Grijalva (the cochair of the Congressional Progressive Caucus), and in the past, they helped elect Phoenix Congressman Ed Pastor (1943–2018), a founding member of the Congressional Progressive Caucus, and a member who supported Planned Parenthood 100 percent of the time. When Pastor retired (2012), the CPUSA helped elect long-time CPUSA supporter Krysten Sinema to Congress, and the communists backed her successful US Senate bid in 2018 as well.[223]

Senator Sinema, an openly bisexual woman, now identifies as a Democrat. She decided to be sworn in as a US senator not on the Bible, but with her hand on copies of the Constitutions of the US and Arizona. Previously she served as the spokeswoman for the Green Party, and, after earning her law degree from Arizona State University, she worked as an adjunct professor for the leftist Center for Progressive Leadership, an organization bankrolled by George Soros' Democracy Alliance.[224]

Ms. Sinema's Democratic Party allegiance is suspect not just because of support from the Communist Party. She launched her political career as a member of the Arizona Green Party and ran for local offices as an independent. She also worked on Ralph Nader's 2000 presidential campaign and showed her socialist views in an *Arizona Republic* letter to the editor criticizing capitalism, in which she wrote, "Until the average American realizes that capitalism damages her livelihood while augmenting the livelihoods of the wealthy, the Almighty Dollar will continue to rule."[225]

The Houston, Texas, area has Communist Party members very active in the Democratic Party. In 2018, Houston Communist Party member Ali Khorasani unsuccessfully ran for Congress. Meanwhile, Houston Communist Party chair Bernard Sampson is a Democratic Party precinct chair.[226]

San Diego has CPUSA members active in the California Democratic

Party as well. Carl Wood, a lifelong communist, ran for the California Democratic Party's central committee. Years earlier, then Democrat Governor Gary Davis appointed Wood to the California Public Utilities Commission.[227]

CPUSA leaders in Minnesota, Doris and Erwin Marquit, were active in the Democratic-Farmer-Labor Party, a local Democratic Party affiliate. They raised funds for Democrat Keith Ellison's three congressional campaigns. Mark Froemke, another Minnesota communist, reportedly had a "good relationship" with disgraced former Minnesota US Senator Al Franken and former Governor Mark Dayton, a big supporter of the AFL-CIO unions and abortion on demand who received top billing from Americans for Democratic Action, a progressive social justice group.[228]

Communists like Pepe Lozano (CPUSA member and worker for progressive political campaigns) helped Chicago native and Mexican-born Jesús G. "Chuy" García's congressional campaign, and CPUSA leader John Bachtell (chairman of the National Committee of the CPUSA, 2014–2019) was a precinct chairman for then US Senate candidate Barack Obama.[229]

The CPUSA is active in Missouri politics as well. In Democratic Party stronghold St. Louis, Glenn Burleigh, a CPUSA member, managed multiple Democrat campaigns, including one for state senate and another for mayor of St. Louis. Meanwhile, Mr. Burleigh chaired the Missouri/Kansas Communist Party education/ideology committee and was an organizer with the Communication Workers Union as well as the head organizer at St. Louis ACORN (Association of Community Organizations for Reform Now), a far-leftist group.[230]

Anita MonCrief, an ex-ACORN insider and Democratic Party donor, said ACORN is an example of "stealth socialism." She explained that inside ACORN offices, liberals were ingrained with the views of radical Saul Alinsky's style of organizing, which was used on both employees and members. Alinsky, the "father of community organizing," advocates in his book, *Rules for Radicals*, "the path to power necessitated the use of people who would serve as pawns."[231]

America's largest urban center, New York City, has a long history of communist political activism. Dan Margolis, a former communist, was the coordinator for the 2004 Democratic Party congressional campaign in mid-Staten Island. Margolis wrote in his blog:

> I ended up working on many Democratic campaigns during my time in the CPUSA: John Kerry's, Obama's twice, [Senator] Kirsten Gillibrand's, Fernando Ferrer's (he nearly beat Michael Bloomberg to become mayor of NYC), and a host of others known mostly to NYC residents. I am proud to say that I wrote the first official document in the CPUSA calling for support of Obama in the primaries: I wrote this as chair of the party in Brooklyn, in 2007.[232]

The CPUSA is especially successful in Connecticut. It is close to governor Ned Lamont, thanks to the governor's uncle Corliss Lamont (1902–1995), a former chairman of 1940s era National Council of American-Soviet Friendship and someone identified as a communist by former CPUSA leader Louis Budenz.[233] Evidently, the CPUSA also has influence with the state's two US senators, Richard Blumenthal and Chris Murphy. It is noteworthy that Senator Murphy employed a CPUSA member as an aide "while serving on the highly sensitive Senate Foreign Relations Committee." Meanwhile, Connecticut member of the US House of Representatives, Rosa DeLauro, "is very close to CPUSA Connecticut leader Joelle Fishman and her husband Art Perlo—the son of Roosevelt-era Soviet spy ring leader Victor Perlo."[234]

Many communists keep their ideological persuasion and CPUSA membership secret, which means there are likely more of them inside the Democratic Party than publicly known. The reality today might be much like the reported thousands of communists who allegedly worked inside the FDR administration and throughout the federal bureaucracy up to the mid-1950s.

The bottom line for the Democratic Party and the US in general is the presence of communists openly serving or hidden behind the veil of the party endangering America's security because of their true allegiance. After all, the CPUSA's goal remains: to replace the American form of government, and that's a serious threat. Democratic Party members who really love this country ought to identify these people and make certain they don't gain stature in their party or positions of authority in government.

Socialists, Quasi-Marxists Hiding inside Democratic Party Ranks

The CPUSA's cousin is America's largest socialist organization, the Democratic Socialists of America (DSA), which has also burrowed its way into the Democratic Party, especially thanks to many thousands of socialists who worked for Senator Sanders' presidential candidacy. Many of these people, all DSA members, also helped elect Alexandria Ocasio-Cortez to Congress in 2018 and again in 2020.

These DSA comrades are part of a growing international socialist-communist movement thinking they are making America more like Scandinavia, but in reality, they are helping to transform the US into something more like Cuba or Venezuela.

Consider that some DSA members are far more Marxist than simpleton socialists such as convicted East German spy Kurt Stand, a long-time DSA leader who served a prison sentence (1997–2012) for his role in helping the East German Stasi secret police. Further, Theresa Squillacote, Stand's former wife, who worked in the Pentagon as a Defense Department lawyer, also spent time in prison. Evidently, according to news reports, Squillacote passed defense documents to an FBI undercover agent who posed as an intelligence official from a foreign government.[235]

DSA socialists, like Mr. Stand, are really communists. After all, DSA's national strategy was adopted not from a socialist icon but from the late Italian Communist Party theoretician Antonio Gramsci, who recommended a very different approach to the standard Marxist revolutionary model. Gramsci suggested infiltrating communists into all areas of society (e.g., media, education, government), an approach the DSA rank and file adopted.[236]

The Los Angeles, California, branch of the DSA confirmed its use of the Gramsci template in a 1984 newsletter:

> Antonio Gramsci was a founder of the Italian Communist Party. He developed theories on "open ended Marxism" and independent Euro-Communism. His writings have remained influential among European parties of the left for several decades. They have also formed a vital part of the ideas that brought about the formation of today's DSA.[237]

The DSA's wide-ranging success of burrowing Gramsci-style into many American institutions is summarized by Mr. Loudon, writing for the *Epoch Times*. Mr. Loudon's examples include:[238]

- AFL-CIO president and DSA member John Sweeney fundamentally transformed the U.S. labor movement in 1994–95.
- DSA comrades like actor Ed Asner moved Hollywood even farther left through their influence in the entertainment unions.
- Eliseo Medina, a DSA comrade and former executive vice president of the Service Employees International Union, almost single-handedly started the political movement to legalize illegal aliens. Medina became President Barack Obama's unofficial immigration adviser.
- Ron Bloom, who served under Obama directly as "assistant to the president for manufacturing policy," was a member of the DSA's predecessor, the DSOC.
- The movement for single-payer (government-run health care) is and continues to be a DSA operation. It started with Chicago DSA comrade Dr. Quentin Young, another mentor to Obama.

- Academia has been overrun with Marxist professors, who are grooming the next generation of radicals. DSA is well-established through their youth organization, Young Democratic Socialists of America, with chapters on university campuses and even high schools all over the country.
- Thousands of "community organizers"—labor organizers and nonprofit officials—have been trained through the DSA-aligned Midwest Academy in Chicago.
- DSA member Michael Moore has influenced millions through his documentaries, and DSA member Linda Sarsour is a prominent pro-sharia activist and speaker, including her role at the Communist Party USA-sponsored Women's March.
- In the early 1990s, New York Mayor David Dinkins and St. Paul, Minnesota, Mayor Jim Scheibel were DSA comrades. DSA had many state legislators, county commissioners, and local officials in its ranks—almost all under Democratic Party cover.
- Several congressmembers were DSAers, including Rep. Major Owens (New York) and the pro-Cuba Rep. Ron Dellums of California, who shockingly served on the House Armed Services Committee. The Congressional Progressive Caucus will likely gain several new members this coming election, including card-carrying DSA members Ocasio-Cortez of Queens, New York, and Rashida Tlaib of Detroit, Michigan. Both have won their Democratic reelection bids in 2020.

As this section demonstrates, many members of the Democratic Party are avowed communists and/or socialists. Likely, there are others among their ranks who keep their radical views to themselves. Meanwhile, there are many more Marxists outside the walls of the Democratic Party who render support to or do the Democrat's bidding for selfish reasons.

Marxists Who Influence the Democratic Party from the Outside

America's numerous Marxist parties tend to put their full support behind the Democratic Party in all elections.

In the fall of 2018, the Communist Party organizer for Ohio sent out an urgent appeal for "progressives and socialists" to support only Democrats. Mr. Rick Nagin, the communist organizer, said the Democrats are the "only electoral vehicle" that can beat the Republicans.[239]

Mr. Nagin wrote the following on the Communist Party's website, People's World:

> The immediate battle is the November elections in which left forces must accept the reality that the only electoral vehicle capable of defeating the extremists [Republican Party] is the Democratic Party. Therefore, there is no question but that every effort must be made to elect the Democratic candidates.[240]

He wrote further:

> Since the election in 1980 of Ronald Reagan and especially with the subsequent consolidation of control over the Republican Party by right-wing extremism, the main challenge for the progressive and socialist movement has been to build a broad democratic coalition to defeat this threat to living standards, democratic rights, peace, and the environment.[241]

To support his case, Nagin quotes former CPUSA leader Gus Hall, who said in 1969, "The fight against state monopoly capitalism, in general, must always be conducted from the viewpoint of strengthening the forces of the ultimately necessary socialist revolution, and never from the viewpoint of stabilizing the system."[242]

In other words, Nagin said, "While socialists and all Democrats agree for the moment on the need to defeat the Republicans in November, the aim of socialists is to weaken, not stabilize, corporate power [i.e., American business]. This means acting in a way that preserves the independent goals, aims, and organization of the movement for socialism and strengthens and builds the broad grassroots anti-monopoly alliance."[243]

So, while socialists and communists must "seek the best possible outcome for working people in any struggle, electoral or otherwise," they must be guided by *The Communist Manifesto* to "fight for the attainment of the immediate aims, for the enforcement of the momentary interest of the working class.... But in the movement of the present, they also represent and take care of the future of that movement."[244]

Marxists like Nagin understand today that the Democratic Party and specifically Mr. Biden were their only option in 2020. That's why noted Marxist terrorist Angela Davis endorsed Biden; there was simply no alternative.

On August 18, 1970, Angela Davis was named to the FBI's Ten Most Wanted List for kidnapping, murder, and interstate flight until her arrest two months later. She is a Marxist terrorist and leading advocate who endorsed Joe Biden for the presidency in 2020. Davis, who delivered her endorsement of Biden on Russian television, is known for wanting to defund the police, backing the Soviet Union and communist Cuba during the Cold War, and owning firearms used to kill four people. Notably, her endorsement earned muffled cheers from the Democrats, albeit even when Davis said Biden is so politically malleable that he can be made to advance Marxist goals.[245]

Neither the Biden campaign nor a single high-profile Democrat said anything about Davis' endorsement or her rationale. Evidently, the support of a famous American communist terrorist is welcomed by Democrats, and besides, everyone knows Mr. Biden is "politically malleable."

Other American communists joined forces to help elect Mr. Biden. Edward Carson, former chairperson of the CPUSA, said it was critical that fellow communists find common ground with their progressive brethren to avoid sectarianism. "The CPUSA aims to avoid sectarianism at all cost," Carson said. "We have to realize that we have to work, have to operate within an apparatus [Democratic Party] of various different groups." That's when Carson encouraged all leftists to vote for Biden.[246]

"People must mobilize in a way to pull liberals and progressives together," Carson said. "That means voting for Biden, supporting Biden, and by really working in many ways to stop the degradation of certain things that are problematic."[247]

These communists don't intend to just serve as surrogates for the Democratic Party, however. The Democrats are ersatz allies because there is no other choice for now. They are nothing but useful idiots, pawns, and will in time be discarded. The communists' true motivation is to eventually take over—completely replace the Democratic Party with their own party.

WHO ARE THE COMMUNISTS AND THEIR PARTIES?

Trevor Loudon profiles these parties in his 2019 article in the *New American*. He writes that US-based communist groups intend to take over the Democratic Party, and given their diverse membership, finances, and outside support, that outcome shouldn't be ruled out.

The CPUSA, Committees of Correspondence for Democracy and Socialism (CCDS), Freedom Road Socialist Organization (FRSO), the DSA, and many other bona fide Marxist parties are dead set on taking over, and frankly, they are showing progress.

Four US communist groups have formed an alliance with the explicit goal of taking over the Democratic Party at every level. The leaders of those four parties met virtually at an online webinar in May 2018, a convocation sponsored by the front group Left Inside/Outside Project. The intent of the webinar, according to CPUSA party leader John Bachtell, was to discuss "building power inside and outside the Democratic Party." Bachtell said the CPUSA "is collaborating with several left groups and progressive activists to promote unity and coalition building in the electoral arena. Building electoral coalitions with every force possible including with the Democratic Party is key."[248]

Left Inside/Outside Project is aligned with FRSO, which calls for communists to completely dominate the Democratic Party. It seeks leftists to work together in and out of the Democratic Party: "We believe that…only determined, long-term, energetic efforts to breakout of the margins based on a common view of how to engage in our electoral system, while also building mass protest, offer a chance to make the left a force in U.S. politics and, eventually, a contender for power."[249]

The Marxist alliance proposed a strategy of running candidates as Democrats in coordination with socialist forces. That strategy states:

> The fight against the far right is strongest when it is energized by an inspiring vision for economic and social justice. Campaigns for openly socialist candidates and progressive challenges to neoliberal Democrats must all be part of the political mix. And the opportunities for broadening the reach of progressive and left forces will be greatest when they both struggle within and work in tandem with the larger anti-Trump or anti-right front.[250]

You may ask whether four small radical groups (parties) with a combined core membership of 65,000 can make a difference in a country of 330 million souls. The answer depends on their dedication. Keep in mind that, in 1910, as Mr. Loudon wrote, "seven years before the Bolshevik revolution, the combined Russian revolutionary forces of Bolsheviks and the slightly more moderate Mensheviks numbered fewer than 10,000."[251]

These modern Bolsheviks have a lot going for them to include many allies identified in the following chapters in this section. But first, let's briefly consider each of these co-conspirator groups that joined the Left Inside/Outside Project to overtake the Democratic Party.

Communist Party USA (CPUSA)

The previous chapter sketched the beginning of the CPUSA, which grew to more than one hundred thousand members after the Second World War, but rapidly shrank as the Cold War exposed the truth about communism in the mid-1950s. Today, the CPUSA's membership might be five thousand strong, with their most significant presence in New York City, Boston, Chicago, Detroit, St. Louis, and states like Connecticut and California.

The CPUSA's vision for the future is outlined in the document, *Road to Socialism USA*, which was adopted in 2005 and updated at the CPUSA's 100th Anniversary Convention in 2019 in Chicago. That vision statement offers "the path from struggles of the present all the way to socialism, a strategy of struggle, unity, reform, and revolution."[252]

That vision blames most every problem known to man on capitalism, "an inhumane, exploitative, oppressive economic system of greed." The CPUSA argues, "We need to replace capitalism with socialism, a system of cooperation, democracy, and equality."[253]

Predictably, the CPUSA blames the harm done by the COVID-19 pandemic not on the communist Chinese (the source of the deadly virus) or on Democrat governors and mayors (who arguably mishandled the response), but on "the economic weakness of capitalism." The document states that the capitalistic system is "unable to adequately compensate workers for lost income, unable to deal with the economic devastation [of the virus] for both small businesses that crash with only a few weeks of being shut down and workers who are laid off as a result."[254]

The CPUSA's document attacks the wealthy as the source of the problem, stating, "We need a system that prioritizes the needs of the people before the greed of the few, the 1%." And it blames capitalism for the "death of seniors in order to 'restart the economy'" as a system that is "morally and economically bankrupt."[255]

Finally, these communists advocate for a utopia whereby all the social justice issues are magically solved: "We stand with the workers of our country, and the working class of the whole world, for health care for all, for an end to income inequality, against racism, sexism, and all injustice."[256]

Committees of Correspondence for Democracy and Socialism (CCDS)

The Committees of Correspondence split from the CPUSA in 1991 and changed its name to Committees of Correspondence for Democracy and Socialism (CCDS) in 2002. Its membership is perhaps four hundred strong, and includes Maoists, Trotskyists, anarchists, and democratic socialists who also tend to hold active memberships with other Marxist organizations and are found mostly in big cities like Boston, New York, Chicago, and San Francisco.

The group's preamble states it believes in "a society of social justice" and to achieve that ideal society, it requires "a joint struggle to democratically transform our present society, to end the existing vast inequalities of wealth, power and conditions…. we view socialism as the struggle for democracy carried to its logical conclusion."[257]

The CCDS helped some Democrats such as New Yorker Chuck Schumer to win his US Senate seat and California's Congresswoman Barbara Lee her office in the early 1990s as well. Even CCDS leader Paul Krehbiel was instrumental in helping defeat conservative Republican Congressman Robert "Bob" Dornan in Orange County.[258]

Finally, Barack Obama received campaign help from CCDS members like Carl Davidson in his bid for the US Senate seat from Illinois.[259]

Freedom Road Socialist Organization (FRSO)

The FRSO is a Maoist-based group that has a membership of perhaps no more than 1,500 personnel. It is funded by the leftist Ford Foundation, billionaire George Soros' Open Society Foundations, and a variety of other leftist groups, unions, and churches. Its strongest presence is found in Atlantic Coast cities (Boston, New York, Philadelphia, and Washington, DC).

It is a Marxist-Leninist organization that believes capitalism is "inherently a system of inequality, injustice, and war. We want a social system where social wealth is not in the hands of a few billionaires, but is controlled by the people."[260]

FRSO takes a strong stand on so-called social justice issues and it blames capitalism for most problems: "For five hundred years, capitalism has everywhere rested on colonization without and racist oppression of its minority nationalities within its borders." It takes a stand in the "fight for women's liberation and against all forms of male supremacy," promises to "fight against all forms of homophobia and heterosexism," and joins "the struggle for a livable planet," blaming corporate greed for environmental issues, and suggests socialism is the only savior for the planet.[261]

It is like other Maoist groups that promote racial politics, and it became a force supporting Black Lives Matter, and both Asian and Latino activist groups.[262]

The group states on its website: "We intend to build a new communist party. We need to build a party of the working class, which can someday contend for power…. [and that] leadership will be predominantly oppressed nationality members and predominantly women, with Lesbian, Gay, and Bisexual and Transgender representation as well."[263]

Thanks to these race-based groups, FRSO has ties to Massachusetts Senator Elizabeth Warren and helped elect public officials like US Congresswoman Ayanna Pressley (MA).

Ms. Pressley is a staunch progressive, who won her seat promising that "change can't wait" and that she would bring "activist leadership." Once in Washington, she became a member of the informal group known as "The Squad," whose members like Ilham Omar (D-MN), Rashida Tlaib (D-MI) and Alexandria Ocasio-Cortez (D-NY) pushed for progressive changes such as the Green New Deal and Medicare-for-All.[264]

As if those issues weren't radical enough, she filed a resolution in

2019 to start impeachment proceedings against Supreme Court Justice Brett Kavanaugh, and two months later, she introduced a criminal justice reform resolution calling for the decriminalization of consensual sex work, legalizing marijuana, and closure of most prisons.[265]

FRSO is also very active in the US southern states, aiming to win power in cities and rural areas, so as to grow the Democratic Party's influence among minorities. For example, FRSO's New Virginia Majority signed up many thousands of minority voters and helped former governor Terry McAuliffe to restore voting rights for two hundred thousand felons to help flip that state from red to blue in favor of Obama's presidential victory.[266]

These communist policy recommendations—restore voting rights to felons, decriminalize sex workers, and others outlined above—are preposterous ideas tried many times before by failing governments, and as history attests, time and again they end up acting as accelerants to a society's decline because they represent the moral collapse of justice.

Democratic Socialists of America (DSA)

The DSA has been mentioned numerous times to this point. It started in 1982 and, thanks to Senator Sanders, grew to sixty thousand strong during the Vermont senator's presidential campaigns. It claims to have members in many cities from Seattle to Los Angeles, Chicago, New York, Washington, and even Austin, Texas.

The group has considerable and widespread political clout, especially inside the Democratic Party in states like Nebraska, Iowa, Florida, and California, where DSA members run the largest Democrat state party in the country.

The party sponsored numerous candidates as Democrats in recent congressional elections, to include Tlaib and Ocasio-Cortez, while other DSA members won state and local races. DSA also has influence and ties among many members of Congress, such as Omar, Eleanor Holmes Norton (D-DC), Jamie Raskin (D-MD) and Ro Khanna (D-CA).[267]

DSA enjoyed a long-term relationship with former President Barack Obama. In 2020. DSA also worked closely with Democratic presidential candidates Bernie Sanders, Elizabeth Warren, Amy Klobuchar, Tulsi Gabbard, Pete Buttigieg, and Beto O'Rourke.[268]

There is a long list of other Marxist-oriented parties in the United States that seek to influence the Democratic Party. These parties vary in size, location, and histories, but tend to share the same core beliefs: Socialist Party USA (SPUSA), Socialist Workers Party (SWP), Freedom Socialist Party (FSP), Workers World Party (WWP), Party for Socialism and Liberation (PSL), Freedom Road Socialist Organization— Fight Back (FRSO-FB), Solidarity, League of Revolutionaries for a New America (LRNA), International Socialist Organization (ISO), and Socialist Alternative (SA).[269]

There are other communist parties in America that, like the socialists and the CPUSA, seek to influence the Democratic Party. That list notably includes the Party of Communists, USA (PCUSA), and the Revolutionary Communist Party (REVCOM). These parties share in common with the CPUSA the goal of global communism, but may not agree on the best way to achieve that outcome. Some of these groups believe only in revolution through the chaos of violence (a Trotsky formula), others believe in a Mao Zedong approach (race-baiting and dividing people), and yet others endorse the Gramsci theory of "march through the institutions."[270]

REPUBLICAN PARTY:
A DIFFERENT APPROACH WITH COMMUNISTS

Meanwhile, and parenthetically, the Republican Party has consistently taken a different approach with communists than the Democratic Party.

In the early 1950s, US Senator Joseph McCarthy of Wisconsin, a Republican, was a well-known, ardent anti-communist who hosted hearings to expose their presence and influence. He was roundly criticized at the time by President Dwight Eisenhower (a Republican) who worked to discredit McCarthy and pushed the Republican caucus to censure the Wisconsin senator. Eisenhower was not pro-communist, just a political pragmatist at the time. Keep in mind it was President Eisenhower who signed the Communist Control Act in 1954, which outlawed the Communist Party of the US and criminalized membership in, or support for, the party of all communist action organizations in America. That act was subsequently ruled unconstitutional in federal court.[271]

Almost two decades later, Republican President Richard M. Nixon, a one-time arch-Cold Warrior, took advantage of the communist Chinese regime to leverage the Soviet Union's leaders. Mr. Nixon struck up relations with the communist Chinese in 1972 as he said, "We're using the China thaw to get the Russians shook." That relationship during the old Cold War was a threatening development for the Soviets and helped drive a wedge between the two communist giants.[272]

Finally, it was Republican President Ronald Reagan who drove the stake into the heart of the communist Soviet Union. He called it an "evil empire" and said the communist ideology gave Soviet leaders the "right to commit any crime."[273]

Mr. Reagan's "Star Wars" initiative drew Moscow into an arms race it couldn't afford, and then his 1987 declaration to then-Soviet leader Mikhail Gorbachev at the Berlin Wall—"Mr. Gorbachev, tear down this wall"—was the final straw that helped bring an end to the old Cold War.

"Reagan's SDI [Strategic Defense Initiative] was a very successful blackmail," said Gennady Gerasimov, who served for the Soviet Foreign Ministry in the 1980s. "The Soviet Union tried to keep up pace with the U.S. military buildup, but the Soviet economy couldn't endure such competition."[274]

Destroying communism and the Soviet Union in particular was the hallmark of President Reagan's eight-year administration, and it was the force that precipitated the Soviet collapse.

The contrast between the Republican and Democratic parties regarding communism is stark. The Republicans tend to oppose and reject communism, while many within the Democratic Party have tolerated (dating back to FDR), and in some cases warmly welcomed, communists into their ranks.

CONCLUSION

The Democratic Party is significantly influenced by individuals and groups of known Marxists and socialists. Traditional Democratic Party voters may still believe in the party of JFK and LBJ, but that's not the reality of their party today. No, it is becoming the party of Marx and Lenin and heavily influenced by Marxist insiders as well as radicals outside the party and even others in communist China and by European communists as well.

There is little doubt, given the Democrats' 2020 White House victory, that the cultural revolution energized the radicals both inside and outside the Democratic Party, and the transformational efforts will go into overdrive in the coming years.

5

Chinese Marxists
Declare Cold War and Fuel America's Cultural Revolution

No need wasting your time reviewing the rainbow of foreign Marxist entities and their influence on contemporary America. They exist—Russian, European, and more—but no country or movement is nearly as dangerous to America and on the scale as the threat posed by the Chinese Communist Party (CCP), which governs the world's largest population and hosts the globe's largest economy.

Unbeknownst to most Americans, the CCP years ago put that regime on a war footing to become the world's economic and military hegemon by the middle of this century (2049), and to reach that goal, it decided to deal with the threat posed by the United States.

The US threatens communist China on many fronts, but the worst is truly existential for the communist regime: ideological. America stands for human rights, freedom of speech, and an assortment of liberties—all values and principles that Beijing's communist tyrants oppose because, should those intangibles become standard fare among the Chinese people, the CCP won't remain in power. So, Beijing's communist dictators launched a war to prevent the West's values invasion, a new cold war that is similar to as well as distinctive from the one the US fought with the former Soviet Union (1947–1991). Beijing's cold war takes the fight to America's shores in many forms, but particularly in regards to our ongoing cultural revolution—and that includes taking advantage of the COVID-19 pandemic and playing an important role in helping defeat President Trump's 2020 reelection bid.

WHAT NEW COLD WAR?

In December 2020, the outgoing US National Intelligence Director (DNI) warned the nation about the threat posed by communist China. Although Mr. John Ratcliffe didn't use the words "cold war," every bit of the following explanation shouts that in fact America is in a cold war with China.

"Beijing intends to dominate the US and the rest of the planet economically, militarily and technologically," wrote Director Ratcliffe. "Many of China's major public initiatives and prominent companies offer only a layer of camouflage to the activities of the Chinese Communist Party."[275]

"I call its approach of economic espionage 'rob, replicate and replace,'" Ratcliffe wrote in the *Wall Street Journal.* "China robs US companies of their intellectual property, replicates the technology and then replaces the US firms in the global marketplace."[276]

Predictably, a Chinese foreign ministry official dismissed Mr. Ratcliffe's allegations as "false information, political viruses and lies" intended to damage China's reputation.[277]

The DNI said Beijing is preparing for an open-ended confrontation with the US. He continued, "This is our once-in-a-generation challenge. Americans have always risen to the moment, from defeating the scourge of fascism [World War II] to bringing down the Iron Curtain [old Cold War]."[278]

Mr. Ratcliffe concluded: "This generation will be judged by its response to China's effort to reshape the world in its own image and replace America as the dominant superpower."[279]

Indeed, America is in a new cold war, and it was launched by the Chinese Communists. Why? They want to protect themselves from democratic values that threaten the Marxist regime's power. Yes, the motivation for the new war is ideological for the most part.

The fact is the Chinese communist regime fears free speech. That was evidenced in September 2020, when Terry Branstad, the retiring US ambassador to China and former governor of Iowa, tried to publish an article in China's state newspaper, the *People's Daily*. The article, "Resetting the Relationship Based on Reciprocity," was rejected by the *Daily*. Secretary of State Mike Pompeo said that shows just how much the regime fears "their own people's free-thinking" and the "free world's judgment" about Beijing's draconian, anti-freedom behavior.[280]

The Chinese communists have always considered the US their enemy because the Beijing regime is politically dependent on "red" ideology, much as was the former Soviet Communist Party, but the CCP has taken a vastly different approach than did the communist dictators who ran the former Soviet Kremlin.

The Soviets sought so-called peaceful coexistence with the US, primarily in order to avoid nuclear conflict. The CCP already has a very different approach, which is using economic and military means to deter the US and establish itself to gain world domination.

Understandably, some readers may still be doubtful about the new cold war, given what is outlined to this point. Yes, many so-called geopolitical experts and historians still dismiss the idea of a new cold war with China, but the open discussion of the topic has become rather robust in the media, especially in 2020. Why? University of Chicago Professor John Mearsheimer spoke out on the topic in June 2020. He's no longer skeptical. The professor said, "Before the [coronavirus] outbreak controversy, people could argue whether China and the United States were really in a Cold War. But by now, I think it's pretty clear that there is a Cold War."[281]

Just how the Chinese weaponized the COVID-19 pandemic is addressed later in this chapter. However, even the Chinese communists agree that there is a new cold war, but they blame the Trump administration for a "new cold war declaration," which they date back to the 2017 release of the United States' National Security Strategy, which spoke of near peer global competitors, China and Russia.

In early 2020, China's foreign minister accused the US of pushing that country to the brink of a "new cold war" as the two nations exchanged barbs over the handling of coronavirus pandemic. "This dangerous attempt to turn back the wheel of history will undo the fruits of decades-long China-US cooperation, dampen American's own development prospects, and put world stability and prosperity in jeopardy," Foreign Minister Wang Yi said.[282]

The finger-pointing will continue for some time. However, agreeing on whether we are now in a second cold war warrants some reflection on the first cold war and a comparison of the causes, similarities, and differences.

Dr. Cheng Xiaonong, a scholar of China's politics and economy based in New Jersey, identified some of the similarities between the first and second cold wars. Those characteristics include:[283]

1. The biggest socialist country is pitted against the biggest capitalist country.
2. The conflict was launched by the socialist country.
3. The cause of the Cold War in the socialist country was "democracy phobia" and a constant hostility toward the most powerful democracy, the United States, for fear that its citizens might find democracy more attractive.
4. The red (communist) values of socialist countries have global conquest as their goal. Evidence for this can be seen in the post-World War II history of the Soviet Union and in the international relations strategy of the CCP under Mao Zedong.

5. Before these two cold wars, there existed a honeymoon phase, with the United States maintaining the honeymoon with constant courtship and gifts. But in the end, the United States found it had only cultivated and strengthened its adversaries.

6. Although the United States was often ill-prepared before the beginning of the cold war, once it entered into the cold war state, it would exert its institutional advantages and bring great pressure on its opponents.

7. While the Soviet Union and China, the world's two biggest communist countries, both initiated a cold war out of their fear of democracy, they each made different choices. The Soviet Union eventually chose to give up the Cold War, whereas the CCP chose to hide its strength and bide its time for thirty years. Having gained a little bit of a technical and economic foundation, it can't help showing off.

Dr. Cheng surmised in his article, "The communist state that initiates the cold war will inevitably be defeated by its own institutional characteristics." He then explained that the US-Soviet Cold War started at the conclusion of World War II as the Soviet army and the American-led armies faced off in Eastern Europe, neither willing to stand down. Then British Prime Minister Winston Churchill was one of the first to recognize the new reality.[284]

On March 5, 1946, Mr. Churchill spoke at Westminster College in Fulton, Missouri, which came to be known as the "Iron Curtain Speech." In it, he said, "From Stettin in the Baltic to Trieste in the Adriatic, an iron curtain has descended across the Continent."[285]

British George Orwell, the celebrated author of *1984*, a 1949 novel written about a world "fallen victim to perpetual war, omnipresent government surveillance, historical negationism, and propaganda," warned about a "cold war" in the wake of World War II. He wrote, "You and the Atomic Bomb" promised a "peace that is no peace." He explained that nuclear weapons might prevent direct invasions but create otherwise irreconcilable world orders.[286]

The prime minister and author Orwell both knew the nature of the communists at the time and discerned their intent to conquer Eastern Europe, which became a reality with the construction of the Berlin Wall in 1961. Meanwhile, the world's two great powers, the US and the Soviet Union, squared off with each promising to defeat the other. That was the start of the Cold War.

Both the old Soviets and present-day Chinese communists embraced Marxist ideology to a fault, the motivator for both cold wars. Like the Soviets, the CCP leadership today holds to the Marxist view that capitalism will inevitably lose to socialism. Former Soviet leader Nikita Khrushchev expressed that view in 1956 when he promised Western diplomats: "We [Soviets] will bury you!" However, by 1959, Khrushchev modified his confident "bury you" declaration by advancing conciliatory slogans like "peaceful coexistence, peaceful competition, and peaceful transition" between the Cold War camps.[287]

The existential nature of the US-Soviet Cold War became a serious reality in 1962 with the Cuban nuclear missile crisis. The threat of mutual destruction sobered both countries and tempered their rhetoric, but it didn't totally subside until the collapse of the Soviet Union on Christmas Day 1991. What was never in doubt from the beginning of the Soviet Union was that nation's leaders like Lenin, Stalin, and Khrushchev, who firmly believed their Marxist ideology would prevail in the end, while at the same time, they wanted to avoid nuclear war with the United States. Thankfully, pragmatism prevailed in both camps and, as the Soviet's final leader, Mikhail Gorbachev, wrote about the Cold War period: "The nuclear age demands a new political mindset.... There are no winners in nuclear war.... Whatever divides us, we live on the same planet, and Europe is our common home."[288]

That was the old Cold War with Soviet Russia, but the new one with communist China promises to be quite different.

The new cold war started with a series of provocative Chinese actions: naval maneuvers off the American military base on Sand Island (Midway Atoll); Beijing projecting a variety of military platforms (weapons systems) that targeted US Pacific forces; the seizing of islets in the South China Sea to transform them into a "fortress sea" for Chinese military operations' and the claim of sovereignty over a vast area that was previously considered international waters.

These provocations were serious enough, but then China announced its ability to strike America with nuclear-tipped missiles thanks to its modernizing space program. Beijing, if the announcement is true, can now strike the US with precision and destroy any target, according to the *Duowei News*. That 2020 article states: "On June 23, China successfully launched Big Dipper 3, the last global networking satellite, completing the deployment of its Global Navigation Satellite System constellation.... The total completion of the Big Dipper system also means a significant increase in China's military capabilities, with both 'global' and 'precision' capabilities, capable of more precise surgical strikes on global targets and detailed deployments on specific war sites."[289]

These actions by Beijing are red flags for those who understand communist ideology and they are backed up by the Pentagon's 2020 annual report to Congress on the threat posed by the People's Liberation Army. China's aggressive moves and major build-up of military might don't reflect the pragmatism expressed by the Soviet leaders in the old Cold War. Rather, they reflect former Chairman Mao Zedong's teachings, which makes the new cold war something quite different.

Dr. Cheng was a policy researcher and aide to the former Chinese Communist Party leader Zhao Ziyang, when Zhao was the Chinese premier. He explained the influence of the late Chairman Mao for the CCP's present cold war thinking about the United States:

> In November 1957, the conference of communist parties and workers' parties around the world was held in Moscow. At the meeting, Mao Zedong said: "Since our power is so strong, why do we still hold talks with it [the United States]? Just fight! What's

the big deal about nuclear war? There are 2.7 billion people in the world, and even if half of them died, another half remained alive. There are 600 million people in China and 300 million will be left. Then what am I afraid of?"[290]

Mao always adhered to his idea of defeating the United States by force. Speaking at the expanded Central Working Conference on Jan. 30, 1962, he said: "From now on, within and outside the 50 years to 100 years, there will be a great era of radical changes in the world's social system. It will be an earth-shaking era, unmatched by any other historical era. At such an age we must be prepared for a great struggle with many different forms of struggles from the past."[291]

The real meaning of his words was later revealed openly. In the book "Long Live Mao Zedong Thought," printed in China in 1968, there is the following passage of Mao speaking to Chen Boda, Ai Siqi, and other comrades in Hangzhou on Dec. 21, 1965: "The next few decades is [sic] a precious and important period for the future of the motherland and the fate of human-ity! Young people in their 20s now will be in their 40s or 50s in another 20 or 30 years. Our generation of young people will build our impoverished motherland into a great socialist country and take part in the battle to bury imperialism with our own hands. We have a long way to go. The ambitious Chinese youth must strive all their lives to fulfill our great historical mission. Our generation must make up its mind to work hard all one's life!"[292]

Dr. Cheng believes these passages influenced the Chinese people during the Cultural Revolution (1966–1976) to embrace Mao's world-view. For Mao and today's Chinese leaders who grew up with Mao's teachings, the term "burying imperialism" means "burying American imperialism."

China evidenced that view when it helped North Vietnam drag the US into the Vietnam War (1954–1975) because of "American imperialism." That mindset exists today among many Chinese communists, and they are confident the threat of force will deter America and lead to Beijing's global dominance over the United States.

Indeed, the Chinese communists are serious about world dominance. Mr. Frank Gaffney, the executive chairman of the Center for Security Policy, explained how Beijing will reach that lofty goal. He warns the US to focus on what the CCP is saying to itself and what it is doing. Mr. Gaffney said it is clear that the Chinese communists are saying to themselves, "to their leadership circles, [it] is very [clear] that the United States is the enemy. And that Communist China will prevail over that enemy by the cumulative effects of its now decades-long efforts through asymmetric warfare or unrestricted warfare—through predatory trade practices, through their Belt and Road initiative, through their dominance of space or their dominance of the 5G telecommunications universe, through their military buildup—they will prevail over us [and] they will become the world's dominant power."[293]

Mr. Gaffney's assertion about China's goal of dominating global communications must be taken seriously, as it is quite serious, which is dangerous for the entire world. Ren Zhengfei, the founder of China's telecommunications giant Huawei, served as an engineer in the People's Liberation Army during the Cultural Revolution. A study of Huawei states "that they mean to not only dominate but to control the world's means of communications."[294]

China's efforts to become the world leader in developing 5G capabilities is a serious threat. (Fifth generation [5G] is the latest wireless technology that redefines the network and establishes a new standard for speed and bandwidth.) Arthur Thompson writes in his 2020 book, *China: The Deep State's Trojan Horse in America*, "If they dominated 5G they would be able to censor the entire world, plant false information, control the ability of businesses to operate, shut down opposition, implant propaganda, etc.—not to mention building a real Big Brother system of thought control, influencing how Americans think and vote."[295]

There is a very significant caveat to this view, explained Mr. Gaffney. China has a serious vulnerability, he said, remarking further:

It needs to rely on us—the West more generally, mostly the United States—for the liquidity that gives it the wherewithal to do all of those malevolent things. It is the walking-around money, it is the enabling financing of the entire array of asymmetric warfare, economic and non-kinetic as well as the capability to engage in kinetic kinds of warfare as well. And when you look at that vulnerability, and the fact that we continue even in the wake of this pandemic [COVID-19], to believe that we can't possibly restrict its access to funds, we can't possibly deprive it of the means by which it is working to…destroy us, certainly to displace us as the dominant power of the world, certainly to impose its form of governance on the world, and its priorities, its values.[296]

So how do the Chinese thread the needle between relying on the US economically and deterring America on other fronts? Mr. Gaffney reminds us that the West (read "the US") is underwriting the CCP's success. They found that balance, which reminded him of a dictum attributed to Soviet leader Vladimir Lenin: "The capitalists will sell us the rope with which we'll hang them." The CCP put this into practice with the US by arranging for us to finance the purchase of the rope with which they'll hang us.[297]

How does that work? Well, the CCP needs America to partner with it on the corporate and political sides that enable profits for the wealthy and suppress the interests of the working class. To accomplish that, the CCP must take jobs out of the West to remain in power, which they believe will essentially destroy liberalism—the existential threat to communism.

So, to the CCP, success in the new cold war is a combination of intimidation (don't take military action against Chinese aggression) and economic manipulation that leads to Beijing's domination of the globe economically while at the same time destroying any hopes that liberal values will ever infect the Chinese people because Western jobs are gobbled up by the Chinese, leading to discontent and cultural implosion in the West. The end result is the survival of the CCP and perhaps its global expansion.

So, if in fact we are in a new cold war, then just how does the CCP contribute to the cultural implosion in the West?

CHINA'S IDEOLOGICAL COLD WAR: FUELS AMERICA'S CULTURAL REVOLUTION THROUGH A VARIETY OF PROXIES

China needs the US for its markets and technology, but it started the cold war because that communist regime can't tolerate our values: openness, democracy, free trade, human rights, and more. That ideological threat led to the new cold war, but when the CCP's war strategy was undermined economically by the election of a populist, an America-first candidate, Donald Trump, alarms went off in Beijing.

Economically, things were going quite well for the CCP prior to Mr. Trump's arrival in Washington. Back in 2001, the US welcomed China into the World Trade Organization, which led to the slow destruction of the American working class, because literally millions of American manufacturing jobs went to China over the subsequent decade-plus, as did our intellectual property and considerable capital, which enriched Chinese communists and stabilized the CCP's grip on its restless population. Then the political outsider, Mr. Trump, came on the scene pledging to "Make America Great Again"—and that translated into reversing all the past bad economic deals that emboldened the rising Chinese regime.

During the 2016 presidential campaign, Mr. Trump accused China of pulling off "one of the greatest thefts in the history of the world" and "raping" the US economy. Those accusations were backed up by the trade imbalance in Mr. Trump's first full year in office. In 2018, the US imported a record $539 billion in goods from the Chinese communist regime while selling only $120 billion, a $419 billion trade deficit.[298]

That trade imbalance, according to Peter Navarro, Trump's economic adviser, made China "the planet's most efficient assassin," because trade deficits represent an existential threat to US jobs and national security. Added to the mix was China's verified history of intellectual property theft, which, according to the Commission on the Theft of American Intellectual Property, cost $600 billion a year. Then China repeatedly for years dumped subsidized goods like steel and aluminum on the US market, drastically undercutting American producers. Meanwhile, American authorities called out China's manipulation of its currency "to gain unfair competitive advantage in international trade."[299]

Those and other activities gave Mr. Trump cause to challenge the Chinese to stop its malevolent economic practices and outright thievery of American property, or else. Beijing refused to concede, so by the end of his first year in office, Mr. Trump set a new course for America to stop China from "raping" America's economy. He published that new strategy in the National Security Strategy and the National Defense Strategy.

China was mentioned twenty-three times in the National Security Strategy, twice as many times as it was mentioned in Obama's last strategy. Mr. Trump's documents made it clear that Beijing was an existential threat to the US, a regime that embraces a "repressive vision of world order," and seeks to overthrow the free world led by the United States.[300]

The documents loudly outlined a fundamental shift in Washington's priorities away from the post-911 transnational Islamic terrorism focus to great power competition with China and Russia. That message confirmed the CCP's worst nightmare, and more so when Mr. Trump canceled past trade arrangements with China and imposed stiff tariffs on Chinese products.

At that point in early 2018, the CCP decided Mr. Trump had to go, and they began to take measures to ensure that he wasn't reelected. Further, they sought someone to replace him in the Oval Office who would return the China-US relationship to the former status quo that significantly benefited Beijing.

Keep in mind the nature of the Chinese regime. The CCP "exists in a world where it prefers authoritarian regimes," explained retired Air Force Brigadier General Robert Spalding, a China expert and author of *Stealth War: How China Took Over While America's Elite Slept.* So, according to General Spalding, the CCP launched efforts to bolster America's cultural revolution to remove Trump by working "very closely with our own corporate sector, mainstream media, and our political institutions. They emphasized critical race theory, things like applied postmodernism, things like social justice, that really have less to do with equality under the law, and more to do with a very particular form of racism [a Maoist revolutionary tool]."[301]

Soon the communist Chinese became a major behind-the-scenes player in the Marxist revolution tearing at America's foundation. That effort was part of Beijing's new cold war strategy focused on removing Mr. Trump in an effort to put America back in its place, to return to the status quo ante.

What else did Beijing do to advance America's revolution? It recruited American communists to the broader global ideological cause, as well as use its new allies to generate support for a Democratic Party alternative to Mr. Trump. Then it helped seed instability on America's streets through communist proxies, weaponized the COVID-19 pandemic against Trump, and manipulated the public conscience through information warfare using the mainstream media.

The conspiracy with many American entities did precisely what Beijing had to do: remove Mr. Trump and install in his place someone who would return America to the pre-Trump state of affairs. Meanwhile, the new cold war marches ahead and America loses to the more aggressive Chinese communists.

CCP RECRUITS AMERICAN
COMMUNISTS TO THE REVOLUTION

The previous chapter demonstrated the significant communist influence both inside the Democratic Party's ranks and from the outside. That influence contributes to how China is treated by some leading Democrats, which might explain why the CCP targeted that party as a proxy.

There are numerous examples of Democratic Party elite flacking for the Chinese. For example, Democrat leader and US House of Representative Adam Schiff (CA) complained in 2020 when the Trump administration ordered the shutdown of the Chinese consulate in Houston, Texas, because of confirmed spying. The US National Security Council said at the time that the order was made to "protect American intellectual property and Americans' private information."[302]

At the time, Mr. Schiff served as the chairman of the US House's Permanent Select Committee on Intelligence. He routinely received intelligence briefings on Chinese espionage and was fully aware of the rationale for closing the Chinese consulate. However, in response, Schiff acknowledged that China engages in criminal activity against the US, but said the move to close the consulate was a "very dramatic and sudden escalation," and that it was "all about politics."[303]

The Chinese consulate in Houston is not the center of China's spying operations in the United States, which is in San Francisco and New York. In fact, San Francisco is the location of the most prominent consulate for Chinese espionage. *Politico* indicates that foreign intelligence operations "in the Bay Area have focused their sights on collecting trade secrets and technology from nearby Silicon Valley."[304]

The bottom line for America is that it is widely known and documented that Chinese agents spy on America, sell us counterfeit goods and pirated software, steal our trade secrets, and conduct economic espionage (hacking) that could exceed $600 billion and reach as high as $1 trillion annually.[305]

Yet many Democrats like Schiff defend China despite the regime's lies about their cyber activities and proven economic "raping" of American corporations. Further, regarding the COVID-19 pandemic, Democrat Speaker of the House Nancy Pelosi (CA) flacked for China by absolving Beijing for its handling of the coronavirus pandemic by calling it the "Trump virus."[306]

Some prominent Democrats have close associations with Chinese spies or Chinese firms. In 2018, *Politico* reported that a staff member for US Senator Dianne Feinstein (D-CA) was recruited by the Chinese government and worked as Feinstein's chauffeur and as a liaison to the Asian-American community for decades. He reportedly attended Chinese consulate functions for the California senator as well.[307]

In December 2020, the FBI briefed leaders in the US House of Representatives regarding US Representative Eric Swalwell's (D-CA) ties to a suspected Chinese spy amidst calls to remove him from the highly sensitive House Intelligence Committee. After that briefing, minority leader, Representative Kevin McCarthy (R-CA), who was briefed, said the presentation "only raised more questions. The one thing that was fundamentally answered: he should not be on Intel." However, House Speaker Nancy Pelosi (D-CA) said, "I don't have any concern about Mr. Swalwell."[308]

Former California US Senator Barbara Boxer (Democrat) is a registered foreign agent for a Chinese surveillance firm, according to the *San Francisco Chronicle*. Evidently, Ms. Boxer gave a donation to President-elect Biden's inaugural committee, but the gift was returned when the committee learned of the former senator's association with Hikvision, a Chinese firm "accused of abetting the country's mass internment of Uighur Muslims." Justice Department documents indicate that Boxer provides "strategic consulting services" to Hikvision's subsidiary in the United States.[309]

Little wonder the Chinese communists celebrated the outcome of the 2020 presidential election—their man won, thanks to the Democratic Party's ongoing cooperation. Of course, President Biden was well known to the CCP as a malleable friend long before 2020. While serving both as a US senator and vice president to Obama, Mr. Biden defended the Chinese, and he repeated that behavior once again during the 2020 campaign: "They're [China] not competition for us," he said in a reference to Mr. Trump's National Security Strategy, to which Mr. Biden rhetorically asked and then jokingly answered: "China is going to eat our lunch? Come on, man."[310]

The communist Chinese' glee over the Biden victory came in late November 2020, when President Xi Jinping sent a congratulatory message to President-elect Joe Biden, a note that arrived after the regime initially hesitated as to avoid acting prematurely, given America's election laws and procedures.

The Xinhua News Agency, the official mouthpiece of the Chinese communist government, released President Xi's November 25 message to Mr. Biden, in which the Chinese leader expressed hope that both sides could "uphold the spirit of non-conflict, non-confrontation, mutual respect, and win-win cooperation." President Xi continued that he hoped "we will focus on cooperation, control our disagreements, and push the China-US relationship forward in healthy and stable directions."[311]

Evidently, the Chinese leader used that message to help Biden gain support as Mr. Trump contested the election with lawsuits in six key states. Tang Jingyuan, a US-based China affairs commentator, said Xi's message was a bid to "boost public opinion that the former vice president won the election." Another, US-based CCP mouthpiece, Li Linyi, said the gesture was in retaliation to Trump's tough measures against the regime.[312]

How did we get to this point whereby the Chinese are so partisan in America's domestic affairs? What steps did the Middle Kingdom's communist leaders use to help topple Mr. Trump and install Mr. Biden, arguably someone who favors Beijing's best interests? However, and worse, why are the Democratic Party and its leaders hyping for the CCP?

BEGINNING OF THE CCP'S
AMERICAN COMMUNIST FRONT

I address each of these questions in the following pages, beginning with the CCP's actions to build a Chinese communist front through cooperation with American communist parties. Those entities have been especially helpful to Democrats in the last couple years and played a decisive role in bringing Mr. Biden to the White House.

In 2018, the communist Chinese began aggressively recruiting American communists to join their global hegemonic agenda and to employ them as proxies in America's cultural revolution to remove Mr. Trump.

In late May of that year, two CPUSA leaders, Chairman John Bachtell and Carol Widom, joined the two hundredth anniversary of Karl Marx's birth, an event hosted in China. Mr. Bachtell wrote:

> We were invited to attend a forum to celebrate the 200th birthday of Karl Marx with 70 communist, socialist, left, and revolutionary parties in Shenzhen, an eco-planned city, followed by a week touring Beijing, Hefei, Fengyang County, and Xiaogang Village, the site of the first rural economic reforms.[313]

> The event reflected the feeling by the Communist Party of China [CCP] that a qualitative turning point has been reached in socialist construction and that China is playing a new role on the global stage. The meeting is an example of China and the [CCP] opening wider to the world and expanding and deepening relations with communist and workers' parties.[314]

The CPUSA's participation in the event signaled the beginning of a new era for American communists with the CCP's leader, President Xi, who a few years ago began reorienting the global communist community to a more revolutionary path aligned with Beijing. Until that point, CPUSA and other like-minded American groups aligned with the communists in Moscow for almost half a century—especially after the China-Soviet split in the early 1960s—and, as a result most American communists remained hostile to the Chinese communists until recent years.

The Russian and Chinese communists were definitely mutual opponents for a long time after their split. That may explain why the former East German intelligence services hosted a January 1963 meeting with CPUSA's Henry Winston, who met them to provide the East German communists a list of members of the Progressive Labor Party, an American Maoist organization aligned with Beijing. No doubt the East Germans passed the list of "Beijing parrots" to Moscow.[315]

The rival communist regimes (Moscow and Beijing) continued their mutual mistrust until the collapse of the Soviet Union (1991). Meanwhile, the leading American Communist Party, the CPUSA, remained distant with China until the mid-2000s.

The mistrust between the Chinese and American communists began to thaw in 2006, when CPUSA members visited both China and Vietnam. That delegation, which included CPUSA's then-national chairman Sam Webb, returned with a "wealth of political and cultural experiences they say they hope to share with the U.S. public in order to build better understanding and friendship between the peoples of the U.S., China, and Vietnam."[316]

Another delegate on the Chinese trip was Pamela Saffer, the CPUSA's international secretary, who said upon returning from the trip that she was "impressed by the country's socialist construction. In China, laws are made to support working people." Both Saffer and Webb said relations with the Chinese and Vietnamese communist parties "had been further strengthened [as a result of the trip], and they look forward to building even stronger relations in the future."[317]

The China-Vietnam visit led to a number of academic opportunities for American communists to demonstrate their ideological purity (reliability) to the Chinese. Specifically, in 2011, Wadhi'h Halabi, a Massachusetts academic who at the time served on the CPUSA Economics Commission, delivered a presentation titled, "China, the Working Class, Unions and the Economy" at the CPUSA-connected Niebyl-Proctor Marxist Library in Oakland, California. A description of that event read: "China is now developing into the largest economy in the world and this forum will discuss how this affects Chinese working people, unions (official & independent) and the Chinese people. It will also look at how the U.S. government, U.S. unions and media look at this development."[318]

At that event, Mr. Halabi joined David Ewing, a member of the old Beijing line US-China Peoples Friendship Association. That relationship blossomed, and evidently positively impressed Beijing's Marxists. Thus, somewhat later (2017), another event included both Mr. Halabi and Dylan Walker, a Boston Communist Party member, who flew to Beijing to participate in the Eighth World Socialism Forum of the Chinese Academy of Social Sciences. That conference marked the one hundredth anniversary of the October (1917) Revolution in Russia and was "an examination" of the "temporal characteristics of the great transformation era, and socialism with Chinese characteristics."[319]

Mr. Halabi's speech at the conference responded to Beijing's question: "What is the greatest honor we can pay the October Revolution?" He said:

> The Great October Socialist Revolution was probably the single greatest step forward in human history. It strengthened Marxism and the working class. The Revolution gave birth to all Communist Parties worldwide, and to the Communist International.[320]

Mr. Halabi's response seemed to please the ideological minders in Beijing who opened the door in the spring of 2018 to formally invite senior members of the CPUSA to tour China. That two-person American communist delegation included the Chicago-based CPUSA chairman, John Bachtell, and a New York communist official, Carol Widom. The "tour" included the opportunity for the American communist franchise representatives to participate in the Chinese-hosted two hundredth anniversary of Karl Marx's birth.[321]

Mr. Bachtell addressed the anniversary conference with a speech, "Marxism in the 21st Century and the Future for World Socialism." He said, "We enthusiastically join in celebrating Karl Marx on the occasion of the 200th anniversary of his birth and express deep appreciation to the International Department of the Communist Party of China for hosting this event."

He continued, "Marxism is the world's most influential body of thought and has changed the course of human history. It is more relevant than ever for addressing humanity's urgent challenges, despite the desperate efforts by the capitalist class to bury it."[322]

The American communist lauded his host as well. "Only socialism can ultimately restore a harmonious relationship between society and nature and between humans and their labor," he said. "And the remarkable experience in China shows a socialist-oriented system makes the transition to sustainability on a massive scale possible." Then he said words that were music to the ears of the CCP leadership: "The danger of authoritarianism and fascism has grown in the U.S. and Europe. Trump and the so-called alt-right, or fascists, linked to him pose an unprecedented threat to democracy, peace, and the environment."[323]

Mr. Bachtell argued that the Trump administration was a major threat—imperialistic—to world peace; therefore, the moral thing for the communists to do was to defeat Mr. Trump before he did any more damage. To accomplish that, Mr. Bachtell recommended, we need to build "a united front to defeat the extreme right's domination of the US government."[324]

CCP AND AMERICAN COMMUNISTS JOIN
ANTI-TRUMP REVOLUTION

Obviously, Mr. Bachtell's call for a "united front" between the CPUSA and other American communist groups with the CCP was designed to defeat Mr. Trump, what the Chinese considered a moral threat to world peace and, of course, to their own hegemonic ambitions.

That was perhaps the open door Beijing needed to join American communists in a collaborative effort to remove Mr. Trump, which almost simultaneously started with efforts to mobilize millions of new Democratic Party voters.

Beginning in 2018 pro-China, American communist parties began to play important roles in a host of US state elections. Specifically, they were a factor in the gubernatorial races in both Georgia and Florida, and helped flip Virginia to blue (favor the Democratic Party candidates), thanks to a concerted effort that was a proof-of-concept approach by the communists that led to the mobilization of other millions of new voters to eventually defeat Mr. Trump in 2020.

In the previous chapter, I introduced the Freedom Road Socialist Organization (FRSO), a Marxist party that invested heavily in recruiting new voters for Democratic Party candidates from Black, Latino, and low-income white cohorts across America's South and Southwest. Jon Liss, FRSO's leader, is a long-time political operative in Northern Virginia. Mr. Liss' FRSO grew out of the Chinese-inspired Maoist "New Communist Movement" of the 1970s, and today he is a key player in the alliance of communist groups introduced earlier, "Left Inside/Outside Project," that infiltrates the Democratic Party across America.[325]

Mr. Liss and his FRSO comrades in the New Virginia Majority (NVM), an FRSO affiliate, signed up several hundred thousand Virginia voters, mainly minority people who turned the commonwealth from a reliably Republican "red" state to a Democrat "blue" state now led by a Democrat governor (Ralph Northam) and a Democrat legislature. It is noteworthy that the NVM used demographic material produced by the Wuhan University in China to guide their voter-recruiting efforts.[326]

In 2018, NVM's Florida partner, the New Florida Majority (NFM), came very close to pushing leftist Andrew Gillum over the finish line to become that state's governor. Surprisingly, the NFM's efforts reportedly raised the Democrat vote by 40 percent over previous elections. Meanwhile, similar communist-inspired voter-recruiting efforts among minorities almost elected Stacey Abrams to be Georgia's governor and Texas' Beto O'Rourke to the US Senate. To their credit, the FRSO-inspired efforts were successful in Arizona with the election of Krysten Sinema and Alabama's Doug Jones to the US Senate.

Evidently, the FRSO learned many lessons from its state voter-registration campaigns and then applied those lessons on a national scale to help defeat Mr. Trump. FRSO's state power caucus' strategy that prepared for the 2020 election stated:

> Inspired by the disaster of Trump and Trumpism two years out, most organizers are engaged in barroom or coffee shop speculation about the 2020 election.
>
> Among the two dozen announced Democratic candidates, many debate: will it be Sanders or Warren, with their attacks on corporate Democrats? Will it be one of Hillary's heirs, with their cozy relationship with Wall Street? Will Harris be the first Black woman nominated by a major party? If it's Biden, do we sit it out?
>
> All of it is idle speculation unless "we" collectively organize tens of millions of the 108 million eligible voters who didn't vote in 2016. That's right, one hundred and eight million eligible voters chose not to register or to vote in 2016. The non-voting block is disproportionately young, poor, and people of color.[327]

FRSO'S stated solution was:

Dozens of state-based power building organizations have banded together to lead efforts to build a bottom-up long-term front against Trump and Trumpism. Over the last twenty-five years, state power organizations have grown to fill the political space created by the decline of Democratic Party local organization, the breakup and collapse of ACORN, and low levels of voter turnout. This reflects a shift from narrow Alinskyism and its very limited political engagement.[328]

Mr. Liss explained:

Starting in the summer of 2017, many leading state-power organizations have come together as a caucus to support peer-to-peer learning and incubate innovate organizing practices. Included among the organizations that have been leading the State Power Caucus are New Virginia Majority, New Florida Majority, California Calls, Washington Community Action Network, and Kentuckians for the Commonwealth.[329]

All told, there are 22 organizations from 15 states involved in the Caucus. Importantly, these organizations recognized the need to develop a systematic and long-term alternative to Trumpism.[330]

These groups, all affiliated with the communist FRSO, can credibly claim to have had a significant impact on voting patterns since the 2016 election cycle. However, they acknowledge that a much greater effort was necessary to defeat Trump in 2020.

We've also begun to assess the collective impact of state-based organizations. Looking at 2016, our rough estimate is that at most 4 million people were contacted and encouraged to vote. This is our high-water estimate. The actual number who actually voted is probably much lower still.

Now, recall the 108 million people who were eligible but not voting? They are largely our "core" constituency, or in other terms, they are our unorganized social base. This 108 million, when compared to the voting electorate, is more Black [sic], more immigrant, more working class and poor.

If we initially target just half of the 108 million, and we acknowledge that some in that half are going to disagree with our values and politics, some aren't going to vote no matter what, and some are in geographies that we just can't reach, we believe our real voter mobilization target number is 40 million, and we've agreed as a caucus to that number as our target. That's our natural constituency.

Liss saw that goal as a means to elect more socialists and communists to public office, but also to decisively defeat Mr. Trump as a step toward moving the country much farther down the socialist trail to overall control.

"The long game to defeat white nationalism and move past neoliberal corporatism is by building a bottom-up movement of 40 million people," Mr. Liss continued. He said that the state power caucus is intended to go beyond defeating Mr. Trump. It has the goal of building a socialist party that will challenge both major political parties for national control. He wrote:

I'm old, but a little too young to have lived through the New Communist Movement of the 1970s and its battles to form revolutionary parties and pre-parties, that is, to build a disciplined band of professional revolutionaries to carry out a political line … On the other hand, there is a unique, maybe even historic opportunity to build a political-strategic space to carry out electoral organizing.

Increasingly, there is a sector of radical organizations who believe that electoral work is a key area of struggle. That is a huge shift from the last few decades: credit Bernie and his campaign for revitalizing the notion of socialism and the importance of elections, credit many immigrant rights, Occupy and Movement for Black Lives leaders for recognizing the need for mass action and an electoral strategy.

But all this new energy will be wasted without centralized coordination:

It's time to create a "general command" or a place where all organized groups of people who view elections as key area of struggle and who view growing a base of radical "new majority" Democratic voters as a central task. To be explicit, the new majority Democrats refers to women, especially women of color, Black and immigrant voters, and sectors of young and working-class voters.

The FRSO and its communist allies had enough people and resources to help the Democratic Party defeat Mr. Trump through a variety of mechanisms, which was the interim goal of their Chinese partners.

MAOIST PROXY SPARKS DESTABILIZING RIOTS

The FRSO was also the CCP's front organization that claimed credit for "the spark that has inflamed the world"—specifically, the riots of the summer of 2020 that devastated some American inner cities.[331]

The FRSO cadre was incredibly successful at instigating destructive civil unrest and maintaining that insurrection for months on end. Consider the case of FRSO leader Joe Iosbaker, who wrote about his comrade Frank Chapman's influence in Minneapolis. Chapman is credited with "sparking" the riots that devastated Minneapolis and created a groundswell of anti-police protests, according to Iosbaker.[332]

Chapman is a trained Maoist revolutionary who knew exactly

how to spark a nationwide rebellion in the wake of the police killing of #georgefloyd, according to Iosbaker. Chapman wrote in a June 20 Facebook post: "Part of my Juneteenth was spent in Minneapolis/St. Paul with the rebels that gave us the spark that has inflamed the world. I also visited the George Floyd Memorial and discovered in the park next to it this memorial cemetery created by the rebels for the far too many Black, Latinx, Indigenous, LGBTQ and Trans people murdered by the police.... all power to the people!"[333]

A report at the CPUSA's website, People's World, states:

> Community control of the Minneapolis police took a step toward that goal at a forum hosted by the Twin Cities Justice for Jamar Clark Coalition on Thursday, June 18. The Coalition has played a leading role in organizing protests and actions demanding justice for George Floyd.

The unrest created across America, not just in Minneapolis, was also fueled by the instability associated with the CCP's malevolent COVID-19 pandemic actions.

CCP AND THE COVID-19 PANDEMIC

Mr. Trump and his State Department made it clear to the American people that the COVID-19 virus emanated from Wuhan, China. There is powerful circumstantial evidence that it came out of the Institute of Virology in Wuhan, the nation's only biological level-four facility in that country and closely aligned with the CCP's biological warfare program. Mr. Frank Gaffney, vice chairman of the Committee on the Present Danger: China, a Washington, DC-based group, is not certain whether the release was accidental or intentional and whether the virus was engineered or in fact is from an exotic bat species found in a remote part of China.[334]

What's clear to Mr. Gaffney and others, and aside from whether the virus was engineered or intentionally released, is that the CCP exploited the pandemic to further its national interests at the expense of the rest of the world. That is why Mr. Gaffney argues the COVID-19 pandemic is "tantamount to a biological warfare attack…[because] the cumulative effect has been to redound to the benefit of communist China in every respect except for its reputation in the world."[335]

Mr. Gaffney explained Chinese thinking about the crisis and their associated strategy. A crisis, in the Chinese way of thinking, is both a danger and an opportunity. So, argues Mr. Gaffney, CCP strategists turned the virus crisis into an opportunity.

The CCP weaponized the COVID-19 pandemic first by concealing it from the balance of the world by denying other countries time to prepare, and the communist regime in fact facilitated its rapid spread by enabling that through international air travel while sparing the Chinese population by blocking domestic air travel. Meanwhile, by keeping the pandemic a secret, the Chinese quickly took a number of other self-serving actions. Those actions, according to Arkansas US Senator Tom Cotton (R), were a series of conscious, malevolent decisions on part of the regime.[336]

The CCP quickly locked down the supply of parts per millions (PPM) surgical masks and ventilators that allowed them to care for Chinese citizens first, but also to corner the global market for such items. Next, the CCP allegedly pressured the World Health Organization (WHO) not to address the topic of human-to-human transmission. Early on, WHO complied, and on January 14, 2020, it tweeted: "Preliminary investigations conducted by the Chinese authorities have found no clear evidence of human-to-human transmission of the novel #coronavirus (2019-nCoV) identified in #Wuhan, #China."[337]

The CCP also engaged its ideological arm to launch a disinformation campaign to make it appear as if the virus originated elsewhere, like in Spain or even in America.

So, the only logical conclusion attributed to the CCP regarding these actions is that it tried both to inflict maximum harm on the balance of the world and to exploit the crisis for its own economic benefit.

That media campaign was especially self-serving and unfortunately echoed across America's mainstream press as well. The Chinese spin on COVID-19 arguably encouraged economically devastating lockdowns, fed virus-related panic, and seeded the message that only China was correctly handling the response to the pandemic.

Of course, this crisis-to-opportunity strategy had a dual purpose. First, it was to portray China not as the perpetrator of the pandemic, but as a co-victim. Second, it was also to portray the Trump administration as inept at handling the issue, actions the CCP deliberately intended to impact the 2020 American presidential election.

The CCP's COVID-19 strategy worked. The Democratic Party and the mainstream media ran Mr. Biden's campaign mostly on the narrative that President Trump wasn't handling the pandemic well, which deflected attention from the Chinese as responsible for spreading the virus to the United States.

A very significant collateral opportunity came about thanks to the pandemic and the lockdowns. It gave support for the idea of massive, mail-in voting, and the real likelihood that nefarious agents manipulated those ballots.

Did the Chinese play a direct role in the 2020 election? Perhaps, but certainly, they played an indirect role. It is yet unproven whether digital machines used for voting that had either some bit of software or hardware made in China, played a role in the election, according to General Robert Spalding. That potentially may have had a more significant impact on the outcome of the election than anyone realizes.[338]

CCP USES AMERICAN MEDIA TO INFLUENCE CULTURAL REVOLUTION

The CCP fuels the American cultural revolution and efforts to defeat Mr. Trump by feeding—investing in—the mainstream media's reporting against Mr. Trump. After all, the CCP was a role model for America's newsrooms when it fabricates lies to tarnish one's reputation by relying on the dictum, "A lie repeated a thousand times becomes the truth."

That was much of American mainstream media's approach to Mr. Trump, a technique embraced by the CCP at home as well. The Chinese are long accustomed to such practices that repeatedly lie to their citizens about events from the 1989 Tiananmen Square massacre to the genocide of Falun Gong, and they constantly spin lies to cover up the regime's other malevolent behavior.

Much the same messaging takes place in this country as well. America's mainstream media controls the narrative here; it's not that different from the state-owned media in communist China. Remember that America's mainstream media is owned by six major corporations, which creates a one-truth environment and more often than not comports with the Democratic Party's spin.

Not surprisingly, the CCP participated in the American mainstream media's campaign of slander against President Trump for his entire term in office. The media—a leftist propaganda machine—molded how people think. They didn't report the truth, especially regarding Mr. Trump's communications. They ignored facts and furthered a negative narrative.

They fed the cultural revolution by not tolerating other media that chose to report the facts as well. Rather, leftist media influenced public opinion by running mostly negative stories, whether real or fake, to mold public disapproval of the Trump administration. This was supported by the social media giants like Facebook and Twitter as well.

They do what the CCP calls "the justification of the rebellion," and what Marxist Mao said is a core tenet: "To rebel is justified." So, the media takes away the victim's power or convicts him of crimes—Russia-gate, the Ukraine-gate, and so on.

There is another appropriate dictum, "Follow the money." That's particularly true about the mainstream media. Mr. Joshua Philipp, an investigative reporter for the *Epoch Times*, said the social media behemoths like Facebook and Twitter were given a lot of money by the Chinese for advertisements, to hide the CCP's fingerprints. Those ads were used as "doublespeak," an Orwellian term, Phillips explained. Basically, they said two contradictory things while violating the very thing they claim to oppose.

At home in China, the China Global Television Network and the *People's Daily* consistently in 2020 mocked President Trump and praised "President-elect Biden." That biased reporting satisfied the mandate to oust Mr. Trump and was in lockstep with their American mainstream media partners.

CONCLUSION

Predictably, the reader won't learn from mainstream media or even Biden administration "intelligence" spokespersons, much less from Democratic Party officials, that the CCP did anything to influence the outcome of the 2020 election and America's ongoing cultural revolution. However, the CCP's emergent relationship with American communists, the strategic manipulation of the COVID-19 pandemic to favor the CCP, the mainstream media's anti-Trump coverage with communist help, four years of incessant Democratic Party leadership's attacks on Mr. Trump, and the fawning over the Chinese by American communists offer sufficient evidence for the objective, nonpartisan mind to conclude: Yes, the communist Chinese played a role in the 2020 election.

The next chapter addresses the role the American education establishment plays in fueling the cultural revolution.

6

Co-conspirator
Public Education Establishment

Freedom is never more than one generation away from extinction. We didn't pass it to our children in the bloodstream. It must be fought for, protected, and handed on for them to do the same, or one day we will spend our sunset years telling our children and our children's children what it was once like in the United States where men were free.[339]

—Ronald Reagan, 40th President of the United States

The American public education establishment is a freedom-robbing co-conspirator in the ongoing cultural revolution. It trains our children in public schools from an early age to become leftist cultural warriors by socially engineering them to be anti-American—and worse, real Marxist ideologues.

This chapter identifies the state of America's educational establishment by defining its products, indicating when and how leftists took over public education, and identifying the tools used by the taxpayer-funded educational establishment to accomplish its Marxist-inspired, social-engineering transformation of young Americans.

OUR PUBLIC EDUCATION
ESTABLISHMENT IS AWFUL

American public education fails this country and its children, and robs the taxpayers. Instead of educating our children to compete in a tough global marketplace, many public schools indoctrinate their students to hate America and fuel the cultural revolution, while failing to equip them with the skills necessary to compete in this world.

Remember that education is critical to civilization, because it fosters individual well-being, provides social stability, and secures a nation's future economic viability. Education accomplishes these lofty goals by teaching students moral standards and traditional culture, and by imparting the necessary craftsmanship. Unfortunately, America's public education establishment falls far short of these goals, and frankly does just the opposite in some situations.

A study that compares American education results with other nations demonstrates failure. The 2020 report from the Program for International Student Assessment (PISA), which studied a cohort of fifteen-year-old students' performance in reading, mathematics, and science literacy, found a serious shortfall in performance. The PISA results compare American students with their peers in nearly eighty countries and education systems.[340]

The only comparison that really matters is with the communist Chinese, America's peer competitor. In each of the three areas of student performance, China outpaced US fifteen-year-olds in the tests: average reading literacy score (US - 505; China - 555); average mathematics literacy score (US - 478; China - 591); and average science literacy score (US - 502; China - 590).[341] Meanwhile, and just as troubling, at least forty-four million American adults are functionally illiterate, which means they can't read or write simple English sentences. Yet, America's federal and state governments spend an estimated $720 billion annually on K–12 public education, or $14,400 for each of the fifty million students in government schools during the 2017–18 school year, the most recent national data available.[342]

America's marginal performance is an old problem. Back in 1988, only 5 percent of American high school seniors could read well enough to understand our founding documents like the US Constitution. More recently, the 2019 National Assessment of Education Progress published the Nation's Report Card, which addressed the testing of six hundred thousand US students from every state and found a drop in reading ability. On average, reading scores declined for fourth and eighth graders, and Peggy Carr, the associate commissioner of the National Center for Education Statistics, said, "Over the past decade, there has been no progress in either mathematics or reading performance, and the lowest performing students are doing worse."[343]

Alarm over public education prompted then President Ronald Reagan to commission a study about America's education. The final report begins: "We are a nation at risk." That report outlined the dismal state of our nation's educational institution, and concluded:

> If an unfriendly foreign power had attempted to impose on America the mediocre educational performance that exists today, we might well have viewed it as an act of war. As it stands, we have allowed this to happen to ourselves.[344]

Poor academic performance among our public-educated students hurts our nation's ability to compete in the global marketplace. Worse, if that's possible, much of our government schooling from K–12 and especially at the collegiate level not only fails to prepare students academically to properly compete, but it puts considerable effort on the indoctrination of our children regarding leftist thinking, socially engineering them to be the exact opposite of what conservative Christian parents want for their children.

The social engineering is especially radical in our public higher education establishment. Dennis Prager, a national radio talk show host and writer, said many of our college-age offspring come home from their expensive collegiate experiences literally holding "America in contempt"; prefer socialism to capitalism; regard white people and police as racist; believe the Bible and Christianity are "dangerous nonsense"; don't believe men and women are inherently different; are no longer interested in getting married and having children; and believe many of our conservative leaders are fascists or worse.[345]

For Christian conservative parents, this outcome attributable to the radical influence of our leftist colleges and universities is a nightmare, and not just because our adult children end up rejecting most everything their family stands for, but also, as Mr. Prater said, "Young people who are transformed into leftists almost always become less kind, less happy and more angry." That might explain in part the ugly street scenes during the unrest in American cities throughout much of the summer of 2020—youthful responses to perceived conservative inspired injustices.[346]

Prater explains that "whatever the left touches, it ruins; music, art, literature, religion, late-night TV, the Academy Awards, sports, economies, the family structure, the Boy Scouts, and race relations are just a few examples. It also ruins people—their character and their happiness."[347]

Many Americans, especially conservatives, agree with Mr. Prater's assessment of our public education establishment. Candace Owens, a conservative author and activist, said the left-wing leaders of our public education establishment are "replacing education with indoctrination." She continued, "If you are a Black American and you go through the public school system like I went through, you come out and you are basically a propagandist for the left and you don't realize it."[348]

"I started on the left, although I was not politically active," Ms. Owens recalled. "I believed in all of the indoctrination. I believed, just four short years ago, that Republicans were racist, that conservatives were racists, and that being a Black person and being a woman disadvantaged me in life. And I'm a pretty smart person. These were things that I learned actively."[349]

"It wasn't because I wanted to be anti-American," she added. "It wasn't because I wanted to believe these things. It was because it was taught to me via the public school system."[350]

Ms. Owens is the author of *Blackout: How Black America Can Make Its Second Escape from the Democratic Plantation*, which warns conservative Americans that they have "lost the education battle with the left."[351]

"If we continue to allow the Democrat[ic] Party to control education, we are guaranteeing them the future because the youth is the future," she said. Our public school system is "actually failing kids," especially Black kids. She illustrated her point.[352]

"In California, 75% of Black boys cannot pass a basic literacy exam," Ms. Owens said. "That is astounding. You will never hear Black Lives Matter talk about that. You will never hear a Democratic candidate talk about that.... In Baltimore, across five schools, they couldn't find a single child that was proficient in reading and writing and math.... People should be talking about that."[353]

Ms. Owens accuses public educators of using "modernized techniques of the slave replantation" practiced by Democrat leaders and the left.[354]

"What is the one thing Black Americans were not allowed to do?" she asked. "Learn to read. Learn to write. The punishment would have been severe for that. And the reason for that is simple. It's because an educated mind cannot be enslaved. And what we're seeing today...[is] this dumbing down of the education system where kids are learning feelings and they're not learning facts, they're not learning practical skills.... It's problematic and it's something that we need to have a meaningful discussion about. It needs to be more than a discussion. It needs to be action that is taken."[355]

America's public education establishment was taken over by the left many years ago. Today, thanks to its indoctrination agenda, many young people embrace Marxist-like views about life, which leads them to reject much of the goodness of this country historically and culturally, and then to join the cultural revolution to radically transform America. It's an ugly sight to see.

We came to this point thanks to a host of factors, including the abandonment of public education to the left's whims, the topic of the next section.

HOW DID AMERICA'S PUBLIC EDUCATION ESTABLISHMENT BECOME A LEFTIST CAMP?

The left conspired to ruin traditional education in the United States, kindergarten through college. Historically, Marxists accomplish this goal in a country by embracing a strategy that targets deep-seated cultural traditions through indoctrination and incessant propaganda. However, that approach alone is typically insufficient. They must also quickly eliminate the cultural elites to stop them from imparting the nation's heritage to the next generation, and that is accomplished by excluding from the education arena those who are not ideologically onboard with leftist views.

It is truly criminal how the left has sabotaged America's public education establishment, especially over the past few decades. We have two parties to thank for this outcome, however. First, we can thank those who knew better but ignored the problem. Second, we should blame the insidious ambitions of the purveyors of the isms who use education as a revolutionary tool.

Long ago, proponents of the isms decided to capture America's educational establishment as one of the means of dominating society, an Antonio Gramsci institutional approach mentioned earlier. They have mostly succeeded, albeit with the exception of private education (both religious and secular) and homeschooling. Otherwise, beginning arguably with the late nineteenth century and particularly in the last few decades, the left took captive public education, but converted it into a vehicle to radically transform America, one child at a time.

More than a century ago, so-called progressives began to trash America's public school system by adopting a philosophy and methods that moved young minds away from studying academic subjects and put emphasis on learning nonacademic life skills. These "educators" purposed to agree that a "narrow focus" on academic training was insufficient for a progressive country. Rather, they insisted that public education must focus on what they called the "whole child." This mindset came to dominate America's public education system, and the data above shows the results.

The progressive takeover of our educational establishment started before it was taken captive by Marxists in the middle of the twentieth century. However, let's begin with a brief overview of the progressives' war on learning, which was documented by Dr. Andrew Bernstein at the City University of New York in his 2018 article, "Heroes and Villains in American Education." Below are highlights of Bernstein's argument exposing progressive malfeasance regarding our educational system.[356]

Early progressives pushed to distance public education from academics, which were replaced with activities better suited to prepare students for their future work lives either on farms or in factories. Jane Addams (1860–1935), a progressive educational reformer, wrote, "We are impatient with the schools which lay all stress on reading and writing, suspecting them to rest upon the assumption that all knowledge and interest must be brought to the children through the medium of books." Lawrence Cremin (1925–1990), a leading scholar of progressive education, wrote of Addams' theory, "Industry…would have to be seized upon and conquered by the educators." This emphasis on group work was a theme that would be sounded over and over again by progressives and their intellectual descendants.[357]

Those early progressive educators claimed their approach was based on science. That view led them to embrace the Stanford Binet intelligence test (IQ test) to help identify the feebleminded and the gifted. Not surprisingly, those advocating the widespread use of IQ testing were also eugenicists who called for limiting the "breeding" of the "unfit."[358]

Starting in the mid-1920s, according to historian Diane Ravitch, "The public schools employed the [IQ] tests to predict which students were likely to go to college and which should be guided into vocational programs." Ravitch continued: "The decision became a self-fulfilling prophecy, since only those in the college track took the courses that would prepare them for college."[359]

Soon, progressives made another major change to public education; they established "curriculum studies." The progressive view was that only true education experts properly employ science to determine a school's ideal curriculum. The impact should be obvious: No longer would school boards and parents have a say in what children learned in school, because curriculum experts knew best.

Historian Ravitch wrote about the topic:

> The invention of the scientific curriculum expert represented an extraordinary shift in power away from teachers, parents, and local communities to professional experts.... In modern school districts, control over curriculum was transferred from educators who had majored in English, history, or mathematics to trained curriculum specialists.[360]

This was a real coup for progressive educators. They conceived that the new field of curriculum design would establish the criteria for a child's preparation to optimally benefit the student and society. This utilitarian approach to education prepared the student to reach his/her intellectual potential while satisfying what society demanded.

Progressive John F. Bobbitt at the University of Chicago, a proponent of the new field of curriculum design, defended this social engineering approach to education by rhetorically asking, "How would a 20th-century plumber's knowledge of Shakespeare's drama or poetry benefit society? Beyond the basic science training necessary to help a farmer grow crops, how would his understanding of physics or mathematics aid society? For what social purpose should we teach a future factory worker ancient history?"[361]

Then progressives adopted "cardinal principles," a new, "scientific" approach to schooling. Naturally, the source of these "principles" was big government and the professional educational establishment, beginning with the US Bureau of Education and the National Education Association (NEA). [362]

The US Bureau of Education partnered with the NEA to call for revamping American schooling, which spawned the Commission on the Reorganization of Secondary Education (CRSE). That commission issued "cardinal principles of secondary education" in 1918, which remain with modern American education today.

The CRSE directed schools to "concern themselves less with academic matters than with the preparation for effective living." Yes, that's a clear message to educators to get involved scientifically, which resulted in less emphasis on teaching students to reason independently and think for themselves, resulted in more effort on teaching them the "common good." [363]

Evidently, the focus on the "common good" included the "cardinal principles" of teaching personal hygiene, "a love for clean sport," "command of fundamental processes" (evidently a reference to academics), "worthy home-membership" (rules of proper family management), "vocation" (teaching blue-collar employment skills), "civics" (to replace history—no need to study about the US Constitution and the ideas of the founding fathers; rather, focus on group projects), "worthy use of leisure" (training in leisure activities), and "ethical character" (government-run moral training on "collective thinking"). [364]

Historian Ravitch explained: "The driving purpose behind the seven objectives [cardinal principles] was socialization, teaching students to fit into society…. The overriding goal was social efficiency, not the realization of individual desire for self-improvement." [365]

What happened here? The US government stripped academic training from the core of the nation's schooling. Bernstein concludes that academics (reading, writing, and arithmetic) were to become "an afterthought," a view that became entrenched within American colleges of education as well. [366]

The CRSE shut down most of the study of American history as well. Prior to the commission's report, American secondary schools offered four years of history: ancient, European, English, and American. But CRSE created an entirely new field called "social studies," which focused on "social efficiency, or teaching students the skills and attitudes necessary to fit into the social order."[367]

Further, CRSE took a dim view of civics, the study of government, which was folded up on the new social activism field. Instead of studying how our government works, social studies emphasized how local jurisdictions function. After all, according to CRSE'S "social studies" chairman:

> The old chronicler who recorded the deeds of kings and warriors and neglected the labors of the common man is dead. The great palaces and cathedrals and pyramids are often but the empty shells of a parasitic growth on the working group. The elaborate descriptions of these old tombs are but sounding brass and tinkling cymbals compared to the record of the joys and sorrows, the hopes and disappointments of the masses, who are infinitely more important than any arrangement of wood and stone and iron.[368]

Professor Bernstein concludes that the above statement by the "social studies" chairman echoes Marxist ideology. The emphasis is put on the masses and rejects any understanding of past kings and rulers and their achievements. So, as the logic goes, the student will focus on little guys, not the past great achievers like founders George Washington and Thomas Jefferson. The educator was expected to socialize children, not nurture them with a love for learning and thinking.[369]

The cardinal principle of progressive learning, according to Bernstein, was that "independent thinking is useless to society, even dangerous." Rather, rote learning is of little value, according to John Dewey, the founder of progressive education who wrote his doctor of philosophy (PhD) dissertation on German philosopher Immanuel Kant, an eighteenth-century German philosopher and central Enlightenment thinker. Dewey said of the topic:

> The mere absorbing of facts and truths is so exclusively an individual affair that it tends very naturally to pass into selfishness. There is no obvious social motive for the acquirement of mere learning, there is no clear social gain in success thereat.[370]

Dewey believed that children learn best when they experience real-life activities. That's why he and his wife, Alice, founded the Laboratory School at the University of Chicago, where "they continually experimented with different ways of [teaching] young students about primitive life in the Bronze Age…early Greek civilization…Prince Henry of Portugal, Columbus, and other explorers…Shakespeare's plays; science; mathematics; algebra and geometry; English, French, and even Latin."[371]

It was Dewey's view that the purpose of learning was not about acquiring knowledge, rather, it was about "saturating [students] with the spirit of service." And it was to prime students for "social cooperation and community life," not to teach them "science, nor literature, nor history, nor geography."[372]

Dewey had "a brilliant mind trained in academic study," according to Bernstein, and he gave progressives the sanction of "lofty philosophy." However, Dewey's influence was "catastrophic," explained Bernstein, because he gave credibility to opponents of academic training, such as William Heard Kilpatrick. Professor Kilpatrick was the chair of education philosophy at Columbia University's Teachers College, where he influenced an entire generation of American educators on the latest progressive ideas.[373]

Professor Kilpatrick chaired the CRSE committee on mathematics, whereby he argued for severely curtailing math instruction for all but future scientists and engineers. The other students only needed basic arithmetic in high school, according to Kilpatrick.[374]

The Columbia scholar "was interested not in encouraging independence but in engineering social conformity," explained Bernstein. In fact, historian Ravitch quotes Kilpatrick to explain his education aim: "In contrast to the 'customary set-task sit-alone-at-your-own-desk procedure' which promotes 'selfish individualism,' the project method [involves] the pressure of social approval [which] would encourage conformity to 'the ideals necessary for approved social life.'"[375]

The reader won't be mistaken to perceive that American education became similar to the social reengineering seen in the former Soviet Union. Why? Progressive educators like Kilpatrick and Dewey visited the former Soviet Union and came away boasting about that communist regime's successful education system.

In 1929, Kilpatrick visited Stalin's Russia, where he saw his project method in action. Specifically, he observed groups of Russian students "disposing of disintegrating carcasses of animals left frozen by the roadside." Kilpatrick later reported, "No school system in history has been more thoroughly and consistently made to work into the social and political program of the state."[376]

Professor Dewey traveled to the Soviet Union as well (1929), and came away saying he "was deeply moved by what he saw." He explained that Soviet educators "realized that the goals of the progressive school were undermined by 'the egoistic and private ideals and methods inculcated by the institution of private property, profit and acquisition possession.'" Further, Dewey praised his communist hosts for changing the institution of the family, which he considered individualistic and pernicious to communal living.[377]

Columbia University professor and progressive educator, George Counts, twice visited communist Russia. Those visits convinced Counts that America's education establishment must help the country transition from a capitalist into a socialist nation. He came away believing that progressive education must result in political activism to help America become a socialist nation.[378]

From his influential perch at Columbia's Teachers College, Professor Counts seriously launched an effort to use education to promote national socialism. Ravitch wrote in his book *Dare the Schools Build a New Social Order?* that Counts "forthrightly called for elimination of capitalism, property rights, private profits, and competition, and establishment of collective ownership of natural resources, capital, and the means of production and distribution."[379]

Professor Counts' promotion of socialism was music to the ears of fellow progressives. Historian Ravitch explained, "Virtually every prominent progressive in the 1930s agreed that the traditional academic curriculum reflected the failed capitalist economic order."[380]

This pro-socialist, communist-influenced education establishment agenda continues even today. Bernstein explained:

> Intelligent Americans often note two seemingly distinct aspects of America's schools: (1) The teaching of academic subjects is poorly done (if done at all), and (2) the educational system is a hotbed of anti-capitalist propaganda. The fact is that the two observations are intimately related.[381]

Thus, as Bernstein notes, "Progressives and their intellectual heirs severely dumbed down the schools as a necessary means of inculcating conformity, dependency, and obedience."[382]

Marxists Make Inroads into Public Education

The progressives essentially prepared our education establishment for the invasion of more radical (Marxist) ideas, first at the college level, but eventually the poison sank deeply into the balance of the public education establishment.

America's colleges and universities are almost an ideological lost cause, especially the liberal arts part of the academe. They no longer foster open debate and the exchange of ideas. No, they are with few exceptions incubators for Marxism and shaping generations of young people. That's where our young adults learn to hate capitalism and our Judeo-Christian foundation, our Constitution, and basic civility. It is on these highbrow campuses where they're recruited to demolish what our forefathers gave us.

The average professor in our very best liberal arts colleges self-identifies as a member of the Democratic Party, and he/she likely has no Republican Party peers on staff. That statement is backed by published research found on the National Association of Scholars' website. More than three-fourths (78 percent) of academic departments have no politically conservative staff members. However, that imbalance does not reflect American homes, the origin of the students at those institutes of higher learning. A Gallup survey found that almost four in ten (38 percent) of Americans identify as conservative, while less than a quarter (24 percent) identify as liberal.[383]

What is the origin of the leftist ideas promulgated by liberal staffs at our universities? For that, we go back hundreds of years in history.

Societal philosophies such as the radical ideas about government are arguably traceable to the seventeenth century and the Enlightenment, the Age of Reason. That was a time of great change, which includes the emergence of political philosophies that impacted the West, starting with the French Revolution (1789–1799).

Professor Emeritus of philosophy at Emory College, Ann Hartle, wrote in the journal *Modern Age*:

> The Enlightenment was an "emancipation project" intended to create a "new civilization" grounded in the autonomy of human reason and the centrality of man. First and foremost, then, the Enlightenment means emancipation from tradition, especially religious tradition, and the elimination of the transcendence of the divine in favor of an "entirely immanent [human] standpoint."[384]

The "emancipation from tradition" influenced authors Karl Marx and Friedrich Engels in *The Communist Manifesto* (1848), which spawned the idea the proletariat (workers) would rise up in revolution to overthrow the bourgeoisie (the oligarchs, capitalists). Then the workers would piece together a utopia free of crime and poverty.

Marx and Engels influenced many—especially among society's elite and in particular among the staffs at universities. Those radical ideas caught the attention of the educated elite in the US who shared their vision for a new paradise on earth.

There are two groups of note that brought from Europe these radical ideas first spawned by the Age of Reason.

British elite like H. G. Wells (1866–1946) and playwright George Bernard Shaw (1856–1950) became captivated by those ideas and thus helped found the Fabian society as the mechanism to replace capitalism with socialism. The difference for the Fabians was in tactics; whereby Marx suggested violent revolution to overthrow the rich, the Fabians used tools of "stealth, intrigue, subversion, and the deception of never calling socialism by its right name" to achieve their promised utopia.[385]

Mr. Shaw, the British leader of the Fabians, favored the worst of humanity in his time. He praised the Italian dictator, Benito Mussolini, as "the right kind of tyrant"; Joseph Stalin, the communist Russian butcher, as a man without "malice"; and the chief Nazi, Adolf Hitler, as "a very remarkable man." These were Shaw's heroes and the type of dictators he expected to run a global socialist/Marxist government.[386]

The Fabian society was named for the Roman general Quintus Fabius Maximus Verrucosus. Fabius sought victory against the stronger Carthaginian army commanded by General Hannibal by being persistent, wearing his enemy down as opposed to launching direct attacks.

The Fabian society's strategy as outlined in the group's first pamphlet echoes the Roman general's approach: "For the right moment you must wait, as Fabius did most patiently, when warring against Hannibal, though many censured his delays; but when the time comes you must strike hard, as Fabius did, or your waiting will be in vain, and fruitless."[387]

In the twentieth century, Fabian ideas became part of the British establishment, starting with the London School of Economics, a Fabian institution, and the basis for England's Labour Party, and it was affiliated with socialist thought. In fact, according to Jon B. Perdue, author of *The War of All the People: The Nexus of Latin American Radicalism and Middle Eastern Terrorism*, "The logo of the Fabian society, a tortoise, represented the group's predilection for a slow, imperceptible transition to socialism, while its coat of arms, a 'wolf in sheep's clothing,' represented its preferred methodology for achieving its goal."[388]

The British scientific community soon joined the Fabians, which linked them with their scientific counterparts in the communist communities in both the Soviet Union and communist China. Those same British scientists more often than not were embedded in Britain's university system, which became the nose of the camel under the tent. These included such scientists as J. B. S. Haldane, known for his works in physiology, genetics, and evolutionary biology. He was a professed socialist, Marxist, and atheist.

Professor Haldane served in numerous British universities: New College, Oxford; Cambridge; Royal Institution and University College, London. Meanwhile, he was very public about his communist views, and for many years wrote for the *Daily Worker*, a communist newspaper. During those years, he was accused of being a Russian spy codenamed "Intelligentsia." His true allegiance was evident by 1950, when he briefly considered standing for Parliament as a Communist Party candidate. He once described Soviet leader Stalin as "a very great man who did a very good job."[389]

Another British scientist and communist within the academe was Hyman Levy (1889–1975), a mathematician, Scottish philosopher, and professor at the Imperial College London. He joined the British Communist Party in 1931.[390] Other British academics who aligned with the communists included Joseph Needham, Lancelot Hogben, and J. D. Bernal, to name a few.[391]

Like most radical ideas born in Great Britain, the Fabian influence, with its communist supporters, eventually crossed the Atlantic to find enthusiasm among American universities and their staffs.

The radical socialist Fabians were joined by the Frankfurt School Marxists, who together significantly impacted America's educational establishment.

The Frankfurt School morphed from the Goethe University in Frankfurt, Germany, under the name "The Institute for Social Research" to embrace the goal of developing Marxist studies. However, the school's true "research" was not focused on violent revolution vis-à-vis Marxism, but on destroying Western civilization through other means.

Mike Shotwell, author of *Immersed in Red: My Formative Years in a Marxist Household*, wrote:

> A major tenet of the Frankfurt School's philosophy, developed by Georg Lukacs, Adorno, Fromm, Wilhelm Reich, and others, was the sinister belief that unrestrained sex could be a useful and devastating instrument if prompted to run rampant. They promoted "compulsory promiscuity, one-parent households, premarital sex, and homosexuality," which struck at the heart of the core values of family and child-bearing as mainstays of Western society.[392]

> Lukacs, along with a small handful of intellectual theoreticians at the Marx-Lenin Institute in Moscow in 1922, formulated the outline the Frankfurt School would follow, the goals being the "abolition of [Western] culture" and Marx's goal for "the ruthless destruction of everything existing," according to Shotwell.[393]

The theoretical goal of the destruction of Western culture provided the foundation for the creation of the Frankfurt School's governing philosophy, which became known as "cultural Marxism." Professor Paul Gottfried, an American philosopher and historian at Elizabethtown College, explained how Theodor Adorno, Max Horkheimer (Gottfried's teacher), and Herbert Marcuse fused Marx's theory of class struggle and Freud's vision of erotic pleasure to develop "cultural Marxism." Perhaps surprisingly, even orthodox Marxists vigorously denounced the Frankfurt School, said professor Gottfried.[394]

The rise of Adolf Hitler beginning in 1933 convinced Frankfurt School faculty they had to leave Germany, primarily because they were all Jews. Thankfully for them, along came the American father of progressivism and "modern education," John Dewey, who paved their way to travel to the United States.[395]

Evidently, Dewey raised the necessary financing for the relocation of the Jewish Frankfurt School philosophers from institutions like the Rockefeller Foundation to place them on the faculties of top American universities: University of California, Berkeley; Princeton, Brandeis; and Columbia University's Teachers College.

These immigrant cultural Marxists used their new American academe perches to advance radical views about the destruction of Western civilization, and soon the effects were being felt. Ralph de Toledano wrote in his book *Cry Havoc!: The Great American Bring-Down and How It Happened* that the Frankfurt School immigrants advanced teachings that led to "tearing down campuses, vilifying decency, glorifying violence and pornography, and Nazifying the spelling of 'Amerika.' "[396]

Quickly, cultural Marxists became respectable in the US because, according to Gottfried, the Frankfurt School immigrants fought fascism [the Nazi influence] "as a cultural and emotional danger and for advocating for a progressive democratic society." A significant aspect of that "fight" was the legacy of Nazi anti-Semitism, which motivated a key aspect of cultural Marxism, prejudice. They castigated and extrapolated prejudice not just against Jews, but also "blacks, social revolutionaries, homosexuals, and women who were revolting against what they viewed as the patriarchal family."[397]

Even as the Cold War started (1947), cultural Marxism "made powerful inroads" in America. "Leaders of the Frankfurt School were sent back to Germany by the American state department to 'reeducate' the former subjects of the Third Reich and to make them 'good antifascists,'" explained Professor Gottfried. Meanwhile, Frankfurt School pioneers like Eric Fromm became popular thanks to their books on psychological well-being (a Marxist ruse), which were all the rage through book-of-the-month clubs.[398]

So, in conclusion, the influence of Fabian and Frankfurt School socialism and cultural Marxism heavily impacted American college students in the 1960s and 1970s, thanks to the teachings of Frankfurt School professors like Marcuse, who became known as the "father of the new left" and a key proponent of the "sexual revolution." He was especially effective at influencing the emergence of groups like the Black Panthers and the Weather Underground, domestic American terrorist organizations.

Further, it shouldn't surprise any observer of our present culture that young Americans quickly internalize the radical teachings found in our educational establishment. This learning at the feet of true radicals set the tone for cultural and political instability and infected other institutions like our media, the topic of the next chapter.

WHAT MARXIST TOOLS AND METHODS ARE USED BY EDUCATORS TO RADICALIZE OUR CHILDREN?

We established in the previous section the history and motivation of some educator proponents of the isms to initially segregate out the talented students for special preparation and later to simply indoctrinate our children against this country and our traditional, Christian values. In this section, I will profile some of the tools and methods these radicals use to infiltrate American education with the intent of taking captive our children to do the left's nefarious, Marxist bidding.

Some of the following material is thanks to a book authored by the *Epoch Times'* staff, especially the chapter on "Sabotaging Education," which identifies areas in which communism infiltrated American education and identifies where that movement enjoys success.[399]

Start Early Influencing Young Americans

We know that progressive educator John Dewey started the trend of influencing the intellectual development of American children in our primary and secondary public schools. That influence was directly contradictory to the Judeo-Christian principles and values that formed the very foundation of this country, which was the necessary target of the ism philosophers like Dewey.

Today, the left promotes atheism, Darwin's evolution, and communist ideology in public schools using psychological manipulation to undermine the values and principles many parents try to instill in their children. That manipulation instills moral relativism and other corrupted thinking about life, which is precisely what Georg Lukacs formulated at the Frankfurt School to abolish Western culture.

Marxists like Lukacs focused on education at all levels to promote corrupted theories. They began, much like the progressives, to dumb down our students, making them less competitive, as outlined in the first section of this chapter.

In that section, I quoted President Ronald Reagan's concerns about our children's education when he addressed the 1983 US Department of Education report, "A Nation at Risk." That report states:[400]

> For our country to function, citizens must be able to reach some common understandings on complex issues, often on short notice and on the basis of conflicting or incomplete evidence. Education helps form these common understandings, a point Thomas Jefferson made long ago in his justly famous dictum: "I know no safe depository of the ultimate powers of the society but the people themselves; and if we think them not enlightened enough to exercise their control with a wholesome discretion, the remedy is not to take it from them but to inform their discretion."

The fact is, communist ideology robs our children of critical thinking skills, which Thomas Jefferson addresses above, thus creating a serious shortfall for Americans in a complex world. That makes American students especially vulnerable to manipulation, something the Frankfurt School philosophers sought.

The Department of Education report also found that many millions of American adults are functionally illiterate, as are a significant portion of our youth, particularly among minority youth (40 percent). The problem is seen elsewhere as well.[401]

Evidence of the dumbing down of America abounds, with dramatic declines in scores on scholastic aptitude tests, and worse. For example, the report states, "Many 17-year-olds do not possess the 'higher order' intellectual skills we should expect of them." Even comparing contemporary school texts with past editions is obvious. John Taylor Gatto, an education researcher, observed: "Pick up a fifth-grade math or rhetoric textbook from 1850 and you'll see that the texts were pitched then on what would today be considered college level."[402]

The dumbing down of Americans is the consequence of a war against American youth, and our public education establishment is the weapon. Charlotte Thomson Iserbyt, a former senior policy adviser to the US Department of Education, wrote in 1999:

> The reason Americans do not understand this war is because it has been fought in secret—in the schools of our nation, targeting our children who are captive in classrooms. The wagers of the war are using very sophisticated and effective tools.[403]

The secret war began a long time ago.

In my 2019 book, *Progressive Evil* (Defender Publishing), I devote an entire chapter to progressivism's impact on education. That chapter exposes the sham theories, new curricula, radicalized teaching materials, and lower performance standards. These changes seriously damaged traditional education, which up to that point (late nineteenth and early twentieth centuries) was the best in the world.

We can credit much of the progressive education legacy to John Dewey, the same man who raised the funding to bring the Frankfurt School Marxist philosophers to America. Dewey was influenced by Darwin's theory of evolution and believed children must be weaned from the influence of their parents, religion, and culture. He believed in moral relativism, and that children should be allowed to freely act as they see fit, because they are the product of a continuous biological evolution. That view is similar to Karl Marx's "new man" theory.

Evidently, according to American philosopher Sidney Hook, Dewey picked up where Marx left off. "Dewey had supplied Marxism with the epistemology and social philosophy that Marx had half seen for himself and had half sketched out in his early works but had never adequately spelled out," Hook wrote.[404]

What's clear from progressive educators is that they intended to transform their students regarding all aspects of life. Their focus is on personal experience, which is, for them, superior to the knowledge learned in conventional teaching environments with books and teachers.

At the end of his life, Dewey was a tenured professor at Columbia University, along with some of his Frankfurt School colleagues. He taught his progressive philosophy of education, thus infecting thousands of future school teachers with radical views.

Replace Moral Character

An aspect of the isms is the destruction of moral character, or what they would say is a replacement paradigm.

The moral crisis in America's schools is not a new story, however. We've seen rampant social problems invade the public schoolhouse as never before, such as drug abuse, suicide, gang activity, sexual promiscuity, shootings, and much more. The real roots are found with the moral disintegration across society, in part thanks to the left's promotion of atheism, evolution, and economic determinism—all Marxist tenets.

It's no secret that these three tenets—atheism, evolution, and economic determinism—of communism reign large in American public schools today. Of course, it's an abuse of America's First Amendment rights to spread atheism and Darwin's bankrupt theory of evolution in our schools with the objective of destroying morality, a key goal of the Frankfurt School philosophers.

That's exactly what is happening, however. For decades now and thanks to leftist federal judges, God is no longer welcome in public schools. Using the pretext of separation of church and state courts, they shut down Bible study in schools and made prayer unconstitutional speech. The outrage continued with courts ordering public schools to remove references to "Christmas," because it included the name "Christ," yet other courts like one in Virginia favored homosexual newspapers but not religious publications in public schools.

As the left has ejected God from schools in the name of the fabricated constitutional separation of church and state, they insisted on public schools teaching evolution as truth, in spite of its many unresolved gaps. That teaching more often than not confuses children of religious parents who teach them biblical truth about creation at home.

Removing the influence of God from the classroom created a void that the left anxiously replaced with communist ideology. This is obvious in many of our public-school texts. E. Merrill Root, author of *Brainwashing in the High Schools: An Examination of Eleven American History Textbooks* (1958), researched history texts and found they characterized American history as classic economic determinism, the struggle between the privileged and underprivileged (a Marxist tenet).[405]

Employ Psychological Manipulation

Another leftist tool is the psychological manipulation of our children. They use psychological conditioning to introduce moral relativism to public education. Conservative activist Phyllis Schlafly wrote about "education as therapy" in her 1984 book, *Child Abuse in the Classroom*. Ms. Schlafly explained that some teachers use psychological games using surveys on personal issues that require mature decisions on topics like suicide, murder, abortion, and adoption. Allegedly, these courses are for the students' health, but in reality, they are psychological conditioning.

Earlier I established that progressive education and the Frankfurt School use elements of Marx and Sigmund Freud's psychoanalysis theory. We saw that played out in the 1960s and 1970s, thanks to Frankfurt School immigrant Herbert Marcuse, who called for the removal of all inhibitions among young people that led them to indulge their whims, such as that associated with the 1960s Woodstock countercultural, free-love culture.

All moral inhibitions were thrown to the wind when Brock Chisholm, the first director of the World Health Organization and Canadian psychiatrist, promoted a radical moral theory that right and wrong must be neutral. He said:

> What basic psychological distortion can be found in every civilization of which we know anything? It must be a force which discourages the ability to see and acknowledge patent facts... which produces inferiority, guilt, and fear.... The only psychological force capable of producing these perversions is morality, the concept of right and wrong....
>
> We have been very slow to rediscover this truth and to recognise the unnecessary and artificially imposed inferiority, guilt and fear, commonly known as sin, under which we have almost all laboured and which produces so much of the social maladjustment and unhappiness in the world....
>
> If the race is to be freed of its crippling burden of good and evil it must be psychiatrists who take the original responsibility.[406]

Chisholm's moral theory of anything goes worked in tandem with Dewey's moral relativism to undermine traditional Judeo-Christian values, and they were taught in our public schools. This approach led to values-clarification classes in the 1970s that forced young children to make values-based decisions on key moral issues such as drug use and premarital sex.

William Kilpatrick, author of the 1993 book, *Why Johnny Can't Tell Right from Wrong: and What We Can Do About It*, explained that such classes turn "classroom discussions into 'bull sessions' where opinions go back and forth but conclusions are never reached."[407]

Kilpatrick continued:

> It has resulted in classrooms where teachers act like talk show hosts, and where the merits of wife swapping, cannibalism, and teaching children to masturbate are recommended topics for debate.... For students, it has meant wholesale confusion about moral values: learning to question values they have scarcely acquired, unlearning values taught at home, and concluding that questions of right and wrong are always merely subjective.... It has created a generation of moral illiterates: students who know their own feelings but don't know their culture.[408]

Advance Pornographic Sex Education

The left pushes pornographic sex education to confuse students with traditional values. For traditionalists, sex outside of marriage is sin and violates the divine standard. However, Lukacs introduced a perverted concept of sex education intended to help overturn traditional values. He developed sex education that promoted free love and the idea that marriage was outdated.

A co-conspirator regarding destructive sexual mores was Alfred Kinsey, who, also like the Frankfurt School professors, was financed by the leftist Rockefeller Foundation. Kinsey is best known for his books *Sexual Behavior in the Human Male* and *Sexual Behavior in the Human Female*. Although his "research" is thoroughly debunked, Kinsey advanced the idea that children are "sexual beings" and must be explicitly educated in every manner of sexual activity. It is important to understand that the morally depraved Kinsey employed pedophiles to conduct his sex experiments on infants and young children.[409]

Marxists and their allies in the public education arena attack traditional sexual morality in the classroom. No wonder America long ago started to see increased rates of teenage pregnancy and sexually transmitted diseases. Their goal is the destruction of human morality.

Push Self-Esteem in Lieu of Academics

The isms push a cult of self-esteem in the schoolhouse. The traditional meaning of "self-esteem" includes feelings of confidence and self-respect, but that's not what our leftist public schools promote. Instead, our public schools dumb down courses to the lowest common denominator so that even the underachieving students do well, thus they are pumped up on self-esteem.

Maureen Stout writes in her book, *The Feel-Good Curriculum: The Dumbing Down of America's Kids in the Name of Self-Esteem,* that to address student demands for top grades, public school teachers too often reduce the difficulty of tests. The result is predictable: The smart students don't have to try as hard and the underperforming students get top grades and feel good. Unfortunately, as Stout explains, this approach may grant better emotional comfort, but it doesn't deliver the necessary intellectual development and resilience needed for adults in a competitive world.[410]

This self-esteem, psychotherapeutic approach to education ends up indoctrinating our youth to a sense of entitlement and victimhood. Stout explained that it promotes in our next generation a mindset that says: "I want to do what I want, how I want, and when I want, and nothing and no one is going to stop me."[411]

Insert Big Government into Local Schools

For much of our history, public schools were primarily financed and run by local government. Now, just like in socialist/Marxist countries, the national government is rapidly growing its role, which includes not just budgets, but mandating education theory, testing, and faculty. As big government's influence grew, parents and local officials gradually lost power to decide what gets taught and how.

The growing centralizing of authority over public education is wrongheaded, because a single mistake applied across the entire system can lead to major issues. Further, Marxists seek to infiltrate every institution, such as national education bureaucracies, because they can make the entire system change with a single directive (i.e., Gramsci's theory), like flipping a single switch to affect an entire country. That is why locally controlled school systems that include parents in decisions are ideal for fighting off radicalism.

The leftist influence for the educational establishment is broad and deep, which tends to be true of any real insurgency or revolution. That influence goes far beyond the effects of centralized, federal bureaucracies reaching down to local schools, but also includes Marxist ideas impacting teacher unions, publishing houses, and, of course, our institutions of higher learning.

Corrupt Teachers' Unions

We've already established the Marxist influence in the colleges that produce K–12 teachers. Once those same teachers are hired, they have to decide whether to join a union, if in fact the decision isn't already made for them.

Some teachers' unions have immense influence, perhaps the most powerful political lobbying group in the country. Unfortunately, that power isn't used to advance positive reform for the education system, but to push for legislation and make self-serving political donations.

Idealistically, unions are intended to promote teacher interests and address issues like the delivery of quality education. Unfortunately, that's seldom the union's agenda. Teacher unions too often reward failure and incompetence while ignoring the legitimate needs of those they are charged to teach: our children.

The COVID-19 pandemic really exposed teacher unions as a fraud on the taxpayer. Many used in-person learning, their mandate, to leverage their self-serving demands. The *Daily Caller* editorialized that teachers' unions "have a history of bargaining for political advantage without apparent regard for the mental or physical health of the children which are purportedly their primary concern."[412]

The Education Week Research Center called out some concerning statistics, which reinforce what I said earlier about progressivism's influence among public education. The Center states that despite "the fact that only 5% of teachers identify themselves as 'very liberal' and 29% as 'liberal,' teachers unions have pushed progressive policies and have become a mainstay of the Democratic Party."[413]

Teachers' unions show their allegiance to Democratic Party candidates with their donations to down-ballot races. In the 2014 midterm elections, for example, teachers' unions spent over $100 million on political races, on behalf of Democratic Party candidates.[414]

It's no surprise that teachers' unions are closely aligned with the Democratic Party and their radical policy positions. The Unified Teachers of Los Angeles (UTLA) called for, like many of their Democratic Party allies, the defunding the police and Medicare-for-All, and evidently these demands took precedence even over reopening schools shuttered by COVID-19. Further, the UTLA threatened to strike the Los Angeles school system over these demands, which they knew could lead the education district into bankruptcy.

Teachers' unions have used their political influence to fight measures that would criminalize sex between students and teachers, which is not as uncommon as parents might think, accordingly to the *Daily Caller*, something that likely came out of the Frankfurt School's cultural Marxism playbook.

There is also some evidence that the strength of teachers' unions is directly related to the level of teacher accountability. Two university-based researchers, Johnathan Lott and Lawrence Keeny, found "a $233 rise in union dues per teacher causes student math and reading scores to drop almost 4 percentage points," and a "$14 increase in union spending per student results in a 3-percentage point decrease in math and reading scores."[415]

Similarly, the study found a negative correlation between the financial influence of teachers' unions and their students' performance. In states where teachers' union dues were low and strikes are uncommon, almost half (47 percent) of teachers are evaluated based on their students' performance. However, by comparison, where teacher unions are most powerful, half of the teachers may strike, and only 12.5 percent are evaluated based on their students' performance.[416]

Keep Parents Out of Their Children's Education

Progressives and Marxists alike seek to remove children from parents, which strikes at the heart of Western civilization. That technique is used in communist countries that create requirements for the students to spend more time at school, thus minimizing the parents' influence.

The Marxist believes government knows best when molding the next generation. So, it seeks to bring children into its jurisdiction as early as possible and keep them inside the government bubble as much of the day as they can through a variety of mechanisms, such as preventing them from taking textbooks home and encouraging children not to discuss what they learned in class, such as "values clarification" lessons, with their parents.

Most parents don't have the time or take the time to fight with the public school system about such issues. Rather, they tend to hope for the best and remain quiet in the face of a clear radical agenda in the public classroom. On occasion when parents do speak out, they are marginalized by the school authorities, which discourages other parents from speaking out as well.

Use Textbooks to Push Marxist Agenda

Earlier in this volume, I reported on the number of Millennials who have favorable views of socialism and even communism. Some of those favorable feelings are attributable to their education and, in particular, their textbooks, which are a powerful source of persuasion.

"I don't care who writes a nation's laws—or crafts its advanced treaties—if I can write its economics textbooks," that's real power, according to economist Paul Samuelson. Why? Textbooks are required reading among the most impressionable cohort of a population, students, who must absorb the material because their grades depend on retention. The student views the text as authoritative, and it shapes their minds often for their entire lives.[417]

A study of textbooks from the 1930s and thanks to progressive influence found a clear anti-religious bias and the promotion of socialism albeit while diminishing America's heritage. That was a key finding from a 1964 book by John Stormer, *None Dare Call It Treason*. However, at the time, the textbooks were being used by millions of students, and evidently too few said anything and the damage was quickly done.[418]

Today, textbooks need to be carefully monitored because, as in the past, their messages might be false or at best misleading. A current history teacher named Annie posted a TikTok video wherein she raved about Howard Zinn's textbook, *A People's History of the United States*. Annie indicated that it was a new and widely used classroom textbook.

Annie complained that she refuses to use Zinn's textbook because it is full of factual omissions and twisted American history. Zinn's objective, according to Annie, is "to fit a narrative of American shame." She illustrates her objection to Zinn's account with a couple of examples. The American Revolution was waged, Annie said and according to Zinn, in order to defeat "potential rebellions and create a consensus of popular support for the rule of a new, privileged leadership." She continued to explain the problem with Zinn's history. She said the text states that Civil War soldiers who fought to preserve the Union were deceived by "an aura of moral crusade" against slavery, which "worked effectively to dim class resentments against the rich and powerful, and turn much of the anger against 'the enemy.'"

Annie's objection to Zinn's radical American history text is warranted because it does influence people. Willem Van Spronsen was an anarchist who attempted to blow up a Tacoma, Washington, ICE (US Immigration and Customs Enforcement) detention facility, what he labeled a "concentration camp" just before police fatally shot him in a standoff. Mr. Spronsen wrote in his manifesto that we are witnessing "fascism ascendant." For proof, "see howard zinn [sic] a people's history of the United States."[419]

Mr. Spronsen was sixty-nine years old at the time of his death and evidently was a consumer of *A People's History of the United States,* like many other millions of students. That text is perhaps the most published American history book ever; it is now in its fifth edition, with three million copies in print.

Zinn has a long and radical history of his own. He led anti-Vietnam War protests and worked on behalf of communists while teaching at Boston University.

Mary Grabar, a resident fellow at the Alexander Hamilton Institute for the Study of Western Civilization, wrote a book about Zinn, *Debunking Howard Zinn: Exposing the Fake History that Turned a Generation Against America.* Ms. Grabar explains that Zinn's history text has remarkable similarities "to the points made by Communist Party USA General Secretary William Z. Foster in his tome, *Outline Political History of the Americans* [1951]."[420]

In 1951, Mr. Zinn, according to his FBI file, writes Grabar, was a Communist Party member teaching a course on Marxism at the party's Brooklyn, New York, headquarters. Grabar writes that Zinn modernized comrade Foster's key ideas.[421]

Ms. Grabar illustrated her point:

Foster, for example, writes that in 1933 Germany, "the workers were in a revolutionary mood" but that "the Social-Democrats blocked the revolution, as they had done in Germany in 1918 and in Italy during 1920. They refused to form a united front with the Communists for an all-out fight against Hitler."...

Actually, the communists were ordered by the Soviet Union to reject efforts by all socialist and leftist groups in order to wait for the opportune moment when the communists, and the communists alone, could sweep in for a revolutionary overthrow. This went along with Marx's and Engels' denouncement in *The Communist Manifesto* of socialists who "wish to attain their ends by peaceful means" and "endeavor…to deaden the class struggle."[422]

Zinn wrote a Marxist view of American history, which is in its fifth edition with millions of copies in classrooms. The text is a Marxist narrative and views American history through a Frankfurt School prism of race and class.[423]

Mr. Zinn makes no excuses for his anti-American text, however. He explains that he became a historian thanks to social revolution. "I came to history with a very sort of modest objective, I wanted to change the world." Zinn believes like other Marxists that the US is, "at its core, and from its inception, a sexist, racist, xenophobic, and bigoted nation." It is irredeemable and therefore revolution is needed to radically reform America.[424]

Annie has good company willing to be critical of Zinn's history of America. To his credit, Stanford University school of education professor Sam Wineburg said *A People's History* was years ago a "quirky outlier" to the "new accepted view of American history." He continued:

In the 32 years since its original publication, *A People's History* has gone from a book that buzzed about the ear of the dominant narrative to its current status where, in many circles, it has become the dominant narrative. For many students, *A People's History* will be the first full-length history book they read, and for some, it will be the only one.[425]

It is indeed frightening that Marxist-inspired *A People's History* is a new (2020) standard in American history curricula. That fact may help explain why America had such a horrible summer of 2020, with race riots, destruction of historical monuments, and the emergence of the thoroughly debunked, *New York Times*-endorsed 1619 Project, which paints all white Americans with the same condemning brush, alleging them racists.

Of course, the root of much of the distress in the classroom isn't solely the fault of Marxist textbooks. A lot of the guilt is shared by America's teachers' colleges which, thanks to the influence of Frankfurt School Marxists, are radicalized, and many of those same teachers' college graduates snapped up Zinn's distorted history because that's all they knew.

The material just covered regarding K–12 public education carries over to the university and college scene, but at a much more intense and dangerous level.

AMERICAN UNIVERSITIES: HOTBEDS OF COMMUNISM

The communist attack on Western universities is worse than what happened with our public K–12 public education establishment. Our teenagers leave their public schools marginally prepared academically and especially ripe for radicalism, and enter today's college campus where they are likely to fully embrace atheism, the theory of evolution, and Marxist materialism. Further, thanks to their public-school indoctrination, these mostly narrow-minded young people can't think for themselves, know very little about their country (history and civics), and lack common sense, yet, they are primed by the counterculture to seek hedonistic lifestyles paid for mostly by their gullible, ill-informed parents and the taxpayers funding this travesty. These young people are truly vulnerable to campus-based communist deception, which is much of what they get, especially in liberal arts schools.

Consider the facts about America's higher learning academe. Let's begin with the faculty. The vast majority—no exaggeration—of staff at

American universities lean hard left. You wouldn't talk to a liberal arts faculty member if one of them was your next-door neighbor because they are just plain weird.

A 2020 report by the National Association of Scholars, "Partisan Registration and Contributions of Faculty in Flagship Colleges," considered voter registration and candidate contributions by twelve thousand professors at top colleges. Mitchell Langbert with Brooklyn College and Sean Stevens with Heterodox Academy, the researchers, found that "48.4 percent are registered Democrats and 5.7 percent are registered Republicans, a ratio of 8.5:1." The donations were more lopsided, with 2,081 professors who gave exclusively to Democrats while only 22 gave exclusively to Republicans, a 95:1 ratio.[426]

Another study in *Econ Journal Watch* asked about the voter registration status of professors of history and social science at forty leading universities. Once again, Democrats (liberals) overwhelmed Republicans (conservatives) 11.5:1. And it was worse in history departments, a 35:1 ratio.[427]

Other studies find much the same results. The fact is leftists own our universities, and panelists at a conservative seminar in 2016 claimed that 18 percent of social scientists who are found mostly on US college campuses self-identify as Marxist, while only 5 percent identify as conservative.[428]

Conservative Texas US Senator Ted Cruz anecdotally confirmed as much about his Harvard Law School faculty:

> There were more self-declared communists [in the faculty] than there were Republicans.... If you asked [them] to vote on whether this nation should become a socialist nation, 80 percent of the faculty would vote yes and 10 percent would think that was too conservative.[429]

Why are our universities so radical, full to the brim with leftists? Remember the 1960s and early 1970s and those who protested the Viet-

nam War and burned the American flag? Those same people were part
of the counterculture movement that consumed Marxism and Frankfurt
School theory and appeared to fade away after President Richard Nixon
withdrew our troops from Vietnam. The problem is that many of those
young people left the anti-war movement for graduate school, especially
the humanities, and never left the campus.

Rather, they embraced Italian Marxist Antonio Gramsci's theory of
"the long march through the institutions." They made careers in our
universities to radicalize our children and grandchildren. America is paying a price for their decision to occupy the academe.

One such radical professor explained:

> After the Vietnam War, a lot of us didn't just crawl back into our
> literary cubicles; we stepped into academic positions. With the
> war over, our visibility was lost, and it seemed for a while—to the
> unobservant—that we had disappeared. Now we have tenure,
> and the work of reshaping the universities has begun in earnest.[430]

In time, an entire generation of former Vietnam War protesters
who matriculated from graduate programs became what Roger Kimball labeled "tenured radicals." Kimball's 1989 book, *Tenured Radicals*,
explains the entire anti-war, civil rights and feminist movement 1960s
crowd who became tenured in the 1980s and haven't left campus. Today
many of these radicals are department heads and deans, and they use their
positions to undermine Western civilization by subverting mainstream
society, producing more revolutionaries just like their former selves.[431]

There is also an active, foreign communist influence fueling on-
campus views about Marxism. The Chinese communist regime heavily
invests in US universities, according to a *Washington Free Beacon* review
of federal records. Although those investments appear to be part of an
extensive espionage campaign, they inevitably influence university decisions regarding the treatment of the communist regime and its ideology,
which evidently many radical faculty members endorse.[432]

The *Free Beacon's* review of donations to our universities found a lot of Chinese money. For example:

> [Duke University operates] a joint-campus in China with Wuhan University, a public university that repeatedly carried out cyber-attacks on behalf of the Chinese military. Northwestern University and the University of California Irvine have together received more than $4 million in research funding from an entity controlled by the Aviation Industry Corporation of China, a Chinese defense contractor that used stolen designs of American F-35 fighters to build planes for the Chinese military.[433]

Between the years 2014 and 2019, according to US government records, Chinese government-controlled institutions donated at least $315 million to American colleges, and more than a quarter (27 percent) of those donations came from Chinese organizations aligned with the Chinese military.[434]

"Americans must know how the CCP is poisoning the well of our higher education for its own ends, and how those actions degrade our freedoms and our national security," said then Secretary of State Mike Pompeo. "If we don't educate ourselves, we'll get schooled by Beijing."[435]

Communist Ideology Prevails

Ever since Dewey helped bring Frankfurt School Marxists to America, their ideology has significantly influenced liberal arts colleges and challenged the essence of academic freedom.

According to a historian at the University of Pennsylvania, the most influential books for the humanities in the US academe today were authored by acknowledged Marxists. Alan Charles Kors reportedly named Gramsci's *Prison Notebooks*, Paulo Freire's *Pedagogy of the Oppressed*, and Frantz Fanon's *The Wretched of the Earth*, all radical volumes, as "the most influential books for humanities in the US academe today." Of course, Gramsci was an Italian Marxist, Freire was a Brazilian theorist who favored Mao Zedong, and Ernesto "Che" Guevara and Fanon, born on Martinique Island (Caribbean), called on people in the colonies to engage in violent revolt. He called "violence" a "cleansing force. It frees the native from his inferiority complex and from his despair and inaction; it makes him fearless and restores his self-respect."[436]

Obviously, the liberal arts departments in American colleges are heavily influenced by Marxism, the Frankfurt School, Freudian theory, and postmodernism—a front for communism.

Colleges: Ground Zero for Promoting Leftist Ideology

David Horowitz and Jacob Laksin identified 150 leftist courses offered at twelve universities that "closely resemble political courses that are mandatory in communist countries." Their book, *One-Party Classroom: How Radical Professors at America's Top Colleges Indoctrinate Students and Undermine Our Democracy*, cites a number examples of these courses. The Community Studies department at the University of California, Santa Cruz, offered a course that read: "The goal of this seminar is to learn how to organize a revolution. We will learn what communities past and present have done and are doing to resist, challenge, and overcome systems of power including (but not limited to) global capitalism, state oppression, and racism."[437]

Leftist ideology leads to moral corruption and is ruinous to a culture.

Marxist Brainwashing and Moral Corruption

Marxist ideology helped to create the "snowflake" phenomenon on campuses across America and the college staffs adjusted their rules to address the issue. In the 1980s, there arose an effort to prevent "offensive" remarks, some might call it free speech, especially when targeted at minorities and women.

Donald Downs, an American political science professor at the University of Wisconsin at Madison, found from 1987 to 1992 about three hundred US universities had policies that regulated speech and governed that speech via a fabricated and questionably constitutional paralegal system.[438]

These paralegal systems have for the most part been struck down as unconstitutional in federal court. However, they clearly represent the cultural Marxism and prejudice that the Frankfurt School philosophers created while still in Nazi Germany. The rules target any behavior considered prejudice regarding virtually all differences—culture, ancestry, skin color, gender, sexual orientation. Naturally, the leftists on campuses supported the system, which granted special treatment for those who claimed victimhood.

This view beckons to the Marxist treatment granted the "oppressed" proletariat by the oppressor "bourgeoisie." This type of groupthink eventually infringes upon traditional views of good, evil, right, and wrong.

Ultimately, this communistic influence causes some college students to abandon what's left of their morality in favor of a perverted view that the oppressed are always morally correct.

CONCLUSION

This chapter demonstrates that America's public education establishment is corrupt and for the most part ineffective—another co-conspirator in the ongoing cultural revolution. In spite of our tremendous investment in public education, our publicly educated children are not prepared academically for a very competitive world, and meanwhile, they are aggressively indoctrinated by a cabal of ism advocates hell-bent on transforming America into something our founders would never recognize.

The next chapter will peel back the truth about our mainstream media's radical views and how it, too, is a co-conspirator in the ongoing cultural revolution to transform America.

7

Media's Role in Society; Marxist History and Influence in the Cultural Revolution

Whoever controls the media, controls the mind.[439]

—Jim Morrison (1943–1971),
American singer, songwriter, and poet

This chapter demonstrates how America's media is infiltrated by Marxists and Marxism's ideology to promote anti-traditional, certainly anti-Christian, and dare I say too often demonic messages. They deliver what President Trump called "fake news," which means the media no longer embraces objectivity and plays the role of society's moral conscience. No, they betray their profession—the fourth estate—and our country, especially free speech. Ultimately, this assault on speech represents an invasion to take captive the minds of Americans, and it is happening all too often with our full knowledge, much less our gullible permission.

We are all influenced by contemporary media, unless you are the rare person who lives off the grid without outside contact. The rest of us are influenced by a variety of media blasted at us every day—advertisements, news reports, contact via social media platforms, and entertainment either via television, Netflix, or a growing plethora of other electronic devices and streaming platforms. Yes, media permeates most aspects of our everyday lives, and thanks to the Internet, that impact is growing exponentially.

Admit it, we live in an ocean of media influencers driven by various tools—radio, film, websites, iPhone, television, and more. Our first impressions about virtually every electronic encounter are shaped by outside sources, and there is nothing too personal that isn't unearthed by today's outlets. And yes, media's psychological manipulation can be quite persuasive and effective in terms of what we buy, who we choose for a mate, how we occupy our leisure, our political views, and what we come to believe is truth about others and current issues.

Traditionally, media outlets play a key societal role by fostering and guarding cultural values. For much of the history of the United States until recently, most of us relied on journalists to report facts—the truth about our complex and rapidly changing world. We long held the public media (journalists)—the fourth estate, a term first used to accentuate the freedom of the press—in high esteem, because it protected us and itself from outside influence, especially government manipulation.

Today, especially in light of the media's dramatic turn to the far left, the vast majority of Americans no longer believes the "fourth estate" is a reliable guardian of truth. Rather, most consider the mainstream media to be lost in the wilderness of bias, especially political and ideological partisanship. A 2020 Gallup/Knight Foundation poll found that 86 percent of Americans believe the media is ideologically partisan, with half (49 percent) saying it demonstrates "a great deal" of political bias. That view tracks along political lines with 70 percent of Democrats saying attacks on media bias are unwarranted, while 61 percent of Republicans think it is justified.[440]

Allegations of media bias, especially as it regards government, are very serious. Historically, Americans expected our media to safeguard society's morality, to call out government overreach, but confidence in that role evaporated as well. With good reason, most Americans see media's bias on full display because too often journalists put their finger on the scales of truth. The fact is too many media outlets long ago abandoned all virtue and caved to pressure, thanks to the temptation and manipulation of powerful people, institutions, and big government.

Serious doubts about journalistic integrity and objectivity are currently almost always suspect. In fact, long ago, media icons understood the fourth estate's obligation to society and warned against compromise. Joseph Pulitzer, the newspaper publisher for whom the Pulitzer Prize for journalism is named, said:

> Our Republic and its press will rise or fall together. An able, disinterested, public-spirited press, with trained intelligence to know the right and courage to do it, can preserve that public virtue without which popular government is a sham and a mockery. A cynical, mercenary, demagogic press will produce in time a people as base as itself. The power to mold the future of the Republic will be in the hands of the journalists of future generations.[441]

Mr. Pulitzer's warning came true if the polling concerning our mainstream media is correct. Indeed, most Americans believe our press is "cynical, mercenary, demagogic" and ideologically biased. It became that way for a host of reasons, but what's evident to most Americans is that the media consistently favors those with a similar leftist, progressive, or socialist leaning.

The corruption of media happens when journalists, their schools, and their employers fall under the control of influencers like communist China, leftist ideologies, or big social media billionaires and their globalist corporations. You see, media outlets today aren't at all what they were only a few decades ago, when television, radio, and printed materials were mostly independent and locally owned.

Today, the vast majority of mainstream media is owned by six conglomerates that foster an ideological and mostly leftist agenda. That matters, because these powerful mega-media groups control the distribution of information to most Americans—both in terms of content and interpretation—through twenty-four-hour cable news networks, newspapers, publishing houses, Internet utilities, entertainment, and even video games. They influence Americans directly and indirectly every day.

Those six powerful conglomerates are, in no particular order: Time Warner, Walt Disney, Viacom, Rupert Murdoch's news corporation, CBS corporation, and NBCUniversal.[442] They are joined by social media giants such as Facebook, YouTube, WhatsApp, WeChat, Instagram, TikTok, Twitter, and more.

Joining the powerful conglomerates and the social media platforms are a collection of Internet information platforms such as Google and Microsoft. These platforms use algorithms (computer-programmed actions) to influence not only search results via "search engines," but also the interpretation of that content. However, and far more sobering, the emergence of artificial intelligence makes these platforms and their associated "search engines" quite significant in the information age. There is a real and growing ability by these platforms to compromise standards for transparency and accountability, which infringes on our First Amendment rights, an issue Congress repeatedly calls out in regulatory hearings, but has yet to rein in these often anti-free speech monopolies.

Entering this sphere of social influence are a host of people with nefarious anti-American intentions. These actors appreciate the role media can play in a society, and their efforts at manipulation began long ago. This is especially true for Marxist regimes like the former Soviet Union and the People's Republic of China, who use their national media as their regime's mouthpiece to keep citizens controlled through propaganda. Unfortunately, that approach and the concentration of media outlets in a few hands, along with the introduction of artificial intelligence, threatens Western free speech today. That's what is happening in America, and it is gravely serious.

HISTORY OF MARXIST INFLUENCE ON AMERICAN MEDIA

The seeds of the communist influence in America and ultimately an insurgent move to take our media captive are traceable to the publication of Marx's *Communist Manifesto* (1848) and the uprisings and strikes that began with the Russian Revolution of 1917.

The Bolshevik (Marxist) Revolution persuaded US President Woodrow Wilson to send troops to aid Tsar Nicholas II, the Russian monarch and the last ruler of the Romanov Dynasty. The "Red" army of the Bolsheviks, led by Marxist Vladimir Lenin, fought the "White" armies of the tsarists and Russian capitalists, aided by the United States and its allies, the French and British. That coalition invaded Russia from both the east and west in 1918, with thousands of troops to "restore order," and what became known in the US as the "Midnight War" because President Wilson never secured congressional consent.

What motivated the US to rush to the aid of the Russian tsar? It had little to do with the restoration of order in Russia. No, at the time Americans opposed Bolshevism, according to Professor David Foglesong, Rutgers University, because of a growing fear of immigrants, anti-Semitism, and racism. The professor notes that Jews, immigrants, and militant American Blacks at the time were associated with the Bolsheviks, and thus they created a perceived threat to American security.[443]

After the Soviets successfully toppled the tsar, Washington brought our troops home, but that didn't end the American hostility with the new Marxist regime in Moscow. No, Washington's hostility to the Bolsheviks led President Wilson to sever aid to the new Soviet government, and he also extended the World War I maritime blockade of Germany to include Soviet Russia. At the time, US Secretary of State Robert Lansing said the Bolsheviks were "dangerous—more so than Germany. They threatened us with revolution."[444]

In the wake of World War I and the Soviet victory over the tsar, there was at home a widespread fear of the rise of communism, anarchism, which revolved around the American labor movement and political radicalism. Political scientist and a communist Murray B. Levin wrote that the "Red Scare" was "a nationwide anti-radical hysteria provoked by a mounting fear and anxiety that a Bolshevik revolution in America was imminent—a revolution that would change church, home, marriage, civility, and the American way of life."[445]

It was a very tense time that followed on the heels of the midterm elections of 1918, in which Republicans had swept the Congress. Then, in January 1919, radical workers started walkouts that lasted much of the year, and meanwhile, a postal clerk intercepted sixteen mail bombs addressed to notable Americans such as Supreme Court Justice Oliver Wendell Holmes, capitalist John D. Rockefeller, and Attorney General A. Mitchell Palmer. Although the bomb attack was foiled, it was quickly followed in the late spring of 1919, when bombs exploded in eight different cities targeting a federal judge, a textile manufacturer, a mayor, and once again Attorney General Palmer.

Those attacks fueled a nationwide response, with state legislatures banning red flags, and a growing endorsement for the government to act against the radicals. Soon the US Justice Department and the newly minted Federal Bureau of Investigation launched what came to be known as the "Red Scare," a series of "attacks on dissident immigrants and some American citizens accused of being Bolshevik agents." That government-led campaign reflected distrust in the waves of new European immigrants, who were condemned as alien and "un-American."[446]

These attacks became known as the "Palmer Raids," which culminated in December 1919 with a massive sweep by FBI agents who arrested thousands of resident aliens, of which 249 were loaded on the *Buford*, a ship with a secret destination. Once at sea, the *Buford's* captain opened the sealed envelope that contained orders to land in Finland.

The ship was met at a Finnish port by American soldiers who escorted the prisoners to the Russian border.[447]

The widespread American distrust of the new European immigrants became such a problem that in 1934, Congress created a new committee, the House Un-American Activities Committee (HUAC), to protect America's political purity from outsiders. The HUAC was initially set up to thwart Nazi propaganda, but came to focus on rooting out communist subversion, an effort that President Roosevelt opposed at the time and that is mentioned in the previous chapter.[448]

World War II presented a special ideological challenge for the United States, because most Americans at the time distrusted both the German Nazis and the Soviet Communists. However, the Nazi invasion of the Soviet Union in 1941 left the US with a tough decision. Then Senator Harry S. Truman outlined that stark choice when he compared the two dictatorships, Adolf Hitler and Joseph Stalin, to "a tarantula and a scorpion locked in a bottle." Senator Truman cautioned the US about aiding either party.[449]

In time, President Roosevelt decided to provide Stalin assistance via the Lend-Lease program, an Act to Promote the Defense of the United States, Public Law 77-11, enacted March 11, 1941. That program allowed the US government to supply ally countries like the Soviet Union with food, oil, as well as warships, planes and weapons.[450]

President Roosevelt soberly understood that aligning with Russia in World War II, much less supplying it via Lend-Lease, was a marriage of convenience that would quickly evaporate once the Nazi threat ended. It is noteworthy, even given Roosevelt's apprehension about the Soviets, that he met with Stalin in Yalta (Crimea, Russia), in February 1945 and essentially gave away postwar Eastern Europe to the communist tyrant. But in his defense, President Roosevelt understood the US could not impose its will to keep Eastern Europe out of Moscow's hands without going to war with the Soviets. At the time, few Americans understood the communist threat, and besides, they had no appetite for extending the Second World War. Further, the Yalta agreements called for "free" elections in Eastern Europe, a sop to the naïve West about the Soviet's true intentions.[451]

Soon the Cold War (1947–1991) started as Moscow used force to impose its will and communist ideology on Eastern Europe. Meanwhile, and more daunting, transforming America in Russia's Marxist image was part of Moscow's strategic global goal and a big part of that effort began by coopting America's media.

MARXISTS: MASTERS AT MEDIA MANIPULATION

Communists see media as a tool to manipulate, to brainwash, an entire society. That view dates back to Marx and Engels, who wrote the book *Rules of the Communist League*, which called on comrades to have "revolutionary energy and zeal in propaganda." These radicals used a variety of terms to describe the purpose of the media: "party battlefield," "political center," and "tool for public opinion."[452]

The Russian Bolshevik leader, Lenin, used media to promote his Marxist views leading up to and during the 1917 Revolution. He filled communist newspapers at the time with propaganda. Meanwhile, after the Soviets toppled the tsar, they immediately began using the national Russian media for political indoctrination both at home and abroad. It is noteworthy that former Soviet prime minister Vyacheslav Molotov outlined the communist intent to infiltrate the media abroad:

> Who reads the communist papers? Only a few people who are already communists. We don't need to propagandize them.... We have to influence non-communists if we want to make them communists or if we want to fool them. So, we have to try to infiltrate in the big press.[453]

The Chinese Communist Party (CCP) considers media a tool much like their former Soviet colleagues. The Chinese communists said, "The guns and the pens are what it relies on for seizing and consolidating power."[454] Even before Mao Zedong took the reins of the Chinese government in 1949, his secretary expressed a similar principle: the CCP newspaper "has to carry through the party's viewpoints and understandings in all articles, every essay, every news report, and every newsletter."[455]

Once in power, the CCP imposed strict control over Chinese media, which remains the case today. That is evidenced by a Chinese phrase describing the Chinese media's role: "I am the Party's dog, sitting by the Party's door. I'll bite whomever the Party tells me to bite and however many times I am told."[456]

Communist regimes across the world gained control of domestic media to serve their party's interests. That control translated into the regime's success and proved to be a useful template to gain traction in America.

The Marxist infiltration into America's media was a gradual process linked to the era between the world wars. At the time, many Europeans, including the Frankfurt School Marxists, immigrated to America and then settled in our education establishment as outlined in the previous chapter, but also into our mainstream media, especially our film industry—Hollywood—a prime target for Marxist takeover, but also in leading print publications.

Soviet spies worked behind the scenes to influence prestigious American media outlets. That communist infiltration included the prestigious *Time* magazine. Whittaker Chambers, the once editor of *Time* (1939–1948), was a Soviet spy who previously defected from the Soviet underground, later detailed in his book *Witness*, the communist subversion of *Time*. Mr. Chambers went on to become a senior editor at *National Review* and was awarded by President Ronald Reagan the Presidential Medal of Freedom posthumously in 1984.[457]

In 1938, Chambers abandoned the communists, but at the time had no plans to tell the US government about his espionage activities. However, that changed, according to author Daniel Oppenheimer, who noted that Chambers soon substituted his passion for communism with his passion for God. Chambers said in his autobiography that, after his defection from Marxism, he saw his actions as an "absolute evil."[458]

In 1939, Chambers met with Assistant Secretary of State Adolf Berle and agreed to reveal what he knew about communist agent infiltration in the US government on the condition of immunity from prosecution. It was during the meeting with Berle that Chambers reportedly named several current and former government employees as spies or communist sympathizers. Among those named were Alger Hiss, his brother Donald Hiss, and Laurence Duggan, all midlevel officials in the US State Department, as well as Lauchlin Currie, a special assistant to President Roosevelt.[459]

Secretary Berle took Chamber's information to the White House, but President Roosevelt dismissed it. Later, Berle notified the FBI of Chamber's information. However, it wasn't until more than a year later that the FBI interviewed Chambers for the first of two times, May 1942 and June 1945, but the Bureau did not take any action at that point. It wasn't until November 1945, when another communist spy, Elizabeth Bentley, defected and corroborated Chamber's account, that the FBI began to take Chamber's story seriously.[460] It appears that the FBI's failures echo down the corridors of time right up until today, e.g., Russiagate.

On August 3, 1948, Chambers testified before the HUAC to identify individuals he said were part of the underground "Ware Group," a covert organization of Communist Party USA operatives within the US government in the 1930s.[461]

Other journalists were suspected of being communist agents as well. Walter Duranty, the Moscow correspondent for the *New York Times* and a 1932 Pulitzer Prize winner, flacked for the communist regime, such as when he denied the Ukraine famine that ravaged that country and killed millions. At the time, Duranty wrote, "Any report of a famine in Russia is today an exaggeration or malignant propaganda." However, Jay Lovestone and journalist Joseph Alsop believed Duranty was indeed a Soviet agent.[462]

The broader problem of Marxist infiltration was chronicled in a novel. Scottish-born novelist Helen MacInnes wrote twenty-one novels describing the struggle against totalitarianism, first at the hands of Nazi Germany prior to and during the Second World War, and later, after the war, she turned her attention to the Russian communists and their infiltration of America's media.[463]

Ms. MacInnes wrote in her 1951 novel, *Neither Five nor Three*, a description "of the methods the left used to take almost complete control of a once-noble institution: the American media." American David Jenkins, photographer and writer, summarized Ms. MacInnes' view on how Marxists took over America's media: "By undermining, discrediting, and marginalizing honest reporters, writers, and editors, the left gradually replaced them with people who would oh-so-subtly (and sometimes not so subtly) parrot the [communist] Party line."[464]

The subversion of America's press likely began with the 1917 Bolshevik Revolution, but, as explained in the previous chapter, the spread of Marxism in America was well underway by the 1930s with the immigration of the Frankfurt School Marxist philosophers.

CONTROLLING HOLLYWOOD:
KEY OBJECTIVE FOR COMMUNISTS

Willi Münzenberg, one of the Frankfurt School faculty John Dewey brought to America in the 1930s, went on to introduce his communist ideology in Hollywood by promoting pro-Soviet, communist propaganda. Recall from the previous chapter that Münzenberg said his goal was to make "the West so corrupt; it stinks. We're going to rock them from within, and we're going to teach immorality to the young people. We're going to try to push pornography and we're going to try to increase alcoholism."[465]

Mr. Münzenberg found fertile ground in California's Beverly Hills to realize his goal of corrupting America. He joined other Marxists in

Hollywood, where they followed much the same script outlined by Lenin and Stalin in Soviet Russia. They used the entertainment business to spread their ideology. That cabal of communists included pro-Soviet artists like Yip Harburg, a songwriter best known for his work on the *Wizard of Oz*. Harburg and other communists used their talents to psychologically manipulate the gullible American population by producing films that contained favorable portrayals of communism and socialist ideals, while denigrating capitalism and American morality.[466]

Kenneth L. Billingsley addressed the use of movies to propagandize the public in his book, *Hollywood's Missing Movies*. Billingsley said that dictator Stalin was an ardent cinephile who firmly believed in the use of film as a tool to spread ideology.[467]

Early in the life of communist Russia, Lenin reportedly told his commissar of education, Anatoly Lunacharsky, "You must always consider that, of all the arts, the motion picture is for us the most important." Evidently, that concept captured the attention of the communists in the Frankfurt School, and they brought that view to America, especially Marxist Münzenberg.[468]

Long before Münzenberg came to America (1925), he wrote an article for the communist newspaper *Daily Worker*, in which he said that "one of the most pressing tasks confronting the Communist Party in the field of propaganda, is the conquest of this supremely important propaganda unit [entertainment media], until now the monopoly of the ruling class." He continued, "We must wrest it from them and turn it against them."[469]

Münzenberg apparently believed that America was especially ripe for the spread of communism because of the Great Depression, which didn't end until just prior to the Second World War. His rationale was that the Americans needed a distraction from the Depression, and movies provided both a relief from life's travails and gave Münzenberg a perfect venue to promote Marxism.[470]

Yet another book by Billingsley, *Hollywood Party: How the Communist Party Seduced the American Film Industry in the 1930s and 1940s,* indicates that the Communist Party USA opened a branch in Hollywood specifically to infiltrate film industry guilds and unions.[471]

The operation of communist fronts—guilds and unions—in Hollywood drew the attention of federal authorities in Washington. Congress responded to the promotion of communist propaganda in movies with the formation of the HUAC, identified earlier in this chapter.

Allan H. Ryskind, author of *Hollywood Traitors: Blacklisted Screenwriters, Agents of Stalin, Allies of Hitler*, provided details about the communist campaign in Hollywood thanks to the work of his father, Morrie Ryskind, a Pulitzer Prize-winning playwright and screenwriter in Hollywood in the mid-1940s. At the time, Mr. Ryskind was considered one of the leaders opposing communism in Hollywood.[472]

Mr. Ryskind said that "hard-core" communists descended on Hollywood intent on taking "over the movie industry and nearly succeeded." This cabal of communists, explained Ryskind, carried Communist Party cards and gave their allegiance to Joseph Stalin and the Soviet Union. He explained that his father, Morrie, said at one time there were as many as three hundred Communist Party members in Hollywood. "They were part of a broad conspiracy of subversives who had penetrated America's more critical institutions, including our intelligence agencies, the State Department and even the White House."[473]

"By 1944, the American communists, who viewed the murderous Joseph Stalin as their political leader, were deeply imbedded in the Hollywood guilds and unions, and even appeared to control movie content," Ryskind said. He said the "Screen Writers Guild was saturated with communists," and the editors for its publication, *The Screen Writer*, were devoted Communist Party members, Dalton Trumbo and Gordon Kahn, "our next-door neighbor in Beverly Hills."[474]

Hollywood communists were indeed useful to their Soviet masters in Moscow. They were often able to prevent the production of movies that might be critical of the regime. Not only did the communists help organize the Screen Writers Guild, but more importantly, they organized the Story Analysts Guild as well. Those people judge scripts and film treatments to make recommendations for production. So, the careful positioning of communists in those positions helped quash scripts and treatments that contained anti-Soviet content.

Evidently, some talent agents answered to Moscow as well. Communist organizer Robert Weber worked at the William Morris Agency, where he evidently represented fellow communist writers and directors. Also, George Willner, a communist agent for screenwriters, purposely sank non-communist clients, and other party members hosted smear campaigns and blacklists against non-communists, targeting some of the best known in Hollywood like Lana Turner and Bette Davis.[475]

There are numerous examples of communist propaganda movies in Hollywood's productions from that time. Mr. Ryskind called out *Song of Russia* and *Mission to Moscow* as examples. "*Song of Russia,*" Ryskind explained, "made you think that pre-World War II Russia was a slice of paradise and *Mission to Moscow* that Joe Stalin was the wisest statesman on the planet." The film praised Stalin's collective farm system, but ignored mentioning the horrendous famine at the time. Further, many of those same communists attacked their opposition and gave "tons of money to communist-run causes, leftwing political candidates, far-left unions and publications defending the Soviet Union."[476]

Leading up to World War II, most Hollywood communists flipped allegiances to satisfy their masters in Moscow. Mr. Ryskind said, "When the Soviet Union viewed Hitler as a threat to Moscow, the communists in Hollywood—who never deviated from the Soviet line—were in the forefront of the fight against Hitler and fascism."[477]

Mr. Ryskind illustrated that relationship. "Donald Ogden Stewart, a major communist screenwriter…headed the Hollywood Anti-Nazi League, which he admitted was controlled by the communist party," he explained. However, the Hollywood communists quickly changed their tune when Stalin entered a pact with Hitler in August 1939. Soon "the entire Soviet apparatus in America…allied itself with the Nazi dictator."[478]

The Hollywood "Reds," as Ryskind said, "enthusiastically supported Hitler when he invaded Poland on September 1, 1939." However, very soon those same communists became anti-Nazi because Hitler "double-crossed his friend [Stalin] in the Kremlin, launching a massive invasion of the Soviet Union in June of 1941." Then, all of a sudden, American communists "became super-patriotic," because only "the United States had the industrial and economic might to defeat Hitler." Mr. Ryskind concluded, "If Hitler hadn't invaded Russia, it's a safe bet to think Stalin and his fifth column in America would never have turned against the führer."[479]

After the war, the communist influence in Hollywood came to the attention of Congress. In 1947, the HUAC found many movie people volunteering stories of communist intrigue in Hollywood, enough for the committee to launch an investigation and host hearings. Almost fifty witnesses were called to testify, which included communist heavy-weights such as Dalton Trumbo, a Communist Party member and one of the highest-paid screenwriters in Hollywood, who described his trade as "literary guerrilla warfare."[480]

Tragically, the HUAC focused on the wrong content of the movies, not on the communists' behind-the-scenes influence, and that was despite key testimony from Walt Disney. They ignored the fact that the films excluded all anti-communist, anti-Soviet material.

Those hearings featured Stalinist writers, who denounced the HUAC for its probe, and these writers became known as the Hollywood Ten. Eventually, "these prominent screenwriters and directors...received jail sentences and were banned from working for the major Hollywood studios. Their defiant stands also placed them at center stage in a national debate over the controversial anti-communist crackdown that swept through the United States in the late 1940s and early 1950s."[481]

One of the Hollywood Ten, Edward Dmytryk, cooperated with the government. In 1951, Mr. Dmytryk testified before the HUAC to provide the names of twenty Hollywood colleagues "he claimed were communists."[482]

The HUAC investigation led to the movie industry becoming serious about the communist threat, and as a direct result, it instituted a "blacklist to convince the public that Hollywood was not 'soft on com-munism.'" Mr. Ryskind explained that just as the Cold War with the Soviets began, Hollywood "producers laid down the law that the studios would not hire anyone who was a [Communist] party member and who refused to cooperate with the [HUAC] committee."[483]

Hollywood never apologized for its history of aiding either the Soviet or Nazi totalitarians, however. In fact, it did just the opposite. Rather, it turned to making anti-American films "and frequently embracing middle-weight Stalinists like Cuba's Fidel Castro and Che Guevara and Venezuela's late Marxist ruler Hugo Chavez." Mr. Ryskind said, "Stalin's champions in Hollywood are still being lavishly celebrated."[484]

Johnathan Gray, a pen name for a current Hollywood-based author and filmmaker, wrote, "Hollywood's romance with communism—an ideology that has led to famine, wars, and genocide around the world, and that has claimed the lives of over 100 million people—continues to this day."[485]

In 2017, Mr. Gray warned, "Lenin seems to be next up to receive his Hollywood makeover, with actor Leonardo DiCaprio courting the Russian film industry for the role of the dictator who Russian novelist and historian Aleksandr Solzhenitsyn estimates killed between 60 mil-lion and 66 million people."[486]

The infiltration of Marxists into America's entertainment media was by design and thorough. Although the influence waxed and waned beginning in the 1930s, as you will quickly see, it is very strong today, thanks to both outside and inside American forces.

MARXIST INFLUENCE IN CONTEMPORARY MEDIA

Most Americans agree that the mainstream media leans ideologically left, while some believe it is truly Marxist. This section will focus on the media's Marxist influence thanks to domestic influencers and will expose the radical sway of communist China on American journalists and their corporations.

Earlier in this chapter, I cited a poll that indicates the majority of Americans consider the mainstream media biased in its reporting. Certainly, not many would dispute the fact that that bias favors the Democratic Party, while fewer than a quarter believe that coverage favors Republicans. What's at issue, however, is just how much sway Marxism delivers across America's mainstream media. The pregnant question is: Does that Marxist sway influence the ongoing cultural revolution?

Marxist Sway in Mainstream News Media

Previously, I established that Marxists want the complete transformation of American culture. Further, as we have seen, Marxists regard control of the news media as a mechanism for reaching that goal. That's why it is useful to consider exactly what mainstream media has done to facilitate that outcome.

The 1914 Journalist's Creed came from the pen of Walter Williams, the founder of journalism education and the first dean of the Missouri School of Journalism. In it, Williams defined journalism as an independent profession whereby journalists should be "unmoved by pride of opinion or greed of power." He expected the journalist to demonstrate self-control, patience, and fearlessness.[487]

Today's journalists are quite different from that which Mr. Williams envisioned for the profession more than a century ago. Jim Kuypers, a professor at Virginia Tech, researched the evolution of American journalism to conclude that today's mainstream journalists are liberal, progressive, in their personal lives and in their reporting—not at all what Mr. Williams promoted. Mr. Kuypers quoted a liberal editor as saying: "Too often, we wear liberalism on our sleeve and are intolerant of other lifestyles and opinions.... We're not very subtle about it at this paper: If you work here, you must be one of us. You must be liberal, progressive, a Democrat."[488]

What does that really mean when it comes to the actual reporting? It means a number of things. First, it means the liberal journalist selects the stories that advance leftist ideology. Second, stories are reported from a leftist point of view. Lastly, the leftist perspective gets more attention—print lines and soundbites—than other perspectives.

Media outlets also set agendas for the consuming public. Political scientist Bernard Cohen captured this idea well. He said that the press "may not be successful much of the time in telling people what to think, but it is stunningly successful in telling its readers what to think about." There are many examples of media-generated topics that otherwise no one would address or be interested in better understanding—e.g., transgender rights, global warming, et cetera.[489]

It is noteworthy that America's growing cohort of political progressives—mostly in the Democratic Party—enlisted our mainstream media to advance their radical ideas like Medicare-for-All, but that same media refuses to address what former Speaker of the US House of Representatives Newt Gingrich once wrote about: "The academic Left and its news media and Hollywood acolytes refuse to confront the horrifying record of Marxism's endless inhumanity." Meanwhile, those same journalists willingly swim in a sea of Marxist ideas while refusing to acknowledge the consequences.[490]

One of mainstream media's tools that keeps them in the Marxist groove is the self-imposed political correctness of self-censorship. Political correctness is an old communist tool that affects what may or may not be reported. The left uses this tool in cases involving problems associated with such issues as homosexuality, immigrant behavior, failure of progressive policies (education, healthcare, public assistance), and the riots created by leftist ideas that created a war zone in the downtown area of the formerly beautiful Portland, Oregon.

Labeling Conservative Sources to Neutralize Their Influence

In order to create the impression of balanced reporting, the liberal (Marxist-inspired) media sometimes have no choice but to report on the opinions of conservatives. But they typically use labels like "far right," "right wing," or "religious right wing" when quoting these sources, which implies that their opinions are prejudiced and therefore not trustworthy. By contrast, when leftists quote from liberals, they use neutral terms, often applying credibility-granting titles to them such as "scholar" or "expert," suggesting that their opinions are expert, impartial, rational, and trustworthy.

Once the media validates a favored left-wing opinion, it implies that view applies to all of society, a keen leftist twist of the pen. An October 2008 article by leftist *New York Times* headlined "Liberal Views Dominate Footlights" illustrates the point: "During this election season theatergoers in New York can see a dozen or so overtly political plays, about Iraq, Washington corruption, feminism, or immigration; what they won't see are any with a conservative perspective." Translation: "The only views worth considering, thanks to New York's theater scene, are those presented by the left."[491]

The media's true political colors are also reflected in their coverage of the democratic process. More often than not, liberal political candidates are reported positively, while conservative candidates who espouse traditional views receive far more criticism. Such reporting and "expert" analyses have potentially great influence over the voting population.

Entertainment Media: Does Marxists' Bidding

The last chapter on education demonstrated that the academe is quite liberal but not the result of popular will. The same is true with the media; it is leftist because of the types of people it attracts and their ideological training and preferences. We already established that American departments of journalism and most liberal arts colleges are full to the brim with very liberal, some say Marxist, faculty. These schools produce mostly liberal thinkers who are full of idealism and seek to transform their world through reporting.

Hollywood is perhaps the most idealistic community in the media world, which explains why it has become a bastion of left-wing propaganda. Most of Hollywood's products promote what conservatives hate: socialism, immoral behavior, and anti-American sentiment.

Noted author Ben Shapiro confirms Hollywood's ideological preference in his book *Primetime Propaganda: The True Hollywood Story of How the Left Took Over Your TV*. Mr. Shapiro writes that liberalism is "100 percent dominant" in Hollywood, and "anyone who denies it is kidding or not telling the truth." He offers a litmus test of that statement: Ask anyone in the film industry whether a non-liberal political point of view could hinder a person's chances of work. "Absolutely," a producer answered Shapiro's question. Another Hollywood producer admitted that "Hollywood has been selling liberal political views through its works: 'right now, there's only one perspective. And it's a very progressive perspective.' "[492]

Mr. Shapiro, who moved his organization to Nashville and away from California because of that failed liberal state government, writes that "nepotism in Hollywood is ideological," not familial. In other words, friends hire friends based on similar ideological beliefs, and dare I say, Hollywood is not a welcoming place for Christians and conservatives. Leftists and Marxists need only apply.

Hollywood embraces the corrupting Marxist prescription of Willi Münzenberg mentioned earlier: "to make the West so corrupt; [it] stinks. We're going to rock them from within, and we're going to teach immorality to the young people. We're going to try to push pornography and we're going to try to increase alcoholism."[493]

"One of the most pressing tasks confronting the Communist Party in the field of propaganda," wrote the Comintern (Communist International) agent Mr. Münzenberg in his 1925 *Daily Worker* article, "is the conquest of this supremely important propaganda unit [Hollywood], until now the monopoly of the ruling class. We must wrest it from them and turn it against them." In time, Hollywood did turn its efforts in the Marxists' favor.[494]

Consider what Hollywood produces.

Long ago, the motion picture business had a code known as the Hays Code, which set moral standards. For example, the Hays Code upheld the sanctity of marriage and prohibited the glorification of crime, evil, and sin. How things have changed!

In 1968, the Hays Code was replaced with the Motion Picture Association film rating system that loosened the moral self-discipline of the industry and blurred the standards. The new system came about in part thanks to the 1960s counterculture that destroyed traditional morality, and Hollywood jumped at the opportunity to capture some of the baseness of human behavior on the big screen. For example, Hollywood embraced a key tactic of communism by casting criminal behavior as noble, much like the 1967 movie, *Bonnie and Clyde*, which glorified the crime spree of Great Depression-era robbers. The storyline pulled at the heartstrings of some at the time (1930s) who were out of jobs and lost their homes. Hollywood created a Robin Hood-like scenario for the movie that earned compassion for the protagonists. Meanwhile, the authorities (police) were depicted as incompetent, and the movie concludes with the robber characters, Bonnie and Clyde, portrayed as martyrs.

Hollywood does the bidding of the communists through the television as well, which decades ago became a ubiquitous part of life and is culturally transformative, something the communist ideologues understand.

A study by the media watchdog group, Media Research Center, found that the "more people watch television, the less committed they are to the traditional values of honesty, reliability, and fairness, and the more lenient their attitudes are likely to be toward issues related to sexual morality, such as sex outside of marriage, abortion, and homosexuality."[495]

Another benefit of television for the Marxist is that it tends to compromise religious views. Evidently, the Media Research Center's study also found that the more one watched television, "the less likely it was for the person to value religious principles." Specifically, those who watched television the most tended to combine their personal morals (influenced by TV watching) and values with God's teachings. Thus, moral relativism infects the population and distances them from their faith, a desirable outcome for Marxists.[496]

Television also hosts programs that promote opinions or behavior that contradicts traditional values. That's another way to manipulate the population, much like we saw in the examples in public education whereby teachers created discussion scenarios that put traditional Christian values in a poor light.

Situation comedies, sitcoms, act as great levelers for average people as well. American television years ago promoted wholesome family settings of respect and marriage, such as in the program *Leave It to Beaver*. Today, some of the most debased human behavior is depicted as normal, such as in one episode of *Friends* that portrays "pregnant lesbians and three-parent households as not only normal, but admirable," an observation made by Shapiro.[497]

Besides Hollywood's proclivity to drag the culture into the gutter, a Marxist aim, it also uses its propaganda power to promote Marxist philosophy in film. Fortunately, the classic Marxist formula for filmmaking isn't especially popular in Hollywood, so they have to become more creative by weaving Marxist philosophy into the storyline.

So, Hollywood makes movies that reflect the problems introduced by Marxist philosophy: proletariat conditions, bourgeoisie dominance, the evolving technology and its connection to society, and revolution. These problems indicate that communism will soon bring social justice.

Every Marxist-inspired movie shares a common faith in proletariat justice, however. The lower industrial classes are the so-called "soil" for a Marxist revolution and bring the only hope for humanity whereby that outcome requires the death of the bourgeoisie, the industrialized class. Communism dominates the ultimate community where humanity is free from the bourgeoisie-imposed slavery.

Although Marx never described a "communist" society, he did provide some advice about that vision in his critique of the Gotha Program: capitalism is the world where slaves serve the few horrible bourgeoisie, which must be replaced by the honorable values of the proletarian class.[498] (The Gotha Program was the political [socialist] platform of the Social Democratic Party of Germany at its first congress, held in Gotha, Germany, in 1875. That platform called for "universal suffrage, freedom of association, limits on the working day, and for other laws protecting the rights and health of workers.")[499]

The Soviets captured that view in their arts, which explains why most of their movies were documentary in nature. They consistently showed how society and socialism work together. For example, the *Kino-Pravda*, a series of twenty-three newsreels (documentaries), were works by Dziga Vertov launched in 1922 that "focused on everyday experiences, eschewing bourgeois concerns and filming marketplace, bars, and schools instead, sometimes with a hidden camera, without asking permission first."[500]

A typical Marxist film made in the West was *Teorema* ("Theorem") (1968). Pier Paolo Pasolini, the director, depicts a typical Italian bourgeoisie Milanese family reacting to a common man, who represents the proletariat. The film shows the reverse alienation of the bourgeoisie while focusing on its incapacity to understand other humans.[501]

The 1976 film *Novecento* shows communism fighting fascism in Italy during the Second War. The storyline follows two men from the same village; one is born to a worker (proletariat) and the other to the landholder (bourgeoisie). They become friends. During the course of the movie, problems of everyday life come to a head while the politics remain the undercurrent. The Marxist message is clear: "Poor people are too weak and ignorant to potently fight the rising fascist power and only when war comes to Italy, they can start to form partisan rebel armies." The five-hour movie ends as the worker (proletariat) elements rise against the landowner (bourgeoisie) and resolves all of life's problems.[502]

It's not a mistake that the few relatively modern films that address the bloody communist legacy weren't produced in the US. That's by design and not due to ignorance. Rather, it is due to the back story of communism's largely uncharted offensive, influence in Hollywood's studios.

For decades, the Communist Party USA, which lived off Soviet cash, used its influence in Tinseltown (aka Hollywood) to prevent American commercial cinema from exposing the horrible truth about the agony of the millions who suffered under communism. Somehow the Hollywood producers managed to ignore what the *New York Times* called "the holy war of the 20th century."[503]

Marxism influences mainstream entertainment media either explicitly or in subtle ways. What's clear: Marxists have a voice across the culture, and it is especially evident thanks to the contemporary Chinese communists as well.

COMMUNIST CHINA'S INFLUENCE ON NEWS MEDIA

The Chinese communists have America's mainstream media exactly where they serve the Marxist giant's best interests. Specifically, those in most of our national newsrooms parrot the communist regime's propaganda. Why? American media are tied to China's purse strings and do the regime's bidding.

"You often see representatives from American companies with financial ties to China naturally become defenders of the CCP's policies and spreading the CCP's propaganda," said Helen Raleigh, a contributor at the *Federalist*. She continued, "The financial tie means these Americans will be much less likely to challenge China's human rights record or unacceptable demand such as technology transfer."[504]

The link between those with financial ties to China and the news media is an easy nut to crack. Consider a number of obvious connections made between deep-pocket Chinese communist surrogates in the West and their CCP masters.

Carlos Slim, a Mexican billionaire, happens to be close to the CCP through a number of joint ventures manufacturing automobiles and telecommunications. Mr. Slim also happens to own 17.4 percent of the shares of America's paper of record, the *New York Times*. "As the largest shareholder, his investment allows him to vote for approximately one-third of the company's board," writes Ms. Raleigh.

Does anyone doubt the *New York Times* is influenced by Mr. Slim's Chinese interests? Why does that paper use its persuasion to question US trade policies aimed at protecting American jobs at the expense of China? Remember, Mr. Slim's company, America Movil, is teamed with the CCP's Huawei technologies to place 5G networks in the US and must overturn American legislation that prohibits our federal government from using that equipment, a position the *Times* appears to embrace.[505]

Jeff Bezos is Amazon's CEO and the owner of the *Washington Post*. Mr. Bezos has direct ties to numerous Chinese markets, which in that country are regulated by the CCP. It won't come as a surprise that some of Amazon's most popular products are produced by Chinese laborers "who work long hours with low pay and little safety training." Some of those workers may in fact be at slave labor camps. Check out the website, UighurOnline, to better appreciate the abuse of that Muslim ethnic minority and Chinese labor camps.[506] How often does the *Washington Post* call out the Chinese communists for human rights violations and especially their abuse of workers such as those who make products for Mr. Bezos?[507]

Let me answer the question. The *Washington Post* seldom criticizes communist China for worker abuse. Rather, when you purchase a *Washington Post* subscription, you get a free copy of Chinese communist propaganda, *China Watch*. That document is produced by the *China Daily*, a communist Chinese state-run media organization with offices in New York City and Washington, DC. *China Watch* has also been distributed by the *New York Times* and the *Wall Street Journal* as well. And further, the *Washington Post* among other papers openly "accepts money for advertisements from the CCP and distributes Chinese propaganda" beyond copies of *China Watch*.[508]

(It is noteworthy that the *China Daily*, as of this writing, is delivered to every member of the US House of Representatives, free of charge.

US Representative Ashley Hinson (R-IA) petitioned House Speaker Nancy Pelsoi (D-CA) to stop the distribution of the Chinese communist propaganda paper to House offices on Capitol Hill. The *Washington Free Beacon* reported that Hinson, who was elected in November 2020, said "she is 'appalled' that lawmakers receive unsolicited copies of *China Daily*, a Chinese state-controlled newspaper that has been designated as Communist propaganda by the State Department."[509])

WarnerMedia, which owns the Cable News Network (CNN), has significant financial ties with the CCP. WarnerMedia partners with China Media Capital (CMC), a firm overseen by the CCP, which of course means it is subject to the communist regime's censorship and must push Chinese propaganda. In fact, working with CMC means partners are subject to China's global objectives and even its cyber security law, which requires technology transfers and leaves the American firm subject to CCP searches.[510]

Is it any surprise that CNN parrots praise for the communist regime over its behavior related to the COVID-19 pandemic? Meanwhile, CNN demonized President Trump for alleged poor leadership over the pandemic.[511] Consider two examples of CNN's support of Chinese propaganda related to the COVID-19 pandemic.

In March 2020, the Chinese government ran a video montage that included CNN and MSNBC reports that attacked President Trump. The *Global Times*, one of the CCP's official mouthpieces, said the montage was evidence of the backlash Trump received for referring to the COVID-19 pandemic as the "Chinese virus," a reference to the disease's origin. Meanwhile, ABC News' White House correspondent Cecilia Vega appears in the Chinese montage challenging President Trump by asking: "Why do you keep calling this the Chinese virus? Why do you keep using this? A lot of people are saying it's racist." Predictably, the montage featured numerous leftist media figures, prominent Democrats and Hollywood celebrities that are Trump critics.[512]

A month after the montage's release, CNN took communist China's side again, almost word for word from a CCP press release, praising the

People's Liberation Army Navy's efforts to contain COVID-19, while in the same report condemning the US Navy as not doing enough. The CNN reporter said the story was a "single update from our international site's 24-7 live story." The network claimed the Chinese navy report came from the *Global Times*.[513]

Then there is the case of NBC Universal, which owns MSNBC and NBC News, which signed an agreement with Xinhua, a CCP-run media organization, to establish a cooperative effort on international news. That deal brought to American shores at least five Chinese state-run media organizations identified by our US State Department as "foreign missions." Make no mistake, these entities are arms of the CCP brought here thanks to NBC Universal.[514]

Also, in 2018, CMC capital partners, a Chinese investment group led by Chinese tycoon Li Ruigang, purchased NBC Universal's joint-venture animation studio, Oriental DreamWorks. This deal follows a 2016 deal by which NBC Universal inherited a 45 percent stake in Oriental DreamWorks, which was the first major Hollywood-China collaboration in the animation business.[515]

The American Broadcast Company (ABC) is tethered to the Chinese communists through ventures with Walt Disney and ESPN, which are owned by ABC. For example, Disney created a theme park in Shanghai, but retains only 43 percent of the enterprise; the balance (57 percent) belongs to the CCP-controlled Shanghai Shendi Group, which means it makes all the decisions.[516]

Remember the National Basketball Association (NBA) controversy thanks to Houston Rockets General Manager Daryl Morey's tweet: "Fight for freedom, stand with Hong Kong"? The tweet expressed Morey's support for Hong Kong's pro-democracy protestors. That tweet drew a quick condemnation from the CCP. Keep in mind that China makes up at least 10 percent of the NBA's current revenue stream, and that contribution is expected to reach 20 percent by 2030.[517]

The NBA never denounced the CCP's criticism of Morey and ABC's ESPN bowed to the Chinese as well with its silence. Evidently, ESPN's senior news director also instructed his staff to avoid discussing Chinese politics if they were asked about Morey's pro-Hong Kong democracy tweet. They obviously embrace an out-of-sight, out-of-mind view about such flare-ups that threaten their Chinese market.[518]

Before leaving the topic of communist China's influence on the news media, I must point out that the regime owns many US-based radio stations. G&E Studio Inc., a Los Angeles company, is mostly (60 percent) controlled by China Radio International (CRI) in Beijing. It broadcasts programs in both Chinese and English on at least fifteen US stations in major cities, including Washington, DC, Salt Lake City, Houston, Portland, and more.[519] The benefit of these stations for the CCP is that it propagandizes American listeners to support the Chinese communists. For example, WCRW, a radio station in Washington, DC, boasts on its website:

> Welcome to THE BRIDGE, the radio show that closes the gap between people of the world, one episode at a time. This historic program connects East and West, and has as its goal, the building of cultural ties between the United States and China. The Bridge goes beyond the headlines to the lifelines, with conversation that informs, entertains and inspires listeners to a greater awareness of the common connections shared between our two cultures.[520]

Why are these mainstream media outlets so afraid?

They pretend that China is a big, soft panda, but refuse to call out the regime's current and past treachery. Evidently, what's verifiable in history is ignored by these media outlets that advance a delusional consideration of the CCP-run regime.

In fact, much of mainstream media not only downplays the ideological nature of the communist regime, but promotes the idea that China is really a capitalist country. Consider an op-ed run by Mr. Slim's *New York Times* that classified communist China as "authoritarian capitalism."

Even Mr. Bezos' *Washington Post* ran a 2019 article, "No, China and the US Aren't Locked in an Ideological Battle. Not Even Close." That article claims the CCP may be "ideologically bankrupt," but is really only "nominally communist." Why? Because China has "embraced capitalism," so states the author.[521]

Jessica Chen Weiss, a professor at Cornell University and the author of the *Washington Post* article, argues that "China has been shaped by engagement with the outside world and has no coherent ideology with international appeal. As US policy planners fashion a new strategy for dealing with China, understanding the differences between today's China and the former Soviet Union will be critical to their success."[522]

I guess Professor Weiss ought to have a long discussion with the victims of the 1989 Tiananmen Square Massacre, those Chinese in Hong Kong's pro-democracy movement who were jailed and beaten for speaking out; the Falon Gong religious movement; and the Muslim Uighurs facing slave labor, re-education camps and, according to the BBC, Uighur women who experience systemic rape at the hands of their CCP minders. Perhaps they have a very different view about China's ideological nature than do Mr. Bezos' *Washington Post* and Professor Weiss.[523]

Even the capitalist-favoring *Forbes* magazine ran a 2019 article pretending that China is no longer communist. That article, "China's Economic Success Proves the Power of Capitalism," suggests the Chinese communists' control is fading fast. I wonder whether anyone told China's President Xi that he is losing his grip on the country?[524]

Forbes magazine, a must-read for America's economic elite, needs to look past its globalist market spin and realize the CCP's real aim. The fact that China moved away from collective ownership toward allowing private property does not mean the communist ideology or the CCP's grip is fading, but that it is flexible. Allowing limited free markets, albeit strictly under CCP control, is radically different and allowed by Marxism.

One of comrade Lenin's heroes, Sergey Nechaev, explained that "the revolutionary may and frequently must live within society while pretending to be completely different from what he really is." Bottom line: China is pretending to be something it is not in order to strengthen itself.[525]

Comrade Nechaev continued, "For [the revolutionary], morality is everything which contributes to the triumph of the revolution."[526]

China loves capitalism only when it aids the regime's Marxist aims. Yes, the CCP allows private property, but as the idiom wisely states: What government gives it can also take away. Count on a future time when China's wealthy will lose everything to the CCP.

HOW DOES COMMUNIST CHINA CONTROL HOLLYWOOD?

China has captured Hollywood unlike what the Soviet communists did in the last century. Beijing knows the language of Hollywood, and it is green (the American dollar), and in fact China has great leverage because it owns a significant slice of Hollywood moviemakers and theater chains such as Legendary Entertainment, AMC Entertainment, Lionsgate, Carmike Cinemas, Odeon and UCI Cinemas, Universal, and 20th Century Fox. Why? They intend to influence US public opinion.[527]

"Beijing has sent a clear message to the filmmaking world, that filmmakers who criticize China will be punished, but that those who play ball with its censorship strictures will be rewarded," states the 2020 report, *Made in Hollywood, Censored by Beijing*.[528]

In 2020, the Chinese communist influence over Hollywood drew fire from then US Attorney General William Barr, who accused the Beverly Hills executives of "kowtowing" to the communist regime for the sake of profits.

"Every year at the Academy Awards, Americans are lectured about how this country falls short of Hollywood's ideals of social justice," Barr said on July 16, 2020. "But Hollywood now regularly censors its own movies to appease the Chinese Communist Party—the world's most powerful violator of human rights."[529]

The CCP successfully influences Hollywood, which is very important because Tinseltown is the world's most significant storytelling center, "a cinematic powerhouse whose movies are watched by millions across the globe," according to the report identified above, *Made in Hollywood, Censored by Beijing*. Proper storytelling can advance Marxism, and that's the catch.[530]

The CCP's influence in Tinseltown is especially significant for the US, because "the choices it makes, about which stories to tell and how to tell them, are increasingly influenced by an autocratic government with the world's most comprehensive system of state-imposed censorship."[531]

The Chinese government uses that influence over Hollywood studios to "soften the edges or erase depictions of its human rights abuses; it can dampen movies' call for change or encouragement of resistance in the face of oppression; and it can discourage or silence filmmakers interested in making movies that question or critique the Chinese government," according to James Tager, the author of the *Made in Hollywood* report.[532]

Chinese sway in Hollywood has significant global implications, because when Beverly Hills bows to Beijing's demands, others across the media world dare not do otherwise. They fear any resistance will result in loss of opportunity and access to the giant Chinese consumer market. This is a particular problem for the leftists who say they care about issues like human rights and for the Tinseltown capitalists who are money hungry.

Any filmmaker or business executive who dares to expose China's crimes against humanity is immediately ostracized, such as the 2019 Hong Kong-supporting tweet by Houston Rocket's General Manager Daryl Morley, a movie or television program that calls out the atrocities the Tibetans face at the hand of Chinese communists, or virtually any account that puts the regime in a dark place. Stories about such state-sponsored abuse could effect change and galvanize people against the regime. After all, speaking truth to communist power is not tolerated, and the communists will censor and sanitize any attempt to embarrass the regime. How does Beijing leverage Hollywood's decisions about what films to produce? Mr. Tager identifies in his report the CCP's three key points of persuasion.

First, and perhaps the most obvious, is whether or not to grant a filmmaker access to China's theater-going market. It is understandable why movie investors want access to the Chinese economic juggernaut as a pre-condition to a decision to invest in a film project. That reality presents significant challenges up front for a filmmaker.

Chris Fenton, the film producer and media executive who worked on blockbuster films like *Iron Man 3* and *Point Break*, is the author of the book *Feeding the Dragon*. He provided some unvarnished perspective on the CCP's leverage over Hollywood.[533]

"There were a lot of directives that were given by the Chinese government to our company.... I would have to find a way to make it tolerable to our [investment] partners here in the United States," Mr. Fenton explained.[534] "You need to sell your product or service to the Chinese government," he continued. "You need to portray it in a way that the Chinese government feels that it benefits them and their populace to allow you access to their market."[535]

Clearly, China is not a capitalist country; otherwise, Mr. Fenton and other filmmakers would not have to "sell" the CCP on the "benefits" of their film in order to access the Chinese market. No, pragmatically, the film must serve the communist regime's interests before it grants access.

Second, China has a robust censorship system that has total control over which movies gain market access. The rules give the censors "unfettered discretion to demand changes to a specific movie as a prerequisite to this access," writes Mr. Tager. Censorship leads to what some call pandering to the target government.

Mr. Fenton said that in the movie business, there are different sorts of pandering:

There's the premeditated self-censorship. You want the movie to play in the two largest markets in the world and make money, and that's the United States and China. So, you obviously want to make a movie that's going to play to both of those markets. Part of that might entail maybe not making a movie about China winning a huge soccer game in the Olympics against the Americans, and hoping that that movie plays in America. Well, it's the same reason why you might avoid having Chinese villains in a movie that you want to have work in China.[536]

Of course, the Chinese censors are involved in the entire process from the start. Mr. Fenton said that, in the post-production, it is common for the CCP censors to tell you, "You need to change it." An example that US Senator Ted Cruz (Texas) brought to light was regarding the movie *Top Gun*. Evidently the star, Tom Cruise, wore a flight jacket that included the Taiwanese flag on the back side. The Chinese censors insisted that it be removed, and Paramount Studios made the change.[537]

Nothing that puts the regime in a bad light is allowed to screen in the Chinese media market.

Third, the CCP will not tolerate any criticism of the regime. The movie maker either plays ball or takes his bat and glove and goes home. Such a censorship policy is well known by Hollywood directors, who self-censor without prompting.

Hollywood tolerates such draconian leverage because China is becoming the undisputed largest movie market. Specifically, the Chinese box office is predicted to reach an estimated $15.5 billion by the year 2023,[538] much higher than the US box office total for the pre-COVID year 2019 at $11.4 billion.[539]

There is a sobering reality facing Hollywood when it comes to China's massive box office. Chinese movie-making is much better than it was just a few years ago, and before long, Hollywood-produced films may lose their luster. In fact, even with the impact of COVID-19, Chinese audiences are increasingly preferring homemade films.

There is another factor mitigating against Hollywood's access to and profit from the Chinese market: a growing anti-American sentiment among the communist government and the Chinese people, which makes American films less welcome, said Mr. Tager. That shift away from American-made films is evidenced by the box-office numbers before year 2018. Up to that point, Hollywood dominated among the highest-grossing films in China. More recently (2019), that dominance began to fade with only one American film (*Avengers: Endgame*) in the top-grossing films.[540]

The shift away from American-made movies only reenergized Hollywood executives and their cast of supporters to become more focused on delivering what China wants in order to maintain a foothold in that lucrative market. "The size of the Chinese movie-going audience is so huge," one Hollywood executive told Mr. Tager, "that if you happen to be the one that catches their fancy, you can make $100 million in pure profit."[541]

"While some of these alterations may seem minor—the cutting of a Taiwanese flag here or the removal of a minor plot point there—cumulatively such censoriousness cuts against artistic and cultural freedom, silences dissenting voices and can skew the global perceptions that are shaped by powerful films," said Mr. Tager.

It is clear that Hollywood is at the beck and call of the CCP. Self-censorship will get worse as Hollywood acquiesces to Beijing's demands in exchange for a dwindling piece of the economic movie pie.

CONCLUSION

The media is a powerful tool, one the Marxists understand and use to propagandize unsuspecting populations at home and here in America. It is clear that the Soviet communists targeted American media for manipulation starting in the 1930s, which continues—albeit without Soviet support today—and certainly the all-powerful movie industry (Hollywood) and much of our mainstream media are heavily manipulated by the Chinese communists, who use this tool to fuel our cultural revolution.

Never forget that Marxists have three very specific goals in mind. First, they want to deflect any criticism of the regime in order to keep their citizens from revolting. Second, they want to gain total control over their (Chinese) population while keeping out Western values, and third, they want to disrupt, cause revolution among Western nations such as the US to advance their ideology and hopefully bring those populations into the totalitarian, communist realm.

8

Other Revolutionary Co-conspirators
Satan, Secret Societies,
and Violent Subversives

As a rule, what is out of sight disturbs men's minds more seriously than what they see.[542]

—Julius Caesar, Roman general
and statesman (100–44 BC)

To round out this section of *Give Me Liberty, Not Marxism*, we need to address three more revolutionary co-conspirators: 1) One is highly visible at the tip of the spear, armed, organized, compensated, and led by the less visible. 2) The less-visible one is difficult to pin down and is armed with intelligence and money accumulated over generations, but will be further exposed here. 3) The third is the invisible, and will stay that way until it's almost too late to respond; it infects and directs the other two in the past, present, and future (for a limited time). So here we will take a closer look at the triple threat facing America: Satan, secret societies, and violent revolutionaries.

227

The first portion of this chapter is an examination of the history that leads up to the time of Karl Marx and the development of his demonic legacy. There is a clear spiritual dimension—Satan and his army of demons—that is a co-conspirator in America's cultural revolution. This silent partner's presence is evident in the radical ideology (Marxism) and the resulting evil outcomes.

The second portion identifies secret societies—a mostly silent, unseen partner—that often seeks outcomes associated with Marxist ideology, which are evidenced by their mostly behind-the-scenes, supporting role.

The third portion profiles Marxist-inspired violent proxies that are the essential revolutionary "ground troops" aided by a cabal of battlefield supporters.

These co-conspirators join those in the previous four chapters to round out a cadre of evil agents that long planned to destroy America and now are working in unison to realize that goal.

FRENCH REVOLUTION: THE BACKGROUND TO MARXISM'S SATANIC-INSPIRED MOVEMENT

A historical summary of the evolution of modern Marxism begins with the French Revolution (1789–1799) and arrives at the present day with the obvious dark influence from the unseen, spiritual realm.

To better understand that influence, we begin with a review of the history that came to influence Karl Marx's communist ideology. Arguably a good starting point is the French Revolution, and the first true revolutionary communist, François Noël "Gracchus" Babeuf.

Gracchus Babeuf (1760–1797) is regarded as the first true revolutionary communist, also a journalist who called for resistance against the government of France. He espoused the goal to restore "egalitarian communism" under a new system drawn from the then-emerging ideas of socialism. [543]

Babeuf's vision was to eliminate money and force the people to hand over the fruits of their labor to a "common storehouse," and then a central government would be in charge of redistributing the goods. Further, to bring this outcome about, Babeuf proposed the "use of violent revolution to seize control and force its will on society."[544]

Mr. Babeuf's idea took form while he was imprisoned in Paris for "inciting rebellion, murder, and dissolution of the [French] national representative body." He was joined in prison by co-conspirators that included ex-terrorists and neo-terrorists.[545]

Once free, Babeuf tried to spark the envisioned uprising, but French authorities discovered his plot, arrested him, and, on May 27, 1797, beheaded him by guillotine. Meanwhile, Filippo Buonarroti, a Babeuf co-conspirator, documented the failed uprising that gave birth to a secret society known as the League of Outlaws.[546]

Decades later, a German, Wilhelm Weitling, joined the French League of Outlaws in 1835 while visiting Paris, and he quickly embraced Babeuf's violent revolutionary ideas—state-enforced equality and the destruction of private ownership. He mixed in that formula his own ideas of a "Christian apocalyptic vision" attributed to the sixteenth-century Munster (German) Anabaptists, and soon changed the group's name to the League of the Just (1837).[547]

Unlike his French comrades, Weitling maintained his Christian faith and endorsed the work of the Christian radical Hugues-Félicité Robert de Lamennais (1782–1854), who urged installing communism by physical force with the help of a proposed forty-thousand-strong army of ex-convicts. Mr. Weitling's blend of communism and evangelism annoyed his ideological contemporaries Karl Marx and Friedrich Engels, but they weren't always at odds.

In 1844 Marx referred to Weitling's work as the "vehement and brilliant literary debut of the German workers." Marx emphasized Weitling's theoretical and philosophical "brilliance," which Marx compared favorably to the more "economically" inclined English workers and the more practical "politically" oriented French workers.[548]

Eventually, Weitling's and Marx's communist ideas melded in England, but not before each went their separate ways. Marx had to flee Paris because he sought the overthrow of European governments and landed in London, where he crafted his *Communist Manifesto*. Meanwhile, Weitling published his *Das Evangelium Eines Armen Sunders* ("The Poor Sinner's Gospel"), which earned him six months in a Swiss jail for tracing communism to early Christianity, in which he depicted Jesus Christ as a communist and the illegitimate child of Mary.[549]

Then in 1849, Weitling immigrated to the US after failing to spark a communist revolution in his home country of Germany. In 1850, he began the publication of a monthly journal, *Die Republik der Arbeiter* ("The Republic of the Worker"), to espouse his radical ideas in America. Later in his life, Weitling participated with the experimental German American settlement of Communia, Iowa, and turned his activism into technical interests whereby he received nine patents for improvements to sewing machines.[550]

Meanwhile, and years earlier, the League of the Just, which was significantly influenced by Weitling, relocated to London and established itself under the new name "Educational Society for German Workingmen in 1840." In 1847, that group joined with the Communist Correspondence Committee, which formed just one year prior and was headed by Marx and Engels. That new group (the melding of Weitling's and Marx's ideas) soon morphed into the Communist League under the leadership of Marx and Engels, who in 1848 published *The Communist Manifesto*, which, as established throughout this book, became the core philosophical guide for modern communist regimes.

BABEUF, WEITLING, AND MARX: TIME OF CULTURAL EXPLOSION

People like Babeuf, et al., cultivated their ideas in a cultural petri dish that came to maturity at the time of the French Revolution, mostly thanks to massive religious and political shifts in the eighteenth century. One major religious shift at the time was the Protestant Great Awakening (1730s and 1740s), which drew its converts from discontented Catholic ranks. It was also a time when the masses sought alternatives to monarchies—a massive political shift. Meanwhile, in America at the time, our founders created a very different system of personal liberties and limited government.

In Europe arose a system of state-sponsored religion and government focused on equality through state redistribution, which required a totalitarian system not that different from what Babeuf envisioned. It was within this environment that the ideology of communism arose as an alternative system, "an ideology with its own sense of moral structure and allegiance."[551]

Michael Walsh, author of *The Devil's Pleasure Palace: The Cult of Critical Theory and the Subversion of the West* (2015), wrote about the logical future impact of Babeuf's vision for society—a new religion. Mr. Walsh noted that "during the Cold War [1947–1991], critics in the west remarked that the Soviet Union and its doctrine of Marxism-Leninism resembled nothing so much as a new religion."[552]

Indeed, this new religion's occult and anti-Christian nature was reflected in the writings of Karl Marx and his French icon Babeuf. Of course, Marx's "new religion" became known as "Marxism," and his scripture came to be known as *The Communist Manifesto*, and together they had demonic roots.

(Although *The Communist Manifesto* is a significant work, Marx's magnum opus is *Das Kapital: A Critique of Political Economy* [1867] [German: *Das Kapital. Kritik der politischen Ökonomie*], which is a foundational theoretical text critical of capitalism and became "the scientific foundation for the politics of the modern labor movement." *Das Kapital* also became "the most cited book in the social sciences published before 1950.")[553]

To understand Marxism and its demonic aims, one must understand the man himself, Karl Marx.

Paul Kengor wrote the book, *The Devil and Karl Marx: Communism's Long March of Death, Deception, and Infiltration*, which addresses Mr. Marx's evil-inspired personal history that verbally shouts the man's troubled being.

Mr. Kengor is a professor of political science at Grove City College in Grove City, Pennsylvania. He exposes in his 2020 book a very dark side of Marx and one the reader ought to appreciate before dismissing the German philosopher and his radical philosophy as having no relevance today.

Most Americans believe the evil of Marxism died with the collapse of the Soviet Union (1991). That would be fortunate if true, but as we see in the *Black Book of Communism*, edited by Stephane Courtois (1999), the Marxist-Leninist death toll in the twentieth century continued past the demise of the Soviet Union and arguably is evident today. The time from the 1917 Soviet Revolution to the collapse of the Soviet Union claimed an estimated sixty-one million lives, mostly Russian citizens. However, the toll grew in communist China, whereby that regime racked up another seventy-eight million killed. More recently, we saw tragedy strike at Beijing's Tiananmen Square (1989), Cambodia (1975–1979), North Korea, Vietnam, Cuba, and more.

Obviously, the evil philosophy's death was short-lived while its satanic influence crossed the Atlantic to ferment in America to infiltrate our Democratic Party, the academe, media, government, and the culture writ large. It's a very evil, malignant philosophy that is becoming mainstream with the Democratic Party today and evident across our culture as it hides behind the veil of its more popular cousins, progressivism and socialism.

Professor Kengor states in his book, "The reality is that one cannot separate Marxism the ideology from Marx the man. Aristotle observed, 'Men start revolutionary changes for reasons connected with their private lives.'" Karl Marx is an example of Aristotle's observation, which is why a brief review of the man's troubled life history is appropriate.[554]

Marx's idea of a communist revolution sparked first in Russia in 1917 and then elsewhere over the past century-plus at a tragic cost in lives and untold physical carnage and misery. Marx the man is gone, but his evil, arguably his demonic ideas, are very much alive today, and his ideological legacy threatens our future.

Some scholars portray Marx and his philosophy as satanically inspired. Robert Payne, an academic biographer of Marx, wrote in his book, *The Demons*, "There were times when Marx seemed to be possessed by demons." Payne continued: "He (Marx) had the devil's view of the world, and the devil's malignity. Sometimes he seemed to know that he was accomplishing works of evil."[555]

Professor Kengor states up front in his book, *The Devil and Karl Marx*, that his research did not discover direct evidence of Marx conducting séances or engaging in black masses or satanic rituals. However, the professor admits the evidence about Marx is clear. Marx, an apostle of evil, had "a fanatically deep hatred of religion and flirtation with the dark side that is undeniable and chilling, especially Marx's poetry." Marx declares in *The Communist Manifesto* that "communism abolishes eternal truths…[and] all religion, and all morality, instead of constituting them on a new basis."[556]

Those who knew him best understood the evil. Marx's family and friends referred to him with words like "governed by a demon" (his father), "my dear devil" (his son), "monster of ten thousand devils" (his friend Engels), and "wicked nave" (his wife).[557]

Anecdotally, Richard Wurmbrand, also known as Nicolai Ionescu (1909–2201), author of *Marx & Satan* (1986), believed Marx's philosophy is out of the pit of hell. "All the biblical descriptions of hell and the pains of Dante's *Inferno* are nothing in comparison with the tortures in communist prisons," stated Wurmbrand, the international bestselling author of *Tortured for Christ*. Wurmbrand recalled of his Romanian captors, "I have seen communists whose faces while torturing believers shone with rapturous joy. They cried out while torturing the Christians, 'We are the devil!'" He remembered one torturer say, "I thank God in whom I don't believe, that I have lived in this hour when I can express all the evil in my heart."[558]

Mr. Wurmbrand, a Jew who became a Christian minister, once said communism and Christianity were incompatible. He eventually emigrated to America and dedicated his life to publishing and helping Christians who are persecuted for their beliefs. He founded the international organization Voice of the Martyrs, which helps Christians persecuted for their faith.[559]

The evil is very real. Karl Marx was a Johann Wolfgang von Goethe (1749–1832) fan, for whom he memorized many pages from Goethe's *Faust*, a classic German legend and the German's best-known work. Marx was especially fond of the character Mephistopheles, an evil spirit to whom Faust sold his soul. Marx frequently recited Mephistopheles' line from Faust: "Everything that exists deserves to perish."[560]

Professor Kengor said Marx's fondness for Mephistopheles "reflects the very thinking of the man who in letters called for the 'ruthless criticism of all that exists,' who in the [*Communist*] *Manifesto* declared that communism seeks to 'abolish the present state of things,'" and who at the close of the *Manifesto* called for 'the forcible overthrow of all existing social conditions.'"[561]

Marx's writing reveals a very troubled, dark man, such as in his poem, "The Pale Maiden," which states: "Thus Heaven I've forfeited, I know it full well. My soul, once true to God, is chosen for Hell." Biographer Robert Payne dissected Marx's ballad "The Player." Payne states that in the ballad, "A musician summons up the prince of darkness, a lover offers a poison cup to the beloved, and both run headlong to their deaths in a satanic rejection of the world." Payne argues that Marx succeeds in conveying in the ballad "the terror at the heart of terror." Marx, explained Payne, "is not playing games," as these poems not only "reek of fire and brimstone," but constitute "real fire and brimstone." Payne observes that Marx "is here celebrating a satanic mystery, for the player is clearly Lucifer or Mephistopheles, and what he is playing with such frenzy is the music which accompanies the end of the world."[562]

Normal people don't write the evil things that fell from Marx's pen.

He wrote about death, torture, executioners, mutilation, and even rup-
tured wombs. His speech was always guttural and filled with vicious
words, wrote Professor Kengor. Biographer Payne said Marx spent
much of his life in a "helpless rage against the world....in letter after
letter, he roars his disgust at the world and at people, with unbridled
malevolence."[563]

Mr. Payne wrote that those around him remember Marx as evidenc-
ing a wild temper and impetuosity, and he had the habit of leaping upon
his prey. "He would clinch his fist and roar interminably for the remaining forty years of his life."[564] Payne admits, "There were times when
Marx seemed to be possessed by demons, when rage overflowed in him
and became poison, and he seemed to enter into a nightmare."[565]

It is noteworthy that other tyrants like Germany's Hitler displayed
similar behavior. Thomas Horn writes in *Nephilim Stargates* (Defender,
2007):[566]

> During the ascendancy of Nazi Germany, [Hermann] Raus-
> chning, the Governor of Danzig related a strange episode
> in which Hitler had "a being" that came after him from the
> unknown. The incident was quite reminiscent of the paralysis
> and sense of foreboding acquainted with modern "alien" abduc-
> tion reports:
>
> "A person close to Hitler told me that he wakes up in the
> night screaming and in convulsions. He calls for help, and
> appears to be half paralyzed. He is seized with a panic that
> makes him tremble until the bed shakes. He utters confused and
> unintelligible sounds, gasping, as if on the point of suffocation.
> The same person described to me one of these fits, with details
> that I would refuse to believe had I not complete confidence in
> my informant.
>
> "Hitler was standing up in his room, swaying and looking
> all round him as if he were lost. 'It's he, it's he,' he groaned, 'he's
> come for me!' His lips were white; he was sweating profusely.

Suddenly he uttered a string of meaningless figures, then words and scraps of sentences. It was terrifying. He used strange expressions strung together in bizarre disorder. Then he relapsed again into silence, but his lips still continued to move. He was then given a friction and something to drink. Then suddenly he screamed: 'There! there! Over in the comer! He is there!'—all the time stamping with his feet and shouting. To quieten him he was assured that nothing extraordinary had happened, and finally he gradually calmed down. After that he slept for a long time and became normal again. (Rauschning)."

Hitler's behavior speaks for itself, and Marx's "demonic"-like behavior came through in his writing and philosophy. It also inspired similarly dark outcomes for those who embraced his teaching. Kengor wrote that Marx's ideological progeny demonstrated a similar affinity for the demonic.

MARXISM'S DEMONIC LEGACY

Professor Kengor points to Alexander Yakovlev, former Soviet Chairman Mikhail Gorbachev's chief aide, who found evidence of the tragic consequence of those who embraced Marx's demonic philosophy. Yakovlev had the task of looking into the subject of communist crimes during the early post-Cold War years. Specifically, Mr. Yakovlev looked into the Russian Communist Party's archives and was particularly struck by the "merciless mass terror," especially against the religious. The terror was so intense and insidious that Yakovlev described it as "infernal," "evil," and "demonic."[567]

It is important to understand that Marx's anti-religious views are at the heart of his philosophy—Marxism. Noted Russian author and historian Alexander Solzhenitsyn said in 1983 that "within the philosophical system of Marx and Lenin, and at the heart of their psychology, hatred of God is the principal driving force, more fundamental than all their political and economic pretensions."[568]

Solzhenitsyn added, "Militant atheism is not merely incidental or marginal to communist policy; it is not a side effect, but the central pivot."[569]

That view may explain why so many authors associate Marxism with the satanic, demonic. After all, Marx's evil legacy was examined by Cid Lazarou, a British freelance journalist, who provides some insight about the nineteenth-century ideology. Marxism grants the believer what Lazarou calls "subjective morality," which attracts a great multitude of people. It is "the belief that morality is decided by the individual, rather than a universal law independent of people. This leads to the belief that you can do whatever you want, as long as you can get away with it." Mr. Lazarou writes that this "subjective morality" is really a front for satanism, and it doesn't necessarily relate to a literal entity (although it could) but to a state of mind.[570]

This "subjective morality," or Satanism, manifests itself in society within the political left, thanks to Marx and his ideological progeny like Saul Alinsky. Mr. Alinsky's magnum opus, *Rules for Radicals*, acknowledges the origin of his evil thoughts. Alinsky cites Lucifer as the source of his philosophy:

> Lest we forget at least an over-the-shoulder acknowledgment to the very first radical: from all our legends, mythology, and history (and who is to know where mythology leaves off and history begins—or which is which), the first radical known to man who rebelled against the establishment and did it so effectively that he at least won his own kingdom—Lucifer.[571]

Satan and Lucifer are the same even though the former is not addressed by name in the Old Testament. Lucifer is mentioned in Isaiah 14:12 (KJV), "How art thou fallen from heaven, O Lucifer, son of the morning! how art thou cut down to the ground, which didst weaken the nations!" Satan is identified in the New Testament (1 Corinthians 7:5) as the same as Lucifer, but had changed his name because he was defeated by God.[572]

This background is important in order to understand what Alinsky meant. After all, Lucifer fought against the established order and won his own kingdom (hell) and authority on earth (Revelation 12:9 and 1 John 5:19).

Mr. Lazarou wrote that the contemporary ideological left embodies the Luciferian archetype of rebellion against tradition and conservative values, much as Satan uses lies to entice a following, a common leftist strategy.

The left, especially Marxists, seek order out of chaos (Luciferian rebellion), and by creating that chaos, common people become so desperate for order that they surrender their liberties. That's why the French Revolution led to Napoleon Bonaparte's dictatorship, and the Chinese Cultural Revolution (1966–1976) compelled those citizens to embrace communist Mao Zedong as their savior.

That brings us to Marxist-inspired satanic ideology, which is typified by inversion, which we see in satanic symbols and in their behavior. Their chaos, rebellion, "stems from intolerance and injustice in society," writes Mr. Lazarou, "but even when they succeed, their craving for order out of chaos can never be satiated, as they forever move on to the next social-justice cause."[573]

The left's true objective is power, as is the case with Lucifer (Satan). Alinsky's twelve rules shout that motivation, such as Rule #1: "Power is not only what you have, but what the enemy thinks you have." Leftists like Alinksy are motivated only by power and are never satisfied, which is the epitome of the ancient and occult left-hand path, a type of "psychological conditioning perpetuated in society by master manipulators," explained Mr. Lazarou.[574]

The conclusion is clear. We can't reason with the unreasonable—those who see chaos as the means to their end. We must acknowledge, therefore, that, just as Alinsky recognized, the roots of the left are really satanic.

MANIFESTATION OF DEMONIC
MARXISM IN AMERICA

I suspect there are skeptical readers at this point. You might rhetorically ask: Is the American left and those who identify with Marxism really under the spell, influence, of demons or satanism? Consider some indicators from our news that suggest the new left is clearly in Satan's camp.

The new left, especially the Democratic Party's platform for 2020, was chock-full of anti-biblical positions. That party and its followers turned completely away from the old Democrats like President John F. Kennedy to embrace abortion on demand up to the time of delivery; support everything the homosexual community demands; and favor giant government overreach into every aspect of our lives. Further, Democrats are clearly anti-Christian.

In December 2020, a group backed by congressional Democrats calling themselves the "Secular Democrats of America," sent a document to President-elect Biden advising him to strip First Amendment rights from Christians who advocate traditional biblical positions on life, marriage, education, and family.[575]

The twenty-eight-page document, titled *Restoring Constitutional Secularism and Patriotic Pluralism in the White House*, which was presented by a number of Democrat congresspersons, states that Mr. Biden must "educate the American public," particularly those in the "religious right," on keeping their "religious dogma" to themselves. The document calls for purging any social conservatives from government, and labeled them as "white nationalist" and "conspiracy theorists."[576]

Brannon Howse, a conservative radio host, said about the document: "As long as you're teaching a leftist progressive socialist religiosity you'll be just fine, but if you preach anything that is wrapped around a Judeo-Christian value system they're coming after you."[577]

We saw plenty more indicators of this type of Marxist behavior throughout the 2020 presidential campaign and building up to that point. Some are clearly from Satan's camp. Consider some examples.

Remember Democratic Party presidential candidate Marianne Williamson? She's a New Ager, arguably involved in the occult. Consider the article, "Marianne Williamson Reveals the Democrats are a Cult."[578]

That article resurfaces previous evidence of demonic (satanic) activity, such as then First Lady Hillary Clinton hosting séances in the White House that included Williamson and also involved Jean Houston, the author of *The Hero and the Goddess: The Odyssey as Pathway to Personal Transformation*, who allegedly tried contacting the spirit of Eleanor Roosevelt. Evidently, at least one report said that Houston did contact something, likely a demon. The Williamson article states: "When Hillary Clinton wasn't trying to commune with Eleanor and [Mahatma] Ghandi, she appeared to share the obsession [of Marianne Williamson and] John Podesta, her campaign chair."[579]

You will recall the weird activities leaked by WikiLeaks in 2015 that involved John Podesta, Hillary Clinton's 2016 presidential campaign chairman, which detailed his participation in a "spirit cooking" dinner with performance artist Marina Abramovic. Ms. Abramovic is known for her gory art that includes pain and ritual.[580]

Ms. Abramovic's "art" involves blood, bodies, nudity, pain, and tension, which she claims isn't demonic. In fact, Ms. Abramovic told the *New York Times*: "I am personally afraid that any kind of lunatic with a gun will come and shoot me, because they think I'm a Satanist."[581]

Some very bizarre things happened after President Trump's 2016 election. The Williamson article indicates that "tens of thousands of women like [Marianne Williamson] swarmed the streets wearing pink hats to shriek at the sky and repel the dark psychic forces. They believe in everything, ghosts, auras, energy forces, UFOs, and even angels, but no God."[582]

Why do the Democrats and their fellow leftists want riots and violence, to defund the police, and gun control? Why do they want illegal immigration, skyrocketing taxes for the "wealthy," and a weak military? Why do they favor socialistic universal healthcare that includes death panels? Why do they want massive regulation of every aspect of our lives and suppression of free speech? That's their new governing ideology, which represents the entire range of the isms—especially Marxism.

Why do witches, according to many press reports, only pray against conservative (Republican) leaders and not against Democratic Party leaders? In 2017, "Followers of witchcraft across the US performed a mass spell designed to stop the president [Trump from] doing harm."[583] Meanwhile, almost four years later, on Halloween 2020, there were new reports of "thousands" of witches trying once again to cast a "binding spell" on the eve of President Trump's reelection bid.[584]

Marxism is deeply rooted in rebellion with strong demonic influences. Marxism and its associated demonic influences are taking root in America, as evidenced in full view with the Democratic Party, the educational establishment, our mainstream media, and, as you will see in the next section of this chapter, inside secret societies.

CO-CONSPIRATORS INSIDE
MARXIST-INFLUENCED SECRET SOCIETIES

For centuries, secret societies arose, motivated by a variety of agendas to empower the membership. One of the early secret societies was the Knights Templar, a medieval society of Christian knights founded around the year 1118 to protect pilgrims to the Holy Land from rampaging Muslims. They were endorsed by the Roman Catholic Church and became one of the most powerful orders in Europe, with a strong military presence and an expanding territory.

The Templars had a strict code of conduct, "Latin Rule," that forbade them from shrinking from battle, required them to wear white surcoats with a red cross at all times, mandated that they eat in silence, and demanded that they sever all connections with women.[585]

The mystery around the Knights was created by Christian legends, which included the idea that they were in possession of the treasure of King Solomon found beneath the Temple of Solomon in Jerusalem.

Speculation is that treasure was the Ark of the Covenant, the Holy Grail.[586]

The Templars built numerous castles and fought battles with Islamic armies throughout the region. However, in the late twelfth century, Muslim armies retook Jerusalem, and by 1291 with the Fall of Acre, the Templars left the Holy Land. Meanwhile, the order became a threat to the king of France, King Philip IV, in the early 1300s. At the time, the king owed the Knights considerable money, but they denied the ruler additional loans, and as a result the monarch resolved to bring down the order using charges of idolatry, heresy, and devil-worship. Shortly afterward, the pope, who supported the king, disbanded the order.[587]

Many other secret societies emerged in the intervening years for a variety of mostly political and religious reasons, especially during Europe's Enlightenment, the Age of Reason (seventeenth and eighteenth centuries). Some of those secret societies embraced ideologies that coalesced to eventually influence the formation of Marxism in the mid-nineteenth century.

Previously we explored the impact of the French Revolution on the rise of Marxism in Europe. We learned about the emergence of groups that embraced vastly different, often radical ideologies that were mostly opposed to the Christian faith and the governments at the time. Those groups, often secret societies, helped fuel what became the French Revolution. However, they were unlike the organized patriots fighting the British in America at the same time (late eighteenth century). They sought top-to-bottom civilizational transformation.

The most violent part of the decade-long French Revolution was known as the "Reign of Terror," called the "Terror" (*la Terreur*), and was short-lived—lasting only from September 5, 1793, to July 27, 1794. It pitted the revolutionary French government overseen by the Committee of Public Safety and run by Maximilien de Robespierre, also a member of the Jacobin Club, a revolutionary political movement (secret society) that stood for a strong central government, against the monarchist coalition of European nations and counterrevolutionary forces within

France. Robespierre quickly gained dictatorial powers he used to eliminate the revolution's enemies by suspending the rights of public trial that led to the the "Great Terror," which claimed the lives of 16,600 people and coincidentally ended Robespierre's life as well.[588]

Robespierre's radicalism later inspired both Karl Marx and Vladimir Lenin, who erected a statue to the French leader after the successful 1917 Russian Revolution. Albert Mathiez (1874–1932), a French historian who is best known for his Marxist interpretation of the French Revolution, wrote in 1920, "Lenin, like all the Russian socialists, is nourished by the history of our great [French] revolution, is inspired by its example, and puts it into practice while adapting them to his country and the circumstances."[589]

Mathiez wrote that both Robespierre's Jacobinism and Lenin's bolshevism were "class dictatorships operating by the same methods: terror, requisition, and taxes, and proposing as a final outcome the same goal, the transformation of society. And not only of Russian or French society, but of universal society."[590]

Robespierre and his fellow Jacobin revolutionaries showed no mercy. Catholic Father William Jenkins said in a television show, *What Catholics Believe*, that these revolutionaries slaughtered many French peasants. "People here had never seen [violence like this] before, people here had never committed a crime, but they had to die so that France could be transformed into a socialist society."[591]

Frenchmen of faith were especially vulnerable during the revolution. One of Robespierre's associate groups, the Cordeliers Club (Society of the Friends of the Rights of Man and of the Citizen) ruled Paris during much of the French Revolution. The group's September Massacres (September 2–6, 1792) targeted 1,200 priests and other prisoners with the aim of eliminating Christianity.[592]

The Cordeliers Club included Jacques Hebert, who formed the Cult of Reason (*Culte de la Raison*), France's first state-sponsored atheistic religion, intended to replace Catholicism during the revolution. That system rejected the idea of any deity, and in its "explicit religion of man," it constructed a new "goddess of reason" and became the first known state religion of atheism.[593]

Catholic priest Donald Sanborn wrote: "The French Revolution reduced a nation to a mob. Communism feeds off that."[594] The priest continued, "Communism is the complete equalization and socialization of a whole nation…[which] 'works by obliterating individual rights, property rights, families, and even the most basic social structures' and 'you are—every aspect of your life—is controlled by the state.'"[595]

That outcome, according to Sanborn, "is only possible if you break down all of the God-given institutions of men.… If you break that down and say everything is equal before the state, and the state doesn't even look at families, doesn't look at the church, doesn't look at God, and it just looks at individuals, that is the basis of communism."[596]

The French weren't the only nationality to experience the rise of secret societies like the Jacobin Club, thanks to the Enlightenment Era. In Bavaria, part of present-day Germany, there arose the Illuminati, which opposed superstition, obscurantism, religious influence on society, and abuses of government. "The order of the day," the group wrote in its statutes, "is to put an end to the machinations of the purveyors of injustice, to control them without dominating them."[597]

Illuminism embraced occultic philosophies that included elements of ancient Gnosticism and Hermeticism, a religious tradition based on the writings of the ancient Greek Hermes Trismegistus. Illuminism focused on personal enlightenment through reason—a progressive concept that centered on materialism and was very anti-religious and anti-government.

The Order of the Illuminati called for the overthrow of religion and government, much like its French counterparts associated with Jacobinism. Abbe Augustin Barruel, a French Jesuit, wrote in his book, *Memoirs Illustrating the History of Jacobinism*, that the ideas of the Illuminati were included by the Jacobins and played out in the French Revolution's Reign of Terror, thanks to leaders like Robespierre and Babeuf.[598]

Father Barruel wrote about the Jacobins, that "all men were equal and free," but in order to promote true equality and liberty, they must trample "under-foot the altar and the throne; they stimulated all nations to rebellion, and aimed at plunging them ultimately into the horrors of anarchy." The Illuminati's founder, Johann Adam Weishaupt (1748–1830) said as much when he called for the abolition of all ordered government, inheritance, private property, patriotism, family, and religion.[599]

The Illuminati, like Robespierre's Jacobinism, also influenced communism. Leon Trotsky, a Lenin comrade, noted in *My Life*, his autobiography: "In the 18th century, freemasonry became expressive of a militant policy of enlightenment, as in the case of the Illuminati, who were the forerunners of [French] revolution."[600]

Marxist Cycle of Secret Societies

We know from the previous section that Marx adopted his radical ideas from both German and French-inspired secret societies that came to England from the continent in the 1840s. By 1848, that influence helped inspire Marx to coauthor with Engels *The Communist Manifesto* and found the Communist League.

Of course, secret societies significantly predated the French Revolution. In fact, some of these groups date back thousands of years, like the Knights Templar introduced earlier in this chapter, and they continue to thrive even today.

Many of us may dismiss modern secret societies as quaint gatherings or some grown-up version of a college fraternity. Others of us label them as wacko conspirators and grant them zero credibility.

I suspect there were similar views in the mid-eighteenth century about such groups, that is, before those rabble organized to spark the French Revolution. Soberly, and to bring the issue closer to home, the riots that torched some American cities in 2020 were sparked and supported by secret societies and their proxies. Yes, there are groups in America that aren't all that different from those that launched past revolutions. The same or similar groups are likely conspiring even today for a troubled future, and some have Marxist ideas, which were introduced earlier in this section of *Give Me Liberty, Not Marxism*.

Former President John F. Kennedy believed in the power of secret societies. On April 27, 1961, he spoke to the American Newspaper Publishers' Association. He made clear that he believed not only that secret societies were very real, but were a true threat to America:

> The very word "secrecy" is repugnant in a free and open society; and we are as a people inherently and historically opposed to secret societies, to secret oaths and to secret proceedings.[601]
>
> Today no war has been declared—and however fierce the struggle may be, it may never be declared in the traditional fashion. Our way of life is under attack [from secret societies]. We are opposed around the world by a monolithic and ruthless conspiracy that relies primarily on covert means for expanding its sphere of influence—on infiltration instead of invasion, on subversion instead of elections, on intimidation instead of free choice, on guerrillas by night instead of armies by day.[602]
>
> It [secret societies] is a system which has conscripted vast human and material resources into the building of a tightly knit, highly efficient machine that combines military, diplomatic, intelligence, economic, scientific and political operations.[603]

You may not share President Kennedy's concern for these secret "highly efficient machines," but he was the first and only president to raise the issue openly. He believed they impacted our nation and the world. Some believe that this is the reason he was assassinated.

Who are these contemporary secret societies?

Portions of the following material are extracted from my book, *The Deeper State* (Defender, 2017), and the chapter on secret societies.

> Bonnie H. Erickson, a professor of sociology at the University of Toronto, writes in the *Journal of Social Forces* to define such

groups as a social network with "a persisting pattern of relationships which directly or indirectly links the participants in related secret activities. There must be some secret activities in order to have a secret society; there must be a persistent pattern of relationships among participants in order to have a secret society."[604]

Another study of secret societies suggests these groups all share some of the same characteristics. First, they display arrogant pride. They "parlay a sense that they are above and superior to others, an elite class, specifically are chosen because of their innate and rare knowledge of the 'truth' while the rest of the world are mere peons."[605]

Second, they "behave one way when they're with their fellow members and then put on a front for others when out in public." That is a natural and a common human characteristic whereby we all tend to be more relaxed when in familiar settings but more guarded when in unfamiliar situations.

Third, they "prize teaching their ways to new members but doing so only in small bits of information at a time until that member meets the requirements to be part of the upper echelon in the organization." That's true of groups like the Freemasons, whereas only the very top leaders know all the group's teachings and dark secrets.

Fourth, they tend to claim man is "inherently good and should be told the secrets through membership, providing the potential initiate meets the criteria to be considered worthy enough to be a society fellow." Of course, that view is contrary to Scripture, which says of mankind, "The human heart is the most deceitful of all things, and desperately wicked. Who really knows how bad it is (Jeremiah 17:9, NLT)?"

Secret societies mirror many facets of ordinary life like health. After all, the exclusivity associated with membership in a group is found in all human endeavors, even those that are not secret, such as sports teams. This exclusivity of membership is actually one of the secret societies' most powerful weapons, as are the use of signs, passwords, and other tools. America has a rich history of secret societies, and many of those groups are focused on political issues. One such group formed immediately following the American Civil War (1861–65), a period marked by deep bitterness on both sides—and in some ways the war never ended.

Resentful Southerners tried to put African Americans back into their previous place in the post-war Southern society, and when that failed, some resorted to violence and terror to affect political control. They also banned together in a "secret society." Those circumstances saw the emergence of the Ku Klux Klan (KKK), which was formed to reverse the changes imposed on the South and return Southern society to its pre-war, white supremacy era.

Tradition indicates the Klan formed in the summer of 1866 in Pulaski, Tennessee, in the law office of Judge Thomas M. Jones. The group's name comes from the Greek word *kyklos*, translated "circle" or "band," with "clan" spelled with a "K." The group borrowed from the Greeks some of the rituals and titles, such as grand cyclops and grand magi.[606]

Very soon after forming, the Klan became a vigilante "society" perpetrating crime, especially against African American freedmen. The KKK donned costumes and invaded black homes allegedly to protect the public.[607]

"The Klan became in effect a terrorist arm of the Democratic Party, whether the party leaders as a whole liked it or not," wrote Allen W. Trelease in *White Terror: The Ku Klux Klan Conspiracy and Southern Reconstruction*. The KKK's popularity drew membership across the South, and stories emerged of its violence such as beatings, lynchings, assassinations, rape, and destruction of property."[608]

Even today, there are numerous domestic and global secret societies—some seemly quite innocent and others rather threatening. For our purposes, we need to answer three questions about those groups that either embrace Marxism outright or adhere to aspects of the ideology. Specifically, are any of the "best known" contemporary secret societies Marxist? Or, better yet, do any of the current secret societies display Marxist-like characteristics? And/or: Do contemporary secret societies contribute as co-conspirators to the ongoing American revolution?

None of the leading so-called major secret societies admit they are Marxist in their ideology, at least those I identify in *The Deeper State*. However, some do appear to subscribe to Marxist views that fuel their behind-the-scenes activities, and those views may very well contribute to our current unrest.

To answer the three questions posed above, we must go back to Marx's ten planks from his 1848 *The Communist Manifesto* to inform our inquiry. Marx's planks, or goals, for a communist society include: abolition of private property, progressive income tax, abolition of rights of inheritance, confiscation of property, centralization of credit in the hands of the state, state-controlled communication of transportation, state-controlled means of production, equal obligation of work, equable distribution of the population, and a free government school education.

Now we need to match these planks with so-called secret societies.

Below I make a distinction among organizations, those that are classic "secret societies," which appear to embrace some of Marx's ten *Communist Manifesto* planks, and those in the subsequent section of this chapter are secretive, yet may embrace some or all of the Marxist planks—and they certainly employ Marxist-like violent tactics and act as the ground troops in the revolution, such as Antifa and Black Lives Matter.

BILDERBERGER GROUP

The Bilderbergers are called the "high priests of globalization," a label granted them by British journalist Will Hutton. This highbrow, elitist group hosts one annual event, an invitation-only, secret conference of the world's luminaries that first took place in 1954 in Oosterbeek, Netherlands, at the Bilderberg Hotel, thus the origin of the group's name. The guest list for the conferences includes some of the world's most powerful people (members), and others are invited for their special knowledge of relevant topics.[609]

The Bilderberger conference participant list is always unpublished, and the meeting place is off-limits to outsiders. Further, the participants are expected to adhere to Chatham House Rules, which, according to a *New York Times* reporter, means attendees can be candid inside the meeting, but must "understand that they do not talk" about what transpires outside the conference.[610]

A press release for a recent Bilderberger conference claimed the discussions concerned megatrends as well as issues facing the world such as artificial intelligence, cybersecurity and regional issues such as terrorism, and US elections. Secrecy allows the participants to explore scenarios and be frank in their comments. Further, according to the press statement, there were no agendas, no resolutions, no votes, and no final report.

The limited material available from past Bilderberger meetings provides some insights about the group's actual agenda and underlying ideology. Specifically, given the audience—world leaders, industrialists, bankers—it literally shouts that the confab is a shadow one-world government. That fits the Marxist agenda, because the topics considered at the conferences are always related to global banking, communications, production, population control, education, and more.

Yes, one world government in some form appears to be an agenda item at the Bilderberg conferences. Daniel Estulin investigated and then wrote a book about the group, *The True Story of the Bilderberg Group*. In that volume, Estulin describes the attendees as a "shadow world government"—a "private club where presidents, prime ministers, international bankers and generals rub shoulders, where gracious royal chaperones ensure everyone gets along, and where the people running the wars, markets, and Europe [and America] say what they never dare say in public."[611]

The late Phyllis Schlafly, an American constitutional lawyer and conservative activist, identified the Bilderbergers as "globalists who sought to undermine the sovereignty of America through a 'bipartisan' foreign policy aligned to the interests of transnational corporations." They are "kingmakers," Schlafly said, who recruit aspiring politicians willing to do their bidding.[612]

Ms. Schlafly wrote about the March 2016 Bilderberger "kingmakers" conference that took place off the Georgia coast. She wrote that attendees included the CEOs of Apple and Google, media titans Arthur Sulzberger and William Kristol, and top political leaders, including former US House Speaker Paul Ryan and then Senate Majority Leader Mitch McConnell. The group's goal, according to Schlafly, "was to stop Donald Trump from obtaining the Republican presidential nomination" and, as is always the case, "to take power away from 'we the people' and to be kingmakers once again."[613]

Conspiracy theories aside, perhaps the Bilderbergers succeeded in 2020 through various means. Trump to them was merely a temporary obstacle to be tolerated for a brief period of four years and then eliminated. His replacement, most anyone from the Democratic Party's ruling class, would be far more malleable to the Bilderbergers' ambition.

Wiley Claes, a former NATO boss and two-time Bilderberg Conference attendee, agrees with Schlafly. Claes said the meetings have implied outcomes: "The participants are then obviously considered to use this report [the conference discussions] in setting their policies in the environments in which they affect." Further, and to Ms. Schlafly's point, attendees meet in secret to chart our collective future, a one-world agenda.[614]

Former British Chancellor of the Exchequer and Bilderberger participant Denis Healey said a one-world agenda might be a little "exaggerated, but not wholly unfair." He admits Bilderberger's goal is global government, an aim shared by those selected to attend the annual meetings.[615]

Even an American manufacturing executive believes the Bilderbergers seek a one-world government. Richard B. Barnes, president of

Nerpco USA LLC, an American firm that designs and manufactures high-quality machinery, blames the mass exodus of American companies overseas to the Bilderbergers and asks rhetorically: "Why did we… allow bankers [a reference to the Bilderbergers] to manipulate us in such as fashion so that we sold out our country?" He said: "It was the scheming by the most secret organization in the world: the Bilderbergers." Then he explained that the Bilderbergers' ultimate objective is "to have one world government at the United Nations."[616]

From a prophetic perspective, perhaps the Bilderbergers' global, one-world agenda may be fulfilled by the ten kings prophesied in Revelation 17:12–14 (KJV), whereby "these [ten kings] have one mind, and shall give their power and strength unto the beast [the Antichrist]. These shall make war with the Lamb, and the Lamb shall overcome them: for he is Lord of lords, and King of kings: and they that are with him are called, and chosen, and faithful."

British Chancellor Healey continued to confirm the perception:

Those of us in Bilderberger felt we couldn't go on forever fighting one another for nothing and killing people and rendering millions homeless. So, we felt that a single community throughout the world would be a good thing.[617]

David Rockefeller spoke at the Bilderberg meeting in Germany in 1991; his speech is quoted at SourceWatch.org. "We are grateful to *The Washington Post, The New York Times, Time Magazine*, and other great publications whose directors have attended our meetings and respected their promises of discretion for almost 40 years."[618]

The quote continues:

It would have been impossible for us to develop our plan for the world if we had been subjected to the lights of publicity during those years. But the world is more sophisticated now and prepared to march toward a world government. The supranational sovereignty of an intellectual elite and world bankers is surely preferable to the national auto determination practiced in past centuries.

This is evidence of the gradual emergence of autocratic socialism, the proverbial frog-in-the-boiling-water approach.

Another Marxist agenda item that applies to the Bilderberger conferees is the centralization of credit (banking) in the hands of the state, big government. Etienne Davignon, a former European Union commissar and Belgian minister of state, told an online program that in fact the Bilderberger summits "helped create" the euro currency imposed on seventeen formerly sovereign nations. That is certainly a tangible outcome of a conference allegedly focused "just on talk." Will Hutton, a former British newspaper editor, confirmed that the Bilderberger meetings provide a backdrop "against which policy is made worldwide."[619]

The Bilderberg conferences address trade, production, and the need to centralize those activities—a globalist, arguably Marxist plank. Evidently, those conferences include king-making to advance the "club's" broader, global financial interests.

One such instance of "king-making" involved Bill Clinton, an obscure governor from Arkansas at the time, who, thanks to the "club," rocketed to the US presidency. In 1991, according to the *New York Times*, Clinton accepted an invitation to attend the Bilderberger Conference meeting held at Baden Baden, Germany. At that meeting, Clinton was, according to the *Times*, "schooled by influential economists and 'free trade' strategists about the desirability of NAFTA [North American Free Trade Agreement] and why he should join them in promoting its aims and working toward its implementation."[620]

Two years after that conference, the newly minted President Bill Clinton signed NAFTA into law. That agreement was a major payoff to the Bilderbergers, who invested in Clinton's election.[621]

The Bilderberg conference promotes those who embrace progressivism—big government, state-run education, the right to work, and population control. Like with Bill Clinton, much the same happened with Barack Obama, a relatively unknown junior US senator before he was plucked up, made the rounds at a Bilderberger Conference, and then quickly found his way to the White House. He fulfilled the Bilderberg's aim: advancing the globalist agenda through eight years of arguably America's most progressively radical presidency.

Obama was the epitome of the Bilderbergers' success in developing the one-world government and accelerating their agenda. Clearly their intent was to move even faster with the Hillary Clinton election. Trump foiled that plan, but not for long—just four years. President Biden sets them up for the global Great Reset.

The Bilderberger conference does impact American war policy as well. A *New York Times* article argued "that the first intimations of American determination to wage war in Iraq came from a Bilderberger gathering in 2002." In that year, Bush administration neocon members who led the march to war in Iraq joined the conference.[622]

What was the Bilderbergers' goal in creating a war with Baghdad? Was it intended to alter the balance in the Middle East? Or was the goal something more nefarious, such as to alter global rule and press for a one-world system by winning the war?

Most likely, no Bilderberger conference attendee would acknowledge being a Marxist or even starting a war to advance their agenda. However, there is a significant overlap between Marx's goals and the byproducts of the Bilderberger annual meetings. Coincidence or not, it doesn't matter, because Marxism continues to march across modern history, and the Bilderbergers are helping push that agenda on a number of fronts.

FREEMASONS

The Freemasons are a worldwide fraternity—secret society—with an emphasis on personal study, self-improvement, individual liberty, freedom of worship, and social betterment. Although the group is known for its secrecy, much of its charity work is well-known, as is a long list of distinguished members, such as George Washington and Benjamin Franklin.

The group claims to preserve ancient secrets handed down from Solomon's builders via the Knights Templar. Further, they claim to offer "light," unobtainable elsewhere, that leads to a perfect society. Henry Wilson Coil, author of *Coil's Masonic Encyclopedia*, wrote that Freemasonry is "a system of morality and social ethics, a primitive religion, and a philosophy of life."[623]

The earliest mention of the "Masons" dates back to 1390 in the "Regius Poem." However, the first grand lodge of England wasn't established until 1717. Freemasons have always been known as an all-male fraternal organization that keeps secret special handshakes, chants, code words, and private rituals. Today, their worldwide membership is estimated at about six million strong.[624]

They do have a troubling history, however. Freemasons were conspicuous in the formation of the racist Ku Klux Klan, and they are known very much as an exclusive, middle-class, "Protestant" organization that really embraces the religion of naturalism. In fact, Freemasonry treats all religions as equal but inferior to its own gnostic wisdom, which may explain why some Catholics consider it a dangerous, satanic-like conspiracy intended to destroy all faith.[625]

Freemason Gnosticism allows members to believe in any one god, but they are known as anticlerical and are expected to remain aloof from politics. Given this position on religion, it is understandable why Freemasons supported both the French and American revolutions, and yes, they seek a new world order.

At the present, some people believe the Freemasons seek a new world order, perhaps with the help of their "light." There are some well-placed critics who advance troubling allegations against the group and implicate it with Marxist ambitions.

Notably, in June 2020, Catholic Archbishop Carlo Maria Vigaro wrote President Trump to warn him that the worldwide coronavirus response and the violent unrest plaguing American cities at the time (2020) was a tactic of the "Masonic" deep state intended to hurt the president's reelection bid and ultimately "dominate the world" to create a globalist "new world order."[626]

Archbishop Vigaro served as the apostolic nuncio to the US (2011–2016), which is the Holy See's (pope's) diplomat to America. His letter to President Trump states, "We have been witnessing the formation of two opposing sides that I would call Biblical." The archbishop described the unrest shaking America in 2020 as a spiritual struggle between the "children of light" and the "children of darkness." The archbishop continued, "We may easily identify with the deep state which you wisely oppose."[627]

The archbishop indicates that "it will not be surprising if, in a few months, we learn once again that hidden behind these acts of vandalism and violence [riots in the summer of 2020 across American cities] there are those who hope to profit from the dissolution of the social order so as to build a world without freedom: '*Solve et Coagula*' ["dissolve and join together"], as the Masonic adage teaches." *Solve et Coagula* is a Marxist tactic (violent revolution) and is associated with Satanism.[628]

The term *Solve et Coagula* may date back to the Inquisition and the torture of the Knights Templar. At the time, King Philip IV accused the Templars of worshiping a heathen god called Baphomet, which might be a corruption of "Mahomet"—the Prophet Muhammad. One interpretation of the phrase drove the plot in Dan Brown's historical novel *Da Vinci Code* (2006), whereby "Baphomet" was translated to mean "Sophia," the last descendent of the alleged marriage of Jesus Christ and Mary Magdalene.[629]

Another view of the term was expressed in the nineteenth century by the French occultist Eliphas Levi, in his book *Transcendental Magic: Its Doctrine and Ritual*. Levi envisaged a winged hermaphrodite with a torch, horns, and a pentagram on his forehead. The image's arms bore the Latin words *Solve* ("separate") and *Coagula* ("join together"), which, as indicated above means "binding and losing," usurped from God. Evidently, Levi's image was the inspiration for a statue in a Satanic temple in Detroit.[630]

Archbishop Vigaro described the ongoing battle undermining American social order in spiritual terms. There are mercenary infidels (atheists) who seek to scatter the flock of believers and hand over those believers to be devoured by ravenous wolves. These mercenaries, wrote the archbishop, are allies of darkness (satanic) and hate the children of light. He said just as there is a deep state, the powers behind the veil of government, there is also a deep church, which the archbishop believes betrays its duty to God. The archbishop continued:

> That there is a Deep Church can't be doubted in light of Pope Francis' socialist views on everything from climate change to migration. Moreover, the Catholic Church notably named the wealthy Rothschild banking dynasty "guardians of the papal treasure." The Rothschilds, of course, have been some of the chief financiers of the Deep State's agenda and are responsible for building the fortunes of other Deep State dynasties, including the Rockefellers and George Soros.[631]

The members of the deep church, writes the archbishop, are subservient to the "deep state, to globalism, to aligned thought, to the New World Order which they invoke ever more frequently in the name of a universal brotherhood which has nothing Christian about it, but which evokes the Masonic ideals of those who want to dominate the world by driving God out of the courts, out of schools, out of families, and perhaps even out of churches."

Vigano links Freemasonry with the historical subversive infiltration of Masonic lodges in order to leverage their influence to foment revolution and radical social change. We see this in the statement of a leading Marxist.

Leon Trotsky, a Marxist leader at Lenin's side, acknowledged the role of Masonry in the Russian revolution. The archbishop explained that "in the eighteenth century, freemasonry became expressive of a militant policy of enlightenment, as in the case of the Illuminati, who were the forerunners of revolution; on its left, it culminated in the Carbonari."[632]

The Carbonari, Italian for "charcoal markers," was an informal network of secret revolutionary societies in Italy (1800–1831), that influenced other revolutionary groups such as those in France and Russia. The group's expressed purpose was to defeat tyranny and establish a constitutional government in Italy.[633]

The archbishop's reference to the Illuminati is instructive. You will recall that earlier in this section, I explained that the Bavarian Illuminati favored Marxist-like ideas, such as one-world government; collectivism; and the state, not parents, being responsible for the rearing of children as well.

Those ideas migrated to France after the Illuminati was suppressed in Bavaria. Once in France, they infiltrated Masonic lodges and other fraternal (secret) organizations to help orchestrate [empower] the French Revolution.

In fact, the masonic lodges contributed to the occultic involvement in the French Revolution, which Gary Lachman explains in his book *Politics and the Occult*. Specifically, Freemasons contributed to the immaterial destructive forces loosed on the French Revolution, according to Lachman, who wrote:[634]

[Frenchman and author Jacques] Cazotte [1719–1792, who embraced the creed of the Illuminati and became a "mystical monarchist"][635] himself was aware of the dangerous energies unleashed by the Revolution.... Although Cazotte didn't use the term, he would no doubt have agreed that, whatever started it, the Revolution soon took on a life of its own, coming under the power of an egregore, Greek for "watcher," a kind of immaterial entity that is created by and presides over a human activity or collective. According to the anonymous author of the fascinating *Meditations on the Tarot* [*A Journey into Christian Hermeticism*], there are no "good" egregores, only "negative" ones.... True or not, egregores can nevertheless be "engendered by the collective will and imagination of nations." As Joscelyn Godwin points out, "an egregore is augmented by human belief, ritual and especially by sacrifice. If it is sufficiently nourished by such energies, the egregore can take on a life of its own and appear to be an independent, personal divinity, with a limited power on behalf of its devotees and an unlimited appetite for their future devotion." If, as some esotericists believe, human conflicts are the result of spiritual forces for spiritual ends, and these forces are not all "good," then collective catastrophes like the French Revolution take on a different significance.

The association between the Illuminati and the Freemasons is instructive, especially regarding the occult role in human tragedy. Consider that a similar occultic influence was evident more than a century later in Germany, which helped fuel the Nazi regime's march to war—a "collective catastrophe."

History tells us that in 1935, Nazi SS (Schutzstaffel) chief, Heidrich Himmler, the architect of the Holocaust, founded the "H Sonderkommando"—the H stood for Hexe, the German word for "witch." Himmler was obsessed with the occult and mysticism, which explains why he seized the library of the Norwegian Order of Freemasons in Oslo during the Nazi occupation of that country. Subsequently, that thirteen-thousand-volume, rare library of books on witches and the occult was discovered in the Czech Republic in 2016.[636]

Little wonder that Karl Marx traced the history of communism to the Illuminist French Revolution and by association the Freemasons' occultic role. Archbishop Vigano noted in his letter to President Trump that the goal of all of these movements has been the establishment of the new world order. Further, he mentioned the Cercle society (the French social club founded by known Illuminati member Nicholas Bonneville) which was aligned with Babeuf's conspiracy, mentioned earlier in this section. He explained that Babeuf's friend, Buonarroti, also mentioned previously, reintroduced the communist ideas of Babeuf, which promoted the concept of the new world order and were embraced by Marx.

For centuries, the Freemasons believed, very much like Marx, in centralized government control. They were associated with those who favored revolutionary change to realize that outcome. Does that mean they are Marxists, satanic, or involved in the occult? Maybe not, but certainly their history and secrecy today and the indictment by the likes of Archbishop Vigano suggest otherwise.

OTHER SECRET SOCIETIES

There are many other influential secret societies identified in my 2017 book, *The Deeper State*. In that book, I profile the Council on Foreign Relations, the Trilateral Commission, the Order of the Skull and Bones, the Bohemian Grove, and a list of twenty-two other groups.

These societies aren't necessarily Marxist in their ideology, but they do seek influence for their members, and that generally translates into an outcome that closely parallels one or more of Marx's original planks.

Another aspect of the "secret society" phenomenon is the informal club of a growing cabal of billionaires who use their wealth to change the direction of nations via nonprofit organizations, such as an array of foundations related to billionaire George Soros' Open Society Foundation, which undermines America's democratic traditions in ways explained in the next section of this chapter. Another is the Bill & Melinda Gates Foundation, one of the most powerful charities in the world, which involves itself across the world in pushing for a one-world government. Jeff Bezos of Amazon fame uses his platform to advance globalism and support communist China's agenda, and others, like Mark Zuckerberg of Facebook fame, manipulate large swaths of the world's population regarding so-called truth and fact, in some instances not that different than the ways communist regimes propagandize their citizens.

The US government has "secret societies" as well. We saw that evidenced so painfully with the revelation that top-level FBI and Justice Department officials held secret meetings outside of government offices, according to US Senator Ron Johnson (R-WI). The senator referred to secret meetings exposed after congressmen reviewed thousands of text messages exchanged among FBI officials, which showed a true conspiracy against President Trump.[637]

Likely, such secret meetings are part of what former President Kennedy meant when he called out secret societies in his 1961 speech to the American newspaper publishers. Also, it's likely what President Trump meant by the "deep state," which also included the surveillance of Trump election campaign staff using the 1978 law, Foreign Intelligence Surveillance Act.

Although what billionaires and rogue government agents do in secret may not be necessarily Marxist, their actions are certainly similar to the tactics used by communist regimes against their political enemies. Further, those tactics and the warrior class used as proxies by Marxist-leaning groups is the topic of the next section of this chapter. These people are also co-conspirators in America's ongoing revolution.

AMERICAN MARXISM'S GROUND TROOPS AND THEIR FACILITATORS

Every revolution needs ground troops to carry out the orders of their masters. The ongoing American cultural revolution is no exception. We certainly saw some of those "ground troops" in action during the summer of 2020, rioting, killing, and destroying statues and torching city blocks.

Their actions followed the prescription of Karl Marx to violently take over and destroy—no holds barred. They did precisely that. In this final section, I will profile the Marxism-inspired "ground troops" sent to battle across America. They are following the orders of their masters: The Democratic Party, deep-pocketed rogue billionaires, secret societies, and foreign governments. They were prepared ideologically thanks to our Marxist-inspired public education establishment, and they were encouraged by our leftist mainstream media.

Even after the 2020 presidential election, some of these Marxist "ground troops" violently attacked Trump supporters. After the

November 14, 2020, "March for Trump" at Washington, DC's Freedom Plaza, which included an estimated ten thousand people who heard a series of speeches repeating claims of widespread voter fraud, the crowd dispersed and then the radicals attacked Trump supporters.

Press reports indicate those radicals were mostly Black Lives Matter and Antifa (so-called anti-fascists), leftists who violently attacked Trump supporters. Videos from that day show Trump supporters who carried signs and banners were sucker punched, kicked, shoved and having their property stolen from them.

Andy Ngo, a social media journalist, tweeted "Graphic: a close-up angle of BLM rioters knocking a man unconscious who was leaving the #millionmagamarch in dc earlier today. They also steal his phone when he's on the ground."[638]

Jorge Ventura, a *Daily Caller* reporter, tweeted a video that depicted individuals assaulting a man. Ventura shared another video on Twitter with the description: "BLM groups threaten elderly couple and attempts to steal their Trump flag."

Human Events editor Ian Miles Cheong tweeted a video, writing: "Black Lives Matter militants assault Trump supporters." Cheong continued, "Antifa militants and BLM beat a Trump supporter over the head with a metal rod and mace him."

Those attacking were proxies of the Marxists fueling the American revolution, that campaign of violence began in earnest in the spring of 2020 that coincided with the COVID-19 pandemic lockdowns and the race-based terroristic attacks that captured much attention and dragged on through much of the summer.

These events and the support behind the violence is very similar to actions characteristic of color revolutions seen elsewhere, such as in the Ukraine in 2004. The intent of such revolutions is to bring about a change in government, which is more than just removing President Trump from office. America's revolution is a Marxist-inspired vehicle to alter the essence of the American experiment and to vacate our founding document, the US Constitution.

The background for what happened in the 2020 election began with the Obama administration, which arguably seeded its deep-state, ideological allies in key institutions prepared to operate a shadow government supported by a cadre of sycophant media and an armed branch ready to riot across America on command. In part, this explained why Mr. Obama never left Washington after his terms in office ended. Why? He wanted to be near the power—shadow government aided by the deep state—in order to influence its actions.

That shadow government made it very difficult for the Trump administration to rule. The deep state, shadow government miscreants fed the constant conspiracy line with support from the leftist media that included the Russia hoax, the Ukraine impeachment, the COVID-19 pandemic lockdowns, and the racist agenda that fueled the insurrection across American cities that brought out professional revolutionaries and a cadre of supporters.

The cadre of Marxist supporters are no longer hiding in the shadows, however. The 2020 insurgency allegedly began with the arrest of George Floyd, a Minneapolis Black felon who was high on fentanyl at the time. Of course, that incident was hijacked by a violent element ready to launch a communist-inspired insurrection, albeit as the nation was already weakened by the COVID-19 pandemic and associated shuttered economy.

Behind the street revolutionaries were groups like the Democratic Socialists of America (DSA), a six hundred-member-strong local group in Minneapolis that put its shoulder into the violence. The DSA worked closely with the ground troops, Antifa-aligned groups, to form a "national working group to help drive collaboration and resource sharing to support our antifascist organizing." DSA's national convention in August 2020 advocated a common Marxist strategy; in a press release, it stated: "One foot in the institutions, one foot in the streets."[639]

The Twin Cities DSA called for help during the unrest via social media from comrades for "supplies" to fuel the insurgency. "Want to help out your comrades protesting the 3rd precinct at Lake and

Minnehaha?" a Marxist posted on Facebook. "Here's a list of needed supplies from folks on the ground."[640]

The DSA's national political committee issued a statement broadly supporting the revolutionaries:[641]

> We, the National Political Committee of the Democratic Socialists of America, condemn the public execution of George Floyd at the hands of the Minneapolis police. His murder falls into the deeply entrenched pattern of violence, anti-Blackness, and oppression upheld by policing in this country. ... This is white supremacy....
>
> Racist police violence is not incidental to the capitalist system; it is necessary to maintain its operation. We recognize that as we fight for a better world, it will be the police who threaten our protests, the police who will break up our picket lines, the police who selectively wield their monopoly on violence against Black people and working-class people to protect those with power and privilege....
>
> We stand with and share the rage of all those who are making themselves heard on the streets after years of being suffocated by policing and poverty, after years of being looted by corporations, landlords, and billionaires.

The Workers World Party (WWP), a Stalinist-Trotskyist party, has members in at least fifteen American cities. It, too, supported the 2020 violent protests. WWP's Monica Moorhead, in an article, "Against Police Violence and Capitalism, to Rebel Is Justified," wrote:

> Workers World salutes all the brave protesters in Minneapolis, currently ground zero against police terror. We also salute those activists in Los Angeles, Memphis and other cities who are organizing protests and braving the pandemic to be in the streets or in car caravans to show solidarity with the demand: Justice for George Floyd and all victims of police violence.[642]

WWP founder Sam Marcy wrote years prior in defense of the 1992
Los Angeles riots:

> In times when the bourgeoisie is up against the wall, when the
> masses have risen suddenly and unexpectedly, the bourgeoisie
> gets most lyrical in abjuring violence. It conjures up all sorts of
> lies and deceits about the unruliness of a few among the masses
> as against the orderly law-abiding many.[643]
>
> Marxism here again cuts through it all. The Marxist view
> of violence distinguishes between the violence of the oppressors
> as against the responsive violence of the masses. Just to be able
> to formulate it that way is a giant step forward, away from
> disgusting bourgeois praise for nonviolence. It never occurs to
> any of them to show that the masses have never made any real
> leap forward with the theory of nonviolence. Timidity never
> made it in history.

The Revolutionary Communist Party issued a statement about the
death of George Floyd, which the group labeled as a call for "a movement for an actual revolution." The statement reads:

> If you're sick of watching video after video of these murders
> by police…you need to…join with a movement for an actual
> revolution, to prepare for a time when it will be possible to lead
> millions to bring this system down, and replace it with a new
> society based on the Constitution for the New Socialist Repub-
> lic in North America.[644]

There were many Marxist groups that fueled the insurgency on
America's streets—directly and/or indirectly. However, the most vis-
ible part was those doing the actual violence such as Antifa. These
Marxist groups, as well as their allies such as the Communist Party USA,
Liberation Road, Socialist Alternative, and their Black Lives Matter and

Antifa accomplices demonstrated the ability to mobilize tens of thousands of militants and send them across the country on short notice.[645]

Let there be no doubt the communists are fueling these incidents and are prepared for much worse.

Who are the actual ground troops?

Antifa—Anti-Fascist Ground Troops: A Marxist Front Group

The best-known revolutionary ground troops are Antifa and Black Lives Matter.

Andy Cuong Ngo, an American conservative journalist and social media personality, knows much about Antifa from his covering the 2020 violence in Portland, Oregon. He wrote a tweet on May 30, 2020:

> We are witnessing glimpses of the full insurrection the far-left has been working on for decades. Within hours, militant antifa cells across the country mobilized to aid BLM [Black Lives Matter] rioters. The first broken window is the blood in the water for looters to move in. The fires come next.[646]

Ngo continued:

> Media, politicians, public—all of us—have underestimated the training, purpose & capability of left-wing extremists. Every part of the rioting has a purpose. Fires destroy economy. Riots can overwhelm police & even military. All of it leads to a destabilized state if maintained.

Another perspective regarding Antifa comes from Jack Posobiec, a One America News network host, former US military intelligence officer, and author of *4D Warfare: A Doctrine for a New Generation of Politics*. Mr. Posobiec said:

[Antifa] are the street forces that are pushing the front line of communism, not through dialogue, not through learning, not through facts, not through persuasion. They are the militant wing of communism. And Antifa in the U.S., as we see them today, they've gained a lot of notoriety and a lot of popularity. But what a lot of people don't understand is that there's a historical basis to what Antifa is doing. [647]

He continued:

[Antifa] has been part of the toxic ideology that we've seen go across the world. It really encompasses the world from the Soviet Union to the Spanish Civil War to of course, China and the Chinese Communist Revolution to Cuba and many others.... It's very, very much typically a group that's encompassed of youth that's pushing in the streets, that's pushing violence in order to achieve the ends of the political leaders and the organizations that are above them that are pushing for radical change in a system. [648]

Mr. Posobiec explained that Antifa groups "existed in Europe for many, many years, and Antifa goes back all the way, even to prewar Germany. We saw this was funded by the Soviet Union." In fact, he explains:

Trotsky basically said Antifa is going to be the militant arm, the international arm of communism. This was set up by the Soviet Union to push and foment communism in other countries during that sort of prewar time. [649]

Where did Antifa get its start?
Antifa started in Germany and then matured in the US. Its goal is simply anarchy. It creates chaos that is intended to lead to civilizational

destruction—nothing short of a top-to-bottom transformation of America's civilization.

Antifa was initially part of the Soviet Union's front operations intended to force a communist dictatorship on Germany. That "united front" of the Soviet Union's communist international (Comintern) labeled all rival parties in Germany as "fascist," states Bernd Langer, in his booklet, "80 Years of Anti-Fascist Action," which was published by the Association for the Promotion of Anti-Fascist Culture.[650]

Joshua Philipp is a reporter with the *Epoch Times* and an expert on asymmetrical hybrid warfare and historical issues related to Marxism. He wrote about Mr. Langer's explanation of the Soviet's agenda and in particular Langer's expose on the Comintern anti-fascist movement.

Mr. Philipp wrote that the "united front" strategy, according to Langer, was "to bring together left-wing organizations in order to incite communist revolution. The Soviets believed that following Russia's revolution in 1917, communism would next spread to Germany, since Germany had the second-largest communist party, the KPD (*Kommunistische Partei Deutschlands*, translated "Communist Party of Germany")."[651]

The Comintern's plan took shape at the Fourth World Congress in 1922, where the slogan "To the Masses" emerged with the intent of joining various communists and German workers' parties under a single structure. Langer explained the intent was for the communists to dominate. Meanwhile, the German KPD embraced the banner of anti-fascism. Langer explained, for the KPD, the ideas of "fascism" and "anti-fascism" were "undifferentiated." For him the term "fascism" was meant to support the group's aggressive opposition.

At the same time as the KPD advanced its "fascist" agenda, Adolf Hitler, a fascist, became the head of the National Socialist German Workers' Party (Nazi party). Mr. Philips explains that "both the communist and fascist systems [in Germany] were based in collectivism and state-planned economies. Both also proposed systems wherein the individual was heavily controlled by a powerful state, and both were responsible for large-scale atrocities and genocide."[652]

In recent years, Germany's domestic intelligence service, the Federal Office for the Protection of the Constitution (BfV), expressed a similar view to that above. From the viewpoint of the "left-wing extremist," the label "fascism" as advanced by Antifa, according to the BfV, doesn't really mean actual fascism; rather, it is a label for "capitalism."

Mr. Philips said, "While leftist extremists claim to be fighting 'fascism' while launching their attacks on other groups, the report states the term 'fascism' has a double meaning under the extreme-left ideology, indicating the 'fight against the capitalist system.'"[653]

Mr. Langer held a similar view. For the communists in Germany, according to Langer, "anti-fascism" really meant "anti-capitalism." Mr. Philips "notes the labels merely served as 'battle concepts' under a 'political vocabulary.'" And the BfV still holds to that definition of capitalism as being "fascism."[654]

"They argue that the capitalist state produces fascism, or at least tolerates it," the BfV report states. "Therefore, anti-fascism is directed not only against actual or supposed right-wing extremists, but also always against the state and its representatives, in particular members of the security authorities."[655]

Meanwhile, at a 1923 meeting of the Politburo of the Communist Party of Russia, wrote Langer, "All the important officials spoke out for an armed insurrection in Germany." Of course, the KPD used that call to action under the banner of united front action and used the name Antifaschistriche Aktion ("Antifascist Action"), the true root of contemporary Antifa organizations across the world.

Understandably, those years after World War I were very problematic for the German people. As the KPD launched its network of radicals, Hitler and his Nazi Party embraced a similar approach, using political violence and intimidation via their militia known as the "Brownshirts."

To Moscow's great consternation, the KPD's *Antifaschistische Aktion* violence and intimidation drove many Germans into Hitler's camp. Specifically, according to Richard J. Evans in the *Third Reich in Power*, "the Communists' violent revolutionary rhetoric, promising the destruction of capitalism and the creation of a Soviet Germany, terrified the country's [German] middle class, who knew only too well what had happened to their counterparts in Russia after 1918."[656]

"Appalled at the failure of the government to solve the crisis, and frightened into desperation by the rise of the Communists," Langer wrote, "they began to leave the squabbling little factions of the conventional political right and gravitate towards the Nazis instead."

Mr. Philips indicates that "from the beginning, the KPD was a member of the Comintern, and 'within a few years, it became a Stalinist party,' both ideologically and logistically. He states that it even became 'financially dependent on the Moscow headquarters.'"

It is not surprising that, years later, some of the leaders of the KPD joined the Soviet KPD in the communist German Democratic Republic (the former East Germany), and formed the backbone of the ministry for state security, the Stasi.

Antifa Comes to America

Antifa is an anti-fascist strategy that came to America with communist immigrants such as the ideologues from the Frankfurt School fleeing the Nazis. Subsequently, they used their new American education and media platforms to advance Marxist revolutionary ideas.

Astute observers of this strategy understand that contemporary domestic Marxist terrorists grew up in America's public schools, which criticized our system of government and distorted our history. Many of these leftists came to embrace Howard Zinn's Marxists' history of America and learned at the feet of Frankfurt School radicals or their ideological offspring, and so a significant part of America's youth today came to believe the psychological manipulation fostered by many leftist educators and journalists.

Meanwhile, Antifa matured alongside the social justice movement, thanks to the same academia and pop culture (mainstream media), Mr. Posobiec said. He continued:

We see it now [that] corporate America is pushing social justice culture. And that's fed into Antifa. That's fed into the rise of Antifa. We see this hand in hand with the rise of the DSA, that's the Democratic Socialists of America, which is more of the quasi-political wing of this militant left, whereas Antifa is just the straight militant wing.[657]

Mark Bray, a radical Marxist, wrote a book, *The Anti-Fascist Handbook*, which justifies the sort of violence perpetrated by Antifa. "So, they [Antifa] know what they're doing," Mr. Posobiec explained. "And they're just very clever about it. In many cases, very sophisticated as well."[658]

Antifa, the strategy, is an outward expression of mostly violent actions. The approach is organic, much like some Islamic terror groups, with dispersed leadership that spreads like a cancer that has metastasized across our society thanks to the schools.[659]

Sergeant Betsy Brandner Smith, a spokesperson for the National Police Association, said Antifa is a dangerous phenomenon with a similar structure to that of "an Islamic terror cell."[660]

"Antifa is more than just an idea, Antifa has quite a history, going back to the 20s and 30s and Hitler's brown shirts and then we come into the anarchists of the 60s through to today," Sergeant Brandner Smith said.[661]

"The left likes to be able to go to a blue-checked Twitter account and say 'okay, this guy's the head of Antifa.' That's not how it works," she said. "Antifa's structure is really more like that of an Islamic terror cell, something like that. But just because we don't have a paramilitary structure for Antifa, doesn't mean they don't exist and doesn't mean they're not dangerous."[662]

FBI director Christopher Wray confirms that Antifa "is a real thing and not a fiction." He testified before the House Homeland Security Committee, where he explained that Antifa is more of an ideological movement, and there are suspects under investigation who have claimed to be members of the group.[663]

Wray continued:

And we have quite a number—and I've said this quite consistently since my first time appearing before this committee—we have any number of properly predicated investigations into what we would describe as violent anarchist extremists and some of those individuals self-identify with Antifa.[664]

Former Attorney General William Barr agrees with Director Wray. Barr said in 2020 that Antifa is a "revolutionary group" like the "Bolsheviks" who toppled Tsarist Russia one hundred years ago, and it seeks to establish socialism or communism in the United States.[665]

"I've talked to every police chief in every city where there has been major violence and they all have identified Antifa as the ramrod for the violence," Mr. Barr said. "They are flying around the country. We know people who are flying around the country. We know where they're going."[666]

"We see some of the purchases they are making before the riots of weapons to use in those riots," Barr added. "So, we are following them."[667]

President Donald Trump said he was aware of a plane that was "almost completely loaded with thugs" wearing dark uniforms, which took off "from a certain city this weekend" headed to Washington, DC. He later said that a passenger on the plane spoke and relayed details about the trip.[668]

In August 2020, Mr. Barr described Antifa as a "revolutionary group that is interested in some form of socialism, communism." He continued, "They're essentially Bolsheviks. Their tactics are fascistic."[669]

Antifa has an ally in an American original, Black Lives Matter, a violent partner and co-conspirator in the revolution.

Black Lives Matter

Black Lives Matter is a home-grown, Marxist scam that uses natural fear of social rejection to force compliance with its radical goals. The

BLM website hosts a Marxist agenda: anti-Christian, anti-free market, and anti-nuclear family, and it demands power. It uses intimidation and mass delusion, guilt by association, and ignorance to suppress free speech and stoke resentment.[670]

Patrisse Cullors, BLM cofounder, admits to being a "trained Marxist," and Alicia Garza, the other founder, is listed as an "expert" who is "guiding the work" of billionaire George Soros' Institute for New Economic Thinking (INET), which instructs others on how to "oppose capitalism," a classic Marxist goal.[671]

Ms. Cullors described BLM's Marxist influence:

We actually do have an ideological frame. Myself and Alicia [Garza] in particular, we're trained organizers. We are trained Marxists. We are super versed on ideological theories.[672]

In 2016, Garza spoke at Soros' INET conference, saying:

We need to build a different kind of movement that continues to push to take back the things that we've won but also continues to pull in new people into the fight who should've been there in the first place. The way that we do that, in my opinion, is not just by opposing what is wrong, what is fascist, what is xenophobic, what is racist, what is capitalist, imperialist about our president-elect [Trump]. It's not just about opposing those things. It's not just about him [Trump], but it's also very much about organizing and building power.[673]

BLM claims to have a global network, and its mission is "to eradicate white supremacy and build local power to intervene in violence inflicted on Black communities by the state and vigilantes."[674]

The group pushes to defund police departments, and some members want to abolish police altogether. BLM leaders refuse to condemn the rioting and looting that accompanied the protests that marked the summer of 2020 in many US cities. They claim those actions were aimed at police brutality and racial injustice.

Some members, like the New York-area BLM leader Hawk Newsome, are off-the-rails radical. Newsome threatened, "If this country doesn't give us [BLM] what we want, then we will burn down this system and replace it."[675]

BLM is as radical and Marxist as Antifa, with one twist. It claims credit for getting Mr. Biden elected president. "We want something for our vote," said BLM cofounder Cullors in a letter to Joe Biden and Kamala Harris. "Without the resounding support of Black people, we would be saddled with a very different electoral outcome. In short, Black people won this election."[676]

Of course, BLM doesn't speak for all Black Americans, but it does for enough of them to garner some attention in the new administration.

CONCLUSION

This chapter identifies the last of the co-conspirators in the ongoing American cultural revolution. It is clear that Karl Marx and his ideology are influenced by Satan and his army of demons.

Marxism emerged from radical philosophies spawned by the Enlightenment era. Those ideas led to the creation of a host of secret societies that sought radical change across much of Europe and eventually in the US. Modern secret societies exist, and like those associated with the French and Russian revolutions, the modern editions embrace aspects of the goals espoused by Marx in his *Communist Manifesto*.

The final section of this chapter identified the ground troops behind Marxist-inspired revolutions. We reviewed how the Marxist Soviets were in league with their German counterparts to deploy a fascist strategy. That concept eventually came to the US in the twentieth century, but didn't become a true co-conspirator in the revolution until it sank its claws into the social justice movement. Thus, by the summer of 2020, we saw communist-led Antifa joined by the American franchise, BLM, fill the ranks of the ground troop units fighting alongside each other in the American cultural revolution.

Might what we are seeing in the streets of America be the beginning of the fulfillment of the lawlessness in the end times? I'll address that issue and much more in section IV.

Section III

What Does a Marxist Great Reset Mean for America?

The first two sections of *Give Me Liberty, Not Marxism* laid the foundation regarding the Marxist revolution attacking America. Section I provided an understanding of the family of isms—capitalism, Marxism, socialism, communism and progressivism—that are present and impacting America, how they came here, and the characteristics of the ongoing revolution they created across this country.

Section II identified the many co-conspirators engaged in the Marxist revolution—the Democratic Party, communist China, the public education establishment, mainstream media, Satan and his army of demons, secret societies, and last but not least, the violent revolution's ground troops. Their collaboration is fueling the transformation of America.

This section addresses what a Marxist reset could mean for America. A Biden administration with leftists at the helm of government like former Secretary of State John Kerry, complemented by a chorus of congressional radicals, likely means a significant transformation of America to something more pleasing to the Marxists—especially if the American people fail to vigorously push back against their Marxist agenda. The vehicle for the Marxist reset is the ongoing revolution, with some aspects having started decades ago in our education establishment and others more recently, such as the ramped-up efforts thanks to the weakened condition of this country because of COVID-19-related shutdowns and the violence that visited many American cities in the summer of 2020.

Just how serious is the Biden administration about a total reset of America, and what does that really mean? John Kerry said the Biden administration supports a broad-based global Great Reset—and, he added, it "will happen with greater speed and with greater intensity than a lot of people might imagine."[677]

Mr. Kerry speaks for the Biden administration when he said the Great Reset already started for America. "In effect, the citizens of the United States have just done a Great Reset. We've done a Great Reset. And it was a record level of voting [a reference to the 2020 presidential election]," explained the former secretary of state for President Obama.[678]

What does the "Great Reset" really mean? The idea began with a World Economic Forum (WEF) initiative announced in 2020. Global lefty elites—billionaires, business executives, and celebrities, all globalists—want to take advantage of the economic chaos thanks to the COVID-19 pandemic to "remake nations across the planet, because desperate populations are now 'more receptive' to big visions of change," said Justin Haskins, the editor of the Australian-based Heartland Institute.[679]

Another Australian, Pauline Hanson, a senator and leader of One Nation, a populist political party, said the Great Reset would "push socialist and neo-Marxist policies." She continued that it would "pave the way for big controlling government, suppression of free speech, and reduced property rights."[680]

Who would oversee the Great Reset? Senator Hanson said the global elite, who are Marxists at the core, would make it happen, those "who think they know better than us how to run our own country."[681]

One of those global elite is Britain's Prince Charles, who said the Great Reset is "a chance to remake nations across the planet."[682] For Prince Charles, the primary target of the global reset is capitalism, the enemy of all Marxists and evidently elite "leaders" like the British crown.

They favor the elimination of the world's current capitalist system and want to push Marxist-like policies such as wealth redistribution, Green New Deal-like programs, and national job guarantees.[683]

Klaus Schwab, the head of WEF, is the most ardent supporter for the global Great Reset. "Every country, from the United States to China, must participate and every industry, from oil and gas to tech, must be transformed," Schwab wrote on WEF's website. "In short, we need a 'Great Reset' of capitalism."[684]

Schwab also said that "all aspects of our societies and economies" must be "revamped," "from education to social contracts and working conditions."

The vision for the Great Reset is outlined at WEF's website. It includes:[685]

> "The Great Reset" is a commitment to jointly and urgently build the foundations of our economic and social system for a more fair, sustainable, and resilient future.
>
> It requires a new social contract centered on human dignity, social justice, and where societal progress does not fall behind economic development.
>
> The global health crisis has laid bare longstanding rupture in our economies and societies, and created a social crisis that urgently requires decent, meaningful jobs.

How would this Marxist-like vision come about? These globalist elites would insist that the US turn its economy over to them, or to an international body like the United Nations, which would then "reset" America.

Of course, the US Constitution is the very foundation of America's economic and social system. Private property, the rule of law, capitalism, and individual rights are all the building blocks of a free people. Those must be scrapped to make the Great Reset transform to the elites' vision for the planet.

Mr. Schwab and his fellow elites don't think Americans have a say in the matter of the Great Reset. "We only have one planet and we know that climate change could be the next global disaster with even more dramatic consequences for humankind," he said. "We have to decarbonize the economy in the short window still remaining and bring our thinking and behavior once more into harmony with nature."[686]

Evidently Schwab, Prince Charles, and John Kerry (a Biden surrogate for such matters) are using the COVID-19 pandemic as the excuse to reset the world, which includes trampling on the rights of sovereign nations.

The pregnant question is whether or not this Marxist idea is supported by President Biden and his phalanx of ism elite supporters. And if that's indeed the case, what does the Great Reset mean for America?

Arguably, the ongoing American revolution, influenced by Marxist ideas, is ripe for more change, thanks to the Biden election and his allegiance to globalists elite who endorse the so-called Great Reset. I answer what that could mean for America in three chapters.

Chapter 9 addresses the Marxist plan for our liberties. They mean to rob us of our freedoms outlined in the Bill of Rights: faith, speech, bear arms, privacy, and states' rights. Part of their plan is also to undermine our confidence in the election system, something they accomplished thanks to the many irregularities associated with the 2020 presidential election.

Chapter 10 addresses the Marxist plan for our critical institutions. They mean to forever change the American economy, faith, family, education, media, and military—a Marxist outcome.

Chapter 11 addresses the Marxist plan to create a new America that is subordinate to a coming one-world government. This is a globalist aim, a one-world government with no borders, ruled by so-called elite totalitarians, who are opposed to all religion except the worship of big government.

Marxists' Plans for Our Civil Liberties

The privacy and dignity of our citizens is being whittled away by sometimes imperceptible steps. Taken individually, each step may be of little consequence. But when viewed as a whole, there begins to emerge a society quite unlike any we have seen—a society in which government may intrude into the secret regions of a life.[687]

—William O. Douglas (1898–1980), Justice,
US Supreme Court

A Marxist Great Reset could produce a very different America, especially one without the basic freedoms we take for granted—our civil liberties given to every American by the US Constitution.

I doubt there are that many Americans who really expected the 2020 election of Joe Biden to the White House to translate into the loss of those liberties. However, a liberty-robbing process is well underway, and President Biden may be only the latest instrument to accelerate the transformation of America into something more akin to a Marxist regime that denies our civil liberties.

This chapter begins with a review of our civil liberties—the rights granted every citizen by our Constitution—and then I summarize the state of those civil liberties for citizens in past and present Marxist countries. The chapter closes with how leftists, Marxists, might go about robbing us of what's left of our civil liberties.

WHAT ARE OUR CIVIL LIBERTIES AND THEIR SOURCE?

On November 9, 2017, President Trump proclaimed that day "World Freedom Day" to celebrate the fall of the Berlin Wall (November 9, 1989), but also to mark the one hundredth anniversary of the Bolshevik Revolution (November 7, 1917), which ultimately claimed more than one hundred million lives thanks to Marxism.[688]

The fall of the Berlin Wall, which once separated East Germany from West Germany, represented the triumph of freedom over communism. "The fall of the Berlin Wall spurred the reunification of Germany and the spread of democratic values across Central and Eastern Europe," Mr. Trump said. "Through democratic elections, and a strong commitment to human rights, these determined men and women ensured that their fellow and future citizens could live their lives in freedom."[689]

President Trump added, "Today, we are reminded that the primary function of government is precisely this, to secure precious individual liberties."[690]

"On World Freedom Day, we recommit to the advancement of freedom over the forces of repression and radicalism," Mr. Trump said. "We continue to make clear that oppressive regimes should trust their people and grant their citizens the liberty they deserve. The world will be better for it."[691]

What are those "precious individual liberties" the government should protect?

Civil liberties are simply personal freedoms, guidelines guaranteed by our founding documents. For Americans, those freedoms, rights, are delineated in our Constitution.

They include the following:[692]

- Freedom of conscience, which means the right to hold any opinion.
- The right of privacy restrains government from threatening the privacy of individuals.
- Freedom of the press, which allows us to communicate and express our thoughts and information.
- The right to a fair trial, which means the power to get a judgment that is fair and unbiased, thus we don't face punishment if found innocent.
- Freedom of assembly, which allows us to associate with whomever we choose without fear of interference by government.
- The right to defend ourselves when law enforcement is not available to help.
- Freedom of religion, which allows us to follow any faith.
- The moral principle that grants us the right to life, which helps build harmony in society.
- Freedom of speech, which grants us the right to articulate our thoughts and opinions.
- Freedom of equal treatment under the law and due process.
- The right to own property in our name.

Of course, America's founders had the wisdom to call out two particular rights that are not always seen in other constitutions: the right to bear arms (2nd Amendment) and the rights of the individual states relative to the central federal government (10th Amendment).

These civil liberties, rights, are important because of what they ultimately produce: true equality, a sense of security, protection of our personal space, and power to retrieve that which is ours.

Unfortunately, these civil liberties are seldom if ever present in countries run by Marxist regimes, and that's what is at risk should America move in the direction of a totalitarian, Marxist government.

HOW DO CIVIL LIBERTIES FARE IN
CURRENT AND PAST MARXIST REGIMES?

This review of history is necessary because the left refuses to admit the utter evil of Marxist-influenced ideologies like socialism, and many among their ranks are ready to repeat that history. In fact, many of those in the West born after the Cold War (1947–1991) demonstrate an indulgence, amnesia, and total ignorance about Marxism and its most virulent form, communism.

In 2017, Bret Stephens, a columnist, wrote a compelling article for the *New York Times*, "Communism Through Rose-Colored Glasses." That article asks some pretty indicting questions for especially America's leftists enamored by Marxism and its cousins.[693]

How many know the name of Lazar Kaganovich, one of Stalin's principal henchmen in the [genocidal Ukrainian] famine [of 1932/33]? What about other chapters large and small in the history of Communist horror, from the deportation of the Crimean Tatars to the depredations of Peru's Shining Path to the Brezhnev-era psychiatric wards that were used to torture and imprison political dissidents?[694]

Why is it that people who know all about the infamous prison on Robben Island in South Africa have never heard of the prison on Cuba's Isle of Pines? Why is Marxism still taken seriously on college campuses and in the progressive press? Do the same people who rightly demand the removal of Confederate statues ever feel even a shiver of inner revulsion at hipsters in Lenin or Mao T-shirts?[695]

Andrew Stuttaford responds to Stephens' article by reminding us in his contribution to the *National Review* that "man's crimes are indeed often forgotten, minimized or explained away in a manner that would rightly never be acceptable in the case of Hitler, Stalin's accomplice for a while and a mirror image of sorts."[696]

The "sheer monstrosity of the Soviet dictator has allowed many on the left to portray the triumph of Stalinism as a terrible wrong turning that crushed the (supposedly) bright promise of 1917," wrote Stuttaford. "Trotsky, no mean mass murderer himself, gave the book in which he described Stalin's Soviet Union the title *The Revolution Betrayed*, the encapsulation of a myth that has stuck. Trotsky may have been a liar, but he was a brilliant one."[697]

Stalin may have matured the revolution that Lenin started, but "compared to Lenin, Stalin was a pussycat," wrote Vyacheslav M. Molotov, a leading figure in Soviet government from the 1920s.[698]

Unfortunately, Mr. Stephens in his *Times* article tries to excuse today's leftists:

> There is an essential difference between Nazism and Communism—between race-hatred and class-hatred; Buchenwald and the gulag—that morally favors the latter. They will attempt to dissociate Communist theory from practice in an effort to acquit the former. They will balance acknowledgment of the repression and mass murder of Communism with references to its "real advances and achievements."[699]

He continued:

> Progressive intelligentsia "is moralist against one half of the world, but accords to the [communist] revolutionary movement an indulgence that is realist in the extreme," the French scholar Raymond Aron wrote in "The Opium of the Intellectuals" in

1955. "How many intellectuals have come to the revolutionary party via the path of moral indignation, only to connive ultimately at terror and autocracy?"[700]

Then he wrote, "And a good number have continued to do so since 1955, cheering on China's Cultural Revolution, Castro's Cuba, 'Bolivarian' Venezuela and all the rest."[701] Then, Stephens strikes the nail on its head, continuing:

> It's a bitter fact that the most astonishing strategic victory by the West in the last century [the Cold War] turns out to be the one whose lessons we've never seriously bothered to teach, much less to learn. An ideology that at one point enslaved and immiserated roughly a third of the world collapsed without a fight and was exposed for all to see. Yet we still have trouble condemning it as we do equivalent evils. And we treat its sympathizers as romantics and idealists, rather than as the fools, fanatics or cynics they really were and are.[702]

Stephens quotes former British Prime Minister Winston Churchill, who referred to Lenin, the leader of the Bolsheviks in the 1917 Russian Revolution as the "bacillus" of revolution which wasn't "eradicated, and our immunity to it is still in doubt." Stuttaford responded: Communism is, in reality, little more than a twist on ancient millenarian ideas so enduring that there must be something about them that does indeed appeal to human nature, or, at least aspects of it, whether spiritual, a simple craving for revenge or both.[703]

Bottom line: Don't let the leftists dismiss the incredibly serious threat posed by Marxism, as they are likely to try. Remind them of the global costs attributed to communism and the fact that toying with the devil today will not end well.

At this point, it is instructive to take a close look at life under the grip of communism. What follows are descriptions of life from the pens and mouths of those who experienced it firsthand. As you read through these descriptions, think about the civil liberties outlined above and what embracing Marxism, communism, could mean for Americans and their civil liberties.

Life in Communist Czechoslovakia

In 1948, the Communist Party of Czechoslovakia seized power and established a one-party state allied with the Soviet Union. Subsequently, the Czech people lived under the iron fist of an evil communist dictatorship for forty years. In 2007, Megan Sihde wrote about life in that communist country for the *Prague Journal of Central European Affairs.*[704]

Reflecting on life in the former communist Czechoslovakia, Ms. Sihde wrote:

> An "evil dictatorship" held the Czechs in its grips; freedom was no-where to be found, and life was imbued with fear and tyranny. Those looking at this past from a Western perspective know that store shelves were often empty, that demonstrations were brutally suppressed, that central planning destroyed the economy, and citizens were forced to either collaborate or suffer. In the beginning, there were Gulags. In the end, there were protests. Less common, however, are the kind of reflections that shed light on the day-to-day experiences of actual living under a communist regime in Eastern Europe.[705]

"Naturally, the communist party did not believe that it was tyrannical or inhuman—a state ideology, which espoused the inherent goodness of the regime, was either accepted or rejected by the populace," wrote Ms. Sihde. "Many chose to believe it, and many as a result, lived lives of relative comfort. Understanding life during this time also involves understanding many of the seemingly mundane day-to-day issues that are often overlooked. So, what was life really like under the Czech communists?"[706]

Czech elections were "a total farce," wrote Ms. Sihde. She continued:

Though elections were held during Communist rule and citizens were allowed to vote, there was no real ideological variety among candidates. Officially, people were voting for members of parliament, but as parliament was essentially a meaningless organization, the "candidate" of choice would make no real difference to the status quo one way or another. Furthermore, there was no privacy for voters. Rather, they [the citizen voters] were often presented with a piece of paper with a candidate's name, and simply asked to place it in a ballot box. Ironically, voter turnout was always the same: 99.9% and so many people soon realized that the entire system was a farce and simply gave up. Sometimes party apparatchiks would call on people in their homes or places of work, waving a ballot in their hands and pressuring people to mark it.[707]

Truth was what the regime said, so journalists always followed the regime's lead. Loyal communist "journalists" put a regime-spin on all the news. "Legitimate, truth seeking or investigative journalism was rare, even in the realms deemed to not be potentially harmful to the state," wrote Ms. Sihde.[708]

"Prior to the [Soviet] invasion of 1968, every piece of information needed to pass through the Office of Censorship in order to be published," wrote Ms. Sihde. "Media outlets could not indict the Communist regime for any societal problems, nor portray its Western enemies in a positive light. In 1968, official censorship was abolished, but was effectively reestablished step by step after the Soviet invasion."[709]

The Czechs enjoyed neither free speech nor privacy. Mr. Sihde wrote:

As an ideology, communism ultimately sought to find its way into every aspect of human interaction. In Stalin's Russia, communism managed to permeate even the family unit, with "love of the state" deemed more important than love of family. Thus, children would often inform on their own parents, who were then dragged away in the middle of the night, and sent to the gulags or executed. The atmosphere of fear was ubiquitous and unceasing. In communist Czechoslovakia, the situation was never that bad, but the 1950s were nonetheless a very dark era for Czechoslovakia.[710]

Escaped from Communist Romania

Carmen Alexe escaped communist Romania. Today she works as a commercial real estate consultant and writes a blog to express her views about individual freedom. Below, she explains what Americans don't understand about freedom—read "civil liberties"—from someone with firsthand experience of living in a country where freedom didn't exist.[711]

Ms. Alexe wrote:

Individual freedom can only exist in the context of free-market capitalism. Personal freedom thrives in capitalism, declines in government-regulated economies, and vanishes in communism. Aside from better economic and legislative policies, what America needs is a more intense appreciation for individual freedom and capitalism.[712]

"I was born and raised in communist Romania during the Cold War, a country in which the government owned all the resources and means of production," she said. "The state controlled almost every aspect of our lives: our education, our job placement, the time of day we could have hot water, and what we were allowed to say."[713]

Socialism created shortages of most everything. "Despite the fact that Romania was a country rich in resources, there were shortages everywhere. Food, electricity, water, and just about every one of life's necessities were in short supply," said Ms. Alexe. "The apartment building in which we lived provided hot water for showers two hours in the morning and two hours at night. We had to be quick and on time so we didn't miss the opportunity."[714]

"During the late 1970s, life in Romania started to deteriorate even more," wrote Ms. Alexe. "Meat was hardly a consumer staple for the average Romanian. Instead, our parents learned to become good at preparing the liver, the brain, the tongue, and other giblets that most people in the West would not even consider trying." She explained that her family "would wake up at 2:00 a.m. to go stand in line so she'd have the chance to get us these goodies. The store would open at 6:00 a.m., so if she wasn't early enough in-line she'd miss the opportunity."[715]

The media was under the communists' control as well. Ms. Alexe explained, "The one television channel our government provided for us often focused on programs related to crime and poverty in the western world. After all, people were poor and suffering because of capitalism, so we were told, so we needed socialism and communism to solve the inequalities of humanity."[716]

The civil liberty of private property was unknown. "Private property and private property rights are at the core of capitalism," Ms. Alexe said. "When in school, we learned that private property makes people greedy and is considered detrimental to society. Private property was associated with capitalism, the system that our textbooks claimed failed."[717]

Communism undermines innovation that could lead to a better standard of living. However, in contrast to capitalism, "communism, socialism, fascism, or just about any government-controlled system lacks the profit incentive. The people, who are the human resources, have no desire to engage in a business where the reward is not attainable (unless it's done in the black markets). They accept the state and its bureaucratic cronies to dictate their faith."[718]

Freedom is to be cherished. Ms. Alexe recalled being questioned by an American counselor as part of her immigration interview. The counselor asked: "Why I escaped Romania and why I wanted to come to America?" Her response was one word, "Freedom." Then the counselor asked: "If America was to go through a period of economic devastation with shortages similar to Romania, would you still feel the same way?" I didn't think too much about it, and I said, "Yes, of course, as long as I have freedom."[719]

Years later, Ms. Alexe said she came to believe "that the human condition of individual freedom can only exist in the context of free markets. Shortages are created by the intrusion of the state into the complex activity of the markets, whether it's price controls or poor allocation of resources." She concluded, "Capitalism is the path to the individual rights and liberty that build the solid foundation of a free society."[720]

Living under Castro's Communist Dictatorship

Jorge Castellanos was a professor and chairman of the history department in the Cultural Relations Department at Oriente University, Santiago de Cuba. In 1962, he spoke to the Economic Club of Detroit about living under Fidel Castro's communist dictatorship.[721]

The professor began his presentation with some historic context:

[In] 1958, the Cuban people ousted Fulgencio Batista, and installed Fidel Castro, who helped to unite the country against the dictator. The Cuban people and Americans believed Castro would restore freedom in Cuba, but they were wrong. Castro posed as a democratic leader and promised liberty but betrayed them by establishing a Communist, totalitarian dictatorship.[722]

"Before Castro took over, Cuba had experienced a trebling of annual per capita income in less than twenty years. The country was rapidly joining the modern world with radios, television, automobiles, telephones and much more," explained Professor Castellanos. Then, "in the last months of 1958 Castro admitted the Cuban Communist Party into the great National anti-Batista Coalition."[723]

"Castro was a Communist posing as a democrat," said the professor. He continued:

He established from the first days a true reign of terror. At the beginning it was said that the summary executions were only for the assassins of the former regime, but soon Castro was shooting the democratic leaders who opposed Communism. Thirdly, he seized control of all communication media. An absolute monopoly was necessary to squelch opposition, and give the people a massive Marxist-Leninist indoctrination. Propaganda and terror, terror and propaganda became the two main instruments of power.[724]

After these two coups d'etat, Fidel decided to go ahead with his plan. He wanted to nationalize all Cuban wealth, the first important step in every Communist revolution. He disguised this act, however, under the banner of nationalism. He intensified his attacks against the United States, stirring up the people's sentiment against "Yankee imperialism." Nationalism was only a pretext. The true objective was to seize all the wealth of the country, American and Cuban alike. It was not, then, a nationalist but a Communist measure.[725]

Religious freedom was abolished. (There are only 153 priests left in Cuba to serve a population of 7 million Catholics.) Academic freedom was destroyed. Young hoodlums in olive-green fatigues, armed with Czech sub-machine-guns took over all University Councils two years ago. Since then, they name and fire Professors, they determine curricula and select the textbooks. Vigilante Committees have been set up everywhere; in every Club, to spy, upon the people day and night. Secret police (the dreaded G-2) terrorizes [sic] the population. No elections— not even the rigged elections of totalitarian countries—have been held. Private property (factories, banks, stores, mines, land) have been confiscated without compensation and their owners were imprisoned, killed or exiled. All communication media, all newspapers and magazines, all radio and TV stations, have been taken over by the government. All parochial schools, all private schools and universities have been also confiscated. In a couple of years, the country was enslaved by its Communist rules. And then it was turned over to the rulers' masters: Cuba was invaded by Soviet troops.[726]

Another Opinion about Life in Communist Cuba

Orlando Gutierrez-Boronat is the cofounder for the Cuban Democratic Directorate, a group that rejects socialism and communism, which participated in October 2020 protests in Florida to call attention to the scourge of Marxism.[727]

Mr. Gutierrez-Boronat said his group's intention behind the protests was to point out that "in the Western hemisphere the sanctuary of communism is in the island of Cuba." He explained that most Cuban-American families experienced communism firsthand to include how the ideology destroyed Cuban family, private property, and individual freedom. He continued that many of the families protesting have a relative "who has spent years in political prisons or has been murdered by the Castro regime."[728]

Communist Cuba is a threat to the US, said Mr. Gutierrez-Boronat. He indicated that FBI veterans told him "how they saw firsthand the links between the communist regime in Cuba and the subversive violent groups in the United States."[729]

"It's a very dangerous regime," Mr. Gutierrez-Boronat added.[730] "Communism is first and foremost a doctrine of power, a doctrine of history, and a strange new type of religion, a religion that seeks to turn the material world into the replacement of heaven."[731]

Gutierrez-Boronat continued, "The last thing [communism] is, is an economic system. Communism has experimented continuously with capitalism to survive," as Lenin, Mao, and the Castros did.[732]

"Even if a communist regime or a totalitarian regime can generate some prosperity it always needs scarcity because the ultimate argument of the totalitarians is that the world is a limited place with very limited resources where scarcity is the primary mandate," Gutiérrez-Boronat explained. Therefore, there is a need for a "strong state that administers what is scarce," every communist regime even in prosperity including the Chinese regime works with this idea of scarcity.[733]

Communism "sought to create individuals with no history, no culture, no spirituality who could be transformed into members of a mass and that mass would simply proclaim 'yes' to anything the state said," Gutiérrez-Boronat continued. "That is a diabolical plan to destroy human beings, to reduce the transcendent dimension of human beings, to make them more easily controlled by the state, which becomes the only god that people can worship and look forward to."[734]

Why do people embrace communism? There has been a takeover of culture, media, and education by Marxists, which in turn created a rejection of the values, the sacredness of individual freedom, private property, the right to life, or the rule of law "which are basic to people being free," to people being able to have moral responsibility over their own lives, Gutiérrez-Boronat said.[735]

This "strategy has created a mass of people who are enamored of a utopia that will never take place and don't appreciate the reality of living in a free society," Gutiérrez-Boronat explained.[736]

Living in a free society as a free person is very rigorous, compared to living in a communist society. Gutiérrez-Boronat continued:

You have to make a lot of decisions, you have to be responsible for your own actions, you have to be accountable to yourself, whereas socialism promises to liberate you from all that. If you give full allegiance to the state then the state will alleviate the tension of your daily life. That is a utopia, it doesn't exist, it's just a way to fool you, and trap you, and imprison you.[737]

However, even in a socialist society, "nothing is free, there is no free health care, there is no free education," Gutiérrez-Boronat said.[738]

Free health care "means that doctors cannot practice independently and the state will use health care to deprive you of it if you disagree with the state," he explained, and the state will mandate what children will learn in schools as well.[739]

"Everything has to be paid [for] in some manner and the way that people in communist regimes pay for education, health care is by surrendering other freedom and other rights," Gutiérrez-Boronat said.[740]

Modern Communist China: An Oppressive Place to Live

Diana Zhang, a pen name, is a staff writer for the *Epoch Times*, grew up in communist China but now lives in the United States. She wrote the following about the 2020 American presidential election: "We thought China was going to become America. Instead, America is becoming China." She explained what that means.[741]

"Fifty years ago, in communist China, if you made casual comments about communists, you would end up in jail or a labor camp," Ms. Zhang wrote. It's becoming almost as bad in the US regarding political correctness. She continued, "If you say one word wrong, you could lose your job. If you don't follow the mainstream narrative, you will get attacked by the mainstream media."[742]

"A person who made one comment not in line with the CCP [Chinese Communist Party], even in the comfort of his or her own home, would be punished," wrote Ms. Zhang. "A son would report on his father, a daughter on her mother, and a husband and wife on each other. Fear of the Communist Party, and indoctrination by it, had become second nature, pushing out one's natural feelings."[743]

She used to tell people that "America is the least discriminatory country in the world." But no more, because today in America, "discrimination" and "racism" have become political weapons—the moral principle is gone. That's a Marxist tactic, to create divisions based on social class. Specifically, by turning one group against the other, Marxists create chaos in society, which opens the door for them to seize power.[744]

Ms. Zhang indicates that her global travels put her in touch with people who used to seek to immigrate to America because it meant more opportunity and a better life. However, she notes that contemporary America has changed for the worse. "America has become more and more like the socialist country they are trying to flee," Ms. Zhang said.[745]

Much more could be said about the oppressive regime in China. I've written about communist China's human rights violations in my 2020 book, *Collision Course*, and especially its terrible record regarding religious groups—Christians, Muslims, and Falun Gong.

What's clear from the above firsthand accounts demonstrate just how anti-freedom Marxist regimes are for their citizens. Unfortunately, there are many in the West who are naïve about the Marxist threat to our civil liberties. Some of these same people are easy prey to charlatans like Mao, Castro, Lenin, and others who peddle promises that only result in ruthless and evil human rights catastrophes—stripping away all their civil liberties.

HOW MIGHT AMERICAN MARXISTS AND THEIR SUPPORTERS STRIP AWAY OUR CIVIL LIBERTIES?

The 2020 presidential election was arguably a referendum on whether America should maintain the status quo or turn left, toward socialism, or worse. Evidently, there is at least a sizeable minority of Americans who believe the election of President Biden, whether legitimate or not, answers that question. Yes, they will argue, socialism or worse is in our future.

We've seen this movie before in history, however. Certainly, the profile of Cuba's fall to communism illustrates the pattern.[746]

"I am sure that at this time, there are strong forces inside the United States pushing hard to turn to socialism," said Luis Zuniga, who was imprisoned for his opposition to communism in Cuba. He warned those pushing socialism here in the US may not in fact be true socialists, but it's only because "they don't tell you."[747]

As indicated in the previous section, Fidel Castro hid his ideological bias when seeking popular support, Mr. Zuniga explained. But once in power, he used the full weight of the government to impose socialism using the government's totalitarian might.[748]

Two years after taking power, Castro abolished all elections, stating: "The revolution has no time for elections. There is no more democratic government in Latin America than the revolutionary government." Then he finally revealed his true motivations in a televised broadcast on December 2, 1961: "I am a Marxist-Leninist and shall be one until the end of my life." He continued that, "Marxism or scientific socialism has become the revolutionary movement of the working class."[749]

Those pushing the US toward a radical Marxist transformation are in some cases as subtle as was Castro in the late 1950s. But be fairly warned: They too seek a much more dangerous outcome for America, one that promises to make this great country much like those outlined in the previous section of this chapter.

TAKE THE LEFTISTS AT THEIR WORD

We established in the second section of *Give Me Liberty, Not Marxism* that the Democratic Party was hijacked by leftists, arguably Marxists. Although some within that party continue to fight for America's founding principles of free speech, freedom of religion and conscience, freedom of association, and the other civil liberties, the tragedy of our time is that they are betrayed by their own party. Imposters inside the Democratic Party and outside allies like communists openly reject the ideals expressed by the American founders.

The so-called democratic socialists and their woke allies seeking social justice have little in common with the old version of the Democratic Party. No, the emergent authoritarian, Marxist, American left intends to deny our civil liberties, our freedom.

US Senator Bernie Sanders (I-VT), a self-described "democratic socialist," lusts after the opportunity to remake America in the image of Marxist regimes by taking over healthcare and confiscating our wealth and all means of production, much like Castro and other communist leaders in history, radically transforming this country. Yes, the threat is that serious.

Consider a sampling of contemporary radicals ready to remake America a socialist country.

Remember former US Representative Robert "Beto" O'Rourke (D-TX), who ran for the Democratic Party's presidential nomination in 2020 and insisted that all religious organizations must embrace homosexual marriage or lose their tax-exempt status—a Marxist idea? "There can be no reward, no benefit, no tax break for anyone, or any institution, any organization in America that denies the full human rights and the full civil rights of every single one of us," O'Rourke said at a CNN town hall.[750]

Bill de Blasio, New York City's radical mayor, promised to pass a law making it a crime to use the words "illegal alien," which would be punishable by a fine up to $250,000. Sounds like China's PC agenda.[751]

Other Democratic Party authoritarians, like US Representative Ted Lieu (D-CA), said "I would love to regulate free speech. The First Amendment prevents me from doing so." Therefore, he'll find a way—and thankfully for him, big tech such as Facebook and Twitter are making inroads to deny freedom of speech.[752]

Representative Lieu added, "I would urge these private sector companies to regulate it [speech] better themselves." The message is that if for now government can't regulate speech, then woke leftists that monopolize the social media will.[753]

In fact, the Democratic Party and their woke allies aim to abolish the basic civil liberties ensured in our Constitution. At the present time, there are roadblocks in their way to a complete transformation of America's civil liberties embedded in our founding documents, however.

So where do leftists look for a model to follow when transforming our freedoms—stripping away our civil liberties? Peter Beinart wrote in the *Atlantic*, "They're more likely to look abroad—to the Soviet Union or Cuba in past eras, and to Scandinavia today—for alternatives to America's political and economic models."[754]

The question is, which model will President Biden and his leftist friends, supported by a very ideologically sympathetic Congress, select? After all, their policy objectives were outlined in the Democratic Party's 2020 campaign agenda, which was packed full of socialist policies such as the redistribution of wealth, guaranteed job programs, healthcare for all, and the Green New Deal. And besides, what they can't accomplish via congressional legislation, they'll seek to accomplish in the courts by packing the Supreme Court given the opportunity with ideologically charged leftist jurists.

DEMOCRATIC PARTY'S "VICHY" AND "NAZI-SOVIET" PACT STRATEGIES FOR AMERICA

So, what is the left's (Democratic Party's) and, by association, President Biden's strategy to transform America? My concern is that President Biden will lead this country down one or the other paths followed by the French Third Republic or one chartered by the Nazis and the Soviets in 1939.

Both strategies or analogies, if either is pursued as a model, are a trail of surrender from which this nation may never rise again, and our civil liberties will vanish with it.[755]

The first analogy, strategy, began with the German invasion of France in May 1940. French forces were quickly subdued on the battlefield, so Paris pursued a strategy that led to an armistice with the Nazi regime. France's prime minister resigned, and the mantle of leadership passed to French Marshal Philippe Petain, who signed an agreement with Hitler, which dissolved the French Third Republic. Meanwhile, Petain's government left Paris for the town of Vichy, where it oversaw the civil administration of France as Berlin's puppet.

Petain used his dictatorial powers to establish an authoritarian regime that closely regulated the French economy, tightly controlled the media, and paid reparations to Berlin. Thus, "Vichy France" was an ally of the National Socialist Germany until all power eventually migrated to Berlin in 1942. As in past national house cleanings, the Vichy rounded up "undesirables" at Berlin's command. More than seventy thousand Frenchmen were eventually executed, a reminder of the Reign of Terror at the end of the French Revolution.

Meanwhile, French patriots who opposed German occupation and the obedient Vichy regime went underground. They resisted the German occupation and their own puppet government's collaboration with the enemy.

France was freed, starting with the June 1944 Allied landing on French beaches and the subsequent, hard-fought campaign that ended with the surrender of the Nazi regime in early May 1945.

The Vichy armistice with the Nazi regime was a convenient and cost-saving agreement for Berlin and analogist in purpose to an agreement struck between Hitler and Stalin, a second comparable strategic alternative to resisting war.

The August 1939 Nazi-Soviet Nonaggression Pact was concluded a few days prior to the beginning of World War II, which divided Eastern Europe into German and a Soviet sphere of influence. That pact came about because the Soviets wanted to avoid a direct confrontation with the Germans, so they searched for a solution. In May 1939, Stalin sent Vyacheslav Molotov to negotiate with the Nazi foreign minister, Joachim von Ribbentrop. The aim of the negotiations was to keep the Soviet Union at peace with Germany in order to gain time to build up the Soviet armed forces for the inevitable conflict with the Nazis. Meanwhile, Hitler saw the value in a nonaggression pact with the Soviets so his forces could quickly invade Poland unopposed and then turn his might against France and Britain in the west without having to fight the Soviets in the east.[756]

On August 23, 1939, Ribbentrop and Molotov signed an agreement in Moscow. The terms of the pact were simple: Both countries agreed not to attack the other and not to support any third power that might attack the other party. The pact cleared the way for the Germans to invade Poland on September 1, 1939, and Soviet troops then invaded Poland weeks later (September 17); both forces met two days later near Brest-Litovsk, effectively partitioning Poland. However, over the intervening months, a series of moves and countermoves by both the Nazi and Soviet forces killed the pact, especially once the Nazi forces attacked the Soviet Union in Operation Barbarossa, June 22, 1941, which signaled a crucial turning point in the war.[757]

Meanwhile, American progressives like President Franklin D. Roosevelt were pleased to come to the aid of Stalin once the Nazi regime trashed the nonaggression pact. Evidently, as discussed much earlier in this volume, American progressives like Roosevelt and not a few communists in and out of the US government celebrated their new ally in Moscow, and Washington quickly added the Soviets to our Lend-Lease program. Also, communists went to work both in Hollywood and in Washington to serve Stalin's best interests, thanks to the naïveté and generosity of Uncle Sam.

These historic analogies—the puppet Vichy regime and duplicitous Nazi-Soviet Pact—illustrate potential strategies that America's left (mostly the Democratic Party) and their fellow Marxist co-conspirators outlined in section II of this volume might use to transform America. Specifically, the Vichy regime's strategy was one of collaboration with the enemy rather than resisting, something we saw occur between Cuban democrats who initially collaborated with Castro, until the communist rogue made his intentions clear and then it was too late. This approach is much like the incremental changes and more recent open embracement of the isms by the Democratic Party, especially with the progressive wing of that party—a Vichy-like strategy.

The Nazi-Soviet Pact was destined to fail from the start, because neither party was sincere about the commitments. However, the more vicious side of the two at the time was arguably Hitler, who from the start let Stalin play the fool to buy time to settle issues in the west against France and Great Britain, and then get serious in the east. Much the same happens strategically when the Democratic Party made a pact with the "devil," the Marxists (socialists and progressives) who pledged their support for Mr. Biden's 2020 campaign in exchange for more influence. Once Senator Sanders and a host of other leftists signed the "pact," the Democratic Party quickly moved to the far left, kicking the remaining moderates overboard, and they took charge with the nomination of Kamala Harris, the most liberal US senator at the time, thus cementing the Marxist hold on the party and the future direction of the Biden administration.

CIVIL LIBERTIES QUICKLY FALL VICTIM TO LEFTIST TAKEOVER

Whether the left embraces a Vichy or a Nazi-Soviet strategy to seize control of the US government vis-à-vis the Democratic Party is of little consequence. Either strategy will deliver the power base they seek to transform the country and begin to erode away our freedoms.

How might that happen?

The process of destroying our civil liberties once the country is under the control of "democratic socialists" like Bernie Sanders (true Marxists) is rather straightforward, and it begins with their first priority: destroying capitalism.

Matthew Harwood, the managing editor at the American Civil Liberties Union, exposes so-called democratic socialists as hostile to individual freedom. He cites the work of the socialist economist and best-selling author Robert Heilbroner to expose the left's agenda regarding the truth about socialism.

Mr. Heilbroner wrote in the democratic socialist magazine, *Dissent*, to answer the question "What is Socialism?" Harwood explains, Heilbroner's answer to the question isn't particularly revealing: Socialism is "not a more generous welfare state along Nordic lines. Instead, it is something entirely different, an economic and cultural configuration that suppresses if not eliminates the market economy [capitalism] and the alienating and selfish culture it produces."[758]

The process of harnessing socialism, according to Heilbroner, is that some "form of command" must underpin the socialist order. It doesn't have to "be totalitarian. But an aspect of authoritarianism resides inextricably in all planning systems. A plan is meaningless if it is not carried out, or if it can be ignored or defied at will." Interpretation: Socialism needs the strong arm of government to make it work, because there will be resistance.[759]

Next, Mr. Heilbroner acknowledges that socialism and individual rights can't coexist. Rather, under socialism, culture must produce "some form of commitment to the idea of a morally conscious collectivity." Thus, according to Heilbroner, individualism, civil liberties, are "directly opposed to the basic socialist commitment to a deliberately embraced collective moral goal."[760]

Evidently, the faux concept that there will ever be a democratic socialist is at best a misnomer and certainly a non sequitur. Mr. Heilbroner explained that there is only one kind of democracy for the true socialist, an illiberal one, whereby the "majority" engages "in massive experiments in social engineering in an attempt [to] purge people of their nasty [read "capitalist"] habits."[761]

Socialists have "two historic problems," according to Heilbroner. First, they must completely take over the economy "to establish the socialist order." Second, they must continue to control all aspects of the economy to make it work. There is a tertiary effect for the civil libertarian in a socialist country, explains Mr. Harwood.[762]

"But no social engineer, as any Marxist knows, can separate the economy from its political and cultural milieu," he said. "And so ruthless intervention in the economy necessitates ruthless intervention in politics and culture."[763]

Mr. Harwood presents a straw-man scenario to explain the second- and third-order effects of a socialist economy, one that could well be applied to the Biden administration. "Say a democratic socialist...does one day achieve the presidency of the United States and...[also controls the] Congress," said Harwood. He continues:

> Could democratic socialists abide a free press that criticize the party for its economic illiberalism? Could writers and artists critical of the regime work without fear of political repression and surveillance? Could citizens of the United States rest assure that democratic socialists would follow tradition and peacefully relinquish the reins of the government...to a party they deem "capitalistic" if they lose the next election when their goal is to abolish capitalism?[764]

Mr. Heilbroner answers these questions by pointing out that socialists have an authoritarian problem:

> But under socialism, every dissenting voice raises a threat similar to that raised under a democracy by those who preach antidemocracy. Because socialist society aspires to be a good society, all its decisions and opinions are inescapably invested with oral import. Every disagreement with them, every argument for alternative policies, every nay-saying voice therefore raises into question the moral validity of the existing government, not merely its competence in directing activities that have no particular moral significance.[765]

The outcome is pretty predictable. The "democratic socialist" cannot remain democratic if ever he wants to reach his utopian vision. Neither can he be a civil libertarian, argues Heilbroner. State power, for the socialist, must always triumph "over the individual's liberty to think, speak, write, work, and associate. Democratic socialism is not freedom, rather it is authority paternalistically dressed up in the language of liberation and wielded on behalf of that fuzzy abstraction, 'the people,' regardless of what flesh and blood individuals want."[766]

Exactly. That's what Americans saw across this country in 2020. So-called democratic socialists relied on government authority to force their agenda on the rest of us, and in the process trashed our civil liberties.

The COVID-19 pandemic brought out the true colors of the left and their disregard for civil liberties. They used the excuse of a virus to deny many Americans of their civil liberties. The issue before us is whether the Biden administration will launch down the same path that at other places and times led those people to embrace versions of Marxism, that ultimately meant government tyrants robbed the citizens of their civil liberties.

CONCLUSION

President Ronald Reagan said in his 1989 Farewell Address to the nation:

> For we must consider that we shall be as a city upon a hill. The eyes of all people are upon us. So that if we shall deal falsely with our God in this work we have undertaken, and so cause Him to withdraw His present help from us, we shall be made a story and a by-word through the world.[767]

America's attractiveness is wearing thin and could be easily extinguished if Marxists gain the power to take captive the country and steal away our civil liberties. As we saw in this chapter, communist, socialist countries such as Cuba and China deny their citizens the civil liberties we enjoy in this country. Our concern with the growing influence of so-called democratic socialists (real Marxists) is that they will use their access to the Biden administration and/or subsequent like-minded administrations to "reset" America by flushing capitalism and imposing socialism that inevitably lead to the abuse of government power to rob our citizenry of the very civil liberties that have always made the US the "shining light on the hill."

The next chapter addresses the Marxist plan for our critical institutions, using much the same strategy outlined in this chapter.

10

Marxists' Plan to Reset
America's Key Institutions

The most fundamental fact about the ideas of the political left is that they do not work. Therefore, we should not be surprised to find the left concentrated in institutions where ideas do not have to work in order to survive.[768]

—Thomas Sowell, American economist, author (1930)

A Marxist "reset" could produce a very different America, especially one that reconfigures our critical institutions—education, media, government (politics), religion (faith), and family. Unfortunately, the left has already mostly captured our education and media institutions, as explained in the second section of *Give Me Liberty, Not Marxism.*

Taking captive American institutions is an effective way for Marxists to completely transform (reset) our country, which was evidenced by the firsthand testimonies about life under communism in the previous chapter.

Why are institutions so important? They provide structure, are identified with a social purpose, fix roles of authority and decision-making, and transcend individuals and intentions by mediating our behavior. Geoffrey M. Hodgson, a professor of management at London's Loughborough University, said institutions are "integrated systems of rules that structure social interactions."[769]

Indeed, there are both formal and informal institutions. Formal social institutions include government, economy, education, and media, while informal institutions include family and religion.

Consider how modern Marxists are attempting to completely capture critical American institutions with the ultimate aim of "resetting" the US.

MARXISTS CAPTURING INSTITUTIONS

Marxists are best known for their violent takeover of countries. Earlier in this volume, I profiled the violence associated with the 1917 Russian Revolution and the violence associated with the takeover by communism in Eastern Europe. Similarly, both Cuba and China fell thanks to violent actors. However, Marxists have at least five nonviolent strategies for taking over countries. We see evidence of each strategy playing out across America today.

Strategy #1: Infiltrating Defining Institutions

A nonviolent strategy to capture Western institutions is a viable alternative to Lenin's violent revolutionary approach. That alternative strategy is attributed to the Italian communist Antonio Gramsci, who explained, and introduced earlier, that in order to subvert Western societies from within, the Marxist needs to fight a "war of position," a concept that came to be known as "the long march through the institutions."[770]

Mr. Gramsci believed that for revolution to work against a legitimate government grounded by a mostly faith-based people like America (65 percent of Americans self-identify as Christian), there must be an army of those who have a contrary view of morality, faith and tradition. Thus, the would-be successful revolution begins by subverting religion, morality, and civilization itself—God's influence on society.

That view explains why American Marxists years ago targeted the subversion of the academe (education establishment) with the intent of sending degreed, ideologically perverted graduates into mainstream society to corrupt the defining institutions that are gatekeepers of morality in Western society: church, government, education, media and more.[771]

After all, democracy only works when the citizens are disposed toward civic virtue and rest on a moral standard. Thus, the infiltration by Marxists into the academe with the objective of attacking the roots of Western society—its institutions—is an aspect of Gramsci's long march.[772]

Once the indoctrinated graduates fan out across America's institutions—education, medicine, media, religion, government, business, et cetera—they began infecting them with the "politics of intent" as opposed to the "politics of achievement." The Marxists' "intent" is to manipulate the culture in such a way as to create politics that favor the left, or as Andrew Breitbart explained, because "politics is downstream from culture." Change comes first to culture and then to politics.[773]

A Marxist culture within a key institution like education happened directly through infiltration, thanks to groups like the Frankfurt School cadre who came here prior to World War II. Once they were strategically placed in our most prestigious educational institutions, the damage was done. They began to influence the other faculty and students with their Marxist political philosophy. In time, they impacted the entire culture, which in turn influences the politics of the nation and by association those who are elected to government.

Strategy #2: Reshaping Public Policy

Another strategy is to capture the institution of government through public policy. Of course, this approach depends upon having enough leftists in government to press their radical policies, which is associated with the first strategy. We saw an example of this in 1966, thanks to a Columbia University couple (Richard Cloward and Frances Piven), who happened to be card-carrying members of the Democratic Socialists of America. Their idea was to bankrupt the US by swelling the public welfare rolls, thanks to one of Saul Alinsky's rules, "Make the enemy live up to its own book of rules."[774]

These socialist policy authors of the Cloward-Piven strategy believed that the number of welfare-eligible recipients would eventually exhaust the federal government's coffers. That would force government to reform the system, resulting in more central control and a move invariably toward a socialized system. That model proved rather potent, at least in the case of New York City, so that "by the early 1970s, one person was on the welfare rolls in New York city for every two working in the city's private economy."[775]

One can see a similar scenario playing out today as the nation sinks deeper into debt thanks to COVID-19 pandemic relief packages. There are also the harebrained ideas pushed by progressive Democrats regarding Medicare-for-All, the Green New Deal (to reduce carbon production), and a host of other extremely expensive, federal, bank-breaking strategies. Each of these ideas could significantly strain America's coffers to the point of jeopardizing its financial viability and thus forcing us to embrace a new system of government.

The election of leftist US politicians makes this strategy far more viable going forward.

Strategy #3: Taking Over a National Political Party

Another strategy is to take captive a national political party. That idea was first promoted by Cleon Skousen in his book, *The Naked Com-*

munist (1958). One of the forty-five communist goals he identifies is to "capture one or both of the political parties in the United States."[776] This would create "crises" and "revolutions" that could be used to the party's advantage, and thus transmit Marxist views to the masses. Arguably, as I developed in the last section of this book, I believe the evidence is rather conclusive that the Democratic Party is already seriously compromised by Marxists both inside and outside their ranks. The process of transmitting Marxist ideology has already begun, especially now that the Democratic Party holds the reins of power in Washington.

Strategy #4: Controlling All Communications and Public Thought

Marxists must control speech and thought in order to capture culture and, by association, politics/government. Speech control is now commonplace across America, enforced by "thought police" under the rich banner of "political correctness," arguably a tool used by Marxists to collar American institutions.[777]

Besides, as I outlined in the media chapter, the "thought police" includes much of mainstream media, Hollywood, and the social media giants—all leftists. They are aligned with the Democratic Party and are useful to Marxists in terms of silencing truth-speakers and those today who expose the left.

This strategy takes advantage of the much-discussed, very important tool: political correctness (PC). It is a tool used to classify people into groups, such as Marx's use of the terms "proletariat" (working class) and the "bourgeoisie" (the wealthy class). Some call this "identity politics," whereby some groups are identified as oppressed while others are targeted for discrimination. This was a tool used in communist China during the Cultural Revolution (1966–1976) to distinguish among the classes, such as the "Five Red Categories" (those favored by the communist regime) and the "Five Black Categories" (the enemies), a distinction between the "black" capitalists and the "red" working classes.[778]

The policy term "PC" also tends to be like a binary switch (either on or off), because only those people who are both sympathetic with the "victim" and disdain the "oppressor" are considered moral, or appropriately PC. The American categories of people who fit this PC description include the alleged racists, sexists, homophobic persons, Islamophobic people, and more.

Ultimately, PC is culturally translated as "same thinking," the true goal of Marxists. Raymond V. Raehn, an author and founder of the US Global Strategy Council, wrote, "Political Correctness seeks to impose a uniformity of thought and behavior on all Americans and is therefore totalitarian in nature."[779] Author Jeff Carlson agrees when he writes that PC "is the translation of Marxism from economic to cultural terms. And once you've changed the culture you can change the laws." Further, as Carlson writes, PC's ultimate goal is globalism (one-world government), the topic of the next chapter.[780]

PC as a tool helps the Marxist move the culture closer to the absolute control necessary for a communist state. A country is moving to a point of absolute control when it embraces legally binding "hate speech," such as public expression that targets race, sex, and sexual orientation. Then government enforces those laws across all institutions: school, work, media, and even cyberspace.[781]

Yes, such restrictions are contrary to America's First Amendment (free speech) but that's the point. Civil liberties, as outlined in the previous chapter, are out the window for Marxists, and in their place is PC speech enforced by the all-controlling government. The worst offenders of PC speech in America today are our universities, which shouldn't surprise anyone who watches the left's tyranny across the culture, but discriminating against the right is okay because the woke crowd is inherently blind to objective truth.[782]

American college campuses are the epicenter for wokeness and PC speech. Dare go against that status quo at an American college campus, and you are jeered at and/or shouted down, if not physically attacked, which is happening more every day when anyone dares to speak truth to the left's numerous lies.[783]

Let me illustrate. Ben Shapiro, a conservative commentator, frequently engages the woke left in college-based settings. In September 2017, Mr. Shapiro spoke at the University of California-Berkeley's Free Speech Week, which predictably earned him threats of violence from the leftists—so much for free speech. Subsequently, Mr. Shapiro appeared at the University of Utah. There, some students vowed to shut him down; in fact, one student said about the First Amendment right to freedom of speech: "I don't care. I don't think that's a, like, relevant document [US Constitution] right now."[784]

Political correctness is an ideological weapon meant to suppress dissent and obscure truth. It forces institutions to change in ways that make them more vulnerable to manipulation by Marxists to control speech and even the public expression of thought.[785]

Strategy #5: Controlling Language

Another aspect of that is a key tool for the left: the transformation of language. Barbara Kay, a columnist for the *National Post*, wrote:

> The most expedient and effective capture-the-culture tool is domination over language. Ideologues know that we cannot have dominion over our ideas if we do not have dominion over our words. We literally do not know what we think unless we are able to speak without self-censorship.[786]

The domination over language—what words mean—is genius, because when done properly, anarchists create uncertainty within a culture, which leads to fear about speaking freely. Ms. Kay explains, "The impulse to implant the fear [to speak] is nevertheless totalitarian." Thus, the fear to speak freely inhibits the ability to discern actual truth from ideological "truth."[787]

Consider the case of the "trans activists" who mastered the "politics of intent." Specifically, those within our population who identify their sex as opposite of their biological gender are creating for themselves an oppressed category of people, and therefore, according to Ms. Kay, their invented class for a group of people trumps "all other considerations in policy-making," which leads to more control for the left's guardians of culture.[788]

The concept is straightforward. The words "man" and "woman" may be biological realities, but when juxtaposed with psychological well-being, the later trumps the former. A biological "man" who psychologically identifies as a woman and pretends to physiologically look like a woman through dress and make-up is oppressed if you don't agree. And it's not enough even if you refer to "her" as a woman—for "her," that view must be enforced by law. Thus, self-identified gender selection earns the same legal standing as sex-based rights, a Marxist tool.

So, as explained above, the PC thing to do, the "intent," is that all people must voice their support for the lie that a "man" who self-identifies as a "woman" is indeed a "woman," no matter that biology obviously indicates otherwise. After all, in the new PC reality, the counterculture insists that we lie to use "their" pronouns in public and "as if pronouns were individual possessions, and as if compulsion to voice 'your' pronouns were commensurate with the principle of freedom of speech," explained Ms. Kay.[789]

When we refuse to conform to pronoun demands, we are confronted in a hostile manner. "Today, an evolutionary biologist who insists that human biology is dimorphic and who refuses to assent to anti-science mantras untethered to reality can see tenure denied on that basis," wrote Ms. Kay. That's why commonsense people leave academia such as Russia's Alexander Solzhenitsyn who said he refused to "live not by lies."[790]

The logical outcome of such craziness is that environments that embrace such lies are abandoned by truth tellers, and what's left are those who wholly grasp the lies, such as many students of American college campuses. A similar draconian language manipulative rule takes place within the culture regarding race, "white privilege" and other nuanced terms.

Briefly, it's important to say the obvious regarding the tragic manipulation by so-called transgenders. John F. MacArthur Jr. is the pastor of Grace Community Church in Sun Valley, California, and the chancellor emeritus of the Master's University and Seminary. On the issue of transgenders, Mr. MacArthur said, "Simply stated, there is no such thing as transgender. You're either XX or XY. That's it."[791]

He continued, saying that God made us men and women. "That is science," he said. "That is reality." Transgenderism is an assault on God, explained the pastor, and "you are something other than your biology is a cultural construct [language manipulation] intended as an assault on God."[792]

The notion of transgenderism "is a kind of personal suicide" and it is cutting oneself off from "the way God designed you." The pastor explained that a transgender person is nineteen times more likely to kill him or herself: "You have cut yourself off from reality and normal relationships."[793]

Pastor MacArthur concluded by emphasizing that we need to show love when addressing a transgendered person. The most important thing to communicate, he explained, is that "God made you. And God made you exactly the way he wanted you to be [male or female]." Further, he explained that a so-called transgendered person is "fighting God in his sovereignty" by trying to redefine himself, herself.[794]

In conclusion, these five strategies are tools American Marxists use to transform American institutions. Some are used more often than others, but together, they are a lethal collection of instruments that truly threaten America's future.

The application of these strategies could further radically transform three critical American institutions into something akin to the left's Marxists' vision: government, family, and religion. Each is addressed in the following pages.

WHAT DOES A MARXIST RESET MEAN FOR THE US GOVERNMENT?

> The purpose of government is to enable the people of a nation to live in safety and happiness. Government exists for the interests of the governed, not for the governors.[795]
>
> —Thomas Jefferson, 3rd US President

A Marxist reset of the US government must be understood in the proper context. Therefore, we begin with a review of the founding purpose of the US government.

Our founders stated the purpose of the US government in the Preamble of our Constitution, which is to "establish justice, insure domestic tranquility, provide for the common defense, promote the general welfare, and secure the blessings of liberty to ourselves and our posterity."[796]

Founder James Madison explained the background for this Preamble. He warned that government is necessary because we live in "a state of nature, where the weaker individual is not secured against the violence of the stronger." Thus, it is government's primary role to help regulate man's behavior to his fellow man.[797]

The US Constitution satisfies that aim through government's form and structure for our federal democratic republic based on three principles: inherent rights, self-government, and separation of powers. Further, a key founding objective of America's federal government is to prevent it from ever becoming oppressive, a legacy concern from our war against British tyranny. That's why our founders instituted checks and balances in our Constitution-based government granting the executive just enough power to govern while creating mechanisms to restrain that authority by the legislative and judicial branches.

Those same founders anticipated a time when government might depart from the original design, however. That's why founder Thomas Jefferson warned that "to take a single step beyond the boundaries [of the Constitution]…is to take possession of a boundless field of power."[798]

Further, founder Madison cautioned that government must "keep close to our chartered authorities."[799]

Those warnings are valid for today, because Marxists and their cousins (leftists, progressives, socialists, and communists) are taking steps well beyond those boundaries, and if not further restrained, they will completely transform our government into something radically different from what our founders intended.

Unfortunately, Marxists have already advanced their radical agenda far beyond the boundaries of our original government. Specifically, many leftists long ago and especially today work inside government, and others occupy seats in our Congress and judicial branches who use their authority to feed social unrest, divide us, undermine traditional morality, and push socialist policies—the very strategies outlined in the previous section of this chapter. Those advances are having an obvious effect.

Marxist Process for Capturing the US Government

Many of the measures outlined in Marx's *Communist Manifesto* are already implemented, as indicated in a previous chapter. The left's purpose going forward is to establish Marxist political control under the guise of whatever name might fit their fancy—liberalism, progressivism, democratic socialism, socialism, or communism...but not democracy.

There are numerous indicators of Marxist success in America's recent governmental history: a progressive income tax, centralization of credit, massive welfare programs, excessive government spending, significant government regulation of most every aspect of life, national healthcare programs (Medicare, Medicaid, Obamacare), discrimination against people of faith, and much more—all a reflection of aims attributable to Marx's ideology.

What's clear is that Marxists are mostly interested in seizing and keeping power, not in making life better for the citizens. After all, Marx and Engels said as much:

The first step in the revolution by the working class is to raise the proletariat to the position of ruling class to win the battle of democracy. The proletariat will use its political supremacy to wrest, by degree, all capital from the bourgeoisie, to central-ize all instruments of production in the hands of the State, i.e., of the proletariat organized as the ruling class; and to increase the total productive forces as rapidly as possible. Of course, in the beginning, this cannot be affected except by means of des-potic inroads on the rights of property, and on the conditions of bourgeois production; by means of measures, therefore, which appear economically insufficient and untenable, but which, in the course of the movement, outstrip themselves, necessitate further inroads upon the old social order, and are unavoidable as a means of entirely revolutionizing the mode of production.[800]

Many Americans watched over the past decades as leftists battled for control of the branches of government, at first in subtle, incremental ways, but more recently in a brazen fashion. Beginning in 2016, we saw the first credible national effort to advance a true, massive, socialist transformation. Self-identified socialist US Senator Bernie Sanders ran for the presidency, and at the time, he enjoyed credible national support. That's an alarming fact, because socialism is the "primary stage" of com-munism. Meanwhile, the level of national acceptability of socialism is quite robust, especially among young Americans, as illustrated in previ-ous chapters.

Then in 2020, the siren call of idealistic Marxism's promises, such as Marx's claim that "from each according to his ability, to each accord-ing to his need" resonated with enough Americans to grant election victories to many leftist democrats, especially Joe Biden, who ran on a progressive/socialist, big-government platform. Unfortunately, many of Biden's naïve voters fell for the communist deception, and now we must live with the consequences: leftists controlling the Congress and the presidency.[801]

We can thank our sold-out leftist educational establishment for cramming radical ideology into our youth. Many of our younger generations naïvely embraced the fantasy that life under socialism will ultimately lead to an earthly utopia, and thus they voted to install into positions of authority savvy and power-hungry, likeminded leftist politicians who are set to push a Marxist agenda.

The history of socialism (the precursor to Marx's communist society) delivers something far different than what those promoting its virtues claim today, however. American economist Milton Friedman captured the essence of the problem:

> A society that puts equality—in the sense of equality of outcome [a socialist's promise]—ahead of freedom will end up with neither equality nor freedom.... on the other hand, a society that puts freedom first will, as a happy by-product, end up with both greater freedom and greater equality.

This non-sequitur (the promises of socialism) is addressed in a previous chapter whereby then US Senator Kamala Harris publicly made the faulty argument about equity and equality of outcome.[802]

The fact is that high-welfare socialist programs—forced give-away programs—grow big government and rob citizens of their freedoms, a key Marxist goal. We know from history that governments that transition to socialism inevitably abandon freedom thanks to their socialist leaders' predictable turn to totalitarianism. After all, socialism demands the elimination of private property and democratic processes, and the only way that can happen for a free people is through tyranny.

The US government has embraced elements of Marxism over the past decades, and, given the election of Mr. Biden and a Democratic Party-controlled Congress, the country will inevitably continue to move in a Marxist direction until such time as America is something akin to the former Soviet Union or the citizens turn the current momentum away from the fast-approaching ideological cliff.

WHAT DOES A MARXIST RESET MEAN FOR OUR FAITH COMMUNITIES?

Religion…is the opium of the masses.[803]

—Karl Marx

Perhaps Marx's most famous line is *"Die Religion…ist das Opium des Volkes,"* which is translated, "Religion…is the opiate of the masses." That quote originates with Marx's *Critique of Hegel's Philosophy of Right.* The full quote is more helpful: "Religion is the sigh of the oppressed creature, the heart of a heartless world, and the soul of soulless conditions. It is the opium of the people."[804]

What did Marx mean by this metaphor? He refers to organized religion in this quote, which provides the believer with practical functions similar to that provided by a drug that reduces pain (analgesic) and provides strength to keep living. Marx considered religion harmful in this context, because it prevented people from realizing the class structure and associated oppression around them, thus it could prevent the socialist revolution, the aim of his ideology.[805]

For Marx, the problem with religion is that it may strengthen the will to live, but it doesn't necessarily address the physical injury, the pain and suffering, especially the underlying cause of that pain. Rather, religion for Marx helps man forget why he is suffering and projects him to an imaginary future (heaven) where there is no pain. Thus, the allegation is the "drug" (religion) is administered by the same oppressors (the capitalists) who are responsible for the pain in the first place. Create a society with conditions that remove that pain and suffering, and the need for religion will cease—a religion-free, Marxist utopia.[806]

The challenge for a Marxist is removing religion's influence from a society.

That's quite an undertaking, especially in America, where most citizens believe in a deity and pray regularly, and where half attend religious services at least monthly. They tend to view religion as very personal.

However, religion as a social institution is important in a broader sense, because it helps society understand the meaning and purpose of life, which governs the principles and values that provide a nation's foundation. Marx would replace that influence with his ideology.

So, in order to capture America, Marxists must completely destroy—"reset"—religion's influence, which is why the subversion of it is such an important goal outlined in *The Communist Manifesto*. Further, earlier in this volume, I addressed Marx's personal motivation and indicated that many of those who knew him best considered him an evil person who was often referred to as demonic—arguably a follower of Satan. No wonder he advocated atheism, but critically, he understood that his advocacy of communism required the abandonment of religion. That is why he once said, "Communism begins from the outset of atheism."[807]

To make Marx's ideology function, there must be no god (deity) for the people to depend upon. That view was embraced by the Soviet leader Vladimir Lenin, who used the machinery of state (the Soviet Union) to begin a campaign to eliminate all religion in order for the Marxist revolution to succeed.

Lenin's attack on religion used high-pressure tactics to oppress all faiths in order to force people to abandon God. From the start, he passed a resolution that ordered the confiscation of all valuables from churches and religious institutions "with ruthless resolution, leaving nothing in doubt, and in the very shortest time." The resolution continued:

> The greater the number of representatives of the reactionary clergy and the reactionary bourgeoisie that we succeed in shooting on this occasion, the better because this "audience" must precisely now be taught a lesson in such a way that they will not dare to think about any resistance whatsoever for several decades.[808]

Soviet dictator Joseph Stalin, who ruled the Soviet Union from 1929 to 1953, picked up where Lenin left off to pursue a campaign to eliminate all religion in communist Russia. Stalin launched a Five-Year Plan of Atheism with the goal of closing all churches and ending with the Soviet Union embracing communist atheism. Although he wasn't completely successful, Stalin by 1941 reduced the number of orthodox churches from 46,000 before the revolution to 4,225 after it. Further, 95 percent of all orthodox monasteries were destroyed, and most of the religious elite were either in gulags or executed.[809]

The Soviets also exported their anti-religious strategy to occupied Eastern European countries. Bulgarian historian Momchil Metodiev, after extensive research into the Cold War-era archives of the Bulgarian Communist Party, exposed the fact that the Eastern European communist intelligence network closely collaborated with the party's religious committees to influence and infiltrate international religious organizations, and copy Stalin's "atheism" strategy.[810]

Similarly, the same type of communist anti-religious tyranny is evident in modern communist China even today. Consider two recent examples of anti-religious persecution.

A top-secret communist Chinese government document obtained by the *Epoch Times* confirms that the Beijing regime abuses its judicial system to commit genocide against a religious group. The Falun Gong is a spiritual meditation practice that focuses on truthfulness, compassion, and tolerance. In July 1999, China's then-communist leader Jiang Zemin launched a persecution campaign that called for detaining, torturing, and murdering members of that spiritual group. That campaign continues to this day.[811]

Communist China persecutes other religious groups, especially Christians who are not properly registered with the state. On December 9, 2018, Chinese communists raided a Sunday service at the Early Rain Covenant Church, Chengdu, Sichuan Province, taking more than five hundred worshippers into custody. The raid by more than two thousand police officers that became known as the "129 Crackdown," included the arrest of the pastor, Wang Yi, who was charged with "inciting subversion of state power," and, if convicted, could face up to fifteen years in prison.[812]

One might expect the anti-religious persecution to be worst in communist regimes. However, Marxists also target religious believers in America. They use money and spies to infiltrate religious institutions under the pretext of "religious exchange," and their rationale is to introduce Marxist concepts into religious teachings.

In the US, Marxists infiltrated Christian churches and seminaries with the objective of influencing the faith groups throughout the country. Back in 1953, the US House of Representatives' Committee on un-American Activities heard testimony from Manning Johnson, a high-level Communist Party member. Johnson testified:

> Once the tactic of infiltrating religious organizations was set by the Kremlin, the actual mechanics of implementing the "new line" was a question of following the general experiences of the living church movement in Russia, where the Communists discovered that the destruction of religion could proceed much faster through infiltration of the church by Communist agents operating within the church itself....
>
> In general, the idea was to divert the emphasis of clerical thinking from the spiritual to the material and political—by political, of course, is meant politics based on the Communist doctrine of conquest of power. Instead of emphasis towards the spiritual and matters of the soul, the new and heavy emphasis was to deal with those matters which, in the main, led toward the Communist program of "immediate demands." These social demands, of course, were of such a nature that to fight for them would tend to weaken our present society and prepare it for final conquest by Communist forces.[813]

Not surprising to many Christians is the fact that the World Council of Churches (WCC) was long ago compromised by communists. Unveiled KGB (Russian secret police) documents indicate that Cambridge University professor and historian Christopher Andrew wrote that during the Cold War, communist agents held seats on the WCC central committee. In 1989, KGB files showed that these agents ensured the WCC-issued public statements that aligned with socialism. Further, in 1975, Russian orthodox bishop Nikodim, a Communist Party agent, was elected to be one of the WCC's six presidents.[814]

Meanwhile in the US, the "separation of church and state" argument often made by the left and the more contemporary tool of "political correctness" are both used to marginalize believers and their religious institutions, which advances the Marxists' anti-religion agenda. Thus, when Bible-believing people speak out of conviction against issues like abortion and homosexuality, they are roundly attacked by leftists, who make them the objects of derision using these faux blunt tools to diminish the influence of religion on society. Do that enough over an extended period of years, and the broader culture begins to believe the lies, which happened.

There are many examples of the leftists aggressively attacking religious people for exercising their faith-based freedom of religion to address any issue from a biblical position. Even in secular schools, leftists prohibit people of faith from expressing their contrary views informed by the Bible. Teachers are not to speak of Creation (just Darwin's flawed theory of evolution), and any mention of God, much less prayer, is strictly forbidden. This is evidence of the Marxists' influence across our culture.

Not surprisingly, Marxists seek to create religious chaos, one of the forty-five goals for communists trying to destroy the US, according to *The Naked Communist* (1958). The twenty-seventh goal on that list states: "Infiltrate the churches and replace revealed religion with 'social' religion. Discredit the Bible." That's exactly what Marxists and their allies have done and continue to do.[815]

Unfortunately, America's faith community has lost much of its past influence, thanks to the disobedience of many believers to recognize and confront apostasy, but also due to Marxists' influence. Communists have infiltrated and altered many American religious groups (churches, Christian colleges, seminaries), resulting in new denominations, which alter fundamental principles and concepts that more often than not end up denying clear biblical teaching and promoting radical Marxist ideology.

The impact of Marxism within the religious institution is predictable. Americans see a waning, faith-based influence on their lives that, given time and cultural encouragement, could inevitably lead to agnosticism or outright atheism. Consequently, many Americans end up abandoning their faith. And if man does not believe, the divine will not protect him, and, ultimately, humankind will be destroyed. Then the Marxists' objective is satisfied: God is expunged from society, which becomes ripe for humanist (read "Marxist") manipulation.

Marxists not only infiltrate American religious groups (churches and affiliated colleges, seminaries, etc.) to gain a foothold for their radical ideology, but they also use the courts and public policy to attack people of faith—all part of a broader strategy to expunge religion from our society.

Conservative author David Horowitz, in his 2019 book, *Dark Agenda: The War to Destroy Christian America*, provides evidence of the rising attacks on Christians and their beliefs, which threatens all Americans and more broadly our society. Mr. Horowitz argues that American progressives seek to overthrow American society; they view it as a system of oppressive hierarchies based on such issues as race and sexual orientation. He said this "collectivist ideology, rooted in Marxism, is opposed to the American ideas of individual rights, individual accountability, and individual equality."[816]

Some of the attacks on Christian America include the Supreme Court's interpretive approach to the Constitution. Horowitz discusses a number of cases, such as the *Engel v. Vitale*, 370 U.S. 421 (1962) case that challenged the role of religion in schools. The High Court in that case ruled that voluntary prayer in public schools violated the US

Constitution's First Amendment prohibition of a state establishment of religion. He called that decision "the creation of a 'constitutional right' that never existed. There is no right for a nonbelieving minority to deny the majority of Americans their right to express their belief in god [sic] while in school."[817]

The Supreme Court also struck down a law that prohibited birth control because it violated the right to marital privacy. Mr. Horowitz argues that in the *Griswold v. Connecticut*, 381 U.S. 479 (1965) case, the Constitution does not provide the right to privacy, but once again the High Court created a new right (access to birth control) in the law.[818]

President Barack Obama showed his radical progressive ideology when he issued a federal mandate as part of the Affordable Care Act (Obamacare), which required employers to provide all FDA-approved contraceptives in their health insurance plans. A Catholic charity, the Little Sisters of the Poor, said Obama's mandate violated their religious convictions. Besides, these celibate nuns served the elderly and had no rational reason to comply with the mandate. In 2020, the High Court agreed with the sisters, that Obamacare exempts nonprofit religious organizations from complying with the mandate, which upheld their First Amendment religious liberty argument.[819]

My 2020 book, *Collision Course: The Fight to Reclaim Our Moral Compass before It's Too Late*, identifies numerous anti-Christian groups doing much the same as Marxists are doing across our society. Those culprits are mostly identified in earlier chapters as Marxist proxies that attack Christianity: Satan and his army of demons, mainstream media, and various nonprofit associations and corporations.

No doubt, Marxists are enjoying significant success using government and cultural tools (media, education, nonprofits, legal groups) to expunge from our society the institution of religion so that America abandons God and embraces atheism, the big totalitarian state, as their god.

WHAT DOES A MARXIST RESET MEAN FOR
AMERICAN FAMILIES?

The only rock I know that stays steady, the only institution I
know that works is the family.
—Lee Iacocca (1924–2019), American businessman

The family is the building block of society, a concept defined in the
Bible: "Therefore a man shall leave his father and his mother and hold
fast to his wife, and they shall become one flesh" (Genesis 2:24, ESV).
This text establishes marriage by one man and one woman becoming
"one flesh," and then they obey God's command to "be fruitful and
increase in number; fill the earth and subdue it" (Genesis 1:28, NIV) to
establish a family.

The family is at the heart of civil law, defining and regulating the
marriage relationship. It is the nucleus of civilization, the basic unit of
society, a critical part of all cultures and religions. It is the source of both
meeting our physical needs—food, water, shelter—and our psychological needs for affection, appreciation, a sense of belonging, and love. Further, it prepares us for life by teaching us how to survive and prosper in
society, while preserving our heritage and morality.

Much of the material that follows regarding Marxism is from a book
by the *Epoch Times*' editorial staff, *How the Specter of Communism Is Ruling Our World*, specifically chapter seven on the family.[820]

Marx hated the traditional family because he considered it a form of
private ownership, which he wanted to destroy. The individual's love and
devotion must be for the Communist Party, according to Marx, not for
one's parents, spouse, or children. Therefore, that ideological decision
requires Marxists to capture the American culture, especially the institution of the family, by promoting a host of attacks using anti-traditional
(mostly anti-Christian), Marxist-inspired movements: feminism, sexual
liberation, "gay" rights, and more. These radical movement attacks on

the institution of family use ideological concepts such as equality and emancipation to distort the God-ordained bonds between the sexes, to corrupt our children, and to drag humanity into the moral gutter.

These social assaults on the family are infused with Marxist ideological factors. For example, Marx's partner, Friedrich Engels, called for widespread "unconstrained sexual intercourse," a tool for accelerating the dissolution of traditional monogamous marriage, the elimination of the family unit as a key social institution.[821]

Part of that campaign against the family came about thanks to government-passed laws that made it easier to gain a divorce. In the US, that amoral avalanche started with no-fault divorce law in California (1969). Soon, we found widespread divorce and, partly as a consequence, a significant number of out-of-wedlock births, which quickly accounted for almost half of all newborns.[822]

Soon, sex outside of marriage became the norm, whereby once it was considered shameful—a sin. Today, however, sex outside of marriage is normalized and, in some cases, encouraged by our leftist educational establishment and certainly by mainstream media. In fact, Hollywood and social media hypersexualize our children and expose them to deviant sexual behaviors that contribute to the destruction of traditional morality and, by association, marriage and the family.

Marxism also aims to destroy the traditional family by blurring Western traditional religious beliefs about the roles of the sexes—men working outside the home to earn support for the family, while the wife tends to the home and children. Marxist attempts to alter this arrangement run counter to God's design and prevent both sexes from fulfilling their potential, but those ideas long ago died with the Marxist-inspired sexual liberation movement.

The fact is that Marxists believe that the private, exclusive family unit undermines human liberation, an economic unit that must be revolutionized into a form of public ownership. Specifically, Marxists believe that the patriarchy of traditional families oppresses women and traditional sexual morality represses mankind. Therefore, those aspects of culture must be eliminated and Marxist revolutionaries long ago set out to replace those conventions with their own radical, anti-biblical ideas.

To that point, Marxists promote promiscuity to undermine the family, to force mankind to abandon private relationships in order to realize their "utopian" society. One such early effort came about in 1825, thanks to socialist Robert Owen, who established such an amoral model "society" in New Harmony, Indiana. Owen wrote:

> I now declare, to you and to the world, that Man, up to this hour, has been, in all parts of the earth, a slave to a Trinity of the most monstrous evils that could be combined to inflict mental and physical evil upon his whole race. I refer to private, or individual property—absurd and irrational systems of religion—and marriage, founded on individual property combined with some one of these irrational systems of religion.

Although Mr. Owen's "utopian" experiment quickly failed, the concept lived on.[823]

French philosopher Charles Fournier (1772–1837) evidently influenced Marx's thinking about the necessity of dissolving the family for society's best interests. At the time, Fourier's influence was behind the concept of "feminism," and his ideal communist society opposed traditional family while favoring bacchanals (wild and drunken revelry) and orgies. He also called for society to care for those sexually rejected to make certain they have the right to sexual gratification, which included sadomasochism ("giving and receiving of pleasure from acts involving the receipt or infliction of pain and humiliation"),[824] incest ("sexual intercourse between closely related persons"),[825] and bestiality ("sexual relations between a person and an animal"),[826] with the caveat that it was consensual.

Evidently, Owen and Fourier influenced the start of the Marxists-influenced, anything-goes, "utopian" communes in nineteenth-century United States. The longest-running such group was the Oneida Commune, near Oneida, New York. It lasted thirty-three years (1848–1881), while abandoning traditional marriage for polygamy, group sex, and selective breeding. The commune's founder, John Noyes, later wrote *Bible Communism*, which advanced the view that Jesus Christ returned in AD 70, "making it possible for them [Noyes' followers] to bring about Jesus' millennial kingdom themselves, and be free of sin and perfect in this world."[827]

As we've indicated previously, Marxist ideology rejects religion and all moral restraints, and encourages base urges, such as that described above. It teaches that if men abandon private property and exclusive (private) relationships like monogamous marriage that then becomes public, then there will no longer be societal friction. This amoral, anti-biblical view of human relationships led to Marxists' open advocacy of promiscuity and "free love," something that became popular during the 1960s in America.

Evidently the idea of common wives—at so-called utopian communes like Oneida—failed, an idea found in *Communist Manifesto*. However, even though it failed, that didn't deter Marx and Engels from their anti-family goal. Rather, they refocused their attention on marriage as an instrument of oppression.

In 1884, Engels published a book, *The Origin of the Family, Private Property, and the State: In the Light of the Researches of Lewis H. Morgan*, which was based on material from both Marx and Lewis H. Morgan's book, *Ancient Society* (1877), which addressed family economics. In that volume, Engels expressed a new view on marriage:

> [The emergence of monogamy] is based on the supremacy of the man, the express purpose being to produce children of undisputed paternity; such paternity is demanded because these children are later to come into their father's property as his natural heirs. It is distinguished from pairing marriage by the much greater strength of the marriage tie, which can no longer be dissolved at either partner's wish. As a rule, it is now only the man who can dissolve it, and put away his wife.[828]

Mr. Engels went much further to argue that monogamy is based on the view that the married spouse is private property. However, he rationalized that once all property is shared in a Marxist utopian society, there will emerge a new marriage model based on "sexual love." Then, this evil man boasts that in a utopian communist society, all property becomes public (no monogamous relationships defined by marriage), thus unrestrained sexual intercourse, housework is professionalized, and childcare is a state responsibility. Engels continued:

> This removes all the anxiety about the "consequences," which today is the most essential social—moral as well as economic— factor that prevents a girl from giving herself completely to the man she loves. Will not that suffice to bring about the gradual growth of unconstrained sexual intercourse and with it a more tolerant public opinion in regard to a maiden's honor and a woman's shame?[829]

These bankrupt ideas about morality fail because feelings are unreliable. "Without traditional norms of courtship and marriage, the inevitable result is sexual promiscuity and the breakdown of social order," writes the *Epoch Times*. This view led to very serious societal problems for Marxist-inspired regimes.[830]

Early efforts by communist regimes like the Soviet Union to implement Marxian ideology to turn love and family into instruments of state power failed. The view that turning love and family into state instruments was based on Marx's and Engels' personal views and evidently was a reflection of their own behavior. Both men engaged in rank immoral behavior—rape, cohabiting, employing prostitutes—which might explain their aberrant ideology, and besides, their ideology is evidently demonically inspired, as outlined in a previous chapter, but did influence the practice of some of their most loyal adherents like Lenin, Trotsky, and Stalin.

Prior to the Russian Revolution, Trotsky wrote a letter to Lenin (1911):

Undoubtedly, sexual oppression is the main means of enslaving a person. While such oppression exists, there can be no question of real freedom. The family, like a bourgeois institution, has completely outlived itself. It is necessary to speak more about this to the workers. [831]

Predictably, Lenin replied:

And not only the family. All prohibitions relating to sexuality must be abolished.... We have something to learn from the suffragettes: Even the ban on same-sex love should be lifted. [832]

Once the Bolsheviks seized power in 1917, they instituted the practice of wife-sharing, an aspect of Lenin's view about abolishing sexual prohibitions. Evidently, the Soviet Union from its inception was very much a pioneer of sexual liberation until the time of the fall of that regime in 1991. A Soviet-run Russian magazine at the time, *Rodina* (translated "Motherland"), published an article about wife-sharing that described some key leaders saying that they were "as casual as dogs" regarding sexual activities. Leaders like Lenin excused such amoral behavior by stating that sexual "lust can emancipate the energy of the spirit; not for pseudo-family values, but for the victory of socialism must this blood-clot be done away with." [833]

That's quite a statement. So, according to Lenin, promiscuity is a victory for socialism, the precursor to communism—everyone, so goes the thinking, should be "as casual as dogs" regarding sexual activities.

The early twentieth-century Bolsheviks promoted sexual promiscuity with the slogan, "Down with shame!" This slogan became a psychological tool used to justify abolishing marriage and decriminalizing homosexuality to create the "new man." Some Bolsheviks swallowed the concept so completely that they ran naked through the streets screaming slogans like, "Shame is in the bourgeois past of the Soviet people." [834]

Early in the Soviet Union's life (1920s), the former People's Commissar for Social Welfare, Alexandra Kollontai, promoted a similar sick theory about sexuality known as the "glass of water." Her theory was an allusion to sexual indulgence that held that in a communist society, satisfying sexual urges should be as easy as drinking a glass of water. Evidently, the theory was quickly embraced by the country's teenagers with overactive libidos.[835]

The newspaper *Pravda* published an article in 1925 about the results of the "glass of water" theory. "The current morality of our youth is summarized as follows," wrote communist Madame Smidovich. "Every member, even a minor, of the Communist Youth League and every student of the Rabfak [Communist Party training school] has the right to satisfy his sexual desire. This concept has become an axiom, and abstinence is considered a bourgeois notion. If a man lusts after a young girl, whether she is a student, a worker, or even a school-age girl, then the girl must obey his lust; otherwise, she will be considered a bourgeois daughter, unworthy to be called a true communist."[836]

Another communist effort to destroy marriage was to normalize divorce. Paul Kengor wrote in his 2015 book *Takedown: From Communists to Progressives, How the Left Has Sabotaged Family and Marriage*, "The divorce rate skyrocketed [in the Soviet Union] to levels unseen in human history. In short order, it seemed as though everyone in Moscow had a divorce."[837]

The Soviet communists also experimented with the phenomenon known as "Swedish families," where many men and women live together and engage in casual sex, a take-off on the nineteenth-century Oneida Commune. The consequences of this anti-family experiment were predictable: broken families, significant cases of sexually transmitted diseases, rape, and moral collapse.[838]

A version of "Swedish families" was known as the "socialization" of women whereby, for example, after the Bolsheviks seized a city during the 1917 revolution, they would collect young women and force them to "socialize" with the Red Army soldiers.[839]

Eventually, even the amoral Soviet communists stopped the "glass of water" practices because of the consequences, such as the influx of unwanted babies. In time, the regime demanded that women return to the traditional role of mother to produce more children and raise them to become good communists.

MARXISTS TURN PERVERTED SEXUAL IDEAS ON WESTERN FAMILIES

The history of Marxist sexual perversions is important to appreciate so to better understand how the proponents of that sick ideology infiltrated the US to begin the destruction of the American family. That transformation came to the fore in the Vietnam era, the 1960s.

The 1960s were marked by great cultural tension, not just because of the Vietnam War and the related conscription (military draft). Mixed into the cultural milieu at the time were Marxist ideas such as feminism and the sexual revolution. This phalanx of immoral, anti-Christian ideologies had a very negative impact on traditional values and our social fabric, especially with regard to issues of family and sexual mores. The turmoil hosted many aberrant outcomes: proliferation of pornography, drug abuse, implosion of sexual morality, a surge in juvenile crime, abortion on demand, and a significant increase in Americans on the welfare rolls due to out of wedlock births.

Each of these issues had consequences for the culture and the American family. Thus, the emergence of the "free love" movement, adopted by the 1960s-era youth culture, was described as "the ultimate rejection of capitalist culture," a Marxist aim that led to the further erosion of traditional family values. Disturbingly, the religious-based social stigma of sex outside of marriage waned when the government washed its hands of its former role to protect biblical marriage, as well as to discourage abortion and adultery.[840]

This Marxist-inspired free-love movement also propelled the rise in pornographic media as more acceptable, and the portrayal of sex outside of marriage as socially tolerable. About the same time, the term "sexual revolution" made its debut, which is attributed to Wilhelm Reich, the Austrian founder of communist psychoanalysis, which combined Marxism and Sigmund Freud's sex-focused psychoanalysis, that espoused the view that while Marxism liberated people from "economic oppression," the latter idea freed people from "sexual repression," evidently something akin to the views embraced by early ideologues like Lenin and Stalin that pushed "the glass of water" theory.

It isn't surprising that such sexual "liberation" brought about some truly bankrupt thinking in the US culture. An agent of that amoral thinking was Alfred Kinsey (1894–1956), an American sexologist who wrote two books, *Sexual Behavior in the Human Male* and *Sexual Behavior in the Human Female*, which promoted the craven concepts of extramarital sex, homosexual sex, and pedophilia (sex with children). He advocated the normalization of such ideas across the culture, and today he is best known for his support for the normalization of homosexuality.[841]

Marxism has a very amoral history when it comes to the family. It seeks the complete destruction of what God created (marriage and family) and to replace it with relationships that only serve the communist state. Of course, the Soviets came to the conclusion that replacing monogamous, private marriage relationships with public, free-sex relationships inevitably fails and results in terrible social consequences. Unfortunately, Western Marxists are more than willing to follow the same bankrupt path hoping to utterly destroy America's institution of family.

CONCLUSION

Marxists must reset America's key institutions if ever it succeeds in taking this country captive. However, taking captive our key institutions is a long process and, fortunately for them, their efforts over multiple decades have been relatively successful regarding our education establishment and mainstream media. Now, they are wrestling with God-fearing American patriots to reset the three remaining critical institutions: our federal government, faith communities, and our families.

This chapter identified five strategies Marxists use to reset American institutions to favor their ideological aim. Now that the US government is under the leadership of leftist President Joe Biden and a Democratic Party-controlled Congress, arguably heavily influenced by Marxists, the outlook for preserving our critical institutions isn't promising.

The next chapter addresses the potential for the current situation to actually get worse. One-world government under a totalitarian, globalist, Marxist regime is possible, the topic threatening every nation, and possibly a sign that we are indeed in the prophetic end times.

11

Marxists' Great Reset for One-World Government

The "elite" left's Great Reset of the world is supportive of the Marxists' efforts to trash our civil liberties (chapter 9) and capture our key institutions (chapter 10) in order to transform America and by extension all of human government. I argue in those chapters that the Biden administration is being used as a vehicle to advance that agenda as well. However, the true outcome of the proposed global Great Reset is a Marxist-controlled, one-world government that could be led by the communist totalitarians in Beijing.

Let's follow the logic of this allegation. To reach that conclusion, we must answer three questions: Is the proposed Great Reset a Marxist initiative? Is the Great Reset intended to lead to a one-world government? Finally, is China poised to use the Great Reset as a tool to dominate a future one-world government?

I firmly believe the answer to each question is "yes." So, if the allegation is true, then that conclusion prepares us to consider the fourth section of *Give Me Liberty, Not Marxism*, which addresses the prophetic implications and what, if anything, we might do to sidestep that outcome.

IS THE PROPOSED GREAT RESET
A MARXIST INITIATIVE?

There is reason to believe the proposed, Biden-supported Great Reset is in fact a Marxist-like initiative. President Biden's spokesman for such issues is former President Barack Obama's Secretary of State John Kerry, who told the 2020 World Economic Forum (WEF) that the Biden administration will use the globalist Great Reset proposal to transform the world's economy. Part of that "transformation" includes rejoining the Paris Climate Accord, which targets private industries and places global actors in an oversight position—a clear anti-capitalist move, one Karl Marx would approve. That was done by executive order the first week of the Biden administration.[842]

In September 2020, Canadian Prime Minister Justin Trudeau called for a similar Great Reset when he spoke to the United Nations (UN) General Assembly. Mr. Trudeau called on the UN to use the COVID-19 pandemic as an "opportunity for reset," a chance to "accelerate our pre-pandemic efforts to reimagine economic systems [read capitalism] that actually address global challenges like extreme poverty, inequality, and climate change." What does Trudeau mean by "reimagine economic systems?"[843]

Brietbart editor James Delingpole explained how this Great Reset could "reimagine economic systems." He describes it as a plan to install "unelected global bureaucrats" like those at the UN to abolish money, private property and democracy—all part of an effort to create a "new world order" and a Marxist anti-private property, totalitarian, and anti-capitalist outcome.[844]

Both what Kerry and Trudeau said are an assault on capitalism and freedom, and ultimately will require the strong arm of a global totalitarian government to make it happen. We are being set up for such a Marxist-like government. In fact, "the Biden administration will focus on every sector of the American economy," explained Kerry. "There will be a 2035 goal to achieve net neutrality [on carbon production] with respect to power and production." That can only happen through draconian measures from a totalitarian-like government that strains out capitalism to transform entire private industries to some form of centralized control.[845]

Klaus Schwab, the founder and executive chairman of WEF echoed what Kerry and Trudeau favor—a Great Reset. Mr. Schwab explained that "to achieve a better outcome, the world must act jointly and swiftly to revamp all aspects of our societies and economies, from education to social contracts and working conditions." That is a Marxist-like statement that requires the surrender of the control of virtually every aspect of our lives, particularly our liberties and private property ownership, to some to-be-determined global entity.[846]

That all-inclusive statement means every nation. Mr. Klaus said, "Every country, from the United States to China, must participate, and every industry, from oil and gas to tech, must be transformed. In short, we need a 'Great Reset' of capitalism." There is no doubt that the elites' Great Reset is a frontal attack on capitalism as well as on most every aspect of life with the intent to level the playing field—a Marxist idea—whereby a to-be-determined global power dictates outcomes for all countries and puts national sovereignty in the waste can.

Mr. Trudeau's recommendation is similar to that presented by Mr. Schwab, who offered a plan (introduced earlier in this section) to enhance economic growth. These gentlemen are joined by another inspiring (not) leader, Britain's Prince Charles, who embraces the Great Reset as a tool to advance global socialist policies such as wealth tax and sweeping green initiatives like the Green New Deal aimed at curtailing free markets, capitalism.[847]

It isn't surprising that the European Commission president, Ursula von der Leyen, joined the WEF president's call to globally neuter capitalism in order to level the playing field of life. Further, Ms. Leyen said the Biden administration will collaborate with the European Union on a major effort, which is to write "a new rulebook for the digital economy and the digital society." What does that mean? It means George Orwell's

"Big Brother" is among us. Ms. Leyen explained that this "rulebook" will cover everything from data to infrastructure to taxation. "So, ladies and gentlemen," globalist Ms. Leyen said, "the need for global cooperation and this acceleration of change will both be drivers of the Great Reset. And I see this as an unprecedented opportunity."[848]

The fact is that the only governance model that grants enough power to compel nations to surrender their sovereignty to a global entity is Marxism. After all, Marxism (especially the most intrusive franchise, communism) prioritizes the "functioning of the collective over the sanctity of the individual and justifies curtailment of individual freedom for the benefit of the 'greater good.'" That's true tyranny and what is necessary for the proposed Great Reset to work![849]

This outcome isn't a contradiction in terms, either. You must appreciate that globalists harness capitalism as a vehicle that can actually favor a Marxist outcome. After all, Marxism describes the world as driven by the capitalist system, through political elites—the bourgeoisie—who dominate the proletariat—the working classes. Thus, the elites control the production of the workers, a situation that confers inequality at the global level. Thus, according to Marx, revolution must subvert this established system to make the world more just.[850]

So how does globalism that is fueled by capitalism support Marxism? That's simple. Marxism calls for the centralized control over all the means of economic production. So, when globalists establish a host of intergovernmental organizations and treaties such as the General Agreement on Tariffs and Trade (GATT), the World Trade Organization (WTO) and the World Bank across most nations, then all sovereign states are forced to become part of a global market that favors a more centralized, regulated economy across the world. That is a major step toward a Marxist model.[851]

Therefore, as odd as it may sound, capitalism is the mechanism that can produce global Marxism overseen by the elite. Now, keep in mind that the Marxist model of governance is the only approach that could work in a global setting. After all, it relies "on mankind's ability to manipulate the environment and social structure according to a theo-retically pragmatic but incomplete view of the world, one that is only interested in the supremacy of the collective [read 'the Marxist ideal']."[852]

This horrendous and frightening approach could put the globalists elite in position to govern the entire world, except it is doomed from the start. Remember, Marxism on any scale has never worked and given the nature of mankind, will never deliver the often-promised "utopian" outcome. Rather, any global, Marxist Great Reset is not an opiate for what ails the world, but will push the countries across this globe in a direction that redefines rights, institutions, and sovereignty, and in its place delivers tyranny and deprivation. It could potentially lead to a true World War III as men rise up to resist or alternatively a one-world, com-munistic government, worse than the failed former Soviet Union.

One aspect of the Great Reset that is seldom examined is the fact that this is a harebrained idea generated by intellectuals, the so-called elite such as those identified above (Schwab, Trudeau, Charles) who really believe they are special, gifts to a corrupted world. They seek to reshape (reset) the discourse of global institutions like the UN, where value neutrality reigns supreme and, when given the power, they will fall back on Marxist ideas about equality and equity, except for themselves.

The idea that global intellectuals pushing the Great Reset are high on themselves isn't original with me. Raymond Aron said in his book, *The Opium of the Intellectuals*, that Marxism is the opium of the intel-lectual, a wordplay on Marx's infamous statement that "Religion…is the opiate of the people." Mr. Aron explains that Western intellectuals "retain an affection for Marxism despite its historical record for totalitar-ian rule, mass violence, suppression of liberty, and abject poverty."[853]

The reality is the so-called Great Reset advocated for by mostly Western "intellectuals" is both Marxist and by association a power grab by those same elite, not all that different from what happened with the 1917 Bolshevik Revolution but on a much grander and nuanced scale. These elite could care less about the impact this effort has on the climate, the average person's civil liberties, or the sovereignty for any country—especially the United States.

So, I conclude that the Great Reset is in fact a Marxist initiative. But could it necessarily lead to a one-world government?

IS GREAT RESET INTENDED TO LEAD TO A ONE-WORLD GOVERNMENT?

The Great Reset is a Marxist idea that harnesses globalism that could lead to one-world government. The evidence of that view is found in history by which globalists seek the formation of a coming single power, global rule. Just what are the tools for that formation, and what might that government become for the citizens? I will answer each of those three questions in this section.

Marxism and its franchise, communism, is ultimately the globalists' goal for governance that seeks to persuade the proletariat, the global citizenry (workers), to surrender their rights and privileges in exchange for the security the elites promise.

It is important at this point not to confuse the terms "globalization" and "globalism." "Globalization" is an economic process that results in increased economic integration of national economies marked by the unfettered cross-border movement of goods, services, technologies and capital—a term for global capitalism.

By contrast, "globalism" is not about trade, commerce, but about governance. It is the global rule of law by which nations cede their authority to a supranational jurisdiction. That supranational government could have limited authority over a few sectors of society, or it could become an all-encompassing global government with unlimited power.

There are many among America's so-called elite who are totalitarian and deep-state globalists who see the proposed Great Reset as an opportunity to put in place a Marxist-feudalistic future, one to solve the many daunting problems facing mankind: pandemics, violence, racism, economic distress, and much more.

Globalists elite across the world who called for one-world government reach back at least a century, and they were never shy about their goal.

DO GLOBALISTS REALLY SEEK A ONE-WORLD GOVERNMENT?

The concept of one-world government requires a review of the history of supranational organizations, their genesis, and their demise.

The early supranational, international organizations were limited in scope and served common purposes that did not infringe on national sovereignty—for example, the concept of global governance, international organizations that consolidate nation-state authority started in the late nineteenth century with the formation of the International Telecommunication Union (1865) and the Universal Postal Union (1874). Both organizations are now special agencies under the banner of the United Nations.[854]

At the turn of the twentieth century, the International Peace Conference was held in The Hague, Netherlands, with the intent of settling crises peacefully and to codify rules for warfare. Eventually that effort resulted in the establishment of the Permanent Court of Arbitration (1902), not a court per se, but an arbitral tribunal to resolve disputes over international agreements such as maritime boundaries between member states.[855]

The Treaty of Versailles (1919), which brought World War I to an end, also created the League of Nations, the forerunner of the United Nations, "to promote international cooperation and to achieve peace and security." The intent was to not repeat the "war to end all wars," aka the First World War (1914–1918), but the US never embraced the League. Eventually, the globalist League of Nations ceased to exist when it failed to prevent the Second World War.[856]

Many Americans called for globalist outcomes, especially thanks to the global events associated with World War II. For example, Wendell Willkie challenged President Franklin D. Roosevelt for the presidency in 1940. In 1943, Mr. Willkie published his book *One World,* which was a travelogue of sorts that described his round-the-world trip wherein he argued for the nations of the world to embrace a single world order, something akin to one-world government. He wanted something much more than what became the United Nations; rather, he wanted world government based on the so-called Atlantic Charter.

The Atlantic Charter was a statement issued in 1941 that set out American and British goals for the world after the Second War. Its aims included: no territorial aggrandizement, no territorial changes, restoration of self-government, reduction in trade restrictions, global cooperation, freedom from fear, freedom of the seas, abandonment of the use of force, and disarmament of aggressor nations. The Charter became the basis for the modern United Nations, the formation of the North Atlantic Treaty Organization, and the General Agreement on Tariffs and Trade (GATT).[857]

Eleanor Roosevelt, the former First Lady, had much the same idea as Mr. Willkie. She called for the creation of a new world founded on American notions of rights and freedoms. She wrote an op-ed in 1945 that called for a globalist outcome in the post-World War II era. "Willy-nilly," Ms. Roosevelt wrote, "everyone [sic] of us cares more for his own country than for any other. That is human nature. We love the bit of land where we have grown to maturity and known the joys and sorrows of life. The time has come however when we must recognize that our mutual [sic] devotion to our own land must never blind us to the good of all lands and of all peoples." Her idea joined with those of her husband to propose a one-world government under the soon-to-be-created United Nations.[858]

President Roosevelt coined the name "United Nations" in 1942, when representatives from twenty-six nations pledged that their governments would fight together against the Axis Powers of Germany and

Japan. Three years later, representatives from fifty nations gathered in San Francisco to form the United Nations Conference on International Organization that drew up the United Nations charter, which was signed June 26, 1945.[859]

A man very much pushing for the creation of the UN at the time was John Foster Dulles (1888–1959), who would serve as the secretary of state for President Dwight D. Eisenhower. Mr. Dulles had a very distinguished foreign policy record having been a member of the League of Free Nations Association, which supported America's entrance in the League of Nations. He also served as the chief foreign policy adviser to Thomas E. Dewey, the Republican presidential nominee in 1944.[860]

Mr. Dulles, the cofounder of the globalist Council on Foreign Relations (CFR), a secret society, and author of *War or Peace*, was the author of the preamble to the United Nations Charter and served as a delegate to the first United Nations General Assembly. It was during this period that Dulles favored turning the reins of world government over to the United Nations. He said as much: "I have never seen any proposal made for collective security with 'teeth' in it, or for 'world government' or for 'world federation,' which could not be carried out either by the United Nations or under the United Nations Charter."[861]

Mr. Dulles was rather sanguine about the formation of a world government. Back in 1942, he called for a unified world government to be given "strong immediate limitation on national sovereignty, international control of all armies and navies, a universal system of money, worldwide freedom of immigration, progressive elimination of all tariff and quota restrictions on world trade and a democratically controlled world bank." He also favored at the time a worldwide redistribution of wealth, a Marxist concept.[862]

President John F. Kennedy favored a move to a quasi-world government as well. Back in 1961, the State Department under President Kennedy issued Document 7277, which promoted the concept of dismantling the US military and turning it over to the jurisdiction of the

United Nations. That document, *Program for General and Complete Disarmament in a Peaceful World*, called for "complete disarmament" across the world, which the document argues could "only be achieved through the progressive strengthening of international institutions under the United Nations and by creating a United Nations Peace Force to enforce the peace as the disarmament process proceeds."[863]

The ultimate goal of the Kennedy State Department's proposal was the "disbanding of all national armed forces and the prohibition of their reestablishment in any form whatsoever other than those required to preserve internal order and for contributions to a United Nations Peace Force."[864]

The establishment of such a force would make every sovereign nation subordinate to one-world government. Might such a military go rogue? Possibly. And further, the US would become a subordinate entity to that global government without checks and balances or separation of powers, and it wouldn't protect civil liberties. Finally, as a cautionary note about such an arrangement, when all military power is vested in one centralized global government, there is an obvious question: Who or what is in the position to contest or override its decisions?

After Kennedy, there continued to be globalist calls for one-world government, thanks to the Council for Foreign Relations. The CFR's publication, *Foreign Affairs*, published an article in 1974 by globalist Deputy Assistant Secretary of State Richard N. Gardner, who wrote, "In short, the 'house of world order' will have to be built from the bottom up rather than from the top down.... An end run around national sovereignty, eroding it piece by piece, will accomplish much more than the old-fashioned frontal assault."[865]

Zbigniew Brzezinski was a globalist and a longtime CFR member as well, who helped fellow CFR, world banker David Rockefeller, to establish the Trilateral Commission, another secret society, and served as President Jimmy Carter's national security advisor. In 1995, Brzezinski spoke at former Soviet leader Mikhail Gorbachev's State of the World Forum when he outlined a globalist agenda. "We cannot leap into world government in one quick step.... In brief, the precondition for eventual globalization—genuine globalization—is progressive regionalization, because thereby we move toward larger, more stable, more cooperative units."[866]

About the same time as Brzezinski's speech, the UN's Commission on Global Governance met to draft a similar strategy for reaching the goal of one-world government. That commission published its *Our Global Neighborhood* report, which states:

> The UN must gear itself for a time when regionalism becomes more ascendant worldwide and assist the process in advance of that time.... Regional co-operation and integration should be seen as an important and integral part of a balanced system of global governance.[867]

A few years later, globalist David Rockefeller confessed to his ambition to realize a one-world government. Rockefeller stated that goal in his 2002 autobiography, *Memoirs*:

> For more than a century, ideological extremists at either end of the political spectrum have seized upon well publicized incidents such as my encounter with Castro to attack the Rockefeller family for the inordinate influence they claim we wield over American political and economic institutions. Some even believe we are part of a secret cabal working against the best interests of the United States, characterizing my family and me as "internationalists" and of conspiring with others around the world to build a more integrated global political and economic structure—one world, if you will. If that's the charge, I stand guilty, and I am proud of it.[868]

Both the Clinton and Obama administrations had their share of globalists. A member of Hillary Clinton's State Department endorsed what she called "vertical government networks" in a book, *New World Order*. Ms. Anne-Marie Slaughter, who ran Secretary Clinton's office of policy and planning at state, explained the networks as "those between national government officials and their supranational counterparts." She continued, "The prerequisite for a vertical government network is the relatively rare decision by states to delegate their sovereignty to an institution above them with real power–a court or a regulatory commission." This is a call for the destruction of the nation-state and the imposition of global law—one-world government.[869]

Ms. Slaughter, who serves as the president and CEO of the leftist New America (indeed) that includes George Soros' son, Jonathan Soros, on the board of directors, elaborated on the vertical government concept. She wrote:

> Vertical government networks pierce the shell of state sovereignty by making individual government institutions—courts, regulatory agencies, or even legislators—responsible for implementation of rules created by a supranational institution.... Vertical government networks make it possible for a supranational court, regulatory entity, or parliament to create a relationship with its national counterparts to make those rules directly enforceable.[870]

It is evident that given an opportunity like the left's Great Reset, some so-called elite, anti-God, arrogant Americans favor surrendering our sovereignty to a world government, whether that is a supranational organization like the United Nations or a yet-to-be-created entity. They are incredibly naïve and dupes of Satan to believe that they will last very long at the top of the heap—likely, and soon, others will emerge to remove them. Yes, globalists really do seek a one-world government, but with themselves at the helm.

How Might Globalists Transition to a One-World Government?

The elite must have leverage over governments in order to address the Great Reset aims to fundamentally reengineer industries, societies, education, and even human beings. As WEF president Schwab declared, we must revamp "all aspects of our societies and economies." This is a global social contract focused on "social justice."

How will this revamping happen? There are at least four strategies that might advance toward that outcome.

STRATEGY #1: UN AGENDA 2030

No doubt the UN will play a role by serving as the foundation stone for a future one-world government. That brings to mind UN Agenda 21/2030, aka "Sustainable Development Goals," whereby all nations embrace those goals that include one-world government, cashless currency, government-controlled schools, end to single-family homes, and Goal 10, to "reduce inequality within and among countries" which is a Marxist aim, because it happens only "if wealth is shared and income inequality is addressed."[871]

The UN proposals in this "agenda" are a national socialist approach to combating "inequality" across the world. "By 2030, ensure that all men and women, in particular the poor and the vulnerable, have equal rights to economic resources," the UN document states. Not surprisingly, that statement is quite similar to both WEF's Great Reset goal and something out of the ten planks of Marx's *Communist Manifesto*.[872]

Predictably, the WEF and the UN are in lockstep regarding Agenda 21/2030. Mr. Schwab said the WEF "is committed to supporting this effort [Agenda 21/2030], and working with the United Nations to build a more prosperous and equitable future." The WEF-UN partnership was celebrated by the UN secretary general, former prime minister of Portugal, and socialist Antonino Manuel de Oliveira Guterres, as well.[873]

Secretary Guterres is practically giddy about the WEF's Great Reset, which he said "is a welcome recognition that this human tragedy [COVID-19] must be a wake-up call.... We must build more equal, inclusive and sustainable economies and societies that are more resilient in the face of pandemics, climate change and the many other global changes we face."[874]

Not surprisingly, the Chinese communists are in league with the globalists at WEF and the UN; perhaps the outcome is something they know well.

The communist Chinese perhaps favor the Great Reset because it represents the development of the Chinese economic system in the West. A blog, *Niger Business*, wrote:

> Whereas the Chinese political elite began with a socialist-communist political system and implemented "capitalism" later, the elite in the West began with "capitalism" and is aiming to implement a socialist-communist political system now. It's as if the Western oligarchy looked to the "socialism" on display in China, and said, "yes, we want it."[875]

The writers at *Niger Business* continue:

> The Great Reset aims to reproduce in connection with Western capitalism would resemble the totalitarianism of the CCP. It would require a great abridgement of individual rights—including property rights, free expression, freedom of movement, freedom of association, freedom of religion, and the free enterprise system as we understand it.[876]

STRATEGY #2: GLOBAL CRISIS

The late Maurice Strong (1929–2015) was a rich Canadian known for significant influence across the world and is referred to as the "Godfather of Global Warming." The left embraced Mr. Strong's global-warming panic as the lynchpin of their ideology to wrest control across the planet, another strategy meant to push for one-world government.[877]

Mr. Strong wielded great power, having served as a director for WEF and a senior adviser to the president of the World Bank. He used his significant influence at the UN by working with that organization's Environmental Programme and World Resources Institute, the Earth Charter Commission, and the UN's World Commission on Environment and Development. These organizations came to embrace Mr. Strong's climate change alarm.[878]

Mr. Strong used those and other organizations as instruments to transform the UN into a permanent world government-like group dominated by elites. In fact, thinking about an eventual world government, Mr. Strong proposed decades ago a tax on every financial transaction on earth, which would generate sufficient funding for the proposed global government. However, when that scheme failed, he promoted the idea that the earth faced an existential threat—climate warming, change. His solution to that alleged existential climate threat was to empower the UN to address the global problem and invest all power in that one-world government.[879]

The outcome of Mr. Strong's strategic formulation around climate change was the UN's Agenda 21/2030 that started at the 1992 UN Earth Summit in Rio de Janeiro, Brazil, which proposed the transfer of power from sovereign states to the UN. "It is simply not feasible for sovereignty to be exercised unilaterally by individual nation states," Mr. Strong argued. No, "the global community must be assured of global environmental security."[880]

This strategy is very much at work within the Biden administration. After all, one of President Biden's first acts was to sign an executive order rejoining the Paris Climate Agreement, the landmark international agreement allegedly to limit global warming. President Trump withdrew the US from that agreement, because "the Paris accord is very unfair at the highest level to the United States."[881]

STRATEGY #3: GLOBAL CITIZENSHIP

Maurice Strong is also the spiritual father for the concept of global citizens, defined as those who travel the world encouraging others to become "conscientious global citizens," a view expressed by Sheryl Wudunn, author of *A Path Appears* and the wife of *New York Times* columnist Nicholas Kristof. The book's thesis is explained by Ms. Wudunn's publisher as "a roadmap to becoming a conscientious global citizen."[882]

Global citizenship isn't universally endorsed, however. In fact, on September 24, 2019, President Trump told the UN General Assembly that "the future does not belong to the globalists. The future belongs to the patriots." However, a few days later, New York City played host to the Global Citizen Festival, an event for "top artists, world leaders, and everyday activists to take action."[883]

Attendees, according to the Global Citizen Festival, included celebrities and global influencers focused on taking "a series of actions to create lasting change around the world." Some heavyweight firms were represented at the event, including Johnson & Johnson, Proctor & Gamble, and Cisco Technologies. A Verizon corporate statement said, "We focus our business and resources to uplift people and protect the planet."[884]

Everyone at the festival was labeled a "global citizen," and that included US Representative Adriano Espaillat (D-NY), who called the audience to a "powerful" image of "global citizenship" and asked them to change the world. Mr. Espaillat continued, "They're doing it now [changing the world].... Tonight, is about community, connection—the world coming together," the representative offered.[885]

The elites' campaign for global citizenship hides behind the façade of the "undocumented persons" label. A growing number on the left argues that there is no such thing as an "illegal person," an idea that is becoming mainstream. These "undocumented persons," according to leftists, evidently are deserving of all the rights and privileges of American citizens, which includes healthcare, schooling, housing, welfare checks, and even a driver's licenses—no questions asked.

Proponents of this global citizenship movement ignore what it once meant to be a citizen, however. It's an ancient idea attributed to the Greeks, when citizenship was precious and it came along with certain protections, rights, and obligations. Roman citizenship was important, as we saw in the New Testament regarding the Apostle Paul, who used his citizen status to get out of jail (Acts 16). For this ancient people, citizenship meant order, prestige, respect, and rights.

Global citizenship is a campaign to recruit people across the world to abandon their nationality for a universal allegiance, arguably a Marxist concept.

STRATEGY #4: REGIONAL GOVERNMENTS = ONE-WORLD GOVERNANCE
The fourth strategy is about creating regional power centers that ultimately come together as a global entity. There are already a number of regional power centers. However, the pregnant question is whether the Great Reset can fold them together into a single global entity, a one-world government.

The European Union is the most developed supranational regime and a model for others. Former Soviet dictator Mikhail Gorbachev described the EU as "the new European Soviet." But it didn't begin that way. Rather, it started as a "coal and steel" agreement among post-World War II nations, then morphed into the European Economic Community (Common Market), the European Community, and finally into the European Union (1993).[886]

Jose Manuel Barroso, the former EU Commission president and a former Maoist revolutionary, once boasted: "We will need to move toward a federation. ...this is our political horizon." Arguably the EU has arrived because it boasts a single currency (the euro), a law-enforcement agency, and a military, and has robbed member nations of considerable sovereign rights over national budgets and even their elected legislative branches of government.[887]

The EU is joined by other supranational organizations that aren't quite as mature. The African Union has a cadre of bureaucrats performing the roles of legislators and judicial overlords, but with limited real authority. It doesn't print a currency as yet, but does promote a "Tripartite Free Trade Area" plan. What makes the AU's future suspect is the fact that Robert Mugabe, the former genocidal Marxist dictator of

Zimbabwe, served as the AU's chairman. Further, the AU enjoys a tenuous supraregional power status because its funding comes from outsiders like the EU and the US governments.[888]

South America has its own emergent supra-state—the Union of South American States (UNASUL). It tries to emulate the EU by seeking to realize a single currency, military, and parliament. Of course, the UNASUL bumps heads with other Latin American regional organizations such as Mercosur, the Bolivarian Alliance for the Peoples of Our America, the Community of Latin American and Caribbean States, and more.[889]

Even Moscow's strong man, Vladimir Putin, is creating the Eurasian Economic Union, or EEU. That organization brings under Russia's umbrella of influence former Soviet states like Belarus and Armenia. Putin hopes in time other states will be added. He explained, "It took Europe 40 years to move from the European coal and steel community to the full European Union." He added that the EEU is "proceeding at a much faster pace because we could draw on the experience of the EU and other regional associations." Putin also suggested that, in time, the EU and the EEU could create a "harmonized community of economies stretching from Lisbon to Vladivostok, a free trade zone and even employing more sophisticated integration patterns" that would pursue "coordinated policies in industry, technology, the energy sector, education, science, and also to eventually scrap visas."[890]

Other supranational organizations are either growing or emerging. The Middle East has the functioning Gulf Cooperation Council, and there are discussions about creating a "Middle East Union" and even an Arab NATO-like security force. South East Asia has the Association of South East Asian Nations (ASEAN), and until President Trump killed it, there was the North American Free Trade Agreement (NAFTA), which Henry Kissinger touted as an aspect of the "New World Order" and "the most creative step toward a new world order taken by any group of countries since the end of the Cold War." NAFTA was replaced by the US-Mexico-Canada Agreement (USMACA) in July 2020.[891]

Globalists like Henry Kissinger explain how these regional supranational organizations will eventually merge. "The contemporary quest for world order will require a coherent strategy to establish a concept of order within the various regions and to relate these regional orders to one another," Kissinger wrote in his book, *World Order*. He boasted that "Europe has set out to transcend the state" as a prelude to the "new world order" finale.[892]

The EU and its globalist sponsors want to recruit other regions to join their quest. In 2016, the EU vowed to "support cooperative regional orders worldwide," which includes the US, albeit as it touts global governance based on a "strong UN." "We will invest in regional orders, and in cooperation among and within regions," declares the EU's *Global Strategy* document.[893]

Kissinger said once this collection of regional governments is in full control, the plan to merge them into a global network begins and "trade" is the pretext. The trade rubric includes the likes of the Transatlantic Trade and Investment Partnership, which intends to join the EU and the United States.[894]

The Great Reset in the hands of globalists has a number of strategies, some of which are outlined above. What's not in question is that the Great Reset is being used as an opportunity by globalists to press the world to form a supranational, one-world government.

WHAT WOULD A GLOBAL ONE-WORLD GOVERNMENT BE LIKE?

So far, this section has established that globalists do seek a one-world government and outlined four of their strategies to attain that goal. We now consider what a one-world government might be like for its global citizens.

One way of approaching this question is to consider what the most successful regional supranational model, the EU, provides its citizens.

Evidently, many British citizens found the EU model unacceptable; after all, they rejected the EU in a national referendum (2020). There were many British objections expressed as part of Brexit, a portmanteau for the "British exit" from the EU.

One of the complaints from the Brits was that the EU makes decisions without regard to public opinion, and if extrapolated globally, it could become much worse under a one-world government. Remember that the National Socialist Germany under Adolf Hitler made life difficult for many of its citizens, especially the millions of Jews put to death. The German tyrant seized power to destroy autonomy, all civil liberties, and all police powers were turned over to the central government, specifically the German secret police under the Nazis known as the Gestapo.

The EU is also especially insensitive to the rights Americans take for granted, like religious liberty. Consider that in 2004, Rocco Buttiglione, a political science professor and devout Roman Catholic, served as a justice commissioner in the EU. He said at one of the EU's committee meetings on civil liberties that homosexuality was a sin, which earned Professor Buttiglione the charge that he was guilty of "hate speech," which led to his ejection from the commission.[895]

Mr. Buttiglione, responding to the committee's politically correct reaction to his statement, said, "The new soft totalitarianism that is advancing on the Left wants us to have a state religion. It is an atheist, nihilistic religion—but it is a religion that is obligatory for all." That's a real danger in a global government.[896]

Richard Gardner, a world government advocate, said the act of melding regional "governments" into a whole could be "an end run around national sovereignty, eroding it piece by piece." The sovereignty issue is especially sensitive for nations like the United States that guard their sovereignty. After all, in the EU, member nations lost control of their borders because immigration is governed by EU bureaucrats in Brussels. The resulting lack of any border control resulted in hundreds of thousands of North Africans and Middle Eastern refugees illegally pouring into Europe in 2015.[897]

Another major concern regarding one-world government is the concentration of power. Lord Acton, a nineteenth-century politician and author, said, "Power tends to corrupt, and absolute power corrupts absolutely." That outcome would invariably become true of a global government, which would then trash everything many Americans treasure: civil liberties, limited government, free enterprise, and replace them with fear and an abusive bureaucracy—all in the name of faux equality, a socialist ideal.[898]

A one-world government that embraces the UN-like charter would also replace America's criminal justice system with something more akin to the International Criminal Court model, which has no jury system and would likely be similar to the UN's Treaty Against Genocide, for which there are "penalties for causing 'mental harm'" to a member of a minority group based on race, ethnicity, or most any psychologically made-up status. It would be especially dangerous for biblical Christians who disagree about the alleged moral rights of homosexuals and the importance of following the teachings of the Bible regarding issues like abortion, marriage, and more.

Many Americans are understandably disgusted with the World Health Organization's (WHO) lack of transparency regarding the COVID-19 pandemic and especially for its covering-up for communist China's denials of culpability. The WHO's constitution, an example of what a global government might embrace, states:

> Health is a state of complete physical, mental and social well-being and not merely the absence of disease or infirmity.... Governments have a responsibility for the health of their peoples which can be fulfilled only by the provision of adequate health and social measures."

Arguably a world government that embraces such a view about "health" would be obligated to provide all that a person requires to live—housing, food, job—clearly a Marxist, big government outcome.[899]

That prescription also means the US, or any other nation, under a one-world government is bound to promote unlimited government intrusion into every human affair, which is something our founders opposed and the reason for our Revolutionary War with the British.

Additionally, one-world-government-run healthcare would also primarily serve the purposes of the elite, not the interests of the global citizens. Yes, the elite would get the best healthcare, but the rest of us would get what government wants to afford. Thus, rationing of care would deny what's truly needed by the ill, poor, and elderly.

Wealth redistribution is another aspect of a one-world government that tracks back to Marxism. In fact, a summer 1992 edition of the *World Policy Journal* published the idea that the world needs to "move to a system of value-added taxes that could be collected automatically when goods and services cross national borders." That revenue would be automatically credited to international organizations like the United Nations. Such thinking, if extended to a world government, would mean a global internal revenue service and be the vehicle for wealth redistribution.[900]

How might a one-world government function? Jeff Deist wrote for the Mises Institute that globalism would only work through force, because blending diverse cultures across the earth would meet significant resistance. Civil liberties would be abandoned: freedom of speech, faith, and the right to bear arms. Once America crumbles to such a global government, then the US ceases to be the light on the hill and a beacon of freedom.[901]

What would the standard of living be for the average American under a one-world government? Most likely our standard of living would degrade—smaller homes, cars—and there would be far more regulation of our businesses. This is inevitable, because of the socialist economic policies the globalists will see as necessary to promote global equity, a Marxist aim.

In conclusion, this section demonstrated that globalists in fact seek a one-world government, a result of the Great Reset. That outcome emerges thanks to a host of strategies, some of which are developed above. Further, the result of the formation of a global government is a radically different lifestyle for all global citizens, especially those in the West accustomed to civil liberties and a good quality of life.

COMMUNIST CHINA: BENEFACTOR OF GREAT RESET AND POISED TO LEAD ONE-WORLD GOVERNMENT?

To this point, I've argued that the Great Reset is a Marxist-like initiative that could lead to a one-world government. Finally, this section of the chapter answers the question: Is communist China poised to take the reins of a future one-world government?

What's not in dispute is that outcome fits China's Marxist ideology and its preparations. Below I will answer three questions to demonstrate that China is indeed a global hegemon that is using the leftists' Great Reset as a mechanism to gain the throne of a future one-world government.

Does communist China see the Great Reset as a mechanism to grow its global influence? The Chinese communists participated in bringing the world to its knees through the COVID-19 pandemic and is using Klaus Schwab's Great Reset to grow its global influence as a result. That may sound like a conspiracy, but the facts speak for themselves.

On January 23, 2020, China imposed the first lockdown in the history of humankind to address the COVID-19 pandemic and quickly the World Health Organization's director, Tedros Adhanom Ghebreyesus, praised China's method as "precedent-setting." Very soon, every country copied China, and in the meantime, the WEF's Mr. Schwab found his once-in-a-lifetime opportunity for a Great Reset. Those COVID-19 lockdowns brought unbelievable profits to big tech, big pharma, and big money; China's influence skyrocketed.[902]

Michael P. Senger, an American lawyer and investigative journalist, saw the brewing conspiracy. He said the COVID-19-related lockdowns came as a result of a large-scale "information operation," a CCP info war. His thesis in the article, "China's Global Lockdown Propaganda," according to cultural anthropologist Aya Velazquez "is that lockdowns are not evidence-based, but rather Chinese state propaganda in the interest of a flu *d'état* – of a government coup on the basis of a virus, with a little help from the export of damaging, pseudo-scientific measures."[903] Mr. Senger documented overwhelming evidence of the conspiracy found on his Twitter account (@michaelpsenger), in a thread entitled "Open Letter to Xi Jinping." He said the core message of the CCP was "China is the only country in the world to have perfectly managed the pandemic. The Chinese system is superior. Whoever doesn't do it like China is inhumane."[904]

Meanwhile, most nations, including the US, stopped in their tracks and ran their economies into the ground while China portrayed itself as morally superior. By late 2020, while most countries were locked in a deep recession, the communist Chinese regime enjoyed a growth rate of of 4.9 percent, and according to Reuters, it will grow 8.4 percent in 2021 (David Lague and Yew Lun Tian, "China expected to unveil hike in military budget as tensions rise," Reuters, February 26, 2021, https://www.reuters.com/article/us-china-parliament-military-idUSKBN2AQ150.)[905]

How did the Chinese do this? They enjoy significant influence over both the WHO and WEF, co-conspirators of sorts and propagandist and globalist centers that favor China. This influence has been building for decades.

Klaus Schwab, "Mr. Great Reset," is one of the most powerful friends of China in the West. His WEF long ago fostered the closest relationships with the communist central government in Beijing, and the Chinese communists leveraged that relationship, and that rapport is amplified by the fact that Mr. Schwab's son, Olivier, is married to a Chinese woman and leads the WEF office in Beijing.

For more than a decade, Chinese officials have come to WEF's annual conference at Davos, Switzerland. Those officials have included Premier Wen Jiabao and Li Keqiang as vice premier, as well as hundreds of Chinese entrepreneurs like Ren Zhengei, the founder of the telecommunications giant Huawei. President Xi Jinping attended in 2017 and at that time, Mr. Schwab introduced the communist leader as the savior of free world trade: "In a world marked by great uncertainty and volatility, the international community is looking to China."[906]

At the 2017 Davos conference, President Xi spoke prophetically when he began his speech with a Charles Dickens quotation: "It was the best of times, it was the worst of times," a reference to the first Industrial Revolution and an oblique allusion to these new "revolutionary" times. Xi used the occasion to juxtapose his country with the USA, which was moving to protectionism under President Trump, while China, promised Mr. Xi, "will keep its doors wide open."[907]

China's economic and political good fortunes come at a time when the West experiences a decline in global economic and military influence, thanks to the COVID-19 pandemic and the associated economic turbulence. Until this point, there was a widespread belief that China would move closer to a Western model regarding rule of law and compliance with world economic standards. That's not happening; just the opposite is.

The communist Chinese regime continues to break all the rules across the international system. It exploits the openness of Western economies and destroys entire Western industries while moving jobs and factories to the communist pariah's homeland.

This is exactly what Marxists do. The Bolshevik Revolution of 1917 set the stage for the emergence of the CCP. Even though the communist Chinese embraced some of the trappings of a market economy, the regime never abandoned its defining characteristics: deceit, malice, and never-ending revolution. The CCP's economic front is necessary to fuel the ongoing revolution to strengthen the socialist nation.

President Xi and his comrades play the WEF and the West for fools. They manipulate the world's greed to bring nations into alignment with Beijing in order to capture them for world domination.

Yes, the WEF's Great Reset is a tool in the hands of the Chinese to gain global influence.

Does Communist China seek to gain superpower status? The Chinese are not satisfied with just being a regional power. They seek to control the entire world and the evidence of that view is mounting.

Marxism is never satisfied with the status quo. It seeks constant revolution that expands its domain and crushes anything in its path. By their very doctrinal nature, the Chinese communists are globalists and totally hegemonic.

The Hudson Institution's Michael Pillsbury agrees. Pillsbury states in his book, *The Hundred-Year Marathon: China's Secret Strategy to Replace America as the Global Superpower*, that "China has a long-term strategy to subvert the US-led world economic and political order and to replace it with communion by 2049, the one-hundredth anniversary of the communist party's rise to power in China."[908]

Mr. Pillsbury also calls attention to a film produced by the National Defense University of China, *Silent Contest*, which claims the regime's "great cause" is dominating the world, "will inevitably run into constant wear-and-tear and struggle with the US hegemonic system," and "is a centennial contest, not to be shifted by the human will."[909]

Of course, Mr. Pillsbury is correct, and the globalists at WEF cheering the Chinese dictator are incredibly naïve because they actually believe that Beijing's partnership in globalization is about furthering democracy and free trade. They couldn't be more wrong. The Chinese communist aim will always be to use globalization as a mechanism to take over the world by imposing their ideology of globalist control.

Although Karl Marx never used the term "globalism," his *Communist Manifesto* claims that capitalism will produce a large proletariat (working class), which would revolt across the globe, destroy capitalism, and result in a communist utopia. Marx and Engels wrote, "The proletariat can thus only exist world-historically, just as communism, its activity can only have a 'world-historical' existence." That's a statement about the future working class spawning a revolution that captures the entire world.[910]

Even Vladimir Lenin shared a global vision. The Soviet leader, who established the Communist International in Moscow, said the aim was to establish a World Soviet Republic, a Marxist one-world government.[911]

Joseph Stalin, who followed Lenin at the helm in Moscow, espoused a policy of "socialism in one country," yet he embraced a global revolution. He wrote in *Marxism and the National Question*, a strategy that ultimately divides the world into regional groups as a transitional stage toward the ultimate objective of one-world government. That sounds very much like the supranational organizations like the EU developed earlier in this chapter or Bible prophecy about a ten-nation alliance in Daniel 7:23–24 and ten kings in Revelation 12:12–14.[912]

Even the American William Z. Foster, the former national chairman of the Communist Party USA, confirmed as much:

> A communist world will be a unified, organized world. The economic system will be one great organization, based upon the principle of planning now dawning in the USSR. The American Soviet government will be an important section in this world government.[913]

So, given statements by the founders of Marxism and the contemporary dictators in communist China, is there any doubt the CCP seeks to dominate all of humanity?

What is communist China's strategy to gain global influence that leads to its dominance in a future one-world government? To this point, we've established that the communist Chinese are using the leftists' Great Reset to bolster their global influence, and the Beijing regime seeks to become the world's hegemon. But, how might the regime reach that lofty goal?

The Beijing communist regime is pursuing global control via five lines of effort.

1. The first line of effort (LOE) is to support the formation of supranational bodies that eventually morph into a one-world government. It is to back the globalists' aim of supporting the creation of regional governments such as those identified earlier in this chapter, like the European Union. The CCP backs these regional structures with funding and business contracts as well as political assistance in world assemblies like the UN. The regime's intent is that once these regional bodies form and collapse into a global super-government, then the Chinese will move in to impose communism eliminating private property, national sovereignty, and culture.

    Realizing the formation of regional supranational structures ready to form a global governance entity is a necessary step but insufficient without other complimentary LOEs.

2. The second LOE is to wage economic leverage to gain global influence.

    China's One Belt One Road Initiative (OBOR) is the regime's global LOE to gain influence. This strategic approach is adopted from what they experienced first-hand prior to World War II thanks to their neighbor, Japan.

    Beginning in the 1930s, the Greater East Asia Co-Prosperity Sphere, was an imperialist effort to support Japan's expansionist ambitions to soak up raw materials from other nations to help sustain its economy. Japan's colonization efforts benefited only the tyrants in Tokyo, a lesson the Chinese never forgot.

    Communist China's dictator Xi Jinping evidently took a lesson from Japan's aggressive history when developing the OBOR strategy. Instead of leading with the bayonet as did the Japanese, the Chinese communists invaded other countries economically vis-à-vis the likes of China's OBOR, which quickly defeats economically weaker partners through the sleight-of-hand enticements.

Beijing sells the foreign partner under the guise of OBOR loans for massive infrastructure and economic development projects, but quickly those nations inevitably fail to repay their debt and then, like a vulture waiting for the victim to die, the communist regime leaps on the victim nation with draconian collection claws. China leverages the partner's assets and immediately harvests raw materials at bargain prices to fuel its homebound and resource-hungry manufacturing sector.

This LOE gives the Peoples Republic of China global economic and political leverage unlike any of its opponents.

3. The third LOE is to steal and entice Western technology to China.

This LOE is known as "Made in China 2025," a CCP initiative that involves the theft of Western technology and firms. The vision is that China will transform from a big manufacturing country to a manufacturing power, so that by 2035, it surpasses the industrially advanced Germany and Japan. Further, "the endgame is the destruction of European and American technological industrial bases, leaving China in top position in artificial intelligence, robotics, microprocessors, pharmaceuticals, and other technologies," according to James Gorrie, writing for the *Epoch Times*.[914]

This LOE makes China the go-to source for advanced technological solutions, a world leader.

4. The fourth LOE is "unrestricted warfare."

The fourth LOE is introduced by the *Epoch Times'* 2018 book, *How the Specter of Communism Is Ruling our World*, which addresses communist China's global ambitions and in particular its use of "unrestricted warfare."[915]

China's intent is to subvert and contain the United States, its primary global adversary. It accomplishes this by engaging the West in "unrestricted warfare," which means anything goes.

In 2013, President Xi identified a national aim of making China the world's leading economy and military power by the regime's one hundredth anniversary (2049). For Xi and his Communist Party, that global ambition means there will be no moral limitations on that quest. What that translates into is the party's nine inherited traits that will be on full display across the world: "evil, deceit, incitement, unleashing the scum of society, espionage, robbery, fighting, elimination, and control."[916]

Those traits are a backdrop to the CCP's strategy of "unrestricted warfare." Although this concept was first used as a communist military strategy, thanks to two Chinese colonels, it has taken on a new character by employing all the regime's national power. The colonels explain the concept in their book *Unrestricted Warfare*: "[It is] a war beyond all boundaries and limits... forcing the enemy to accept one's own interests by all means, including methods of force and non-force, military and non-military, killing and non-killing.... The means are all-inclusive, information is omnipresent, the battlefield is everywhere... beyond all political, historical, cultural, and moral restraints."[917]

The term "unrestricted warfare" in a broader sense can be understood as "all weapons and technologies can be used at will; it means that all boundaries between the worlds of war and non-war, military and non-military, are broken." Translation: The full range of China's capabilities across many domains are employed: finance, trade, media, law, outer space and more. Beijing's no-holds-barred strategy includes cyber hacking, terrorism, atomic weapons, electronic warfare, drug trafficking, ecological warfare, intelligence (spying), psychological warfare (propaganda), and much more.[918]

How might this unrestricted warfare be executed? The Chinese colonels write that "the generalization of war" is the direction of the future, and executing that campaign includes the robust employment of nonmilitary personnel across all "battlefields" at all times, such as those introduced above.

This approach to modern all-domain warfare is not necessarily new for the communist Chinese. During the Chinese Civil War (1927–1949), the CCP used a variety of tools to defeat the nationalist government (Kuomintang), such as economic warfare and espionage. Today, the communists use a much larger set of tools—"unrestricted warfare"—but on a much broader scale, and they don't follow any conventional rules, much less allow themselves to be constrained by morality.

The *Epoch Times* identifies the Chinese communists' "unrestricted warfare" means, across all domains, to achieve the following goals:[919]

- Exporting Party culture and lies to the world through foreign propaganda
- Controlling global media and carrying out ideological warfare
- Using fame, honey traps (sexual entrapment), interpersonal relationships, bribery, and despotic power to gain leverage over the leaders of global organizations, important political figures, experts in think tanks and academic circles, business tycoons, and influentials from all walks of life
- Supporting, inciting, and allying with rogue regimes to distract the United States and Western governments
- Using trade diplomacy to make free countries compete against one another, using the market of more than one billion Chinese consumers as bait
- Deepening economic integration and interdependency to tie up other countries
- Violating World Trade Organization trade rules
- Making false reform commitments to accumulate trade surplus and foreign exchange reserves

- Using the market, foreign exchange, and financial resources as weapons to suppress human rights through economic unrestricted warfare and to force other countries to abandon moral responsibility and universal values
- Forcing Chinese working in private enterprises abroad to steal information from them
- Making hostages of China's citizens and those of other countries

I address many of these goals in detail in my 2018 book, *Alliance of Evil*, which declares that the US is very much in a new cold war with China across four distinctive battlefields: cyber, economic, military/technological, and ideological. The evidence for that new cold war is overwhelming.

5. The fifth LOE is to grow China's armed forces into a world-class military.

A world power must be able to defend its interests as well as that of its allies and partners. Over the past two decades, the communist Chinese heavily invested in the Peoples' Liberation Army (PLA) to "become a practical instrument of its statecraft with an active role in advancing the PRC's foreign policy, particularly with respect to the PRC's increasingly global interests and its aims to revise aspects of the international order," according to the US Department of Defense.[920]

The PRC is quite serious about using its military to globally advance its interests. Twenty years ago, the PLA was a weak force. The Pentagon assessed in 2000 that the PLA focused on waging large-scale land warfare along China's borders. Beyond her borders at the time, China had little capability: an obsolete navy, inaccurate missiles, rudimentary cyber capabilities, nominal space assets, and a struggling defense industry.[921]

Two decades later, the PLA is rapidly approaching "world-class" status, a goal set by General Secretary Xi in 2017. The PRC invested resources, technology, and political will over the past decades to strengthen and modernize the PLA in every respect. Today, the PLA is ahead of the United States in some very important areas: shipbuilding (350 versus 293 ships and submarines); land-based conventional ballistic and cruise missiles; and integrated air defense systems.[922]

More significant than these advantages, the PLA deployed incredible amounts of new military hardware and completely restructured its forces for joint operations, improved overall combat readiness, embraced radically new operational concepts, and is rapidly growing its global military footprint.

By any objective standard, the evidence is clear. Communist China intends to become the world's hegemon and is on track to become the leader of a future one-world communist government.

CONCLUSION

This chapter answers three questions to conclude that the left's Great Reset is a Marxist initiative that aims at a long-held globalist goal—one-world government. Communist China is preparing itself through a variety of strategies to take the reins of that government to rule the world into the future.

Section IV

How Marxists Take Over the World, and What Follows

It may be hard for some readers to believe, but there is a brewing conspiracy to take over the world. Some of the players in this global takeover are useful idiots (mostly ideological liberals), while others, seen and unseen, are true co-conspirators; many are identified in chapters 5–8. This global Great Reset coup has historic precedents beginning in heaven, when Satan tried to topple God, as well as throughout history. There have been conspiracies, but most have failed, and the perpetrators have suffered the consequences.

To this point, *Give Me Liberty, Not Marxism* has established that we face a true global conspiracy by Marxists. However, not until recently have all the pieces of the global *coup d'état* puzzle come into focus. Today, we have globalist billionaires, nation-state actors, international organizations like the UN, big tech, and multinational corporations all pushing for the global, Marxist Great Reset with considerable international support from naïve "global citizens" helping make it possible to reach Marx's goal of a one-world, Soviet-style government. Further, there is gathering evidence that the unseen realm includes a host of real evil spirits (Satan and his army of demons) who are furiously pushing for the new world order that will bring about the one-world government. It is a final, desperate effort to avoid their God-ordained inevitable eternity in hell. While it will ultimately fail, they will unleash hell on earth in the meantime (Revelation 20:8–10).

Let's not get ahead of ourselves, however. At the present, the globalist campaign to unseat sovereign governments including that of the United States is a work in progress, and the Biden administration is part of the team of co-conspirators, whether President Biden knows it or not. This globalist cabal has a campaign plan profiled in the previous section of this book (chapters 9–11) that demonstrates a genuine, rising worldwide threat and the means to follow through. But, as you are about to see, past coup attempts inevitably have failed. It is yet to be seen whether this global takeover with its army of co-conspirators both seen and unseen can succeed, and if indeed the Great Reset becomes the mechanism to usher in the biblical end times.

This final section of *Give Me Liberty, Not Marxism* will address in two chapters the indicators of the global coup (markers of the prophetic end times), the parallel fight in the unseen realm egging on their earthbound co-conspirators, and, in the final chapter, speculation about what pre-Rapture Christians should expect if the coup succeeds and what must be done in response until Christ returns.

12

Great Reset Conspiracy, Prophetic End Times, and Demonic Partners

Will the global, Marxist Great Reset conspiracy coup crush world governments and press them into an alliance of nation-states under a Chinese-led one-world government? Clearly this is the Marxists' ambition, and no doubt there is a global conspiracy underway seeking that outcome. Further, it appears that this revolution corresponds with an increase of prophetic markers suggesting that these are the biblical end times bolstered by an increase in a complementary, parallel spiritual war.

So, the first question we address in this chapter is: Will the Marxist Great Reset coup work? It certainly has promise, and thanks to the fumbling of the right, the chances are improved.

THE GREAT RESET: WILL IT MOVE THIS COUNTRY AND THE WORLD TO A SOVIET MODEL?

In 2021, the Communist Party USA celebrated the Democratic Party's trifecta—their ascension to leadership in both houses of Congress and the presidency. That was a long-awaited outcome, and evidence their

Great Reset coup is progressing, arguably a significant step toward the eventual Sovietization of America and then the world.

The CPUSA's website included a December 2020 post that read: "In this context—the ever-present capitalist system and the temporary two years of a democratic-controlled congress and White House—what we do in the next two years is crucial." Indeed, time is short for America's communists and their allies in the Democratic Party to launch an earnest Marxist class struggle to advance their globalist Great Reset.[923]

The 2020 election outcome wasn't enough, however. The congressional majority is razor thin, but then the left got an unexpected gift: the right gave them a present on January 6, 2021—the Capitol Hill riot.

President Trump never called on his supporters to storm down the mall to the Capitol, much less to stage a riot or a coup. But the establishment media and social media giants created from whole cloth an absurd indictment that Mr. Trump incited the January 6 riot to install himself as a dictator by means of the assault by a host of mostly right-leaning wingnuts. Contrary to that bizarre fantasy of the left, the real fascists are the leftists and their cheerleaders who took a page from the history of one of the world's worst tyrants.

On February 27, 1933, shortly after Adolf Hitler was sworn in as Germany's chancellor, the Reichstag, the German parliament building in Berlin, caught fire and quickly a Dutch communist, Marinus van der Lubbe, was charged with the crime. The newly minted German führer used the alleged arsonist's communist affiliation to press German president Paul von Hindenburg to approve an emergency law, the Enabling Act, that gave Chancellor Hitler dictatorial powers to hunt down and arrest communists, as well as granted him total control over the German people.[924]

There is reason to believe the Reichstag fire was staged as a pretext to grant Hitler the mechanism to remove his political opponents and solidify his control of Germany. What's not disputed is that the Nazis benefited from the fire, and it's more than curious that years later, during the post-war Nuremberg trials, that German General Franz Halder put the blame for the Reichstag's torching on Hermann Göring, a military officer and minister in Hitler's regime, who denied complicity. Conspiracy or not, that event gave the Nazis the power to silence their opponents, thus controlling the Bundestag (German parliament) and sparking the move to World War II and the Holocaust.

The parallel between the Reichstag fire and the January 6 riot is obvious. The Democrats used the attack to criminalize their opposition, and they were joined in the allegation by most of the mainstream media, high-tech firms, and many major corporations. But they didn't stop casting aspersions at President Trump because he wasn't the real target of the leftists. The seventy-five million Americans who voted for Mr. Trump on November 3, 2020, are the left's real target. In fact, some on the left, like *CBS News* anchor Katie Couric, said: "The question is how are we going to really almost deprogram these people who have signed up for the cult of Trump."[925]

The left used the disgusting Capitol Hill event to justify the suppression of free speech for all Trump supporters, an existential threat to our civil liberties, but a necessary Marxist-like step and part of the globalists' Great Reset conspiracy.

Radio talk show host and columnist Dennis Prager said of the Capitol Hill event: "The left suppresses liberty everywhere it takes power—there is no exception." He added, "They're using January 6 [riot] as the excuse to do so" now.[926]

Mr. Prager said Amazon taking down Parler, a social media platform frequented by ideological conservatives, was an example of the left's suppression. On January 11, 2021, leftist Jeff Bezos' Amazon Web Services took down Parler, sparking allegations that the suspension was stifling free speech.

Amazon Web Services replied to Parler's lawsuit with the statement: "This case is not about suppressing speech or stifling viewpoints. It is not about a conspiracy to restrain trade."[927]

Amazon corporate wrote, "Instead, this case is about Parler's demonstrated unwillingness and inability to remove from the servers of Amazon Web Services (AWS) content that threatens the public safety, such as by inciting and planning the rape, torture, and assassination of named public officials and private citizens."

Really? Their hypocrisy is hardly palpable. After all, Amazon and its friends on the left did absolutely nothing during the summer of 2020 when the nation burned at the hands of leftist groups like Antifa and Black Lives Matter.

In late February 2021, Parler relaunched itself using a new web hosting service. At the time, it had more than twenty million users. The service that first launched in August 2018 states its "new platform is built on robust, sustainable, independent technology."[928] Evidently, taking down Parler wasn't enough to tame the right's speech. Both Twitter and Facebook announced stricter measures on their platforms. Facebook took special umbrage against Trump supporters who posted news about "Stop the Steal," a reference to claims by the right that the left was guilty of election fraud, and meanwhile, Twitter took special aim at accounts focused on the QAnon movement, an anonymous user named "Q Clearance Patriot" who posts conspiracy theories on social media, and, according to the *New York Post*, QAnon "claims to have insider knowledge of the Trump administration and touts the theory that the president [Trump] is waging a secret war against a global cabal of pedophile elites that includes an array of Hollywood actors and Democratic politicians who allegedly worship Satan."[929]

The left's Nazi-like ploy may not work, however. Americans have a long tradition of freedom of speech, and won't accept the left's woke totalitarianism like the Germans in the 1930s. Although the American left is reveling in its Reichstag fire moment for now, it is a dangerous path to follow, and one that could spark much more than a fire or an assault on Capitol Hill.

Arguably what's happening in Washington is not just about facing a Great Reset, but a conspiracy, a *coup d'état*, French for "blow of state," or, as the Cambridge dictionary states, "sudden defeat of a government through illegal force by a small group, often a military one." Certainly, from President Trump's perspective, the Democrats and their globalist partners did everything possible to destroy his presidency and remove him from power. They succeeded in removing him via the ballot box in 2020, in spite of countless allegations of fraud, but they failed after four years of Russian collusion attacks and two impeachments. Now, they have a green light with all the power of government in their sails to advance their radical agenda—the Great Reset coup, which is outlined in the previous chapter.[930]

Similar efforts—coups—mostly fail in time, however. The current conspiracy seeks to radically transform America and, given the globalists' agenda, if successful, this country could end up becoming something akin to a nation-state member of a global, Soviet Union-like government led by the Chinese communists.

We've seen in the first three sections of this book that Marxism gains power through division. That's the technique Hitler used after the Reichstag fire, and that's what is happening now with the Democrats using the pretext of the Capitol Hill riot. They are dividing us in their coup attempt to take over and transform this country. But coups don't always work out; history is full of failed efforts, and the costs for the citizens is always steep.

Consider prior coups through history and decide for yourself whether the current effort is likely to succeed.

Satan staged a coup in heaven to take the reins of the world, but he failed. He conspired with other angels, as revealed in several Scriptures: Ezekiel 28:12–19, Isaiah 14, Jude 6, 2 Peter 2:4, and others. Piecing together these biblical passages, we understand that Satan was a captain of the cherubic hosts, a chief angel. Somehow, he became vain and was convinced that he should replace God. So, he divided the legions of angels, recruited some to his heavenly conspiracy, and then attempted a coup that failed. As a result, he and his army of fallen angels were expelled from heaven (Luke 10:18, 2 Peter 2:4, Jude 6, Revelation 12:4). Ever since that expulsion, Satan and his demonic legion have warred against God and will continue to do so until they are ultimately confined to hell for all eternity (Revelation 20:10).

Another biblical example of a coup finds mankind rebelling against God when they built a tower to "reach to the heavens" with the intent of replacing God. Genesis 11 explains that the descendants of Noah were living in the area of Mesopotamia in Babylon, present-day Iraq. At that time, they spoke one language and decided to build a tower, a proud symbol of their great nation. These Babylonians built the tower of Babel, as the Scripture states, to "reach to the heavens" so they could be like God. But God saw their pride and arrogance, and defeated their plans by confusing their tongues, causing them to speak different languages, which ended their tower project. The language confusion divided the people into tribes, causing them to scatter across the world and their conspiracy to fail.

Modern coups also began with the strategy of dividing the people into factions, delivering totalitarian governments, and ending with tragic outcomes.

Napoleon Bonaparte returned triumphant from Egypt to conspire to overthrow the ruling French Directory (the government leaders). He divided the Directory members, then abolished that authority, but had those who remained loyal to quickly appoint him France's first consul; by 1804, he crowned himself emperor. Obviously, the coup worked for a time, but eventually the emperor's arrogance got the best of him when he launched an invasion of Russia, which eventually led to the collapse of the Grande Armée. By the spring of 1814, Napoleon abdicated and fled into exile to the island of Elba off the coast of Tuscany (Italy).[931]

Idi Amin rose to become Uganda's top general, and initially he was an ally of President Milton Obote, who won the nation's independence from Britain in 1962. Evidently, President Obote was suspicious of General Amin and ordered his arrest, but word of the conspiracy got to Amin, who moved his troops to the capital to quickly seize the airport and other important sites, and then the general announced his successful coup. Although Amin promised democracy, he ruled Uganda with an iron fist, slaughtering three hundred thousand of his political opponents over the course of his reign.[932]

Coups seldom advantage the citizenry, who invariably suffer and those who are toppled typically pay a high price as well. Whether the current Great Reset conspiracy ends in a totalitarian, one-world government depends on a host of issues, which includes the topic of the next section, a review of the indicators of the prophetic end times—the last true coup.

GLOBAL COUP, ONE-WORLD GOVERNMENT, AND ANTICHRIST

The day of the Lord will come like a thief in the night.... So then let us not sleep, as others do, but let us keep awake.

—1 Thessalonians 5:2,6 (ESV)

The prophetic Scriptures speak of a coming global coup overseen by the Antichrist. What we don't know at this point is whether or not the Great Reset coup conspiracy will be marked by the apocalyptic events described in the Scriptures that play a role ushering in "the day of the Lord."

There is plenty of speculation and many theories about the timing and circumstances of the last days. The Scriptures provide some insight, and Jesus speaks of the time just before His return. He specifically tells believers to watch for those signs (Matthew 24), and one of those indicators is the topic addressed in the previous section of this book, a one-world government.

In the past, many people have tried to achieve a one-world government, but no one has succeeded. Alexander the Great conquered a large swath of the earth from Greece to India, but he never succeeded in uniting those territories. Even the Roman Augustus Caesar held sway from Spain to Turkey, but world government never materialized.

Many centuries later, Adolf Hitler promised a thousand-year reign for his Third Reich, and the Soviet's Nikita Khrushchev threatened that

Russia would take over the world. Both outcomes never materialized. Even the post-World War II United States, arguably the most powerful nation in history, failed to rule the world. One-world government remains elusive, but there could be such an outcome on the horizon.

Scripture tells us only one person will set up and rule over that one-world government, and that person is the Antichrist, the horned goat (Daniel 8) and the beast of Revelation 13 and 17. Yes, one-world government is coming, but whether it is on the near horizon and associated with the Marxists' Great Reset coup is to be determined.

Scripture also provides indicators, signs, of that coming one-world government. The first is the threat of a "new world order"; perhaps that's what the current Marxists are promising with their Great Reset. In this volume, we've considered many of the historical milestones across the years that suggest a coming new world order: the UN founding in 1945; creation of the World Trade Organization; the stand-up of supranational organizations like the EU; the creation of the Internet that links the world through cyber technology; and the all-pervasive moves to constantly surveil mankind, thanks in part to the world-changing COVID-19 pandemic.

Scripture tells us that the Antichrist will unify ten nations around the territory of the old Roman Empire (Daniel 8) to establish a one-world government. Is that about to happen? Let's consider the indicators.

Jesus warns us in Luke 21 about false christs, and He mentions birth pains—wars, plagues, famines, great earthquakes, and signs in the heavens. He also speaks of Christians being persecuted (verses 9–11), with that persecution fueled by hate that is religious and political in nature. Although this suffering is difficult for Christians, it leads to great opportunity; Jesus says this "gospel of the kingdom shall be preached in the whole world as a testimony to all the nations, and then the end will come" (Matthew 24:14, NASB).

Dr. Roger Barrier, a retired senior teaching pastor from Casas Church in Tucson, Arizona, suggests signs of the emergent one-world government. For example, the pastor calls out the emergence of technology that tracks everyone—that's already here in terms of GPS locators and facial-recognition tools all guided by artificial intelligence-enabled 5G technology. He also suggests that there will be mass financial changes that empower one-world government, rampant fraud, and economic sanctions used as a tool to identify those who follow the Antichrist (mark of the beast), and a worldwide common currency.[933]

Certainly, our understanding of Marxism shows that it could be the instrument to create the coming one-world government through war and economic intimidation.

We also see in Matthew 24:7 (EHV), "Nation will rise against nation, and kingdom against kingdom." This could mean that communist China becomes the global military superpower as planned by President Xi, which uses its might to conquer the US and brings it under Beijing's control—to become a vassal of a Marxist-led, one-world government.

The description in Luke 21:25–26 by which Christ speaks of the "roaring of the sea…people fainting with fear" could describe modern warfare associated with the fight China wages to conquer America and the balance of the world. Certainly, modern weapons like hypersonic missiles, nuclear-powered cruise missiles, and weapons mounted on orbiting satellites could lead to "people fainting with fear."

Marxism also demands total control, and that's what the Apostle John describes in Revelation 13. The Antichrist receives his power from Satan, is worshiped by "all of the world" (13:3–4), and rules over "every tribe, people, language and nation" (13:7). Thus, he becomes the leader of a totalitarian one-world government that perhaps is formed thanks to disasters or man-made catastrophes like wars, which are described as the seal and trumpet judgments in Revelation 6–11 and the devastation that leads to a true global crisis.

The circumstances behind the formation of a one-world government are not enumerated in the Scriptures. However, what's clear is that the Antichrist, with Satan's support, moves to establish absolute control over all the nations, perhaps by war as described above. Alternatively, that control could come about thanks to commerce, a one-world currency that requires the satanic mark in order to buy and sell.

What's certain in the Scriptures is that mankind will ultimately bow to the one-world government leader simply to survive, and will then carry the mark of the beast on their hand or forehead. Whether that's an actual, visible mark, a technological signal emitted by an implanted chip, or a device carried on the person, or digitized facial recognition technology, isn't clear, nor does it matter.

Another aspect of Marxism that fits the prophetic end-times scenario is the ideology's disdain for all religions, especially Christianity. The absence of a global Christian influence results in the morally bankrupt culture described in 2 Timothy 3:1–4, ESV:

> But understand this, that in the last days there will come times of difficulty. For people will be lovers of self, lovers of money, proud, arrogant, abusive, disobedient to their parents, ungrateful, unholy, heartless, unappeasable, slanderous, without self-control, brutal, not loving good, treacherous, reckless, swollen with conceit, lovers of pleasure rather than lovers of God.

Note: Many biblical scholars have adopted the finding that the words "difficult times" or "perilous times" can also be translated as "raging insanity," which at this moment in history seems to be a more accurate description of the world environment.

MARXIST, ONE-WORLD GOVERNMENT: MIGHT NOT BE IN PROPHETIC SCRIPTURES

Just perhaps this future Marxist, one-world government is only a step in the direction of the coming Great Tribulation and the emergence of the Antichrist. After all, Jesus Christ said, "For then there will be a Great Tribulation, such as was not since the beginning of the world to this time, no, nor ever shall be" (Matthew 24:21, KJV). Further, this one-world government could come about prior to the Great Tribulation, which begins at the midpoint (three and a half years) of the seven-year Tribulation period. What we are looking for is a "convergence" of signs of the Second Coming, which are in effect simultaneously for the first time, though not as yet to the degree they will be, but all are accounted for. If in fact those signs are manifesting, then the Rapture is much closer.

There is no mention of Israel in this mix, which is key to end-times prophecy. That's a significant missing piece that could emerge in the near term. Further, Jesus is specifically addressing the Jews in this portion of Scripture, and in Jerusalem in particular—which must be considered when interpreting the times.

What's clear is that Marxism could play a role in end-times prophecy, and it could be the driving ideology behind the formation of the Antichrist's one-world government. However, the Great Reset conspiracy that eventually leads to a one-world government under a Marxist regime like communist China does not address, at least at this point, all the elements of end-times prophecy. So, we must keep watching, praying, and listening as that time approaches.

What we do know is the Great Reset coup is a true conspiracy, and a key member of that effort resides in the unseen realm, the topic of the third section of this chapter. Further, the Great Reset may be the actual mechanism that destroys America to the point that it is no longer relevant to world events that would warrant mention in the prophetic Scriptures.

DEMONS CONSPIRE WITH
GREAT RESET GLOBALISTS

A global conspiracy to take down all the world's nations and fold them into a one-world government may sound outrageous. But what if I told you the princes of darkness—the UN, Soros, Gates, Bloomberg, Biden, Klaus, Obama, Trudeau, Xi, et al.—had supernatural help? Yes, these builders of a "new world order" conspired with the evil world—a true Great Reset to take over all of mankind.

The *New York Times* labeled the Great Reset a "conspiracy theory."[934] It's noteworthy that the *Times* is right for once. After all, Webster's dictionary traces the word "conspire" to the Latin term *com spirare* or "to breathe, more at spirit." Translation: There is a spiritual aspect to every conspiracy. Noah Webster elaborates that conspire is "to plot; to breathe. But the primary sense is to throw, to wind; hence spira, a fold, circle, wreath or band; and the sense of the verb is, to breathe together, or more probably, to wind or band together… [and] To agree, by oath, covenant or otherwise, to commit a crime; to plot; to hatch treason."[935]

The Great Reset is a true Luciferian (guiding spirit to evil) conspiracy, according to Leo Hohmann, an investigative reporter and author. He writes, "To truly understand evil, you must understand the nature of conspiracies because evil people never tell their intended victims the truth about their plots."[936]

"Now, if God is Truth and wants His people to 'walk in the truth,' then Satan is the opposite," writes Hohmann. "He (Satan) wants as many people as possible to be shielded from truth and walk-in falsehood." Hohmann labeled Satan "the most crafty" of the beasts and the first to successfully pull off a worldwide conspiracy, albeit a failure, an issue addressed earlier in this chapter.

"Truth, Marxism, conspiracy and Satan—sort them out. Satan wants to hide the truth. Marxists lie to hide the truth and then you give them whatever they want in exchange for security," explained Hohmann. "Every communist revolution throughout history has been conspiratorial and therefore Luciferian. They use deception to win power. Once in power, their lies are exposed but it's too late. They use their power to brutally repress their enemies."[937]

Mr. Hohmann argues that communists launch revolutions in a time of crisis, such as during the 1917 Russian Revolution. Those communists promised "bread and peace" to a war-weary Russian people who lost hope and were desperate. That's what is going on today with the Great Reset. The agents of darkness, the Great Reset co-conspirators, are using the COVID-19 virus to shut down the world, to make the people desperate.

Is it just a coincidence that a cabal of globalists with the help of their comrades in communist China brought the world to its knees with a virus? Or, is it just a coincidence that those same people—princes of darkness—are launching a "new world order" to answer the world's desperate people? The answer to both questions is a resounding "no."

This conspiracy is different than the others, however. Past communist revolutions were confined to single nations like France, Russia, and China. However, the conspiracy behind the Great Reset coup is the first in history of a communist revolution that has gone global. However, to fool the "global citizens," it will be modeled after China's variation of communism with state capitalism in the mix, "where the state picks the private enterprises it wants to partner with and dooms the others to forced impoverishment," said Hohmann.[938]

Success at the global level takes more than all the power available to the princes of darkness, however. It requires a partnership much bigger—a co-conspirator with considerable power and an army deployed across the world. Yes, they need the father of lies, Satan and his army of demons, to join forces and perhaps lead them to a one-world government and into the prophetic end times.

Before further developing this conspiracy view, it's necessary to address the readers' doubts about the unknown. Some readers will never accept that there is anything beyond our five senses (touch, sight, hearing, smell, and taste), much less a Marxian conspiracy with Satan. But bear with me to consider that there is much we humans don't know that is beyond our science and senses. Does that mean anything outside our senses and scientific knowledge really doesn't exist?

Do you believe in unidentified flying objects (UFO) and/or demons?

Evidently, there are those at the Pentagon who are now believers in UFOs, even though our best science can't explain them. On September 8, 2004, off the coast of San Diego, California, US Navy Commander David Fravor, an F-18 pilot, encountered what he described as a "Tic Tac" (mint)-shaped UFO, which he believed committed an "act of war."[939]

Commander Fravor was dispatched from his aircraft carrier to investigate radar anomalies he described as "like nothing I've ever seen," an object able to turn on a dime and make itself invisible to radar.[940]

Fravor said the flying conditions were perfect—crystal clear—that day, and the object he saw was watched by four other trained observers. When he tried to fly close to the object, Fravor said, it accelerated so quickly, it was gone in half a second.

Fravor aimed his radar at the UFO. He explained, "The radar is smart enough that when the signal comes back if it's been messed with, it will tell you—it will give you indications that it's being jammed… it's being jammed into about every mode you can see…you can tell it's being jammed."[941]

Luis Elizdono was a former military intelligence official and previously led the Pentagon's Aerospace Threat Identification Program (ATOP). He tried to explain the unexplainable in an op-ed for Fox News.[942]

Mr. Elizdono said in 2004 the USS Nimitz (an aircraft carrier) launched top gun-trained fighter pilots—including Commander Fravor—who engaged with and attempted to intercept "something that could only be described as extraordinary."[943]

The object the pilots pursued "defied all logic and our current understanding of aerodynamics…the technological feat they encountered was further verified by the impressive Aegis AN/SPY-1 radar, America's premiere system at the time, and even gun camera footage and sonar systems from submarines accompanying the carrier."[944]

The ATOP tried to decode the mystery object. Further, such incidents, according to Mr. Elizdono, "continued for at least a decade later and involved other carrier battle groups around the world."[945]

The Pentagon's ATOP was "utterly unprepared to address something that can easily out-maneuver our best-in-class pilots, in our very own tightly controlled airspace," wrote Mr. Elizdono.[946]

Then he said, "Our leaders need to have the courage to ask the question, did a foreign adversary just leapfrog ahead of the U.S.? Or is this something else?"[947]

Just because we don't understand something doesn't mean we ignore it and conclude that it doesn't exist. That takes me back to the unexplained Great Reset co-conspirators, Satan and his army of demons. For the Christian and others who believe in the unseen realm, Satan is very real and working his evil today.

Juxtapose what the Scripture says in 2 Kings 2:11 (KJV) with the above UFO account. That verse states: "And it came to pass, as they still went on, and talked, that, behold, there appeared a chariot of fire, and horses of fire, and parted them both asunder; and Elijah went up by a whirlwind into heaven." A writer 2,500 years ago describes something he saw using objects he understood—"chariot of fire, and horses of fire…and a whirlwind into heaven." Just perhaps that's not much different from Commander Fravor's "Tic Tac" that was "gone in half a second."

As Mr. Elizdono asked, "Or is this something else?" Indeed. There are many things we can't explain, much less sense, and it would be incredibly naïve to suggest, as some even today claim, that there is nothing, no powers, beyond our senses and the reach of science. At a minimum, we can say that angelic forces, good and bad, use technology that is far superior to anything known on the earth. We are not talking about disembodied spirits that are armed with simple swords; rather, the spiritual realm enemy is immeasurably equipped with sophisticated technology with which they will deceive most of the world.

The truth of the matter is the unseen realm is very real and is engaged in events all over this globe. The battle firing up the heavens is very real; Satan is very present and is partnering with earth-bound dark princes.

What Do the Scriptures Say about Satan and His Army of Demons?

I devote an entire chapter in my 2020 book, *Collision Course*, to describing a scriptural view of Satan, his demonic army, and his work on earth. Extracts of that chapter are provided below to answer the question: What do the Scriptures say about Satan and his army of demons? It should become obvious that what Marxists and globalists seek is very much aligned with Satan's goals.

Satan means "the adversary" in Hebrew, and his *nom de guerre* is *devil*, a Greek word meaning "false accuser." He is a fallen angel thanks to his rebellion against God, and he is among us humans on earth (albeit in another dimension) to accuse the saved of their sins that are already forgiven and to encourage unsaved people to reject the salvation Christ offers to all of humanity.

Scripture provides some insight into Satan's character. Isaiah and Ezekiel refer to him as the "morning star," translated "Lucifer." He rules over all the fallen angels, the evil spirits known as demons in the Bible (Matthew 12:24–27). Numerous times in the Gospels, Jesus Christ is identified by demons who without exception cower from His authority as God.

Satan is not only deceiving, as seen above, but he is a prideful and bloodthirsty murderer. Ezekiel 28:17 (NIV) identifies Lucifer (Satan) as full of himself: "Your heart became proud on account of your beauty, and you corrupted your wisdom because of your splendor." He is evidently a narcissist who sought the honor and glory that belonged to God alone.

Jesus identifies Satan as a murderer as well. The Lord confronts the scribes and the Pharisees in the Jerusalem temple:

"You belong to your father, the devil, and you want to carry out your father's desires. He was a murderer from the beginning, not holding to the truth, for there is no truth in him. When he lies, he speaks his native language, for he is a liar and the father of lies." (John 8:44, NIV)

Satan came to destroy life and make our earthly existence eternally miserable. His greatest strength is that many people don't believe he even exists. Some dangerously and naively portray him as a caricature with horns and a spiked tail. However, Jesus took him seriously, and so He should, because Satan employs his army of demons to cause havoc across the world, often using human proxies to convince the lost to ignore their only path to eternal salvation through Christ.

The ranks of Satan's army are demons, fallen angels, spirits that influence people and take over the bodies of some (possession), as seen in the Bible (Leviticus 17:7 and 2 Chronicles 11:15).

These invisible warriors were banished from Heaven because they rebelled against God:

"Then another sign appeared in heaven: an enormous red dragon with seven heads and ten horns and seven crowns on his heads. His tail swept a third of the stars out of the sky and flung them to the earth." (Revelation 12:3–4, NIV)

Jesus, in His public ministry, dealt with demons. They presented themselves in a variety of ways: making a person mute, deaf, and blind, causing convulsions, manifesting superhuman strength, and displaying self-destructive behavior. The disciple Matthew made the distinction between those with illnesses and those truly demon possessed. He wrote:

"News about him spread all over Syria, and people brought to him all who were ill with various diseases, those suffering severe pain, the demon-possessed, those having seizures, and the paralyzed, and he healed them." (Matthew 4:24, NIV)

Satan's army of demons is real, engaged across the world, and doing his bidding. Revelation 12 provides a picture of the archangel Michael and his angels fighting Satan and his demons. The dragon (Satan) and his cohort are cast to the earth just before Christ returns to bring 'salvation, and strength, and the kingdom of our God, and the power of His Christ have come, for the accuser of our brethren, who accused them before our God day and night, has been cast down" (Revelation 12:10, NKJV).

What are Satan's goals?

Satan seeks to destroy humanity even though he knows he is fighting from a losing position. His strategic goals are to prevent as many humans as possible from coming to salvation, as well as to marginalize those who are saved.

We read in 2 Corinthians 4:3 (NIV) that the gospel is "veiled to those who are perishing." Satan intends to keep it that way and employs all his powers to prevent the message of salvation from reaching the lost.

His secondary goal is to keep the saved defeated—ineffective—because when in that state, they are marginalized; they are ineffective at advancing the kingdom of God. That frees Satan to focus on preventing the lost from being saved."

What Does Satan Attack?

Satan attacks the human mind. We know that psychological warfare is an important tool for the human warfighter, a tool designed to influence the mind of the enemy. The US Department of Defense defines psychological warfare as: "The planned use of propaganda and other psychological actions having the primary purpose of influencing the opinions, emotions, attitudes, and behavior of hostile foreign groups in such a way as to support the achievement of national objectives."[948]

Satan uses a variety of psychological warfare tools to influence our opinions, emotions, attitudes, and behavior. He employs these tools to control our minds, a tool identified in 2 Corinthians 4:4 (NIV), which states, 'The god of this age [Satan] has blinded the minds of unbelievers, so that they cannot see the light of the gospel that displays the glory of Christ, who is the image of God.'

The word for "mind" here is *noēmata*, which means "thought" or "purpose." In other words, what humans think is what Satan wants to control so as to blind them to the truth of the gospel. The Apostle Paul warns Christians about Satan's attack on our thoughts (our minds). He cautions us to be of one mind and guard our thoughts against the ways of this world (Philippians 4:7). Control people's minds and you control all human activity. Saved people have a different way of thinking, because God's Holy Spirit dwells with them, freeing them from Satan's absolute control of their mind. However, Satan is not without the means to distract the believer as well.

What are Satan's weapons to control the mind of unbelievers and to keep Christians distracted? He has a significant arsenal of effective weapons to defend against the spread of the gospel and to keep Christians defeated.

He maintains control of the minds of the unbelievers through lust. The word for "lust" in the Greek is *epithumia*, which means "desire," "craving," and "longing, the desire for what is forbidden." The Apostle John explains this weapon in 1 John 2:16 (KJV): "For all that is in the world—the lust of the flesh, the lust of the eyes, and the pride of life—is not of the Father but is of the world [the devil]."

The physical and psychological manifestation of lust is detailed in Galatians 5:19–21 (NIV). These verses identify the tools Satan has at his disposal to keep the unbelieving human's mind captive. The acts of the flesh are obvious: sexual immorality, impurity and debauchery, idolatry and witchcraft; hatred, discord, jealousy, fits of rage, selfish ambition, dissensions, factions and envy; drunkenness, orgies, and the like. I warn you, as I did before, that those who live like this will not inherit the kingdom of God.

We now turn our attention to how Satan deals with Christians, true Spirit-filled believers. He employs three weapons to keep the believing Christian marginalized: lies, temptations, and manipulations. He uses these covertly to deceive and blind us to God's direction. For example, he presents us with false gods, pollutes our thinking with other worldviews, imbues in us selfish desires, and introduces despair, doubt, fear, anger, and more.

Remember, Satan is the father of lies: "When he lies, he speaks his native language, for he is a liar and the father of lies" (John 8:44, NIV). Also, recall that Satan's first appearance in the Bible is in Genesis 3:1 (NRSV), and there he said to Eve, "Did God say, 'You shall not eat from any tree in the garden'?" Then the father of lies quickly answered his question with a falsehood: "You will not die; for God knows that when you eat of it your eyes will be opened, and you will be like God, knowing good and evil" (Genesis 3:4–5, NRSV). Satan attempts to deceive us similarly today by twisting or changing God's Word and confusing us about sin.

We are engaged in a war for the souls of mankind. Much of the fight is in the invisible realm. Satan and his army of demons with his Great Reset co-conspirators use every trick available to destroy mankind.

So how do you fight the dark princes of the Great Reset when they have Satan on their team? We exorcise the evil.

Yes, we are heading for a clash of spiritual worldviews and arguably the true prophetic end times. The answer to the question "How do we fight evil?" in part is to recognize our enemy and take appropriate action.

Satan and his army have been around earth since the time of Adam and Eve. They know the ropes—humankind's many weaknesses—and won't leave without a fight. So, when entering such a fight, we ought to consider advice from those who have experience with spiritual warfare and exorcisms.

Catholic priest Chad Ripperger is such an expert who understands the dark prince globalist conspirators, and he elaborates on the topic in a December 2020 YouTube video, *Demons and the Great Reset*. The globalist conspirators are "basically in league with Satan," explained Father Ripperger. "They believe the same things that he [Satan] does. They want the same goals. I think what we're seeing is, there's some stark comparisons between what I see in the behavior of some of these [globalist] people and what I see in a [exorcism] session."[949]

"For example, right now, things are leading up to a crescendo," Father Ripperger explained. "And that's what you tend to see right before a person has been liberated [set free from a demon]. So, there's this buildup of the diabolic manifestation that becomes much more drastic, much more open, much more out there, sometimes even more preternatural [outside of the natural] right towards the end, and then the person is actually liberated."[950]

The priest presents the challenge. That is, if this country is to be liberated from the globalist, Marxist Great Reset coup, then it must be freed from the demons that torment them.[951]

"Once Satan thinks he has the upper hand, he presses it all the more," the priest said. "He doesn't wait, he doesn't take his time, he will in certain circumstances take his time but once he thinks he has control over a situation he's going to drive it until he gets ultimately what he wants."[952]

Father Ripperger used a broad brush regarding the dark prince co-conspirators. These are people who are being used by Satan, who are also involved in horrific sins, said the priest, and they're not that different than Jeffrey Epstein, the convicted sex offender who took his own life.

Ripperger elaborated:

And I think that's slowly starting to come out. If you read about it, it's in the public record about some of the behavior of some of the people that have been the most vociferous during this time frame, and it reminds me a lot of how the demons themselves, when they get caught in something, or their shame gets revealed in something they have committed, they sometimes become very vociferous and very angry about it and try to push the envelope even more.[953]

He continued:

Once their sin is revealed and people see it, then what they do is, they'll try to create a distraction onto something else. So, one of the things an exorcist has to constantly be on guard about during a session is, when you start getting to a certain point where the demons actually, where you're starting to gain certain control over them or you're starting to get somewhere in the session where it looks like he's going to start telling you some information, he'll actually start doing things to distract you or he'll dig into the person, the demons.[954]

The priest explained that another demonic trick is to claim victory before it is confirmed. He explained:

The other thing that's very common is, claiming that they are victorious or that they've already won when they really haven't yet, or that they actually have rights, or that there's certain things that they have that other people can't take away from them. So, it's very similar to a lot of things we're actually seeing, on their [evil] side.[955]

Father Ripperger says demoralization of the masses is a demonic trick, one they used effectively via the COVID-19 pandemic and thanks to the cooperation of certain so-called leaders in our cities, states, and Congress:

That demoralization is precisely what you see when demons are attacking people. One of the things we have to do when people are possessed [by a demon], is constantly get their focus back on God. Don't let the demons drag your focus into the stuff that you're suffering and the things that you're dealing with, keep your focus, because that's when things start to go downhill. It's also one of those things that the shift in the focus is what the demons are always trying to get us to do, and to be demoralized.[956]

Demons are like their leader, Satan, who lies. "My concern," said the priest, "is the people on the other side are being used to make us feel demoralized and distracting us so we lose our focus."[957]

Finally, demons are angry about most everything. "They take everything personal," said Father Ripperger. "That's how demons function. That boils down to the fact that, demons are narcissistic, that's pretty much the description of demons and that's the description of communists."[958]

The good news for Christians, explains the priest, is to "stay prayed up, don't lose hope, stay focused on the hope of hopes, Jesus Christ."[959]

CONCLUSION

The global, Marxist, Great Reset conspiracy is real—and it does seek to move America and eventually the entire world to a Soviet model, perhaps ruled by a communist Chinese-dominated, one-world government. This chapter confirms that intent and then considers whether what we are seeing played out today is a coup that might usher in the prophetic end times. Finally, the chapter demonstrates that the key co-conspirator in the Great Reset is none other than Satan, supported by his army of demons, who heavily influences many globalists and how we ought to address their global campaign.

The final chapter in *Give Me Liberty, Not Marxism* assumes that the Great Reset succeeds, then outlines what we can expect from that totalitarian globalist regime and how we ought to respond before the Lord's return.

13

The Post-Great Reset World

What will life be like going forward should the globalist Great Reset coup actually lead to a one-world government under a Marxist totalitarian regime? It may well be what I described in the previous chapter marked by all the biblical end-times events.

That outcome only happens if we repeat some of mankind's darkest history. To illustrate that point, consider the record of post-World War I Europe and how the world turned a blind eye to the rising storm in Germany.

The First World War (1914–1918) is often known as the "war to end all wars," but it only took two decades before the world was plunged once again into a new war, and that time, the second global conflict was more devastating than the first. This outcome was evidence that at least some people in authority refused to learn from past mistakes.

Why did a second world war come so quickly on the heels of the first war's devastation? Evidently, the Europeans welcomed socialism after the first war, which led to anarchy and economic hardship and set the stage for the rise of the German tyrant Adolf Hitler. That half-mad socialist rose to power thanks to the Great Depression that devastated so many Germans and their refusal to learn from history.[960]

Hitler, the elected chancellor of Germany (beginning in January 1933), quickly pushed aside his political opposition to create a one-party state as outlined in the previous chapter vis-à-vis the Reichstag fire, and then he maintained control over the German people thanks to his secret police, the Gestapo. His economic policies spurred a rapid recovery while sparking his dream of a "thousand-year Reich," a true dictatorship, and ultimately launched his vision for a world government. An impressive economic recovery gave Hitler the leverage to destroy the Communist Party's influence in Germany, which was necessary to consolidate Nazi power, and then he began the long march to colonize Europe, beginning with the peaceful incorporation of Austria (1938), the occupation of portions of the Czechoslovak state (1939), and then the 1939 invasion of Poland.[961]

On reflection, I'm afraid Americans, like many pre-World War II Europeans, haven't learned from history. Too many of today's American youth and not a few much older leaders were fed a pro-Marxist public school history that failed to review the horrific devastation associated with past Marxist countries and chronicled in books like the *Black Book of Communism* (1999). Those lessons are still fresh in some of our minds, thanks to the Cold War. However, they are evidently lost on most Americans, which explains in part why especially our younger generations are determined today to retrace the trail of tears others like the Germans and Cold War victims want to forget. Yes, America and much of the free world in 2021 is on the cusp of suffering the consequences of our collective naïveté regarding the Marxist Great Reset coup should we fail to change course.

This chapter addresses three closing issues for *Give Me Liberty, Not Marxism*. First, we will consider the three stages of a Marxist revolution that lead to a possible new America and a one-world government under a totalitarian regime. Second, we will consider just how far we are down that transformational pathway and what such a future might portend. Finally, I provide some recommendations on what we might do to respond to the coming troubled times that could well be the beginning of the prophetic end times.

MOMENTUM BUILDING FOR GREAT RESET

The Democratic Party's stranglehold of Washington and its ideological alignment with Marxist-inclined globalists will give America and the world a wild ride into the future, possibly worse than what we experienced in 2020.

I say that because, during the summer of 2020, the left and those now sitting in the seats of power in Washington did little to stop the thuggery across this country. Leftists sat on their hands as the likes of Antifa and BLM declared "autonomous zones," destroyed or vandalized thousands of state and federal public monuments, torched many hundreds of buildings with impunity, and loudly called for defunding our last line of defense—local police.

Throughout the violent summer of 2020, presidential candidate Biden rarely, if ever, condemned the atrocious violence by his allies on the left. Rather, he contextualized it as an "idea," and then magically, once he assumed the presidency, called for unity and accused our police of racism for not quelling the violence. The left's hypocrisy is palpable.

The left has gone completely rogue. They are now totalitarian, anti-American. Consider what happened to President Trump, whose ability to use social media imploded allegedly because former First Lady Michelle Obama called the likes of the Twitter CEO, Jack Dorsey, to complain about Mr. Trump's use of the social media platform. Like a good leftist, Mr. Dorsey shut down Mr. Trump's account forever, and worse, Trump voters were also blocked temporarily from their Parler apps by Apple and Google. Now that the left has all the power, expect more draconian, anti-speech sanctions against the politically incorrect conservatives.

Victor Davis Hanson with the Hoover Institution illustrated the hardening of the left's anti-free speech monopolist assault. He explained:

In the 19th century, "progressives" sought to curb the power of monopolies and trusts on the logic that the proverbial people had only the railroads or telegraphs to travel or communicate, and should be freed from their octopus "tentacles." The railroad argument, "Ride a horse if you don't like us," never washed.[962]

Now progressives (ideologically Marxist cousins) enlist social media monopolies to ensure that they alone can control, censor, and cancel incorrect communications over the publicly owned airspace. "Just email or use your cell phone, if you don't like us" won't wash either. Progressives are no longer the watchdogs breaking up trusts. They are the trusts breaking up watchdogs.

So, those of us on the right side of justice who treasure our civil liberties are left with less than free speech, and that's until some future time when even our email and cell phones are confiscated.

Yes, we are seeing the Great Reset revolution coming at us at a breakneck speed. We ask: How far and fast will the leftists go at transforming America? Will President Biden end the Senate filibuster, the nine-justice Supreme Court, the Electoral College and a fifty-state union? After all, the left needs the tools to never let absolute control once again slip from their hands, much like Hitler destroyed his political opposition and used the Gestapo to enforce his will on the German people.

Unfortunately, the left has also taken the mainstream media captive. Most journalists long ago abandoned objectivity and reporting only the facts, which explains, as we saw in the 2020 presidential campaign, they are like good sycophants who shielded Mr. Biden from the consequences of his numerous "senior moment" flubs and will continue to twist the truth and the consequences of his policy decisions going forward.

My only conclusion is that, starting with the Biden inauguration, America will ride on a very bumpy road that dead ends. After all, Mr. Biden came to office to oversee a country worn by riot, arson, looting, plague, lockdown, and accusations of election fraud. Will this compilation of crises further snowball into something truly existential?

Consider our current state and the vulnerabilities this creates going forward. The 2020 national shutdown, thanks to some rather irrational government decisions and Chinese propaganda, drove our national debt through the roof ($28 trillion), with hardly any hope of ever reaching a balanced budget again.

Overseas, our enemies drool for a piece of America and literally celebrate our troubles. They know America can't be as strong in the future, because we must service our out-of-control debt and heavily invest in recovering from the ongoing recession. Is America in a meltdown, the dream of so many tyrants across the centuries?

Will our new and often confused commander-in-chief Mr. Biden agree to reset the disastrous Obama 2016 Iran nuclear deal, cementing the Islamists' acceleration to an atomic bomb, lighting the fuse to the next Middle East war? Further, will the Chinese return to their former draconian mercantilism thanks to a Chinese-favoring man in the Oval Office? Will the dictator in North Korea test more nuclear "devices" and missiles? Will the Russians pick up steam on intimidation and their asymmetric global campaign? Count on the answer to these questions being "yes," because those dictators are feeling their oats, thanks to America's new weak, leftist "sheriff."

THREE STRIKES AND AMERICA (THE WORLD) IS MARXIST!

History could indeed repeat itself, and it can happen to America too. The left is much too cozy with Marxists, and they are embracing a basic communist strategy used repeatedly to take over a country—and this time perhaps the entire world—to establish a one-world government.[963]

There are three stages to every communist strategy to take over a country: (1) prepare the ground, (2) destabilize and change basic values, and (3) cleanse by reorganizing to put all power in the hands of a few. Consider each stage and whether it is working or could work in America and more broadly across the world.

Stage #1: Prepare the ground for a communist takeover by eradicating the influence of key institutions and polarizing the worker class. The Marxist revolutionaries, some who are well positioned in America and support the Great Reset coup, are very busy weakening their strongest opponents "by infiltrating and subverting them, while simultaneously strengthening your own forces."[964]

In a previous section of *Give Me Liberty, Not Marxism*, I demonstrated that two key institutions are already coopted by Marxists, our mainstream media, and the education establishment. With those under control, Marxists identified their remaining opposition as two other institutions already under severe attack: family and religion. Why? Because Marxists must turn America against traditional morality, and the family and the church (especially Christianity) are the last remaining strongholds resisting the advances of Marxists.

These opponents of a communist Great Reset coup are tough, as past Marxists discovered, because church and family thrive when oppressed. So that means to be successful, Marxists must alter their strategy.

The problem for American traditionalists is that the Christian church, the primary opposition to Marxists across the globe, is getting fat, undisciplined. The Apostle John found a similar problem with the first-century church of Laodicea. That church wavered in its commitment to Christ, about which the apostle wrote: "I know your deeds, that you are neither cold nor hot. I wish you were either one or the other! So, because you are lukewarm—neither hot nor cold—I am about to spit you out of my mouth" (Revelation 3:15–16, NIV).

A lukewarm church isn't useful to God's purposes, and neither are pastors who forget their God-ordained mission and embrace government mandates that violate God's Word. They cower to Satan and his demonic army aiming to make the church a social club that embraces anti-biblical atrocities such as abortion and homosexuality on the altar of choice and totally misinterpret Romans 13 to embrace government's evil orders over God's mandates when it comes to gathering—yes, even during a pandemic.

Even former Soviet leader Vladimir Lenin understood how to weaken the church's influence, as do his modern students. "We will find our greatest success to the extent that we inculcate Marxism as a kind of religion: religious men and women are easy to convert and win, and so will easily accept our thinking if we wrap it up in a kind of religious terminology," wrote Lenin.[965]

The same is true regarding the family. In times of prosperity, the family unit becomes weak, discarding marriage and permitting extramarital affairs, no-fault divorces, and so-called homosexual marriages. The children pay the price, and so does much of society, when sequential monogamy becomes the norm for such a critical institution.

Why has this happened to the American family? Part of this outcome is by design and thanks to the revolutionary Communist Party's New Programme, which states:

> The right to abortion will be guaranteed.... As far as the policy toward the family, it will be recognized for what it is: Not some holy or sacred institution to be preserved for all time...not only will the family be a secondary form for determining children's upbringing, but its influence in promoting conservatism among its members, especially the women and children, will be actively combatted. While the parents will still have significant responsibility for their children, this does not mean they are "theirs," and there will be struggle to prevent parents from imposing old values, and conservative, non-revolutionary thinking generally on the children.[966]

Marxists also have to polarize, divide society into haves and have-nots, a concept introduced earlier. One group, what Marx called the proletariat (workers), must feel victimized by a second group, the wealthy (bourgeoisie). After all, communists can't abide by wealthy people, but it might surprise you to learn that Marx's "wealthy" classification includes anyone who owns a private business, no matter how small. Marxists loathe and demonize such people to the point of hatred. Yes, Vladimir

Lenin said: "We must hate. Hatred is the basis of communism. Children must be taught to hate their parents if they are not communists."[967]

Altruistic liberals are especially vulnerable at this stage to recruitment. Communists target them because they have big hearts and are full of liberal good intentions, and they are naïve and easily manipulated by emotions. Lenin called them "useful idiots."

Stage #2: Destabilization: Change society's basic values. Arguably, this process is well underway in the United States, thanks to the left's takeover of both mainstream media and the education establishment. It's all about the children, and as Lenin said: "Give me your child for eight years, and [he or she] will be a communist forever."[968]

An earlier chapter in this volume demonstrated in detail the Marxist corruption of our public education establishment, which performs more indoctrination than academic instruction. It distorts our history and fails to instruct our children about American civics, which would otherwise vaccinate them against Marxism.

Perhaps this Marxist indoctrination is best understood in the context of the promotion of the so-called environmental cause, which acts as a catalyst for promoting socialism.

So-called new communism is "based on all the old communist ideological principles and beliefs, but uses environmentalism as its agent of change, to completely alter the core values of western democracy and destabilize (demoralize) society," according to Zuzana Janosova Den Boer, who grew up in a communist country.[969]

She illustrated this process with an excerpt from Captain Eco, a 1991 publication intended to indoctrinate children "to believe that it's their responsibility to 'save the planet'":

> Your planet is in serious trouble—from pollution, toxic waste and the loss of forest, farmland and fresh water.... Your parents and grandparents have made a mess of looking after the earth. They may deny it, but they are little more than thieves. And they are stealing your future from under your noses.[970]

Stage #3: Implement post-revolution cleansing. Once the Marxists gain power either by the bayonet or the ballot box, they seize control and abolish democratic elections. Opposition parties and all opponents are "physically liquidated." Private businesses are seized and confiscated—what they call "nationalized." The "useful idiots" (liberals) who helped the Marxists gain power are either jailed or executed. A new privileged elite of party leaders is formed, and the leaders of every key institution or organization are replaced by an official member of the ruling Marxist party.

"After the Reds have accomplished their bloody Revolution, the entire conquered society must be totally subjugated and transmogrified, and all institutions and entities must be forcibly crammed into an approved Socialist mold, including the Church, all levels of government and schools, and, most importantly, the family," writes the American Life League in a paper entitled *Life Under Communism: Hell on Earth.*[971]

So, what happens next?

> [The Marxists] jail and silence church leaders…and leading lay people. They also immediately disband [B]ible-believing religious organizations and severely restrict their activities, because these entities preach morality and are the antithesis of atheism and communism. The objective of such oppression is the total eradication of the visible church.[972]

The oppression was still in effect as the former Soviet Union crumbled. In 1990, Avraham Shirfin wrote in his book, *The First Guidebook to Prisons and Concentration Camps of the Former Soviet Union,* that "tens of thousands of Christians are still trapped in more than 2,000 slave labor camps for the heinous crimes of '…reading religious books, posting up notices, or demanding religious instruction for their children.' And, in Albania, making the sign of the cross is punishable by three years in prison."[973]

Russia's campaign against the Christian church and the so-called intellectual class was part of a formal program. On August 22, 1922, dictator Lenin sent a letter to the Politburo announcing his program: "The more representatives of the reactionary bourgeoisie and the reactionary clergy that we manage to shoot the better. Now is the time to teach the public such a lesson that for many decades they will not dare even to think of any sort of resistance."[974]

There is no reason to believe modern Marxists wouldn't do to America what is described above.

Unfortunately, America is well into the three stages of a transition to Marxism. Already much of the media and education institutions are aboard the transformation train and are doing their best to support future efforts. The church and family are on the ropes, and it's questionable whether they can survive much longer. Stage two is well underway as well, as basic values are shifting to that of a secularized culture. Once the first two stages are complete, all that is left is for the globalist Great Reset coup elite to declare victory, consolidate power, and clean up the battlefield: jail or execute those of us who won't succumb to their demands.

STARTING MID-TRANSFORMATION, GOING FORWARD TO FULL MARXISM

It may be hard to stomach that Marxists are making good progress in America, much less across the world, vis-à-vis their Great Reset coup. Unfortunately, many of us are fooling ourselves and aren't aware of the very things happening before our eyes.

More than a decade ago, a man by the name of Ken Huber, a former city manager who retired in 2006, wrote the editor of a Tawas City, Michigan paper, the *Losco County News Herald*, to express his concern about just how far the left has brought America. Here are Mr. Huber's words:[975]

What Has America Become?

Editor,

Has America become the land of the special interest and home of the double standard?

Let's see: if we lie to the Congress, it's a felony and if the Congress lies to us its just politics; if we dislike a black person, we're racist and if a black dislikes whites, it's their First Amendment right; the government spends millions to rehabilitate criminals and they do almost nothing for the victims; in public schools you can teach that homosexuality is OK, but you better not use the word God in the process; you can kill an unborn child, but it is wrong to execute a mass murderer; we don't burn books in America, we now rewrite them; we got rid of the communist and the Socialist threat by renaming them progressives; we are unable to close our border with Mexico but have no problem protecting the 38th parallel in Korea; if you protest against President Obama's policies you're a terrorist but if you burned an American flag or George Bush in effigy it was your First Amendment right.

You can have pornography on TV or the Internet, but you better not put a nativity scene in a public park during Christmas; we have eliminated all criminals in America, they are now called sick people; we can use a human fetus for medical research but it's wrong to use an animal.

We take money from those who work hard for it and give it to those who don't want to work; we all support the Constitution, but only when it supports our political ideology; we still have freedom of speech, but only if we are being politically correct; parenting has been replaced with Ritalin and video games; the land of opportunity is now the land of handouts; the similarity between Hurricane Katrina and the Gulf Oil spill is that neither president did anything to help.

And how do we handle a major crisis today? The government appoints a committee to determine who's at fault, then threatens them, passes a law, raises our taxes; tells us the problem is solved so they can get back to their re-election campaign.

What has happened to the land of the free and the home of the brave?

Don't Mr. Huber's observations ring true? What if the leftists' Marxist transformation continues through stage three? What will life be like in that future world?

Mr. Huber isn't the only person who sees signs that America is radically going in a Marxist direction. Rod Dreher is the author of *The Benedict Option*, a book that calls on Christians to withdraw from society in order to preserve their Christian beliefs.[976]

Mr. Dreher warns, "There is persecution coming. Christians need to right now prepare for it." He indicates that it will become difficult to be a physician or lawyer in the future without compromising one's Christian morals. Further, he believes it won't be long into the future before Christians won't be allowed to attend certain schools, hold certain jobs, or even shop at certain stores.[977]

He warns Christians to "pay attention to what is happening in your church, your work place, your local schools[;] it is becoming distinctly more hostile to any kind of social conservatism and religious conservativism." He argues that we are already in a state of "soft totalitarianism" in America. Many of the conditions facing America today were experienced by the Germans in the 1930s and led to them embracing Nazism and likewise the Russians accepting bolshevism in 1917.[978]

Part of that acceptance was thanks to "mass loneliness and alienation," which made the Germans embrace Nazism, said Mr. Dreher. He explained that "mass loneliness and alienation" made the Germans "sitting ducks for people who came in with sweeping new ideologies that could replace the thing that they thought they were missing." Then Mr. Dreher called attention to the loneliness rising in America today, due in part to prolonged COVID-19 shutdowns (jobs, schools, churches, etc.). Those government-ordered closures and shelter-in-place mandates showed low trust by "leaders" in society, a magnifier of loneliness that makes people vulnerable to totalitarianism.[979]

Under those circumstances, truth is up for grabs, argues Mr. Dreher. He said we see the left with their LGBT (lesbian, gay, bisexual, transgender) homosexual agenda, promotion of abortion, and other ideologies that ignore biblical truth. Further, too many people are willing to fictionalize history for ideological reasons such as the 1619 Project, which reframes America's history by placing the consequences of slavery at the center of our national narrative.

The state's surveillance system is something to be feared as well. Mr. Dreher indicates that technology can surveil our every move beyond what we voluntarily give away to Google and other Web services, such as social credit systems like the one in communist China or the emergent COVID-19 tracking system experienced by many.

Given what Mr. Dreher and others mentioned above, we have a pretty good idea about the consequences should America and the world become Marxist. After all, the histories of the former Soviet Union, communist China, and other Marxist regimes are replete with many practical implications of that possible transformation. Consider some common experiences from past communist regimes, not all that different from those shared in previous chapters, but a stark reminder of what is at stake.

Catholic priest Paul Marx of Human Life International describes what living is like under a communist regime. He explains that it is the same as existing under a feudal monarchy: "For the communist overlords, human beings are mere barnyard animals to be bred, aborted, and worked for the benefit of the fortunate elite on top."[980]

Father Marx's description perfectly captures life for the average citizen behind the Soviet's former Iron Curtain. At that time, life was grey, dirty, and mostly lifeless. One could stand in line for hours to buy a low-quality item or some gummy food. But even if you are fortunate enough to find what you seek, it may be impossible to buy, because your wages are so low. Years ago, in communist Eastern Europe, the average wage was $600 per year, or just $12 per week. Why? Communism thrives in a system of universal poverty, which keeps the people helpless and dependent upon big government. Further, it keeps people from plotting to overthrow the leaders because it takes all their energy just to satisfy their hunger.[981]

Want a place to live in a communist country? It could take ten to twenty years for the opportunity to buy a dirty, run-down apartment with one bedroom, cold running water, and occasional electric service.[982]

Drug and alcohol abuse were a serious problem for many living under communism. One report estimates that up to 8 percent of the Soviet population was drunk at any given time, and it shouldn't be surprising that, after weapons sales, the state's chief source of revenue was from 80-proof vodka.[983]

Life in a communist state is also a life-long lesson in corruption. To survive in such a system, you have to network and pay bribes, because corruption is endemic. Yes, education may be "free," but even with top grades and being academically gifted, it still takes a bribe to get into the best schools.

Healthcare is "free" in a Marxist system—that is, unless you want a good, sober surgeon for your operation; then you need to pay a bribe.

Police are mostly corrupt in communist states, primarily because they have such immense power and are poorly paid. Money buys justice in such a system, and without the proper bribe, you can land in jail with no hope.

Government bureaucrats often rely on bribes to supplement their income and there's no getting around paying one if you want a "government service." You can't build anything, drive a car, go to school, or carry on most every other aspect of life without a government-approved document.

Did your car break down? Don't leave it with the local repair shop;

otherwise, you risk it becoming a boneyard for others needing replacement parts.

Perhaps the worst of the corruption is evident when a citizen comes to the attention of law enforcement. You can be arrested, tortured, allowed to die as a political prisoner or in a labor camp in some distant uranium mine, or you can be thrown into an insane asylum because of your religious views. But of course, fear is the primary tool of the regime, because it keeps the population silent and obedient, something the East German Stasi, Soviet KGB, and Nazi Gestapo knew well.

Now reflect with me about changes to American's freedoms over the past few decades. Have you noticed like Mr. Huber that many of the social changes haven't promoted our liberties? Our present diminished liberties and quality of life, if we continue down a Marxist path, will certainly get much worse.

Let me end this section with something former President Ronald Reagan used to remind us about our precious freedoms. He said, "Freedom is a fragile thing and is never more than one generation away from extinction. Those who have known freedom, then lost it, have never known it again."[984]

Will this generation lose forever the freedoms our founders gave this nation?

HOW TO PREPARE FOR A MARXIST WORLD

Preparing for something you've only read about is difficult. It's like getting ready for major surgery or the death of a spouse. You can read up on how others have dealt with those life events or talk to a friend who has gone through a similar tragedy. But no matter what you've done, including giving it up to the Lord in constant prayer, it's still going to be tough for you on many levels.

What follows isn't comprehensive or prescriptive. It's intended as a few ideas to consider if you, like me, are convinced that this world is heading toward the prophetic end times. That means life will become quite challenging and physically uncomfortable, thanks to an emergent Marxist government.

Consider two groups of recommendations.

First, I'll provide some practical advice on how to prepare for a possible future Marxist-like American government that robs us of our civil liberties and gives us a life such as those described above.

Second, I'll address the Christian who sincerely seeks the Lord's direction on this matter: How do I live in a world that hates me and my Savior?

Practical Considerations

I'd rather not think about this country crumbling to a Marxist-like government. Why? I've had a glimpse of communism, albeit briefly, and I found it quite frightening.

I've seen communist North Korea from the demilitarized zone that divides the Korean peninsula. I've seen communist China from Hong Kong and looked across the Iron Curtain's barbed-wire fences and mine-fields, and even once "vacationed" in the Soviet Union. I also twice visited US Naval Base Guantanamo (Cuba) to visit our prison for Islamic terrorists.

These brief encounters with communist states left a deep impression of gloom, doom, and fear. I've also had many encounters with people who escaped communist countries, including a stepmother, and I've listened to their accounts of life, which still haunt my soul.

With this as a background, I suggest the following "advice" with readers who share my concern that it's best to be prepared today than be sorry tomorrow should these concerns become a reality for America.

When investigating this topic, I came across an *American Thinker* article by Judith Acosta, author of *The Worst Is Over* and *The Next Osama*. Ms. Acosta's article, "How to Prepare for a Communist Coup," resonates with my own concerns.[985]

She interviewed a doctor of pharmacy and the daughter of a Dutchman who resisted the Nazis in World War II, saved many Jews and Christians from capture, and escaped three German concentration camps. Ms. Acosta asked the unnamed woman: "If you had a time machine and wanted to warn your father, or the Jews or Ukrainians in the late '20s and early '30s, what would you tell them?"

Below is the woman's advice, which speaks to my understanding of the threat from the perspective of a US Army infantry officer trained on survival and as a strategist.

First, the doctor of pharmacy said: "Keep your eyes open, look for the truth, don't be afraid to speak up, keep the faith and trust in God."

That response surprised Ms. Acosta. Rather, she had expected to hear: "I would tell them to run as fast as they can, now, get out, drop everything and come here, to us." But, as Ms. Acosta explained, there's no "us" anymore. The United States is the last great hope for refugees seeking freedom, and if this country gives in to Marxism, then "we really are on our own."

At that point, the daughter of the Dutch resistance fighter presented five options to be prepared for such an eventuality.

1. ARM YOURSELF

That's still supported by America's Second Amendment. "The first piece of legislation enacted after Hitler took power was the confiscation of weaponry in the civilian population," Ms. Acosta transcribed from the woman's words. "He was a madman, but he was no fool. He knew that you couldn't shove a well-armed populace into cattle cars or ghettos. We know that the next step in Germany was to defund the police. The only weapons then were in the hands of goose-stepping soldiers."

Fortunately, our forefathers knew about the threat posed by monarchists like King George III, the British ruler at the time of the American Revolution. An armed citizenry is the best defense from a tyrannical government, a description of a possible future Marxist state.

Confiscation of our arms could happen in America, however. Keep in mind that President Biden has a record of favoring gun control. In the 1990s, then Senator Biden favored federal background checks and a ban on assault weapons, and he boasted at the time that he has "taken on the National Rifle Association (NRA) on the national stage and won—twice."[986]

2. Build a Cache

Be prepared for the unexpected. "It is a common understanding that Mormons have a year's supply of foodstuffs and other essentials in the basements of their homes," wrote Ms. Acosta. She reminded us about the 2020 shutdown-inspired toilet paper craze, and then she asked "What to store?"

Her list includes: "tools, batteries, warm clothes, paper towels, candles, precious metals, freeze-dried foods, medicines, water, water and water." She also recommends a new backpack, a stack of cash, or "some other form of tender."

I spent decades in the Army's infantry and one assignment in the Alaskan Arctic. I'd add to the mix a source of fuel, stove, water purification tablets or filters, a couple of good knives and hatchet with a sharpening file, a spool of lightweight and strong nylon rope, plastic sheeting, and a copy of God's Word, the Bible, in a waterproof pouch.

Also, store these items in a safe place free of moisture and rodents, out of the reach of children, and yet easily accessible. Become familiar with survival skills and annually practice using these items.

A good source for your "cache" supplies is found at the *Skywatch TV* Store, https://www.skywatchtvstore.com/collections/preparedness-supplies.

3. Prepare for the Worst

By now, you know that Marxists intend to come for those who refuse to obey, especially Christians who won't deny God and worship the state. Ms. Acosta wrote: "At some point you will be called either to stand up for what you believe and what you know is right or to surrender. To take a stand, you may be required to lay down your life."

That's a sobering statement. Few of us other than those who serve in law enforcement or our military services routinely contemplate such issues. However, as Ms. Acosta wrote, "The stakes might just get that high. Take stock. Be honest. What do you stand for? What are you willing to die for?"

I can tell you from personal experience that not only must you train to use a weapon in self-defense, but you also must train your mind. Preparing yourself psychologically for the unthinkable—violently resisting to the death if necessary—isn't pleasant, but it is a necessity when your life and freedoms are in the balance.

The Scriptures remind us: "Who is going to harm you if you are eager to do good? But even if you should suffer for what is right, you are blessed. Do not fear their threats; do not be frightened" (1 Peter 3:13–14, NIV). Years ago, I hosted a Bible study in my military quarters in Germany. Our guest that evening was a Christian man from India. He told us about the time the authorities arrested him and threatened to take his life. His response was sobering. "I will be in heaven with Jesus if you kill me," he said. "That is far better than living here under tyranny." That man's conviction must become the Christian's belief if we are ever faced with denying our faith and confronting an imminent physical death at the hands of an evil government.

4. PREPARE SPIRITUALLY

This goes hand in glove with preparing for the worst. Ms. Acosta wrote that "this is…the most important option. We are still one nation under God, whether or not it 'trends.' It entails that we take the time now to cultivate relationships, spend time in prayer, and trust in the right things, which are overwhelmingly not in this world."

She continued, "We are held together and empowered by the Creator who really does know what He is doing. Even when we can't see it…or understand it. And, when (or if) the time comes for us to show what we're made of, we may be braver and stronger than we can imagine from our more comfy vantage points right now."

5. BE BOLD

Ms. Acosta's friend told a true story about her father's confrontation with the Nazis. She explained that her father, who was about 18 years old at the time, had hidden the family car in a nearby woods, camouflaged by a thicket. He'd kept it so he could smuggle Jews out of Germany and into homes with hiding spaces. On one occasion, with lives literally and immediately in the balance, he arrived at the border between Holland and Germany only to be confronted by soldiers who demanded to inspect his papers. He told them in perfect German that the commander himself had given him his orders. The soldier said, "We need to see the orders. We'll call the commander ourselves."

She continued, "Thinking on his adrenalized feet, he said, 'You go right ahead. He's in a foul mood. Better you than me.' They let him through."

"Can you ever be prepared for something like that? I don't know," said Ms. Acosta in closing.

I'll answer her question. Yes, emphatically yes. In the history of mankind, there are numerous examples of true heroes who stood their ground against tyranny. Our time may come, and if it does, I pray we will count the cost and be found faithful.

HOW TO LIVE IN A WORLD THAT
HATES ME AND MY SAVIOR

Do not treat prophecies with contempt but test them all; hold on to what is good, reject every kind of evil.
—1 Thessalonians 5:20–22, NIV

Let me begin this final section of the last chapter with a reminder: Test, hold to the good, and reject evil. Jesus said, "My kingdom is not of this world. If it were, my servants would fight to prevent my arrest by the Jewish leaders. But now my kingdom is from another place" (John

18:36, NIV). Fellow believer, our home is in heaven and, like the Indian Christian mentioned earlier, we are going to a far better place. That's why the Christian must be bold, willing to take risks in a lost world.

That reminds me of a risky mission trip into the heart of communist China.

Pastor Wayne Cordeiro with New Hope Christian Fellowship in Honolulu, Hawaii, shared about his trip to communist China with twenty-two Christian leaders, eighteen of whom had previously been imprisoned. What was their offense? They had smuggled in Bible passages on small pieces of paper for other believers to memorize.[987]

"If we get caught, what will happen to me?" the pastor asked the Chinese Christians who joined him on a thirteen-hour train ride to the secret leadership training site. One of the Chinese Christians soberly explained, "Well, you will get deported in 24 hours, and we will go to prison for three years."

That's quite a frightening threat to consider, one posed by a current communist regime (China) and perhaps by the very same leaders who might in the future oversee a one-world government.

I have three recommendations for believers going forward into the future that might include a Marxist one-world government: Live like Daniel in Babylon, properly apply Romans 13, and be an uncompromising truth-teller.

Live Like Daniel in Babylon

Christian, remember your home is in heaven. No doubt, someone will say we have to live in this world, which is true. The book of Daniel illustrates how we can live in an alien place (an atheistic Marxist world) without compromising our faith.

Teenage Daniel was taken captive in 586 BC by King Nebuchadnezzar and brought to Babylon. His Babylonian masters tried to reprogram him; their effort started by giving him a new name and erasing his Hebrew identity by quickly assimilating him into the local culture.[988]

Daniel's assimilation included language and literature training and eating rich food from the king's table (Daniel 1:4–5). However, "Daniel purposed in his heart" not to defile himself by eating that food (Daniel 1:8). Bold Daniel asked for a different menu, and trusted that God would honor his faithfulness. At the end of his training, a three-year period, God blessed Daniel and his faithful friends, who were found to be much wiser and healthier than all the other trainees (Daniel 1:20).

Daniel's resistance to the Babylonian assimilation followed three principles that apply generally to Christians who are forced against their will to live in an alien culture.

First, resolve to be holy and not embrace the culture's idolatry. A Marxist culture replaces all religion with faith in government and punishes those who refuse to obey.

Second, demonstrate opposition to the alien culture with genuine humility and grace. Daniel continued his daily devotions while being a good public servant. That earned him respect as a person and for his commitment to his God.

Third, consistently demonstrate faith, trusting in God's promises and expect Him to respond to your obedience. God honored Daniel with wisdom not only for his daily life, but also for times of crises, when he could provide the Babylonian leaders insights uncommon to man.

Daniel's model behavior in the face of great opposition applies to us today. He persevered against temptation and remained obedient to God and he remained faithful to his calling.

Properly Apply Romans 13

Some Christians are apt to recite Romans 13:1 (NASB) and throw up their hands to declare, "I may not agree with the government's ruling, but I'm bound by God's Scripture to obey. After all, the verse states that 'every person is to be in subjection to the governing authorities. For there is no authority except from God, and those which exist are established by God.'"

Does that mean we must obey when a Marxist regime commands us to shutter our churches, stop speaking to others of Christ's promised salvation, and flush our hope of heaven? After all, as Marx said, "Religion… is the opiate of the masses." True. Our Christian faith comforts our hearts, gives rest to our souls, and provides hope for the future. It allows us to stand up against evil and, what Marx wanted to avoid, faith-based opposition to evil, tyranny. That's why Marxists' first efforts when taking over a country is always to round up believers and close their churches.

Christians need to adjust their understanding about their relationship with both the church and the state. R. C. Sproul published a marvelous little book, *What Is the Relationship Between Church and State?* Chapters 5 and 6 address a Christian's proper attitude about church-state issues.[989]

Chapter 5, "An Instrument of Evil," begins with an important statement: "Our first allegiance is to our King and to the heavenly kingdom to which we belong." Mr. Sproul quotes Ephesians 6:10–13, a familiar passage concerning the armor of God, which is a reminder that we ought to stand against the craftiness of Satan.

Satan, the father of lies, was very real to the apostle, and he ought to be for us as well. I explained in the last chapter about Satan's influence as a co-conspirator in the Marxist Great Reset. Translation: Co-conspirators agree about their aim and strategy. To respond to such evil, Paul admonishes Christians to put on the armor of God for spiritual battle, and he points out that our enemy includes rulers and authorities who engage in evil—acts that are specifically called out in God's Word.

In this volume, I've addressed the evil done by leaders like Hitler, Stalin, Mao, and others in the name of Marxist revolutions. At the start of those revolutions, there were good Christian people who were fooled into believing that those leaders were to be trusted. In Germany, for example, Hitler recruited church leaders to join his campaign to help the Nazis, but in time, Christians like Dietrich Bonhoeffer found out the German tyrant quickly turned against believers when they were no longer useful to the regime.

Governments that engage in genocide, such as Germany, Russia, and China become servants of Satan because they destroy what God calls precious: human life. Also, when government fails to protect private property, specifically the rights of individuals to the property they possess, they are abusing their God-given power.

Now back to Romans 13. Yes, God gives governments a right to tax citizens to pay for the necessities of life, and Christians are expected to pay their taxes. However, when government becomes greedy and imposes unjust taxes for wealth redistribution, a socialist dream, then it steps beyond God's authority. As Mr. Sproul writes, "It is still stealing if I take from you to give to someone else, even if I do it with my vote. We call that entitlement."[990]

There comes a time when civil disobedience is required of the Christian, the topic of chapter 6 in Mr. Sproul's book. I cite Romans 13:1 above, which states that we are to be subject to the authorities who are placed over us—the principle of civil obedience. However, it is not an absolute authority!

When those authorities do what God forbids or forbid us from doing something God commands, then we must disobey. Remember the scene in Acts 4, when Peter and John are called before the Sanhedrin for the crime of healing a crippled man?

Peter and John explained that they had healed the man by the power of Christ, and not even the Jewish officials denied the obvious miracle. But those officials called the men before them and charged them "not to speak or teach at all in the name of Jesus" (Acts 4:18). Peter and John responded: "Whether it is right in the sight of God to listen to you more than to God, you judge. For we cannot but speak the things which we have seen and heard" (Acts 4:19–20, NKJV).

The principle is clear. When there is a direct conflict between the law of God and the rule of men, always obey God. Disobey man. Unfortunately, too often we are prone to twist and distort things to our benefit. Mr. Sproul cautions, "Before we disobey the authorities over us, we should be sure to be painfully self-reflective and have a clear understanding as to why we plan to disobey."[991]

We should disobey if government authorities tell us we cannot distribute Bibles or even scraps of paper with verses on them, such as in the case of the Chinese Christians described earlier in this section. What if a government official told you to have an abortion? You should disobey like many Christian women in China who got such orders but who rightly obeyed God, a higher authority.

Never forget that God's law is the ultimate authority. Noted author and evangelist Francis Schaeffer said, "Not to resist tyranny is evil. To not resist tyranny which is Satanic; is to oppose God who is holy."[992]

The choice is yours to make, but as Joshua wrote: "But as for me and my household, we will serve the LORD" (Joshua 24:15, NIV).

Be an Uncompromising Truth-Teller

A Marxist government will separate the Christian wheat from the chaff. Many readers are quite familiar with the biblical metaphor that speaks of God separating those who are worthy and those who are unworthy (Luke 3:17 and Matthew 3:12). That metaphor comes from an age-old practice of literally separating wheat from chaff, which happens when a farmer uses his winnowing fork to toss the combined wheat and chaff into the air. The lighter chaff drifts away in the wind, leaving the valuable grain used for flour.

I expect the coming Marxist Great Reset will demonstrate that metaphor when Christians face tough choices. The wheat represents Christians who are committed to living "righteously" like Daniel, pure and undefiled, led by the Holy Spirit. They will continue to obey God's direction to be salt and light (Matthew 5:13) in a fallen world. The rest, the chaff, represents Christians who are okay with compromise, willing to conform, and who obey the government's evil orders rather than God's commandments.

The "wheat" Christians speak truth to the fallen world, even though they are scorned and face shame and rejection. As Christian apologist Francis Schaeffer said, "This is a time to show to a generation who thinks that the concept of truth is unthinkable that we do take truth seriously." We must also engage the lost with God's truth. Our evangelism and apologetics must be deeply relational and demonstrably reasonable.

CONCLUSION

This chapter outlines the three stages of a Marxist revolution that might lead to a future one-world government and addresses just how far America has traveled down that road. It concludes with a number of Christ-centric recommendations should we find ourselves with that outcome—a Marxist, one-world totalitarian government.

Epilogue

I work in Washington, DC, within the government, where I see the good, the bad, and the ugly on a daily basis. Given the current state of the Biden administration's makeup and their rapid cancelation of numerous decisions and programs instigated by the previous administration to the clear detriment of America, President Biden's questionable state of mental health over the short term, the obvious increasing saber-rattling by China, North Korea, and others, I believe we are entering an unprecedented time of danger militarily, economically, morally, and politically. We and the western nations are plunging headlong into chaos. Can we recover in time to save our nation and Christian influence?

Give Me Liberty, Not Marxism examines what current American leaders like President Biden and his globalist allies intend for America and the world, an outcome that may well usher in the prophetic end times. The evidence for this possible result is provided by an objective review of the histories of past Marxist-regimes, accounts that are juxtaposed with the political proposals of those who, such as Mr. Biden, seek a global Great Reset that produces a radically different America that becomes subordinate to a godless, totalitarian one-world government.

Albert Camus (1913–1960), a French philosopher and Nobel Prize-winning author, said, "Fiction is the lie through which we tell the truth." *Give Me Liberty, Not Marxism* employs truth from history to suggest at this point a possible (fictional) outcome where our political leaders push this country into a "new world order." That cabal of globalists employs "lies" to persuade us to buy their evil Marxist ideology, a fool's errand.[993]

Recall that I reviewed the aims of the distinctive isms that define our current political discourse—capitalism, Marxism, socialism, communism, and progressivism—and their relationship with one another, and if adopted by our nation what that might mean for our future. What's not at issue is the growing push to implement the most radical of these isms fueling the ongoing American cultural revolution that is redefining our very foundation.

That revolution is spurred by a host of co-conspirators aiming not just to divide this country, but also to weaken its resolve. They intend to turn this country into something akin to a "Soviet" America. To that end, I identified eight co-conspirators fueling this revolution: The Democratic Party, the Communist Chinese Party, our leftist public education establishment, America's mainstream media, Satan and his army of demons, secret societies, and a host of Marxist-inspired ground troops like Antifa. Of course, many of them will deny that they are aligned and working together, but their protests are irrelevant. They are blind to the fact that the leader of the group exists in the unseen realm: Satan maneuvers each according to his design, whether they know or believe it.

How do these revolutionary co-conspirators intend to transform America and the world? That effort began many decades ago when they started whittling away at our founding civil liberties and critical institutions. Unfortunately, at this point, they've made great progress on all fronts, and now they are accelerating their efforts, which brings us to their ultimate goal—a Marxist Great Reset that ultimately leads to a totalitarian one-world government.

I am reminded of the many prophecies that describe the world situation just prior to the Rapture of the Church before the Tribulation

Period. Lawlessness and chaos will abound. Liars will be self-evident. Hypocrisy will be the norm. Immoral acts and behavior will be common. Sexual perversion will be accepted. And the list goes on and on. The bottom line is that we are seeing all these things converging now for the first time. This convergence fulfills the prophecy that the world would be like the days of Noah as the end time approaches. We are there.

Right now, a Marxist one-world government and a radically different America are still futuristic, fictional—as Camus said—they are yet "lies." However, the evidence presented here is the truth, and the outcome of this yet fictional account could become a frightening reality and may well explain why many of us firmly believe our world is rushing toward the prophetic end times.

As Christians, we are therefore called to action to spread the gospel to all those we can connect with—at home, in the community, at work, and beyond. We are not called to sit and wait. In the final analysis, this book is my call to action and my warning to all those who read it that they need to be about their Heavenly Father's business as we were commanded by Jesus.

Notes

1. John Kennedy, "The Story with Martha MacCallum," Fox News, November 11, 2020.
2. Lawrence Kudlow, Brainyquote, accessed January 24, 2021, https://www.brainyquote.com/authors/lawrence-kudlow-quotes.
3. Hannah Hartig, "Stark Partisan Divisions in Americans' Views of 'Socialism,' 'Capitalism'," Pew Research Center, June 25, 2019, https://www.pewresearch.org/fact-tank/2019/06/25/stark-partisan-divisions-in-americans-views-of-socialism-capitalism/.
4. Ibid.
5. Ibid.
6. Michael Novak, "How Christianity Created Capitalism," Acton Institute, July 20, 2010, https://www.acton.org/pub/religion-liberty/volume-10-number-3/how-christianity-created-capitalism.
7. Ibid.
8. Ibid.
9. Ibid.
10. Ibid.
11. "What Does the Bible Say about Capitalism?," GotQuestions, accessed January 25, 2021, https://www.gotquestions.org/capitalism-Bible.html.
12. Ibid.
13. Ibid.
14. Novak, Op cit.

15. Karl Marx Quotes, AZQuotes, accessed January 25, 2021, https://www. azquotes.com/author/9564-Karl_Marx.

16. Jared Ball, "A Short History of Black Lives Matter," Real News Network, July 23, 2015, https://therealnews.com/pcullors0722blacklives.

17. Ibid.

18. "Marxist Worldview," All About Worldview, accessed January 25, 2021, https://www.allaboutworldview.org/marxist-worldview. htm#:~:text=The%20Marxist%20worldview%20is%20grounded%20 in%20Karl%20Marx,of%20the%20Marxist%20Worldview%20 across%20ten%20major%20categories.

19. Robert F. Schwarzwalder Jr., "Marx's New Religion," *Journal of the Evangelical Theological Society*, JETS 62.4 (2019): 775–88, file:///C:/ Users/rober/OneDrive/Desktop/C%20S%20BOOK/SECTION%20I/ CHAPTER%201/MARXISM/MARXS%20NEW%20RELIGION.pdf.

20. Ibid.

21. Peter Kreeft, "The Pillars of Unbelief— Marx," National Catholic Register, January–February 1988, https://www.catholiceducation.org/en/ culture/catholic-contributions/3-the-pillars-of-unbelief-karl-marx.html.

22. Schwarzwalder, Op cit.

23. "Thoughts of a Living Christian," accessed January 25, 2021, https://thoughtsofalivingchristian.wordpress. com/2010/11/21/a-christian-critique-of-marxism/.

24. Schwarzwalder, Op cit.

25. Martin Luther King Jr., "Communism's Challenge to Christianity," MLK Research and Education Institute, Stanford University, August 9, 1953, https://kinginstitute.stanford.edu/king-papers/documents/ communisms-challenge-christianity.

26. Jon Miltimore, "Harvard Student Whose Father Escaped Communism Has a Message for Her Fellow Students," Intellectual Takeout, December 5, 2017, https://www.intellectualtakeout.org/article/harvard-student-whose-father-escaped-communism-has-message-her-fellow-students/.

27. David Mikkelson, "Norman Thomas on Socialism," Snopes. com, September 26, 2009, https://www.snopes.com/fact-check/ norman-thomas-on-socialism.

28. Robby Soave, "The 2020 Election Results Look Like a Massive

Rebuke of Socialism, Reason.com, November 6, 2020, https://reason.
com/2020/11/06/socialism-2020-trump-biden-rebuke-left/.

29. "Bernie Sanders Quotes," BrainQuote, accessed January 25, 2021,
    https://www.brainyquote.com/quotes/bernie_sanders_830990.

30. "Ronald Reagon," QuoteFancy, accessed January 25, 2021, https://
    quotefancy.com/quote/902961/Ronald-Reagan-Socialism-only-works-in-
    two-places-Heaven-where-they-don-t-need-it-and-hell.

31. Randy Desoto, "Survey Finds 98% of Americans Who Support
    Socialism Reject Bible's Key Teachings," Westernjournal.com, August
    29, 2020, https://www.westernjournal.com/survey-finds-98-americans-
    support-socialism-reject-bibles-key-teachings/.

32. Lee Edwards, "Socialism: A Clear and Present Danger," Heritage
    Foundation, October 11, 2019, https://www.heritage.org/progressivism/
    commentary/socialism-clear-and-present-danger.

33. "Robert Owen," Wikipedia, accessed January 25, 2021, https://
    en.wikipedia.org/wiki/Robert_Owen.

34. Karl Marx quote, Wikipedia, January
    25, 2021, https://en.wikipedia.org/wiki/
    From_each_according_to_his_ability,_to_each_according_to_his_needs.

35. Krishan Saagar Rao, "The Psychology of 'Communist'
    Liberals," Hans India News Service, October 16, 2020,
    https://www.thehansindia.com/hans/opinion/news-analysis/
    the-psychology-of-communist-liberals-651426.

36. Edwards, Op cit.

37. Mikkelson, Op cit.

38. Lee Edwards, "What Americans Must Know about Socialism,"
    American Spectator, November 30, 2018, https://spectator.org/
    what-americans-must-know-about-socialism/.

39. Ibid.

40. Ibid.

41. James Barrett, "Poll: Who would Jesus vote for?," Dailywire.
    com, May 17, 2016, https://www.dailywire.com/news/
    poll-who-would-jesus-vote-james-barrett.

42. Freddy Davis, "A Worldview Perspective on Socialism,"
    Marketfaith Minstries, March 12, 2020, http://www.marketfaith.
    org/2020/03/a-worldview-perspective-on-socialism/.

43. Marx, Op cit.

44. Mike Baker, "Obama Takes Questions from 5-Year-Old," *USA Today*, November 1, 2007, http://usatoday30.usatoday.com/news/politics/2007-11-01-1567063266_x.htm.

45. Bernie Sanders, Facebook Post, April 29, 2012, accessed January 25, 2021, https://www.facebook.com/senatorsanders/posts/10150781969192908.

46. Colin Campbell, "Hillary Clinton Called for 'Toppling' the 1%," Businessinsider.com, April 21, 2015, https://www.businessinsider.com/report-hillary-clinton-called-for-toppling-the-1-2015-4.

47. Paul Kengor, "Americans Buy into Marxist Family Planning," *Federalist*, June 29, 2015, https://thefederalist.com/2015/06/29/americans-buy-into-marxist-family-planning/.

48. "Bernie Sanders on Children," Feelthebern.org, accessed January 25, 2021, https://feelthebern.org/bernie-sanders-on-children/.

49. Julie Roys, "5 Reasons Socialism Is Not Christian," Christianpost.com, July 12, 2016, https://www.christianpost.com/news/5-reasons-socialism-is-not-christian-opinion.html.

50. Ayn Rand, Gen Z Conservative, accessed January 25, 2021, https://genzconservative.com/socialism-is-suicide-and-communism-is-murder/.

51. Karl Marx, Communist Manifesto, Encyclopedia2.thefreedictionary.com, accessed January 25, 2021, https://encyclopedia2.thefreedictionary.com/Communist+Manifesto.

52. Michael P. Orsi, "Communism and Christianity Cannot Coexist," CNS News, September 9, 2020, https://www.cnsnews.com/index.php/commentary/rev-michael-p-orsi/communism-and-christianity-cannot-coexist.

53. Ibid.

54. Paul Kengor, "Vatican II's Unpublished Condemnations of Communism," *Crisis* Magazine, November 30, 2017, https://www.crisismagazine.com/2017/vatican-iis-unpublished-condemnations-communism.

55. "Why Did the Soviet Union Collapse?" Britannica.com, accessed January 25, 2021, https://www.britannica.com/story/why-did-the-soviet-union-collapse.

56. Ibid.

57. Ibid.

58. Ibid.

59. "Text of Gorbachev's Speech to the United Nations," AP News, December 8, 1988, https://apnews.com/article/1abea48aacda1a9dd520c3 80a8bc6be6.

60. "Why Did the Soviet Union Collapse?" Op cit.

61. Ibid.

62. Glenn Beck, Brainyquote, accessed January 25, 2021, https://www. brainyquote.com/quotes/glenn_beck_411837.

63. "'Socialism is the philosophy of failure...' Winston Churchill, The Churchill Project, Hillsdale College, July 30, 2015, https://winstonchurchill.hillsdale.edu/ socialism-is-the-philosophy-of-failure-winston-churchill/.

64. Mohamed Younis, "Four in 10 Americans Embrace Some Form of Socialism," Gallup, May 20, 2019, https://news.gallup.com/poll/257639/ four-americans-embrace-form-socialism.aspx.

65. Ibid.

66. Ibid.

67. Domenico Montanaro, "Poll: Sanders Rises, But Socialism Isn't Popular with Most Americans," NPR, February 19, 2020, https://www.npr.org/2020/02/19/807047941/ poll-sanders-rises-but-socialism-isnt-popular-with-most-americans.

68. Paul Bedard, "2020 poll: 77 Percent of Democrats Back socialism, But Most Voters Don't," *Washington Examiner*, February 25, 2019, https:// www.washingtonexaminer.com/washington-secrets/2020-poll-77-dems- back-socialism-but-most-voters-dont.

69. Ibid.

70. Younis, Op cit.

71. Ryan Prost, "Report: 37 Percent of Young Americans Favor Communist Manifesto," historyaddicted.com, not dated, https://historyaddicted. com/report-almost-37-percent-of-young-americans-favor-communist- manifesto/.

72. Ibid.

73. "Progressive Congressional Caucus," US House of Representatives, accessed January 25, 2021, https://progressives.house.gov/ caucus-members/.

74. Josh Christenson, "Majority of Americans Support Progressive Policies Such as Paid Maternity Leave Free College," *Washington Free Beacon*, November 8, 2020, https://freebeacon.com/democrats/dems-turn-away-from-defund-the-police-and-socialism/?utm_source=actengage&utm_campaign=conservative_test&utm_medium=email.

75. Steve Liesman, "Majority of Americans Support Progressive Policies Such as Higher Minimum Wage, Free College," CNBC, March 27, 2019, https://www.cnbc.com/2019/03/27/majority-of-americans-support-progressive-policies-such-as-paid-maternity-leave-free-college.html.

76. John Andrews, "If We Don't Stop It, Marxism Will Annihilate the American Way of Life," *Federalist*, July 7, 2020, https://thefederalist.com/2020/07/07/if-we-dont-stop-it-marxism-will-annihilate-the-american-way-of-life/.

77. "Nihilism," Merriam-Webster dictionary, accessed January 28, 2021, https://www.merriam-webster.com/dictionary/nihilism.

78. Ibid.

79. Scott McKay, "Four Stages of Marxist Takeover: The Accuracy of Yuri Bezmenov," *American Spectator*, July 10, 2020. https://spectator.org/four-stages-of-marxist-takeover-the-accuracy-of-yuri-bezmenov/.

80. Ibid.

81. Note: "The Frankfurt School was a school of social theory and critical philosophy associated with the Institute for Social Research, at Goethe University Frankfurt. It comprised intellectuals and political dissidents dissatisfied with the contemporary socio-economy systems of the 1930s. Its perspective of critical investigation is based upon Freudian, Marxist and Hegelian premises of idealist philosophy." Accessed January 25, 2021, https://en.wikipedia.org/wiki/Frankfurt_School.

82. "Intersectionality," Merriam-Webster, accessed January 25, 2021, https://www.merriam-webster.com/dictionary/intersectionality.

83. Yuri Bezmenov, "Fascinating KGB Defector Yuri Bezmenov Reveals Russian Subversion Tactics Full Interview, YouTube, May 20, 2020, FASCINATING - KGB Defector Yuri Bezmenov reveals Russian Subversion Tactics - Full Interview - YouTube.

84. "Letters: Nikita Khrushchev's Chilling Prediction: 'We will take America without firing a shot,'" *Orlando Sentinel*, July 16, 2018, https://www.

orlandosentinel.com/opinion/os-ed-put-trump-online-letters-20180716-story.html.

85. Scott McKay, "Four Stages of Marxist Takeover: The Accuracy of Yuri Bezmenov," *American Spectator*, July 10, 2020, https://spectator.org/four-stages-of-marxist-takeover-the-accuracy-of-yuri-bezmenov/.

86. Ibid.

87. Ibid.

88. Ibid.

89. Ibid.

90. "2019 Annual Poll," Victims of Communism Memorial Foundation, accessed January 25, 2021, 2019 Annual Poll | Victims of Communism.

91. Elaine Godfry, "Socialism, but in Iowa," *Atlantic*, April 2019, https://www.theatlantic.com/politics/archive/2019/04/democratic-socialism-surging-iowa-ahead-2020/586441/.

92. Joel Mathis, "3 Reasons Why socialism Is Gaining Popularity in America," *Week*, April 9, 2019, https://theweek.com/articles/834078/3-reasons-why-socialism-gaining-popularity-america.

93. "Student Loan Debt," Nitro, accessed January 25, 2021, https://www.nitrocollege.com/research/average-student-loan-debt#:~:text=Student%20loan%20debt%20is%20a%20reality%20for%20more,America%20between%20the%20ages%20of%2020%20and%2059.

94. Mathis, Op cit.

95. Emergency Economic Stabilization Act of 2008, Wikipedia, accessed January 25, 2021, https://en.wikipedia.org/wiki/Emergency_Economic_Stabilization_Act_of_2008.

96. Deborah White, "Pros and Cons of Obama's Stimulus Package," thoughtco.com, March 6, 2017, https://www.thoughtco.com/pro-cons-obama-stimulus-package-3325641#:~:text=President%20Obama%27s%20stimulus%20package%20of%20%24787%20billion%20includes%3A,Forest%20Service%2C%20and%20%24515%20million%20for%20wildfire%20prevention.

97. US Debt Clock, accessed January 25, 2021, https://usdebtclock.org/.

98. Connor Boyack, "Why Socialism Is So Popular Among Young People," Fox News, May 15, 2019, https://www.foxbusiness.com/politics/socialism-capitalism-youth-ocasio-cortez.

99. Ibid.

100. Mitchell Langbert, "Homogenous: The Political Affiliations of Elite Liberal Arts College Faculty," National Association of Scholars, Summer 2018, https://www.nas.org/academic-questions/31/2/homogenous_the_political_affiliations_of_elite_liberal_arts_college_faculty.

101. "National Survey Finds Just 1 in 3 Americans Would Pass Citizenship Test," Woodrow Wilson National Fellowship Foundation, October 3, 2018, Woodrow Wilson National Fellowship Foundation | National Survey Finds Just 1 in 3 Americans Would Pass Citizenship Test.

102. Ibid.

103. Alexander Zubatov, "Four Reasons Why Socialism Is Becoming More Popular," intellectualtakeout.org, November 8, 2019, https://www.intellectualtakeout.org/article/four-reasons-why-socialism-becoming-more-popular/.

104. Emily Ekins, "Poll: Americans Like Free Markets More than Capitalism and Socialism More Than a Govt Managed Economy," *Reason*, February 12, 2015,Poll: Americans Like Free Markets More than Capitalism and Socialism More Than a Govt Managed Economy – Reason.com.

105. Robert Knight, "Socialism Howard Zinn and His Fake History," *Washington Times*, January 5, 2020, https://www.washingtontimes.com/news/2020/jan/5/socialism-howard-zinn-and-his-fake-history/.

106. Ibid.

107. Ibid.

108. "Communist Party of the United States of America," Britannica.com, accessed January 25, 2021, https://www.britannica.com/topic/Communist-Party-of-the-United-States-of-America.

109. Ibid.

110. Ibid.

111. James R. Barrett, "What Went Wrong? The Communist Party, the US, and the Comintern," American Communist History, Vol. 17, No. 2, pp. 176–184, 2018.

112. Ibid.

113. "Lincoln Battalion," Wikipedia, accessed January 25, 2021, https://en.wikipedia.org/wiki/Lincoln_Battalion.

114. Herbert Hoover, "A Call to Reason," Vital Speeches of the Day, Vol. VII, June 29, 1941, pp. 580-584, http://www.ibiblio.org/pha/policy/1941/1941-06-29a.html.

115. Ibid.

116. "Hobson's Choice," Merriam-Webster Dictionary, accessed January 25, 2021, https://www.merriam-webster.com/dictionary/Hobson%27s%20choice.

117. Hoover, Op cit.

118. Ibid.

119. Ibid.

120. Ibid.

121. Ibid.

122. Ibid.

123. Ibid.

124. Ibid.

125. Bionic Mosquito, "Communism Comes to America," lewrockwell.com, March 22, 2012, https://www.lewrockwell.com/2012/03/bionic-mosquito/communism-comes-to-america/.

126. Ibid.

127. "Earl Browder," Wikipedia, accessed January 25, 2021, https://en.wikipedia.org/wiki/Earl_Browder.

128. Mosquito, Op cit.

129. Ibid.

130. Ibid.

131. Ibid.

132. Ibid.

133. Robbie Lieberman, "Communism, Peace Activism, and Civil Liberties: From the Waldorf Conference to the Peekskill Riot," *Journal of American Culture*, Fall 1995, p. 59.

134. Ibid.

135. Ibid.

136. "McCarthyism," Britannica, accessed January 25, 2021, McCarthyism | History & Facts | Britannica.

137. Phillip Deery, "Finding His Kronstadt: Howard Fast, 1956 and American Communism, *Australian Journal of Politics and History*, Vol. 58, No. 2, 2012.

138. Ibid.

139. "Robert Eikhe," Wikipedia, accessed January 25, 2021, Robert Eikhe - Wikipedia.

140. Zhores A. Medvedev and Roy A. Medvedev, *The Unknown Stalin* (London, 2006), p.98.

141. Shawn Langlois, "More Than a Third of Millennials Polled Approve of Communism," Marketwatch.com, November 2, 2019, https://www.marketwatch.com/story/for-millennials-socialism-and-communism-are-hot-capitalism-is-not-2019-10-28.

142. Bradley S. Watson, "Progressivism and the Historians," Law & Liberty, March 25, 2020, https://lawliberty.org/progressivism-and-the-historians/.

143. Ibid.

144. Ibid.

145. Ibid.

146. Ibid.

147. Richard Reinsch, "How the Academics Made Progressivism All-American," Law & Liberty, May 1, 2020, https://lawliberty.org/podcast/how-the-academics-made-progressivism-all-american/.

148. "Obama to Business Owners: 'You didn't build that,'" Fox News, December 23, 2015, https://www.foxnews.com/politics/obama-to-business-owners-you-didnt-build-that.

149. Ibid.

150. "Hillary Clinton: I'm Not a Liberal," Newsmax.com, July 24, 2007, https://freerepublic.com/focus/news/1870865/posts.

151. Watson, Op cit.

152. Ibid.

153. Ibid.

154. Ibid.

155. Ibid.

156. Karl Marx, "Revolution," AZQuotes.com, accessed January 25, 2021, https://www.azquotes.com/author/9564-Karl_Marx/tag/revolution.

157. Michael Walsh, "President Trump, Explain to the American People That Survival of the Republic Is at Stake," *Epoch Times*, November 23, 2020, https://www.theepochtimes.com/president-trump-explain-to-the-american-people-the-survival-of-the-republic-is-at-stake_3589556.html.

158. Ibid.

159. Vasko Kohlmaver, "This Is a Marxist Revolution," lewrockwell. com, October 31, 2020, https://www.lewrockwell.com/2020/10/ vasko-kohlmayer/this-is-a-marxist-revolution/.

160. Ibid.

161. "Critical Race Theory," Gotquestions.org, accessed January 25, 2021, https://www.gotquestions.org/critical-race-theory.html.

162. Benjamin Franklin, Bartleby.com, accessed January 25, 2021, https:// www.bartleby.com/73/1593.html#:~:text=%E2%80%9CA%20 Republic%2C%20if%20you%20can%20keep%20 it.%E2%80%9D%20ATTRIBUTION%3A,McHenry%2C%20one%20 of%20Maryland%E2%80%99s%20delegates%20to%20the%20 Convention.

163. Bill Federer, "Lenin Explained, 'The goal of socialism is communism,'" Self-Educated American, December 11, 2017, https:// selfeducatedamerican.com/2017/12/11/lenin-explained-goal-socialism-communism/#:~:text=Centralizing%20power%2C%20Vladimir%20 Lenin%20explained%3A%20%E2%80%9CThe%20goal%20of,as%20 an%20absolute%20dictator%20of%20the%20Soviet%20Union.

164. "Karl Marx," LibertyTree, accessed January 29, 2021, http://libertytree. ca/quotes/Karl.Marx.Quote.EBAB#:~:text=Karl%20Marx%20 Quote%20%E2%80%9CMy%20object%20in%20life,is%20to%20 dethrone%20God%20and%20destroy%20capitalism.%E2%80%9D.

165. Anthony Murdoch, "Vermont Authorizes Schools to Ask Kids to Rat on Parents Who Celebrated Thanksgiving with Others," LifeSiteNews, November 26, 2020, https://www.lifesitenews.com/news/vermont-authorizes-schools-to-ask-kids-to-rat-on-parents-who-celebrated-thanksgiving-with-others.

166. Jan Jekielek, "How the Marxist Agenda Is Taking Over America Today: Curtis Bowers," NTD, October 18, 2020, https://www.ntd. com/how-the-marxist-agenda-is-taking-over-america-today-curtis-bowers_518400.html

167. Ibid.

168. Ibid.

169. Ibid.

170. Ibid.

171. Ibid.

172. Ibid.

173. Ibid.

174. Gene Van Shaar, "The Naked Communist: Exposing Communism and Restoring Freedom in America by Former FBI Agent and Constitutional Scholar Cleon Skousen," *Published Reporter*, August 27, 2020, https://www.publishedreporter.com/2020/08/27/the-naked-communist-exposing-communism-and-restoring-freedom-in-america-by-former-fbi-agent-and-constitutional-scholar-cleon-skousen/.

175. Jekielek, Op cit.

176. Ibid.

177. Ibid.

178. Ibid.

179. Ibid.

180. Ibid.

181. Ibid.

182. Ibid.

183. Ibid.

184. Ibid.

185. Ibid.

186. Ibid.

187. Ibid.

188. Ibid.

189. Michael Ruiz, "De Blasio: New Yorkers can report social distancing violations by texting photos to authorities," Fox News, April 18, 2020, https://www.foxnews.com/us/de-blasio-new-yorkers-report-social-distancing-violations-text.

190. Andrew Stiles, "Virginia Health Department Urges Citizens to Snitch on Churches, Gun Ranges for Violating Democratic Governor's COVID-19 Regulations," *Washington Free Beacon*, June 22, 2020, https://freebeacon.com/coronavirus/northam-blackface-snitch/.

191. "Gore Vidal," BrainyQuote, accessed February 21, 2021, https://www.brainyquote.com/quotes/gore_vidal_704566.

192. Jordan Davidson, "Joe Biden Says Democrats Created 'The Most Extensive and Inclusive Voter Fraud Organization' in American

History," *Federalist*, October 24, 2020, https://thefederalist. com/2020/10/24/joe-biden-says-democrats-created-the-most-extensive-and-inclusive-voter-fraud-organization-in-american-history/.

193. Dan MacGuill, "Did Biden 'Admit' to Voter Fraud?" Snopes. com, October 26, 2020, https://www.snopes.com/fact-check/ biden-admit-voter-fraud/.

194. Tamara Keith, "Wielding a Pen and a Phone, Obama Goes It Alone," National Public Radio, Morning Edition, January 20, 2014, https:// www.npr.org/2014/01/20/263766043/wielding-a-pen-and-a-phone-obama-goes-it-alone#:~:text=President%20Obama%20has%20 alluded%20to%20his%20pen%20and,help%20him%20act%20 without%20waiting%20for%20congressional%20approval.

195. Kevin Breuninger, "Robert Mueller's Russia Probe Cost Nearly $32 Million in Total, Justice Department says," CNBC, August 2, 2019, https://www.cnbc.com/2019/08/02/robert-muellers-russia-probe-cost-nearly-32-million-in-total-doj.html.

196. Ryan Teague Beckwith, Bloomberg.com. 9/22/2020, pN.PAG-N.PAG. 1p.

197. Ibid.

198. Ibid.

199. Scott Detrow, "Democratic Task Forces Deliver Biden a Blueprint for a Progressive Presidency," NPR, July 8, 2020, https://www.npr. org/2020/07/08/889189235/democratic-task-forces-deliver-biden-a-blueprint-for-a-progressive-presidency.

200. Ibid.

201. "Democratic Party on Jobs," On the Issues, accessed January 25, 2021, https://www.ontheissues.org/Celeb/Democratic_Party_Jobs.htm.

202. "Joe Biden's Democrat Party: All Out on Police, All in on Socialism," *States News Service*, 20 Aug. 2020, p. NA. *Gale Academic OneFile*, https://link.gale.com/apps/doc/A633040632/AONE?u=wash9 2852&sid=AONE&xid=489b7522. Accessed 29 Nov. 2020.

203. Ibid.

204. Ibid.

205. Ibid.

206. Ibid.

207. Aesop quotation, Goodreads, accessed January 25, 2021, https://www.goodreads.com/quotes/690104-a-man-is-known-by-the-company-he-keeps.

208. "Joe Biden's Democrat Party: All Out on Police, All in on Socialism," Op cit.

209. Ibid.

210. Alan Gathright and David Armstrong, "Chinese Leaders's Friendly Bay Area Visit," *San Francisco Chronicle*, October 29, 2002, https://www.sfgate.com/business/article/Chinese-leader-s-friendly-Bay-Area-visit-S-F-2758596.php.

211. Ibid.

212. "Lateefah Simon," Keywiki, accessed February 15, 2021, https://keywiki.org/Lateefah_Simon.

213. "Why Is No One (Except the President) Calling Out Kamala Harris's Communist Ties?" AMAC, October 16, 2020, https://amac.us/why-is-no-one-except-the-president-calling-out-kamala-harriss-communist-ties/.

214. Trevor Loudon, "Why Is No One (Except the President) Calling Out Kamala Harris's Communist Ties?," *Epoch Times*, October 16, 2020, https://www.theepochtimes.com/why-is-no-one-except-the-president-calling-out-kamala-harriss-communist-ties_3538284.html.

215. Alex Nester, "'Not a Good Fit': Team Biden Stabs Former MoveOn Chief in the Back," *Washington Free Beacon*, December 2, 2020, https://freebeacon.com/democrats/not-a-good-fit-team-biden-stabs-former-moveon-chief-in-the-back/?utm_source=actengage&utm_campaign=conservative_test&utm_medium=email.

216. Natalie Winters, "Revealed: Kamala Harris's Husband's Firm Reps Chinese Communist Party-Owned Corporates, Employs Ex-CCP Officials," Winter Watch, September 5, 2020, https://www.winterwatch.net/2020/09/revealed-kamala-harriss-husbands-firm-reps-chinese-communist-party-owned-corporates-employs-ex-ccp-officials/.

217. Hannah Bleau, "Kamala Harris Promotes Socialism Two Days Ahead of Election: 'Equitable Treatment Means We All End Up at the Same Place,'" Breitbart.com, November 1, 2021, https://www.breitbart.com/politics/2020/11/01/kamala-harris-promotes-socialism-two-days-ahead-

of-election-equitable-treatment-means-we-all-end-up-at-the-same-place/.

218. Ibid.

219. Tony Perkins, "Kamala Practices Socialism Distancing," Family Research Council, November 2, 2020, https://www.frcaction.org/get. cfm?i=WA20K01&f=WU20K01.

220. Ibid.

221. Trevor Loudon, "Covert Influence! Communist Party Supporters Run as Democrats in Arizona and Texas," *Epoch Times*, April 3, 2020, https://www.theepochtimes.com/covert-influence-communist-party-supporters-run-as-democrats-in-arizona-and-texas_3296990.html.

222. Ibid.

223. "Ed Pastor," Wikipedia, accessed January 25, 2021, https:// en.wikipedia.org/wiki/Ed_Pastor.

224. Loudon, Op cit.

225. "Kyrsten Sinema," Wikipedia, accessed January 25, 2021, https:// en.wikipedia.org/wiki/Kyrsten_Sinema.

226. Loudon, Op cit.

227. Trevor Loudon, "Democrats Allow Communists to Infiltrate Their Party Across the Nation," *Epoch Times*, February 8, 2019, https://www. theepochtimes.com/democrats-allow-communists-to-infiltrate-their-party-across-the-nation_2777771.html.

228. Ibid and "Americans for Democratic Action," Wikipedia, accessed January 25, 2021, and https://en.wikipedia.org/wiki/ Americans_for_Democratic_Action.

229. Loudon, "Democrats Allow Communists to Infiltrate Their Party Across the Nation," Op cit. and "John Bachtell" and "Pete Lorzano,"Wiki, accessed January 26, 2021, https://www.theepochtimes. com/democrats-allow-communists-to-infiltrate-their-party-across-the-nation_2777771.html and https://keywiki.org/Pepe_Lozano and https:// en.wikipedia.org/wiki/John_Bachtell.

230. Ibid. and "Glenn Burleigh," Wiki, accessed January 26, 2021, https:// keywiki.org/Glenn_Burleigh.

231. Anita MonCrief, "Obama, ACORN and Stealth Socialism: Dire Domestic Threat," RedState, May 27, 2010,

https://redstate.com/diary/anitamoncrief/2010/05/27/
obama-acorn-and-stealth-socialism-dire-domestic-threat-n195472.

232. Loudon, "Democrats Allow Communists to Infiltrate Their Party Across the Nation," Op cit.

233. "Corliss Lamont," Wikipedia, accessed January 25, 2021, https://en.wikipedia.org/wiki/Corliss_Lamont.

234. Trevor Loudon, "American Bolsheviks' Marxist Conquest of the Democratic Party," NewAmerican, May 22, 2019, https://thenewamerican.com/print/american-bolsheviks-marxist-conquest-of-the-democratic-party/.

235. "Couple Found Guilty of Spying," CBSNews.com, October 23, 1998, https://www.cbsnews.com/news/couple-found-guilty-of-spying/.

236. Trevor Loudon, "Democratic Socialists of America Is a Communist Organization," The Epoch Times, August 16, 2018, https://www.theepochtimes.com/democratic-socialists-of-america-is-a-communist-organization_2621954.html.

237. Ibid.

238. Ibid.

239. Trevor Loudon, "Communist Party USA Leader: 'Socialists Must Vote Democrat,'" The Epoch Times, September 11, 2018, https://www.theepochtimes.com/communist-party-usa-leader-socialists-must-vote-democrat_2656730.html.

240. Ibid.

241. Ibid.

242. Ibid.

243. Ibid.

244. Ibid.

245. Tiana Lowe, "Return to Normalcy! Biden Endorsed by Marxist Terrorist Angela Davis on Russian State Television," *Washington Examiner*, July 14, 2020, https://www.washingtonexaminer.com/opinion/return-to-normalcy-joe-biden-endorsed-by-marxist-terrorist-angela-davis-on-russian-state-television.

246. "Leftist, Communists Debate Supporting Biden." *UWIRE Text*, 2 Nov. 2020, p. 1. *Gale Academic OneFile*, https://link.gale.com/apps/doc/A640262662/AONE?u=wash92852&sid=AONE&xid=4c443e5d. Accessed 29 Nov. 2020.

247. Ibid.

248. Loudon, Trevor. "American Bolsheviks: Marxist Conquest of the Democratic Party: Communist/socialist-inspired groups have been quickly winning converts and taking control of the Democratic Party, at both the national and local levels." *New American*, vol. 35, no. 10, 20 May 2019, p. 21+. *Gale Academic OneFile*, https://link.gale.com/apps/doc/A592238814/AONE?u=wash92852&sid=AONE&xid=443399bf. Accessed 29 Nov. 2020.

249. Ibid.

250. Ibid.

251. Ibid.

252. "CPUSA Program," Communist Party USA, April 13, 2020, https://cpusa.org/party_info/party-program/.

253. Ibid.

254. Ibid.

255. Ibid.

256. Ibid.

257. "Bylaws," Committees of Correspondence for Democracy and Socialism, accessed January 26, 2021, https://www.cc-ds.org/about-2/bylaws/.

258. Loudon, Trevor. "American Bolsheviks," Op cit.

259. Ibid.

260. "Unity Statement of Freedom Road Socialist Organization," FRSO.org, May 6, 2001, accessed January 26, 2021, https://frso.org/main-documents/unity-statement/.

261. Ibid.

262. Ibid.

263. Ibid.

264. "Ayanna Pressley," Wikipedia, accessed January 26, 2021, https://en.wikipedia.org/wiki/Ayanna_Pressley.

265. Ibid.

266. Ibid.

267. Loudon, Trevor. "American Bolsheviks," Op cit.

268. Ibid.

269. Ibid.

270. Trevor Loudon, "A Beginner's Guide to American Communist

Parties: Part 2," *Epoch Times*, January 22, 2019, https://www.theepochtimes.com/a-beginners-guide-to-american-communist-parties-part-2_2759559.html.

271. "Communist Control Act of 1954," Wikipedia, accessed January 26, 2021 https://en.wikipedia.org/wiki/Communist_Control_Act_of_1954.

272. Iwan Morgan, "Richard Nixon's Opening China and Closing Gold Window," History Today, June 15, 2018, https://www.historytoday.com/history-matters/richard-nixons-opening-china-and-closing-gold-window.

273. "In Russia, Reagan Remembered for Helping Bring Down Soviet Union," NBC News, June 5, 2004, https://www.nbcnews.com/id/wbna5145921.

274. Ibid.

275. Deb Riechmann, "US Intelligence Director Says China Is Top Threat to America," *Washington Times*, December 4, 2020, https://www.washingtontimes.com/news/2020/dec/4/us-intelligence-director-says-china-is-top-threat-/.

276. Ibid.

277. Ibid.

278. Ibid.

279. Ibid.

280. "China Insider: Xi Jinping's Latest Speech Caused a Rebuke of International Criticism," Epoch Video, *Epoch Times*, September 18, 2020, https://www.theepochtimes.com/CHINA-insider-xi-jinpings-latest-speech-caused-a-rebuke-of-international-criticism_3506600.html.

281. "The Chinese Communist Party's Cold War Against the US: A Historical Perspective," JoshWho.net, August 4, 2020, https://www.joshwho.net/the-chinese-communist-partys-cold-war-against-the-us-a-historical-perspective/?shared=email&msg=fail.

282. Yuliya Talmazan, Eric Baculinao and Ed Flanagan, "A 'New Cold War?' China Blames U.S. for Growing Tensions," NBC News, May 25, 2020, https://news.yahoo.com/cold-war-china-blames-u-123409207.html.

283. Cheng Xiaonong, "The Chinese Communist Party's Cold War Against the US: A Historical Perspective," *Epoch Times*, August 4, 2020,

https://www.theepochtimes.com/the-chinese-communist-partys-cold-war-against-the-us-a-historical-perspective_3450439.html.

284. Ibid.

285. "Churchill's 'Iron Curtain' Speech," Writework, accessed January 26, 2021, https://www.writework.com/essay/churchill-s-iron-curtain-speech#:~:text=On%20March%205%2C%201946%2C%20Prime%20Minister%20Winston%20Churchill,initiative%20to%20stop%20the%20spread%20of%20communist%20ideals.

286. "Nineteen Eighty-Four," Wikipedia, accessed January 26, 2021 https://en.wikipedia.org/wiki/Nineteen_Eighty-Four.

287. "We Will Bury You," Wikipedia, accessed January 26, 2021 https://en.wikipedia.org/wiki/We_will_bury_you.

288. "The Chinese Communist Party's Cold War Against the US: A Historical Perspective," Op cit.

289. Xiaonong, Op cit.

290. Ibid.

291. Ibid.

292. Ibid.

293. Jan Jekielek, "Frank Gaffney: How China's Communist Party Is Exploiting American Pension Funds and the Coronavirus Outbreak," *Epoch Times*, May 12, 2020, https://www.theepochtimes.com/frank-gaffney-how-CHINAs-communist-party-is-exploiting-american-pension-funds-and-the-coronavirus-outbreak_3348102.html.

294. Ibid.

295. Arthur R. Thompson, *China: The Deep State's Trojan Horse in America*, (Appleton, Wisconsin: The John Birch Society, 2020) cited in Adelmann, Bob, *The Deep State's Trojan Horse in America.*: "This book does well at showing that not only are the Communist Chinese a threat to our country, but they are also being used to advance a globalist agenda." *New American*, vol. 36, no. 18, 21 Sept. 2020, p. 29+. *Gale Academic OneFile*, link.gale.com/apps/doc/A637032121/AONE?u=wash92852&sid=AONE&xid=486796e7. Accessed 30 Dec. 2020.

296. Ibid.

297. Ibid.

298. Dominic Rushe, "Here Are the Reasons for Trump's Economic War with China," *Guardian* (London), August 23,

2019, https://www.theguardian.com/us-news/2019/aug/23/trump-china-economic-war-why-reasons.

299. Ibid.

300. Michael D. Swaine, "Chinese Views on the U.S. National Security and National Defense Strategies," Carnegie Endowment, May 1, 2018, https://carnegieendowment.org/2018/05/01/chinese-views-on-u.s.-national-security-and-national-defense-strategies-pub-76226.

301. Jan Jekielek, "Video: Has China's Communist Party Interfered in the US Election?—Gen. Robert Spalding," *Epoch Times*, November 12, 2020, https://www.theepochtimes.com/video-has-CHINAs-communist-party-interfered-in-the-u-s-election-gen-robert-spalding_3575866.html.

302. Emily Jacobs, "Chinese Consulates in NYC, San Francisco Identified as Main Spy Hubs," *New York Post*, July 28, 2020, https://nypost.com/2020/07/28/chinese-consulates-in-nyc-san-francisco-identified-as-spy-hubs/.

303. Ryan Saavdra, "Schiff Condemns U.S. For 'Escalation' By Stopping Chinese Spying; Other Democrats Accused of Covering for Chinese Communist Party," Daily Wire, July 25, 2020, https://www.dailywire.com/news/schiff-condemns-u-s-for-escalation-by-stopping-chinese-spying-other-democrats-accused-of-covering-for-chinese-communist-party.

304. Jacobs, Op cit.

305. "The Theft of American Intellectual Property: Reassessments of the Challenge and United States Policy," The Commission on the Theft of American Intellectual Property, National Bureau of Asian Research, February 2017, https://www.nbr.org/wp-content/uploads/pdfs/publications/IP_Commission_Report_Update.pdf.

306. "China's PR Shop in America: The Democrat Party," States News Service, 24 July 2020, p. NA. *Gale Academic OneFile*, https://link.gale.com/apps/doc/A630477069/AONE?u=wash92852&sid=AONE&xid=b563b3df. Accessed 29 Nov. 2020.

307. Jacobs, Op cit.

308. Alana Wise, "FBI Briefs Pelosi and McCarthy on Rep. Swalwell's Ties to Suspected Chinese Spy," NPR, December 18, 2020, https://www.npr.org/2020/12/18/948210355/fbi-briefs-reps-pelosi-mccarthy-on-rep-swalwells-ties-to-suspected-chinese-spy.

309. Eric Ting, "Former Sen. Barbara Boxer Is Now Working for a Chinese Surveillance Firm," *San Francisco Chronicle*, January 12, 2021, https://www.sfgate.com/politics/article/Barbara-Boxer-China-foreign-agent-Uighur-Muslims-15865511.php.

310. Adam Edelman, "Biden's Comments Downplaying China Threat to U.S. Fire Up Pols on Both Sides," NBC News, May 2, 2019, https://www.nbcnews.com/politics/2020-election/biden-s-comments-downplaying-china-threat-u-s-fires-pols-n1001236.

311. Nicole Hao, "Chinese Leader Xi Congratulates Biden as Trump Reportedly Moving to Take Tough Action Against Regime," *Epoch Times*, November 26, 2020, https://www.theepochtimes.com/chinese-leader-xi-congratulates-biden-as-trump-reportedly-moving-to-take-tough-action-against-regime_3593743.html.

312. Ibid.

313. Trevor Loudon, "Chinese Regime Recruits American Communists," *Epoch Times*, July 30, 2018, https://www.theepochtimes.com/chinese-regime-recruits-american-communists_2608647.html.

314. Ibid.

315. Ibid.

316. Ibid.

317. Ibid.

318. Ibid.

319. Ibid.

320. Ibid.

321. Ibid.

322. Ibid.

323. Ibid.

324. Ibid.

325. Trevor Loudon, "Pro-China Communists Working to Mobilize 40 Million New Voters Against Trump," *Epoch Times*, July 11, 2019, https://www.theepochtimes.com/pro-CHINA-communists-working-to-mobilize-40-million-new-voters-against-trump_2983985.html.

326. Ibid.

327. Trevor Loudon, "'People's War': Pro-China Communists Claim Credit for 'Sparking' US Riots," *Epoch Times*, July 2, 2020, https://www.

theepochtimes.com/peoples-war-pro-CHINA-communists-claim-credit-for-sparking-us-riots_3406249.html.

328. Ibid.

329. Ibid.

330. Ibid.

331. Ibid.

332. Ibid.

333. Ibid.

334. Jan Jekielek, "Frank Gaffney: How China's Communist Party Is Exploiting American Pension Funds and the Coronavirus Outbreak," Op cit.

335. Ibid.

336. Steve Watson, "Senator Cotton: China's Actions Deliberately Malevolent; Their Scientists Shouldn't Be Allowed to Study In US," NewsWars.com, April 27, 2020, https://www.newswars.com/senator-cotton-chinas-actions-deliberately-malevolent-their-scientists-shouldnt-be-allowed-to-study-in-us/.

337. Nick Givas, "World Health Organization January Tweet China Human Transmission Coronavirus," Fox News, March 18, 2020, https://www.foxnews.com/world/world-health-organization-january-tweet-china-human-transmission-coronavirus.

338. Jan Jekielek, "Video: Has China's Communist Party Interfered in the US Election?—Gen. Robert Spalding," Op cit.

339. "Ronald Reagan Quote," Goodreads.com, accessed January 26, 2021, https://www.goodreads.com/quotes/13915-freedom-is-never-more-than-one-generation-away-from-extinction.

340. "PISA 2018 U.S. Results," NCES, accessed January 26, 2021, https://nces.ed.gov/surveys/pisa/pisa2018/pdf/PISA2018_compiled.pdf.

341. Ibid.

342. David S. Knight, "Federal Spending Covers Only 8% of Public-School Budgets," The Conversation, July 14, 2020, https://theconversation.com/federal-spending-covers-only-8-of-public-school-budgets-142348.

343. Lauren Camera, "Across the Board, Scores Drop in Math and Reading for U.S. Students," US News & World Report, October 30, 2019,

https://www.usnews.com/news/education-news/articles/2019-10-30/ across-the-board-scores-drop-in-math-and-reading-for-us-students.

344. Andrew Bernstein, "Heroes and Villains in American Education," Objective Standard, August 13, 2018, https://www.theobjectivestandard.com/2018/08/ heroes-and-villains-in-american-education/?add-to-cart=113670.

345. Denis Prager, "Coming Home from College," *National Review*, March 12, 2019, https://www.nationalreview.com/2019/03/ college-indoctrination-leftism-rampant/.

346. Ibid.

347. Ibid.

348. Charles Creitz, "Candace Owens Warns Conservatives Have 'Lost the Education Battle' to Left, Are 'Guaranteeing Them the Future,'" Fox News, September 13, 2020, https://www.foxnews.com/media/ candace-owens-conservatives-lost-education-battle-left.

349. Ibid.

350. Ibid.

351. Ibid.

352. Ibid.

353. Ibid.

354. Ibid.

355. Ibid.

356. Andrew Bernstein, "Heroes and Villains in American Education," *Objective Standard*, 13.3 (Fall 2018), p.14+, http://www. theobjectivestandard.com/.

357. Ibid.

358. Ibid.

359. Ibid.

360. Ibid.

361. Ibid.

362. Ibid.

363. Ibid.

364. Ibid.

365. Ibid.

366. Ibid.

367. Ibid.
368. Ibid.
369. Ibid.
370. Ibid.
371. Ibid.
372. Ibid.
373. Ibid.
374. Ibid.
375. Ibid.
376. Ibid.
377. Ibid.
378. Ibid.
379. Ibid.
380. Ibid.
381. Ibid.
382. Ibid.
383. Mike Shotwell, "The Infiltration of Marxism into Higher Education (Part 1 of 2)," *Epoch Times*, December 3, 2018, https://www.theepochtimes.com/the-infiltration-of-marxism-into-higher-education-part-1-of-2_2718970.html.
384. Ibid.
385. Ibid.
386. Ibid.
387. "Fabian Society," Wikipedia, accessed January 26, 2021 https://en.wikipedia.org/wiki/Fabian_Society.
388. Ibid.
389. "J.B.S. Haldane," Wikipedia, accessed January 26, 2021 https://en.wikipedia.org/wiki/J._B._S._Haldane.
390. "Hyman Levy," Wikipedia, accessed January 26, 2021 https://en.wikipedia.org/wiki/Hyman_Levy.
391. Mike Shotwell, "The Infiltration of Marxism into Higher Education (Part 1 of 2)," Op cit.
392. Mike Shotwell, "The Infiltration of Marxism into Higher Education (Part 2 of 2)," *Epoch Times*, December 3, 2018, https://www.theepochtimes.com/the-infiltration-of-marxism-into-higher-education-part-2-of-2_2718972.html.

393. Ibid.

394. Paul Gottfried, "The Frankfurt School and Cultural Marxism," *American Thinker*, January 12, 2018, https://www.americanthinker. com/articles/2018/01/the_frankfurt_school_and_cultural_marxism. html.

395. Ibid.

396. Mike Shotwell, "The Infiltration of Marxism into Higher Education (Part 2 of 2)," Op cit.

397. Gottfried, Op cit.

398. Ibid.

399. Editorial Team, "The Specter of Communism Is Ruling Our World, Chapter Twelve, Part I: Sabotaging Education," *Epoch Times*, June 11, 2018, https://www.theepochtimes.com/chapter-twelve-sabotaging-education-part-i_2636144.html.

400. Andrew Bernstein, "Heroes and Villains in American Education," Objective Standard, August 13, 2018, https://www.theobjectivestandard.com/2018/08/ heroes-and-villains-in-american-education/?add-to-cart=113670.

401. As cited in Editorial Board, "How the Specter of Communism Is Ruling Our World," *Epoch Times*, June 11, 2018, National Commission on Excellence in Education, *A Nation at Risk* (Washington DC: US Department of Education, 1983), https://www2.ed.gov/pubs/ NatAtRisk/risk.html.

402. John Taylor Gatto, *Dumbing Us Down: The Hidden Curriculum of Compulsory Schooling* (Gabriola Island, BC, Canada: New Society Publishers, 2005), 12, as cited in https://www.theepochtimes.com/ chapter-twelve-sabotaging-education-part-i_2636144.html.

403. Charlotte Thomson Iserbyt, *The Deliberate Dumbing Down of America: A Chronological Paper Trail* (Ravenna, OH: Conscience Press, 1999), xvii, as cited in https://www.theepochtimes.com/chapter-twelve-sabotaging-education-part-i_2636144.html.

404. Sidney Hook, as quoted in Robin S. Eubanks, *Credentialed to Destroy: How and Why Education Became a Weapon* (Scotts Valley, CA: Createspace Independent Publishing Platform, 2013), 48, as cited in https://www.theepochtimes.com/chapter-twelve-sabotaging-education-part-i_2636144.html.

405. E. Merrill Root, *Brainwashing in the High Schools: An Examination of Eleven American History Textbooks* (Papamoa Press, 2018), Kindle edition, as cited in https://www.theepochtimes.com/chapter-twelve-sabotaging-education-part-i_2636144.html.

406. Brock Chisholm, as quoted in B. K. Eakman, *Cloning of the American Mind: Eradicating Morality through Education* (Lafayette, LA: Huntington House, 1998), 109, as cited in https://www.theepochtimes.com/chapter-twelve-sabotaging-education-part-i_2636144.html.

407. William Kilpatrick, *Why Johnny Can't Tell Right from Wrong and What We Can Do About It* (New York: Simon & Schuster, 1993), 16–17, as cited in https://www.theepochtimes.com/chapter-twelve-sabotaging-education-part-i_2636144.html.

408. Ibid.

409. Judith A. Reisman et al., Kinsey, *Sex and Fraud: The Indoctrination of a People* (Lafayette, LA: Lochinvar-Huntington House, 1990), as cited in https://www.theepochtimes.com/chapter-twelve-sabotaging-education-part-i_2636144.html.

410. Maureen Stout, *The Feel-Good Curriculum: The Dumbing Down of America's Kids in the Name of Self-Esteem* (Cambridge, MA: Da Capo Lifelong Books, 2000), 1–3, as cited in https://www.theepochtimes.com/chapter-twelve-sabotaging-education-part-i_2636144.html.

411. Ibid, p. 17.

412. Bradley Devlin, "Why Do Teachers Unions Hate Our Kids?," Dailycaller.com, November 24, 2020, https://dailycaller.com/2020/11/24/teachers-unions-weingarten-pandemic-shutdowns-school-closures-lobbying/.

413. Ibid.

414. Ibid.

415. Ibid.

416. Ibid.

417. Paul Samuelson, as quoted in foreword to Phillips Saunders and William B. Walstad, eds., T*he Principles of Economics Course* (New York: McGraw-Hill Companies, 1989).

418. John A. Stormer, *None Dare Call It Treason* (Florissant, MO: Liberty Bell Press, 1964), 99.

419. Mary Grabar, "America, the Fascist: The Communist Histories of

Howard Zinn, William Z. Foster Used in US Schools," *Epoch Times*, December 3, 2019, https://www.theepochtimes.com/america-the-fascist-the-communist-histories-of-howard-zinn-william-z-foster-used-in-us-schools_3152945.html.

420. Ibid.

421. Ibid.

422. Ibid.

423. Evita Duffy, "High School History Teacher Throws Out Textbooks for Radical Marxist 'History' Book," *Federalist*, June 19, 2020, https://thefederalist.com/2020/06/19/high-school-history-teacher-throws-out-textbooks-for-radical-MARXist-history-book/.

424. Ibid.

425. Ibid.

426. Mitchell Langbert and Sean Stevens, "Partisan Registration and Contributions of Faculty in Flagship Colleges," National Association of Scholars, January 17, 2020, https://www.nas.org/blogs/article/partisan-registration-and-contributions-of-faculty-in-flagship-colleges.

427. Mitchell Langbert, Anthony J. Quain, and Daniel B. Klein, "Faculty Voter Registration in Economics, History, Journalism, Law, and Psychology," *Econ Journal Watch* 13, issue 3, September 2016, 422–51, https://econjwatch.org/articles/faculty-voter-registration-in-economics-history-journalism-communications-law-and-psychology.

428. "The Close-Minded Campus? The Stifling of Ideas in American Universities," *American Enterprise Institute,* June 8, 2016, https://www.aei.org/events/the-close-minded-campus-the-stifling-of-ideas-in-american-universities.

429. Ted Cruz, as quoted in Fred Schwarz and David A. Noebel, *You Can Still Trust the Communists…to Be Communists (Socialists, Statists, and Progressives Too)*, revised edition (Manitou Springs, CO: Christian Anti-Communism Crusade, 2010), 2–3.

430. Jay Parini, as quoted in Walter E. Williams, *More Liberty Means Less Government: Our Founders Knew This Well* (Stanford, CA: Hoover Press, 1999), 126.

431. David Macey, "Organic Intellectual," in *Penguin Dictionary of Critical Theory* (London: Penguin Books, 2000), 282.

432. Yuichiro Kakutani and Jack Beyrer, "Organizations Linked to Chinese

Military Are a Cash Cow for American Colleges," *Washington Free Beacon*, January 11, 2021, https://freebeacon.com/campus/organizations-linked-to-chinese-military-are-a-cash-cow-for-american-colleges/?utm_source=actengage&utm_campaign=conservative_test&utm_medium=email.

433. Ibid.

434. Ibid.

435. Ibid.

436. Frantz Fanon, *The Wretched of the Earth,* trans. Constance Farrington (New York: Grove Press, 1966), 94.

437. David Horowitz and Jacob Laksin, *One Party Classroom: How Radical Professors at America's Top Colleges Indoctrinate Students and Undermine Our Democracy* (New York: Crown Forum, 2009), 3.

438. Donald Alexander Downs, *Restoring Free Speech and Liberty on Campus* (Oakland, CA: Independent Institute, 2004), 51.

439. "Jim Morrison," Brainyquote.com, accessed January 30, 2021, https://www.brainyquote.com/quotes/jim_morrison_167304.

440. Jordan Lancaster, "Poll: 86% of Americans Think the Media Is Biased," Dailycaller.com, September 10, 2020, https://dailycaller.com/2020/09/10/poll-americans-think-media-biased-fake-news/.

441. Joseph Pulitzer, as quoted in Michael Lewis, "J-School Confidential," *New Republic,* April 18, 1993, https://newrepublic.com/article/72485/j-school-confidential.

442. Katharine J. Tobal, "These 6 Corporations Own Most of the Media," ExposingTruth, July 7, 2014, https://www.exposingtruth.com/6-media-corporations-everything-watch-hear-read/.

443. Cited in Michael J. Carley, Review of Foglesong, David S., *America's Secret War Against Bolshevism: U.S. Intervention in the Russian Civil War, 1917–1920*. H-Russia, H-Net Reviews. June, 1996, http://www.h-net.org/reviews/showrev.php?id=489.

444. Ibid.

445. "Red Scare," Wikipedia, accessed January 26, 2021, https://en.wikipedia.org/wiki/Red_Scare.

446. "The Cold War: Prelude in Wartime." *American Decades*, edited by Judith S. Baughman, et al., vol. 5: 1940–1949, Gale, 2001. *Gale*

eBooks, link.gale.com/apps/doc/CX3468301525/GVRL?u=wash92852 &sid=GVRL&xid=443b45bb. Accessed 18 Dec. 2020.

447. Jennifer Luff, *Commonsense Anticommunism: Labor and Civil Liberties between the World Wars* (2012), p.65.

448. Ibid.

449. Ibid.

450. "Lend Lease," Wikipedia, accessed January 26, 2021 https:// en.wikipedia.org/wiki/Lend-Lease.

451. Ibid.

452. Karl Marx and Friedrich Engels, "Rules of the Communist League," in *The Communist League* (1847), Marx/Engels Internet Archive, accessed April 26, 2020, https://www.marxists.org/archive/marx/works/1847/communist-league/index.htm.

453. "Vyacheslav Molotov," Russiapedia, accessed January 26, 2021, http://russiapedia.rt.com/prominent-russians/history-and-mythology/vyacheslav-molotov/?gclid=CPqq5-a1xKcCFSVa7AodgAfrCg.

454. Lin Biao 林彪, "Zai Zhongyangzhengzhiju kuodahuiyi shang de jianghua" 在中央政治局擴大會議上的講話 ("Speech at the Enlarged Meeting of the Politburo"), in Zhongguo Wenhuadageming wenku 中國文化大革命文庫 (*Collection of Documents From China's Cultural Revolution*), May 18, 1966. (In Chinese) as cited in Editorial Team, "The Specter of Communism, Chapter Thirteen: The Media," *Epoch Times*, June 9, 2018, https://www.theepochtimes.com/chapter-thirteen-hijacking-the-media_2684140.html.

455. Hu Qiaomu 胡喬木, "Baozhi shi jiaokeshu" 報紙是教科書 ("Newspapers Are Textbooks"), in *Hu Qiaomu wenku* 胡喬木文集 (*The Collected Works of Hu Qiaomu*), (Beijing: People's Daily Publishing House, 1994), 3:303. (In Chinese) as cited in Editorial Team, "The Specter of Communism, Chapter Thirteen: The Media," *Epoch Times*, June 9, 2018, https://www.theepochtimes.com/chapter-thirteen-hijacking-the-media_2684140.html.

456. Editorial Team, "The Specter of Communism, Chapter Thirteen: The Media," *Epoch Times*, June 9, 2018, https://www.theepochtimes.com/chapter-thirteen-hijacking-the-media_2684140.html.

457. "Whittaker Chambers," Wikipedia, accessed January 26, 2021, https:// en.wikipedia.org/wiki/Whittaker_Chambers.

458. Ibid.

459. Ibid.

460. Ibid.

461. Ibid.

462. Marco Carynnyk, "The New York Times and the Great Famine," *Ukrainian Weekly,* vol. LI, no. 37, published September 11, 1983, accessed April 26, 2020, http://www.ukrweekly.com/old/archive/1983/378320.shtml.

463. David B. Jenkins, "America's Marxist Media," PJ Media, April 3, 2011, https://pjmedia.com/blog/david-b-jenkins/2011/04/03/americas-marxist-media-n11648.

464. Ibid.

465. Ibid.

466. Johnathan Gray, "Spreading the Red Stain: The Communist Infiltration of Hollywood," *Epoch Times*, September 21, 2017, https://www.theepochtimes.com/spreading-the-red-stain-the-communist-infiltration-of-hollywood_2299892.html.

467. Ibid.

468. Ibid.

469. Ibid.

470. Ibid.

471. Ibid.

472. Brett M. Decker, "Hollywood Traitors Supported Hitler and Stalin: An Interview with Allan Ryskind," Dailycaller, May 13, 2015, https://dailycaller.com/2015/05/13/hollywood-traitors-supported-hitler-and-stalin-an-interview-with-allan-ryskind/.

473. Ibid.

474. Ibid.

475. Kenneth Lloyd Billingsley, "Hollywood's Missing Movies: Why American Films Have Ignored Life under Communism," Reason, 32, No. 2, 20-9 Je 2000.

476. Decker, Op cit.

477. Ibid.

478. Ibid.

479. Ibid.

480. Billingsley, Op cit.

481. "Hollywood Ten," History.com, December 16, 2009, https://www.history.com/topics/cold-war/hollywood-ten.

482. Ibid.

483. Decker, Op cit.

484. Ibid.

485. Gray, Op cit.

486. Ibid.

487. "The Journalists' Creed," Fourth Estate, accessed January 26, 2021, https://www.fourthestate.org/journalists-creed/.

488. Jim Kuypers, *Partisan Journalism: A History of Media Bias in the United States* (Lanham, MD: Rowman & Littlefield, 2013).

489. Bernard Cohen, as quoted in Maxwell E. McCombs and Donald L. Shaw, "The Agenda-Setting Function of Mass Media," *The Public Opinion Quarterly* 36, no. 2 (Summer 1972): 177.

490. Newt Gingrich, "China's Embrace of Marxism Is Bad News for Its People," Fox News, June 2, 2018, http://www.foxnews.com/opinion/2018/06/02/newt-gingrich-chinas-embrace-marxism-is-bad-news-for-its-people.html.

491. Patricia Cohen, "Liberal Views Dominate Footlights," *New York Times*, October 15, 2008, https://www.nytimes.com/2008/10/15/theater/15thea.html.

492. Ben Shapiro, *Primetime Propaganda: The True Hollywood Story of How the Left Took Over Your TV* (New York: Broadside Books, 2012), 55–85.

493. Ibid.

494. Billingsley, Op cit.

495. "The Media Assault on American Values," *Media Research Center,* accessed April 26, 2020, https://www.mrc.org/special-reports/media-assault-american-values.

496. Ibid.

497. Ibid.

498. "Critique of the Gotha Programme," Wikipedia, accessed January 26, 2021, https://en.wikipedia.org/wiki/Critique_of_the_Gotha_Programme.

499. Ibid.

500. "Kino-Pravda," Wikipedia, accessed January 26, 2021, https://
en.wikipedia.org/wiki/Kino-Pravda.

501. "Teorema," Wikipedia, accessed January 26, 2021, https://en.wikipedia.
org/wiki/Teorema.

502. Luca Badaloni, "The 10 Best Movies Influenced by Marxist
Philosophy," Taste of Cinema, July 22, 2015, http://www.tasteofcinema.
com/2015/the-10-best-movies-influenced-by-marxist-philosophy/.

503. Billingsley, Op cit.

504. Chrissy Clark, "A Rundown Of Major U.S. Corporate
Media's Business Ties To China," The Federalist,
May 4, 2020, https://thefederalist.com/2020/05/04/
has-china-compromised-every-major-mainstream-media-entity.

505. Ibid.

506. Jen Kirby, "Concentration Camps and Forced Labor:
China's Repression of the Uighurs, Explained," Vox, July
28, 2020, https://www.vox.com/2020/7/28/21333345/
uighurs-china-internment-camps-forced-labor-xinjiang.

507. Ibid.

508. Clark, Op cit. and "China Daily," Wikipedia, accessed January 26,
2021, https://en.wikipedia.org/wiki/China_Daily.

509. Adam Kredo, "Lawmaker Urges House Leadership to Stop
Distributing Communist Propaganda Paper," *Washington
Free Beacon*, January 11, 2021, https://freebeacon.com/
culture/lawmaker-urges-house-leadership-to-stop-distributing-
communist-propaganda-paper/?utm_source=actengage&utm_
campaign=conservative_test&utm_medium=email.

510. Ibid.

511. Clark, Op cit.

512. Joseph Wulfsohn, "China's Government-Run Propaganda Video
Includes CNN, MSNBC Journalists, Hillary Clinton, Celebs,"
Fox News, April 1, 2020, https://www.foxnews.com/media/
china-government-propaganda-coronavirus-cnn-msnbc-hillary-clinton.

513. Becket Adams, "CNN Publishes Chinese Propaganda Praising China,
Degrading the US Navy," *Washington Examiner*, April 15, 2020,
https://www.washingtonexaminer.com/opinion/cnn-publishes-chinese-
propaganda-praising-china-degrading-the-u-s-navy.

514. Clark, Op cit.

515. Patrick Brzeski, "China's CMC Takes Full Ownership of NBCUniversal's Oriental DreamWorks," *Hollywood Reporter*, February 1, 2018, https://www.hollywoodreporter.com/news/chinas-cmc-capital-partners-takes-full-ownership-nbcuniversals-oriental-dreamworks-1081186.

516. Clark, Op cit.

517. Ibid.

518. Clark, Op cit.

519. Koh Gui Qing and John Shiffman, "Beijing's Covert Radio Network Airs China-Friendly News Across Washington, and the World," Reuters, November 2, 2015, https://www.reuters.com/investigates/special-report/china-radio.

520. "The Bridge," WCRM 1190, Washington, DC, accessed January 15, 2021, http://www.wcrw1190.com/.

521. Jessica Chen Weiss, "No, China and the U.S. Aren't Locked in an Ideological Battle. Not Even Close," *Washington Post*, May 4, 2019, https://www.washingtonpost.com/politics/2019/05/04/no-china-us-arent-locked-an-ideological-battle-not-even-close/.

522. Ibid.

523. Matthew Hill et al., "'Their goal is to destroy everyone': Uighur Camp Detainees Allege Systematic Rape," BBC News, February 2, 2021, https://www.bbc.com/news/world-asia-china-55794071.

524. Dolia Estevez, "Billionaire Carlos Slim And China's JAC Motors to Manufacture Cars for Latin American Market," *Forbes*, March 28, 2017, https://www.forbes.com/sites/doliaestevez/2017/03/28/billionaire-carlos-slim-and-chinas-jac-motors-to-manufacture-cars-for-latin-american-market/?sh=61ed0e246ac8.

525. Daniel Ashman, "Media Pretend That China Isn't Communist," *Epoch Times*, October 4, 2019, https://www.theepochtimes.com/media-pretend-china-isnt-communist_3106656.html.

526. Ibid.

527. Adelmann, Bob, "*The Deep State's Trojan Horse in America*: This book does well at showing that not only are the Communist Chinese a threat to our country, but they are also being used to advance a globalist agenda." *New American*, vol. 36, no. 18, 21 Sept. 2020, p. 29+. *Gale*

Academic OneFile, link.gale.com/apps/doc/A637032121/AONE?u=wash92852&sid=AONE&xid=486796e7. Accessed 30 Dec. 2020.

528. James Tager, "Made in Hollywood, Censored by Beijing, The U.S. Film Industry and Chinese Government Influence PEN America," accessed January 26, 2021, https://pen.org/report/made-in-hollywood-censored-by-beijing/.

529. Cathy He, "Hollywood Continues to Cave to Chinese Censorship, Jeopardizing Free Speech, Report Finds," *Epoch Times*, August 5, 2020, https://www.theepochtimes.com/hollywood-continues-to-cave-to-chinese-censorship-jeopardizing-free-speech-report-finds_3451221.html.

530. James Tager, Op cit.

531. Ibid.

532. Ibid.

533. Jan Jekielek, "Inside Communist China's Takeover of Hollywood: Film Exec Chris Fenton," *Epoch Times*, July 9, 2020, https://www.theepochtimes.com/inside-communist-chinas-takeover-of-hollywood-film-exec-chris-fenton_3418527.html.

534. Ibid.

535. Ibid.

536. Ibid.

537. Ibid.

538. As cited in Tager, Op cit., Uptin Saiidi, "China's Box Office Is Expected to Surpass the US in 2020. That's Good News for Hollywood," CNBC.com, November, 5, 2019.

539. As cited in Tager, Op cit., Sandy Schaefer, "2019 US Box Office Falls Below 2018 Despite Avengers: Endgame," *Screen Rant*, January 3, 2020.

540. As cited in Tager, Op cit., "Mainland Box Office Ranking," endata, 2019; Robert Foyle Hunwick, "Chinese Film Studios Are Blacklisting Americans," *Foreign Policy*, May 23, 2019; Tom Hancock, "Chinese Studios Impose Informal Ban on American Actors," *Financial Times,* July 4, 2019.

541. Tager, Op cit.

542. Julius Caesar, AZQuotes, accessed January 26, 2021, https://www.azquotes.com/author/2318-Julius_Caesar.

543. Joshua Philipp, "The Dark Origins of Communism: Part 1 of 3," *Epoch Times*, May 24, 2017, https://www.theepochtimes.com/the-dark-origins-of-communism-part-1-of-3_2249661.html.

544. Ibid.

545. Ibid.

546. Ibid.

547. Ibid.

548. Ibid.

549. "Wilhelm Weitling," Wikipedia, accessed January 26, 2021, https://en.wikipedia.org/wiki/Wilhelm_Weitling.

550. Ibid.

551. Ibid.

552. Joshua Philipp, "The Dark Origins of Communism: Part 3 of 3," *Epoch Times*, May 24, 2017, https://www.theepochtimes.com/the-dark-origins-of-communism-part-3-of-3_2251601.html.

553. "Das Kapital," Wikipedia, accessed February 22, 2021, https://en.wikipedia.org/wiki/Das_Kapital.

554. Paul Kengor, *The Devil and Karl Marx: Communism's Long March of Death, Deception, and Infiltration*, (Tan Books, Gastonia, NC 2020), p. 33.

555. Ibid.

556. Ibid and Karl Marx, Communist Manifesto, accessed February 22, 2021, https://www.marxists.org/archive/marx/works/1848/communist-manifesto/ch02.htm.

557. Kengor, Op cit.

558. Ibid, p. 34.

559. "Richard Wurmbrand," Wikipedia, accessed January 26, 2021, https://en.wikipedia.org/wiki/Richard_Wurmbrand.

560. Kengor, Op cit., p. 36.

561. Ibid.

562. Ibid, p. 40.

563. Ibid, p. 77.

564. Ibid, p. 99.

565. Ibid, p. 78.

566. As cited in Thomas Horn, *Nephilim Stargates* (Crane, MO: Defender Publishing, 2007) 211–212.

567. Ibid, p. 135.

568. Joshua Philipp, "The Dark Origins of Communism: Part 3 of 3," Op cit.

569. Ibid.

570. Cid Lazarou, "How the New Left Is Perpetuating Satanism in Society," *Epoch Times*, February 21, 2019, https://www.theepochtimes.com/how-the-new-left-is-perpetuating-satanism-in-society_2806197.html.

571. Ibid.

572. Ibid.

573. Ibid.

574. Ibid.

575. Rich Swier, "Democrat Document Surfaces Demanding Biden Clamp Down on Conservative Christians, Remove Them from Public Office and Re-educate Trump Voters,"Dr. Rich Swier, December 16, 2020, https://drrichswier.com/2020/12/16/democrat-document-surfaces-demanding-biden-clamp-down-on-conservative-christians-remove-them-from-public-office-and-re-educate-trump-voters/.

576. Ibid.

577. Ibid.

578. Daniel Greenfield, "Marianne Williamson Reveals the Democrats Are a Cult," FrontPage, August 13, 2019, https://www.frontpagemag.com/fpm/2019/08/marianne-williamson-reveals-democrats-are-cult-daniel-greenfield/.

579. Ibid.

580. Cassandra Fairbanks, "Spirit Cooking: The Most Disturbing Podesta Email Yet?," WEARECHANGE, November 4, 2016, http://archive.is/iFRof.

581. Helen Holmes, "Marina Abramović Breaks Her Silence on Being Labeled a Satanist," *Observer*, April 22, 2020, https://observer.com/2020/04/marina-abramovic-breaks-silence-satanist-conspiracy-theories/.

582. Greenfield, Op cit.

583. "Witches Cast 'Mass Spell' Against Donald Trump," BBC News, February 25, 2017, https://www.bbc.com/news/world-us-canada-39090334.

584. Steve Warren and Benjamin Gill, "Thousands of Witches Plot 'Blue Wave' Spell on Oct. 31 and Nov. 2 to Force Trump from Office,"

CBN News, October 31, 2020, https://www1.cbn.com/cbnnews/politics/2020/october/marking-2-rare-cosmic-moments-in-1-month-thousands-of-witches-plot-to-bind-trump-for-last-debate-and-election-day.

585. "Knights Templar Code of Conduct," medievalchronicles.com, accessed January 26, 2021, https://www.medievalchronicles.com/the-crusades/knights-templar/knights-templar-code-of-conduct/.

586. Ibid.

587. Ibid.

588. "French Revolution," Britannica.com, accessed January 26, 2021, https://www.britannica.com/event/Reign-of-Terror and https://en.wikipedia.org/wiki/French_Revolution.

589. "Bolshevism-Jacobinism," Marxists.org, accessed January 26, 2021, https://www.marxists.org/history/france/revolution/mathiez/1920/bolshevism-jacobinism.htm.

590. Ibid.

591. Joshua Philipp, "Dark Origins of Communism: Part 2 of 3," *Epoch Times*, May 31, 2017, https://www.theepochtimes.com/the-dark-origins-of-communism-part-2-of-3_2251602.html.

592. Ibid.

593. Ibid.

594. Joshua Philipp, "The Dark Origins of Communism: Part 2 of 3," Op cit.

595. Ibid.

596. Ibid.

597. "Illuminati," Wikipedia, accessed January 26, 2021, https://en.wikipedia.org/wiki/Illuminati.

598. Joshua Philipp, "The Dark Origins of Communism: Part 3 of 3," Op cit.

599. Ibid.

600. Ibid.

601. "JFK's Speech On Secret Societies," Wakeup-World.com, May 20, 2011, https://wakeup-world.com/2011/05/20/jfks-speech-on-secret-societies/.

602. Ibid.

603. Ibid.

604. Bonnie H. Erickson, "Secret Societies and Social Structure," Social Forces, Vol. 60:1, September 1981, pp. 188-210, https://

academic.oup.com/sf/article-abstract/60/1/188/1938308/ Secret-Societies-and-Social-Structure?redirectedFrom=fulltext.

605. David Bay, "A Transcript of Secret Societies," Cutting Edge Radio Program, accessed May 20, 2017, http://www.cuttingedge.org/ce1037.html.

606. Beth Rowland, "Home Grown Terrorists," America's Civil War, Historynet, July 2015, pp. 49-53. http://www.historynet.com/home-grown-terrorists.htm.

607. Ibid.

608. Ibid.

609. "Bilderbergers Give John Edwards the Nod?" *New American*, August 9, 2004, p. 5.

610. Ibid.

611. Jason Simpkins, "The World's Most Powerful Secret Societies: The Bilderbergs," Outsider Club, January 21, 2014, https://www.outsiderclub.com/secret-societies-the-bilderbergs-david-rockefeller-trilateral-commission-council-on-foreign-relations/751.

612. "Kingmakers Don't Even Change Loation Let Alone Plans for the Nation," States News Service, 8 Mar. 2016.

613. Ibid.

614. William F. Jasper, "Bilderberg Post Mortem: What Is the Trump-Pompeo-Kushner-Bilderberg Connection All About?," *New American*, June 10, 2019, https://thenewamerican.com/bilderberg-post-mortem-what-is-the-trump-pompeo-kushner-bilderberg-connection-all-about/.

615. Alex Newman, "Where Big Business and Big Government Meet," *New American*, July 7, 2014, pp. 21–26.

616. Richard B. Barnes, "Globalization and What It Means to Citizens of the United States," Rubber World, May 2020, http://eds.b.ebscohost.com.pentagonlibrary.idm.oclc.org/eds/pdfviewer/pdfviewer?vid=1&sid=7c24665b-7ec6-46ca-afaf-58b34881fbcf%40pdc-v-sessmgr04.

617. Ibid.

618. Kalee Brown, "David Rockefeller's Chilling 1991 Speech at A Bilderberg Meeting," Collective-Evolution, March 21, 2017, https://www.collective-evolution.com/2017/03/21/the-new-world-order-david-rockefellers-chilling-1991-speech-at-a-bilderberg-meeting/.

619. "Bilderbergers Give John Edwards the Nod?" *New American*, August 9, 2004, p. 5.

620. Ibid.

621. Andrew Glass, "Clinton Signs NAFTA into Law," *Politico*, December 8, 1993, https://www.politico.com/story/2018/12/08/clinton-signs-nafta-into-law-dec-8-1993-1040789.

622. Alan Cowell and David M. Halbfinger, "The Nation: Conspiracy Theorists Unite; A Secret Conference Thought to Rule the World," *New York Times*, July 11, 2004, https://www.nytimes.com/2004/07/11/weekinreview/nation-conspiracy-theorists-unite-secret-conference-thought-rule-world.html.

623. Sandra Miesel, "Freemasons and Their Craft: What Catholics Should Know," *Catholic World Report*, February 7, 2017, https://www.catholiceducation.org/en/controversy/common-misconceptions/freemasons-and-their-craft-what-catholics-should-know.html#:~:text=Their%20foremost%20modern%20commentator%2C%20Henry%20Wilson%20Coil%2C%20describes,into%20the%20guild%20traditions%20developed%20by%20medieval%20stoneworkers.

624. Paul Darin, "The Truth About Secret Societies," *Epoch Times*, November 29, 2014, https://www.theepochtimes.com/the-truth-about-secret-societies_1111841.html.

625. Miesel, Op cit.

626. "Masons, New World Order Warning to the President," Life Site News, June 18, 2020, https://ifapray.org/blog/masons-new-world-order-warning-to-the-president/.

627. Ibid.

628. Ibid.

629. James Morgan, "Decoding the Symbols on Satan's Statue," BBC News, July 31, 2015, https://www.bbc.com/news/magazine-33682878.

630. Ibid.

631. "Masons, New World Order Warning to the President," Op cit.

632. Ibid.

633. "Carbonari," Wikipedia, accessed January 27, 2021, https://en.wikipedia.org/wiki/Carbonari.

634. Gary Lachman, *Politics and the Occult: The Left, the Right, and the*

Radically Unseen (Wheaton, IL: Theosophical Publishing House, 2008), 97–98; as cited in Thomas Horn, *Saboteurs*, Crane, MO: Defender Publishing, 2017) 158–159.

635. "Jacques Cazotte," Wikipedia, accessed February 10, 2021, https://en.wikipedia.org/wiki/Jacques_Cazotte.

636. Allan Hall, "Heinrich Himmler's Stash of Books on Witchcraft Is Discovered in Czech Library after Being Hidden for 50 Years," *Daily Mail*, March 18, 2016, https://www.dailymail.co.uk/news/article-3498908/Heinrich-Himmler-s-stash-books-witchcraft-discovered-Czech-library-hidden-50-years.html.

637. Ivan Pentchoukov, "Senator: FBI Secret Society Held Secret Offsite Meetings, Informant Says," *Epoch Times*, January 24, 2018, https://www.theepochtimes.com/senator-fbi-secret-society-held-secret-offsite-meetings-informant-says_2423143.html.

638. Ryan Saavedra, "Leftists Violently Attack Trump Supporters in Nation's Capital Following 'MAGA March,'" Dailywire, November 14, 2020, https://www.dailywire.com/news/leftists-violently-attack-trump-supporters-in-nations-capital-following-maga-march?itm_source=parsely-api?utm_source=cnemail&utm_medium=email&utm_content=111520-news&utm_campaign=position1.

639. "All LSC-endorsed Resolutions for 2019 National Convention," DSA Libertarian Socialist Caucus, July 16, 2019, https://dsa-lsc.org/2019/07/16/all-lsc-endorsed-resolutions-for-2019-national-convention/.

640. Twin Cities DSA on Twitter: "Want to help out your comrades protesting at the 3rd precinct (at Lake and Minnehaha?) Here's a good list of much needed supplies (except for milk! Water is always better for eyewashing than milk!! Please don't bring milk!) https://t.co/DZxwZlrAIh" / Twitter.

641. "DSA Condemns the Public Execution of George Floyd at the Hands of the Minneapolis Police," Democratic Socialists of America, May 28, 2020, https://www.dsausa.org/statements/dsa-condemns-the-public-execution-of-george-floyd/.

642. Monica Moorehead, "Against Police Violence and Capitalism, to Rebel Is Justified," Workers World, May 28, 2020, https://www.workers.org/2020/05/49008/.

643. Ibid.

644. "Communiqué #6 from the Revcoms: Police mMrder after Murder
      after Murder…," Revolutionary Communist Party USA, May 28, 2020,
      https://revcom.us/a/649/communique-6-police-murder-after-murder-
      after-murder-en.html.

645. Trevor Loudon, "Cities Burn, but None Dare Call It Communist
      Insurrection," *Epoch Times*, May 31, 2020, https://www.
      theepochtimes.com/cities-burn-but-none-dare-call-it-communist-
      insurrection_3371302.html.

646. Andy Ngô on Twitter: "We are witnessing glimpses of the full
      insurrection the far-left has been working on for decades. Within hours,
      militant antifa cells across the country mobilized to aid BLM rioters.
      The first broken window is the blood in the water for looters to move
      in. The fires come next." / Twitter.

647. Jan Jekielek, "Antifa Origins, Tactics Exposed after Assault on Andy
      Ngo at Portland Protest: Jack Posobiec," *Epoch Times*, July 15, 2019,
      https://www.theepochtimes.com/antifa-origins-tactics-exposed-after-
      andy-ngos-assault-at-portland-protest-jack-posobiec_3002841.html.

648. Ibid.

649. Ibid.

650. Joshua Philipp, "The Communist Origins of the Antifa Extremist
      Group," *Epoch Times*, August 18, 2017, https://www.theepochtimes.
      com/the-communist-origins-of-the-antifa-extremist-group_2282816.
      html.

651. Ibid.

652. Ibid.

653. Ibid.

654. Ibid.

655. Ibid.

656. Richard Evans, *The Third Reich in Power*, Google Books, July 26,
      2012, https://books.google.com/books/about/The_Third_Reich_in_
      Power_1933_1939.html?id=EBD6KEMrY5sC.

657. Jan Jekielek, "Antifa Origins, Tactics Exposed after Assault on Andy
      Ngo at Portland Protest: Jack Posobiec," Op cit.

658. Ibid.

659. Roger L. Simon, "Antifa Is the Natural Product of Our Educational

System," *Epoch Times*, August 3, 2020, https://www.theepochtimes.com/antifa-is-the-natural-product-of-our-educational-system_3448074.html.

660. Kaatabella Roberts, "Antifa a Dangerous Organization with Similar Structure to an Islamic Terror Cell: Police Spokesperson," *Epoch Times*, October 30, 2020, https://www.theepochtimes.com/antifa-a-dangerous-organization-with-similar-structure-to-an-islamic-terror-cell-police-spokesperson_3558572.html.

661. Ibid.

662. Ibid.

663. Jack Phillips, "FBI Director: 'Antifa Is a Real Thing,' Confirms Investigations Into 'Violent Anarchist Extremists,'" *Epoch Times*, September 17, 2020, https://www.theepochtimes.com/fbi-director-antifa-is-a-real-thing-confirms-investigations-into-violent-anarchist-extremists_3503958.html.

664. Ibid.

665. Ibid.

666. Zachary Stieber, "Antifa Members Flying Around the Country to Engage in Rioting: Barr," *Epoch Times*, September 3, 2020, https://www.theepochtimes.com/antifa-members-flying-around-the-country-to-engage-in-rioting-barr_3486759.html.

667. Ibid.

668. Ibid.

669. Bowen Xiao, "Barr: Antifa a 'Revolutionary Group' That Wants to Establish Socialism," *Epoch Times*, August 11, 2020, https://www.theepochtimes.com/barr-declares-antifa-a-revolutionary-group_3457627.html.

670. Stella Morabito, "How Socialists Like Black Lives Matter Weaponize Our Fears of Loneliness," *Federalist*, June 15, 2020, https://thefederalist.com/2020/06/15/how-socialists-like-black-lives-matter-weaponize-our-fears-of-loneliness/.

671. "'Trained Marxists' Behind Black Lives Matters Admit Core Issue: 'To get Trump out,'" World Tribune, June 23, 2020, https://www.worldtribune.com/trained-marxists-behind-black-lives-matters-admit-core-issue-to-get-trump-out/.

672. Ibid.

673. Ibid.

674. Zachary Stieber, "Pence: Leaders of Black Lives Matter Pushing 'Radical Left' Agenda," *Epoch Times*, June 29, 2020, https://www. theepochtimes.com/pence-leaders-of-black-lives-matter-pushing-radical-left-agenda_3405479.html.

675. Ibid.

676. Douglas Andrews, "BLM's Big Electoral Fail," *Patriot Post*, November 18, 2020, https://patriotpost.us/ articles/74998-blms-big-electoral-fail-2020-11-18/print.

677. Justin Haskins, "John Kerry Reveals Biden's Devotion to Radical 'Great Reset' Movement," MSN News, December 3, 2020, https://www.msn.com/en-us/news/politics/john-kerry-reveals-bidens-devotion-to-radical-great-reset-movement/ ar-BB1bBu34.

678. Ibid.

679. Caden Pearson, "'Great Reset' of Capitalism a Threat to Our Way of Life: Australian Senator," *Epoch Times*, November 11, 2020, https:// www.theepochtimes.com/great-reset-of-capitalism-a-threat-to-our-way-of-life-australian-senator_3573950.html.

680. Ibid.

681. Ibid.

682. Ibid.

683. Ibid.

684. Ibid.

685. Adrian Monck, "The Great Reset: A Unique Twin Summit to Begin 2021," World Economic Forum, June 3, 2020, https://www.weforum. org/press/2020/06/the-great-reset-a-unique-twin-summit-to-begin-2021.

686. James Gorrie, "What Does 'The Great Reset' Mean for the US Economy?," *Epoch Times*, September 30, 2020, https://www. theepochtimes.com/what-does-the-great-reset-mean-for-the-us-economy_3519155.html.

687. "William O. Douglas," AZQuotes, accessed January 27, 2021, https:// www.azquotes.com/author/4102-William_O_Douglas.

688. Joshua Philipp, "Trump Proclaims 'World Freedom Day' to Oppose Communism and to Uphold Individual Liberties," *Epoch Times*, November 9, 2017, https://www.theepochtimes.com/trump-proclaims-

world-freedom-day-to-oppose-communism-and-to-uphold-individual-liberties_2353983.html.

689. Ibid.

690. Ibid.

691. Ibid.

692. Mayavadi Rajesh, "What Are Civil Liberties? 4 Reasons They Are so Important!," Airtract, May 7, 2019, https://www.airtract.com/article/What-are-Civil-Liberties-4-Reasons-they-are-so-important-.

693. Bret Stephens, "Communism Through Rose-Colored Glasses," *New York Times*, October 27, 2017, https://www.nytimes.com/2017/10/27/opinion/communism-rose-colored-glasses.html.

694. Ibid.

695. Ibid.

696. Andrew Stuttaford, "Communism, Memory and 'Forgetting,'" *National Review*, October 29, 2017, https://www.nationalreview.com/corner/communism-memory-and-forgetting/.

697. Ibid.

698. Ibid.

699. Ibid.

700. Ibid.

701. Ibid.

702. Stephens, Op cit.

703. Stuttaford, Op cit.

704. Megan Sihde, "Everything You Wanted to Know about Communism but Were Afraid to Ask," New Presence, Prague Journal of Central European Affairs, Summer 2007, p. 31f.

705. Ibid.

706. Ibid.

707. Ibid.

708. Ibid.

709. Ibid.

710. Ibid.

711. Carmen Alexe, "I Grew Up in a Communist System. Here's What Americans Don't Understand About Freedom," Intellectual Takeout, March 12, 2018, https://www.intellectualtakeout.org/article/i-grew-

communist-system-heres-what-americans-dont-understand-about-freedom/.

712. Ibid.
713. Ibid.
714. Ibid.
715. Ibid.
716. Ibid.
717. Ibid.
718. Ibid.
719. Ibid.
720. Ibid.
721. Jorge Castellanos, "What Living under Castro Means," a speech delivered before the Economic Club of Detroit, Michigan, November 5, 1962, Vital Speeches of the Day, EBSCO Publishing, 2003.
722. Ibid.
723. Ibid.
724. Ibid.
725. Ibid.
726. Ibid.
727. Ella Kietlinska and Joshua Philipp, "Orlando Gutierrez-Boronat: Cubans Warn Americans Against Socialism, Communism," *Epoch Times*, December 12, 2020, https://www.theepochtimes.com/orlando-gutierrez-boronat-cubans-warn-americans-against-socialism-communism_3614941.html.
728. Ibid.
729. Ibid.
730. Ibid.
731. Ibid.
732. Ibid.
733. Ibid.
734. Ibid.
735. Ibid.
736. Ibid.
737. Ibid.
738. Ibid.

739. Ibid.

740. Ibid.

741. Diana Zhang, "I Grew up in Communist China; Here's My Warning to America," *Epoch Times*, November 24, 2020, https://www. theepochtimes.com/the-2020-election-a-test-for-our-freedom_3592552. html.

742. Ibid.

743. Ibid.

744. Ibid.

745. Ibid.

746. Joshua Philipp and Ella Kietlinska, "Former Political Prisoner: Today's America Has Lesson to Learn from Cuban Socialism," *Epoch Times*, December 21, 2020, https://www.theepochtimes.com/former-political-prisoner-todays-america-has-lesson-to-learn-from-cuban-socialism_3624677.html.

747. Ibid.

748. Ibid.

749. "Fidel Castro Declares Himself a Marxist-Leninist," History, accessed January 27, 2021, https://www.history.com/this-day-in-history/castro-declares-himself-a-marxist-leninist#:~:text=Fidel%20Castro%20 declares%20himself%20a%20Marxist-Leninist%20Following%20 a,bitter%20Cold%20War%20animosity%20between%20the%20 two%20nations.

750. Robert J. Hutchinson, "Robert Hutchinson: AOC, Bernie Sanders and Other Leftist Extremists Have Hijacked Democratic Party," Fox News, October 24, 2019, https://www.foxnews.com/opinion/robert-hutchinson-democrats-republicans-extreme-leftists.

751. Ibid.

752. Ibid.

753. Ibid.

754. Ibid.

755. William Brooks, "Vichy and the Destiny of the West," *Epoch Times*, December 28, 2020, https://www.theepochtimes.com/vichy-and-the-destiny-of-the-west_3631611.html.

756. "German Soviet Nonaggression Pact," Britannica.com,

accessed January 27, 2021, https://www.britannica.com/event/
German-Soviet-Nonaggression-Pact.

757. Ibid.

758. Matthew Harwood, "Civil Liberties and Socialism Don't Mix,"
Reason.com, October 18, 2018, https://reason.com/2018/10/18/
civil-liberties-and-socialism-dont-mix/.

759. Ibid.

760. Ibid.

761. Ibid.

762. Ibid.

763. Ibid.

764. Ibid.

765. Ibid.

766. Ibid.

767. "Ronald Reagan and 'The Shining City Upon a Hill,'"
OurLostFounding.com, accessed January 27, 2021, https://
ourlostfounding.com/ronald-reagan-and-the-shining-city-upon-a-hill/.

768. "Thomas Sowell," Brainyquote.com, accessed January 27, 2021,
https://www.brainyquote.com/quotes/thomas_sowell_371247.

769. "Geoffrey Hodgson," Wikipedia, accessed January 27, 2021, https://
en.wikipedia.org/wiki/Geoffrey_Hodgson.

770. Editorial Team, *The Specter of Communism,* Chapter Five, "Part
II: Infiltrating the West," *Epoch Times*, June 21, 2018, https://
www.theepochtimes.com/chapter-five-infiltrating-the-west-
continued_2562807.html.

771. Ibid.

772. Ibid.

773. Ibid.

774. Bilal Hafeez, "Saul Alinsky's 13 rules for 'have-nots' to gain power,"
Sovereignnations.com, March 7, 2019,https://sovereignnations.
com/2019/03/07/saul-alinskys-13-rules-have-nots-gain-
power/#:~:text=%E2%80%9CMake%20the%20enemy%20live%20
up%20to%20its%20own,weapon.%E2%80%9D%20It%20is%20
almost%20impossible%20to%20counterattack%20ridicule.

775. Editorial Team, *The Specter of Communism*, Chapter Five, "Part II:
Infiltrating the West," Op cit.

776. Gene Van Shaar, "The Naked Communist," *Independent Sentinel*, August 27, 2020, https://www.independentsentinel.com/the-naked-communist/.

777. Editorial Team, *The Specter of Communism*, Chapter Five, "Part II: Infiltrating the West," Op cit. 1.

778. Ibid.

779. Raymond V. Raehn, "The Historical Roots of 'Political Correctness,'" myislam, accessed January 27, 2021, https://myislam.dk/articles/en/raehn%20the-historical-roots-of-political-correctness.php#:~:text=Raymond%20V.%20Raehn%20holds%20an%20M.A.%20degree%20in,Commander%20of%20a%20fighter%20squadron%20some%20years%20later.

780. Jeff Carlson, "The Globalism Threat—Socialism's New World Order," TheMarketsWork, February 24, 2017, https://themarketswork.com/2017/02/24/the-globalism-threat-socialisms-new-world-order/.

781. Editorial Team, *The Specter of Communism*, Chapter Five, "Part II: Infiltrating the West," Op cit. 1.

782. Ibid.

783. Ibid.

784. Ibid.

785. Ibid.

786. Barbara Kay, "Communism's Long March Through the Institutions Has Succeeded," *Epoch Times*, December 28, 2020, https://www.theepochtimes.com/communisms-long-march-through-the-institutions-has-succeeded_3631579.html.

787. Ibid.

788. Ibid.

789. Ibid.

790. Alexander Solzhenitsyn, "Live Not by Lies," Serendipity, accessed January 27, 2021, https://www.serendipity.li/more/live_not_by_lies.htm#:~:text=Alexander%20Solzhenitsyn%27s%20essay%20%22Live%20Not%20By%20Lies%22%20first,and%20circulated%20among%20Moscow%27s%20intellectuals%20at%20that%20time.

791. Megan Briggs, "John MacArthur: Transgenderism Is a Form of Suicide and an Assault on God," ChurchLeaders, December 21, 2016, https://

churchleaders.com/pastors/videos-for-pastors/296543-john-macarthur-transgenderism-form-suicide-assault-god.html.

792. Ibid.

793. Ibid.

794. Ibid.

795. "Purpose of Government," AZQuotes, accessed January 27, 2021, https://www.azquotes.com/quotes/topics/purpose-of-government.html.

796. "The Preamble," Preamble Annotated, accessed January 27, 2021, https://constitution.congress.gov/constitution/preamble/.

797. James Madison and Alexander Hamilton, "The Federalist No. 51," Founders Online, February 6, 1788, https://founders.archives.gov/documents/Hamilton/01-04-02-0199.

798. Thomas Jefferson, Sesquicentenary, Wordpress.com, May 15, 2012, https://sesquicentenary.wordpress.com/2012/05/15/i-consider-the-foundation-of-the-constitution-as-laid-on-this-ground-that-all-powers-not-delegated-to-the-united-states-by-the-constitution-nor-prohibited-by-it-to-the-states-are-reserve/.

799. Ralph Ketcham, *James Madison: A Biography*, (University of Virginia Press, 1990), p. 320.

800. Karl Marx and Friedrich Engels, "Manifesto of the Communist Party," in *Marx & Engels Selected Works,* vol. 1, trans. Samuel Moore, ed. Andy Blunden, Marxists Internet Archive, accessed April 17, 2020, https://www.marxists.org/archive/marx/works/1848/communist-manifesto/ch02.htm.

801. "From each according to his ability, to each according to his needs," Wikipedia, accessed January 27, 2021, https://en.wikipedia.org/wiki/From_each_according_to_his_ability,_to_each_according_to_his_needs.

802. Milton Friedman, *Free to Choose: A Personal Statement* (Boston: Mariner Books, 1990), 148.

803. "Opium of the People," Wikipedia, accessed January 27, 2021, https://en.wikipedia.org/wiki/Opium_of_the_people#:~:text=%22Religion%20is%20the%20opium%20of%20the%20people%22%20is,as%20%22religion...%20is%20the%20opiate%20of%20the%20masses.%22.

Austin Cline, "Karl Marx on Religion as the Opium of the People," Learn Religions, January 7, 2019, https://www.learnreligions.com/karl-marx-on-religion-251019.

804. "Opium of the people," Op cit.

805. Ibid.

806. Cline, Op cit.

807. Karl Marx, as quoted in Dimitry V. Pospielovsky, *A History of Marxist-Leninist Atheism and Soviet Antireligious Policies: History of Soviet Atheism in Theory and Practice, and the Believer, Vol. 1* (London: Palgrave Macmillan, 1987), 80.

808. US Library of Congress, "Translation of Letter from Lenin," Revelations from the Russian Archives, accessed April 17, 2020, https://www.loc.gov/exhibits/archives/trans-ae2bkhun.html.

809. Editorial Team, *The Specter of Communism*, Chapter Six: The Revolt Against God, *Epoch Times*, June 20, 2018, https://www.theepochtimes.com/chapter-6-articles-of-faith-how-the-devil-has-man-revolt-against-god_2562880.html.

810. Momchil Metodiev, *Between Faith and Compromise: The Bulgarian Orthodox Church and the Communist State (1944–1989)* (Sofia: Institute for Studies of the Recent Past/Ciela, 2010).

811. Alex Wu, "Classified Document Reveals Beijing Ordered Eradication of Spiritual Group, Likely Evidence of Genocide: Lawyers," *Epoch Times*, November 9, 2020, https://www.theepochtimes.com/classified-document-reveals-beijing-ordered-eradication-of-spiritual-group-likely-evidence-of-genocide-lawyers_3551573.html.

812. "Church in China Under Intense Attack by Communist Government." *New American*, vol. 35, no. 2, 21 Jan. 2019, p. 8. *Gale Academic OneFile*, link.gale.com/apps/doc/A572716080/AONE?u=wash92852&sid=AONE&xid=8e566d85. Accessed 2 Jan. 2021.

813. US Congress, House, Committee on Un-American Activities. *Investigation of Communist Activities in the New York City Area.* 83rd Cong., 1st sess., July 8, 1953. https://archive.org/stream/investigationofcnyc0708unit/investigationofcnyc0708unit_djvu.txt.

814. Christopher Andrew, "KGB Foreign Intelligence from Brezhnev to the Coup," in Wesley K. Wark, ed., *Espionage: Past, Present,*

Future? (London: Routledge, 1994), 52. and Metodiev, "Between Faith."

815. W. Cleon Skousen, *The Naked Communist* (Salt Lake City: Ensign Publishing Co., 1958).

816. Linda Wiegenfeld, "Is America Losing Its Soul?" *Epoch Times*, August 23, 2019, https://www.theepochtimes.com/is-america-losing-its-soul_3048128.html.

817. Ibid.

818. Ibid.

819. Ibid. And "Little Sisters of the Poor," Wikipedia, accessed January 27, 2021, https://en.wikipedia.org/wiki/Little_Sisters_of_the_Poor_Saints_Peter_and_Paul_Home_v._Pennsylvania.

820. Editorial Team, *The Specter of Communism*, Chapter Seven, Part I: The Destruction of the Family, *Epoch Times*, June 19, 2018, https://www.theepochtimes.com/chapter-seven-destruction-of-the-family-part-i_2661675.html.

821. Friedrich Engels, *Origins of the Family, Private Property, and the State,* trans. Alick West, (1884), chap. 2, part 4, accessed via Marxists Internet Archive on April 17, 2020, https://www.marxists.org/archive/marx/works/1884/origin-family/ch02d.htm.

822. W. Bradford Wilcox, "The Evolution of Divorce," *National Affairs,* no. 1 (Fall 2009), https://www.nationalaffairs.com/publications/detail/the-evolution-of-divorce; US Centers for Disease Control and Prevention, National Center for Health Statistics, "Table 1–17. Number and Percent of Births to Unmarried Women, by Race and Hispanic Origin: United States, 1940–2000," https://www.cdc.gov/nchs/data/statab/t001x17.pdf; and John Elflein, "Percentage of Births to Unmarried Women in the US from 1980 to 2018," Statista, December 3, 2019, https://www.statista.com/statistics/276025/us-percentage-of-births-to-unmarried-women/.

823. Robert Owen, "Critique of Individualism (1825–1826)," Indiana University–Bloomington, July 4, 1826, accessed April 17, 2020. https://web.archive.org/web/20171126034814/http://www.indiana.edu:80/~kdhist/H105-documents-web/week11/Owen1826.html.

824. "Sadomasochism," Wikipedia, accessed January 27, 2021, https://en.wikipedia.org/wiki/Sadomasochism.

825. "Incest," Wikipedia, January 27, 2021, https://www.dictionary.com/browse/incest.

826. "Bestiality," Wikipedia, January 27, 2021, https://www.dictionary.com/browse/bestiality?s=t.

827. "Oneida Communisty," Wikipedia, January 21, 2021, https://en.wikipedia.org/wiki/Oneida_Community.

828. Friedrich Engels, *Origins of the Family, Private Property, and the State,* trans. Alick West, (1884), chapter 2, part 4, accessed via Marxists Internet Archive on April 17, 2020, https://www.marxists.org/archive/marx/works/1884/origin-family/ch02d.htm.

829. Ibid.

830. Editorial Team, *The Specter of Communism*, Chapter Seven, Part I: The Destruction of the Family, Op cit.

831. Alexander Melnichenko Александр Мельниченко, "Velikaya oktyabyr'skaya seksual'naya revolyutsiya" Великая октябрьская сексуальная революция ["The Great October Sexual Revolution"], Russian Folk Line, August 20, 2017, http://ruskline.ru/opp/2017/avgust/21/velikaya_oktyabrskaya_seksualnaya_revolyuciya. (In Russian).

832. Ibid.

833. Ibid.

834. Ibid.

835. Ibid.

836. Madame Smidovich Смидович, as quoted in Natal'ya Korotkaya Наталья Короткая, "Eros revolyutsii: Komsomolka, nye bud' myeshchankoy—pomogi muzhchinye cnyat' napryazheniye!" Эрос революции: "Комсомолка, не будь мещанкой—помоги мужчине снять напряжение!" ("Eros of the Revolution: 'Komsomol Girl, Do Not Be a Bourgeois—Help a Man Relieve Tension!'"), Tut.By Online, November 10, 2012, https://lady.tut.by/news/sex/319720.html?crnd=68249. (In Russian).

837. Paul Kengor, *Takedown: From Communists to Progressives, How the Left Has Sabotaged Family and Marriage* (Washington, DC: WND Books, 2015), 54.

838. Melnichenko, Op cit.

839. Xia Hou 夏侯, "Gongchanzhuyi de yinluan jiyin—xingjiefang"

共产主义的淫乱基因——性解放 ["The Promiscuous Gene of Communism: Sexual Liberation"], *Epoch Times* (Chinese edition), April 9, 2017, http://www.epochtimes.com/gb/17/4/9/n9018949.htm. (In Chinese).

840. Michelle Collums, "Swingers in the '60s," Free Love Movement, October 7, 2014, https://mc3321fall14.wp.txstate.edu/tag/ free-love-movement/.

841. Judith A. Reisman et al., *Kinsey, Sex and Fraud: The Indoctrination of a People* (Lafayette, LA: Lochinvar-Huntington House, 1990).

842. Art Moore, "John Kerry: Biden Presidency Opens Door to Globalist 'Great Reset,'" WND, November 20, 2020, https://www.wnd. com/2020/11/4871642/.

843. Ryan Moffatt, "The Great Reset Smells of a Socialist Experiment," *Epoch Times*, November 26, 2020, https://www.theepochtimes.com/ the-great-reset-smells-of-a-socialist-experiment_3590824.html.

844. Ibid.

845. Ibid.

846. Ibid.

847. Ibid.

848. Moore, Op cit.

849. Ibid.

850. Federico Germani, "Marx's Modern View on Global Capitalism," Culturico, December 28, 2018, https://culturico.com/2018/12/28/ Marxs-modern-view-on-global-capitalism/.

851. Ibid.

852. Ibid.

853. Moffatt, Op cit.

854. "History of the United Nations," United Nations, accessed January 27, 2021, https://www.un.org/en/sections/history/history-united-nations/.

855. Ibid.

856. Ibid.

857. "Atlantic Charter," Wikipedia, accessed January 27, 2021, https:// en.wikipedia.org/wiki/Atlantic_Charter.

858. Bruce Bawer, "The 'Global Citizen' Fraud," *Commentary*, vol. 148, no. 4, Nov. 2019, p. 15+. *Gale Academic OneFile*, link.gale.com/apps/

doc/A606081285/AONE?u=wash92852&sid=AONE&xid=74d20ffd. Accessed 13 Jan. 2021.

859. "History of the United Nations," Op cit.

860. "John Foster Dulles," Wikipedia, accessed January 27, 2021, https:// en.wikipedia.org/wiki/John_Foster_Dulles.

861. Alex Newman, "Global Elite: Regionalism Is Only Path Tt New World Order," Technocracy News & Trends, December 2, 2018, https://www.technocracy.news/ global-elite-regionalism-is-only-path-to-new-world-order/.

862. Steve Byas, "Fear World Government," *New American*, Vol. 33 Issue 13, July 10, 2017, pp. 23–28.

863. Ibid.

864. Ibid.

865. Ibid.

866. Ibid.

867. Ibid.

868. Ibid.

869. Carlson, Op cit.

870. Ibid.

871. Chelsey Cox, "Fact Check: U.N. Agenda 21/2030 'New World Order' Is Not a Real Document," *USA Today*, July 23, 2020, https://www.msn.com/en-us/news/world/fact-check-un-agenda-21-2030-new-world-order-is-not-a-real-document/ ar-BB1773fm.

872. Don Cobb, "The New America: Agenda 21 and the U.N. One World Government plan," Renew America, February 19, 2013, https://www. renewamerica.com/columns/cobb/130219.

873. Ibid.

874. Alex Newman, "The Great Reset: Deep State Globalists Taking over the World and You!" *New American*, December 28, 2020, https://thenewamerican.com/ the-great-reset-deep-state-globalists-taking-over-the-world-and-you/.

875. ASNF, "The Great Reset, Part III: Capitalism with Chinese Characteristics," Niger Business, January 2, 2021, https:// nigerdiaspora.info/the-great-reset-part-iii-capitalism-with-chinese-characteristics/#:~:text=The%20Great%20Reset%20represents%20

the%20development%20of%20the,aiming%20to%20implement%20 a%20socialist-communist%20political%20system%20now.

876. Ibid.

877. Bruce Bawer, "The 'Global Citizen' Fraud," *Commentary*, vol. 148, no. 4, Nov. 2019, p. 15+. *Gale Academic OneFile*, link.gale.com/apps/ doc/A606081285/AONE?u=wash92852&sid=AONE&xid=74d20ffd. Accessed 13 Jan. 2021.

878. Ibid.

879. Ibid.

880. Ibid.

881. Barnini Chakraborty, "Paris Agreement on Climate Change: US Withdraws as Trump Calls It 'Unfair,'" Fox News, June 1, 2017, https://www.foxnews.com/politics/paris-agreement-on-climate-change-us-withdraws-as-trump-calls-it-unfair.

882. Ibid.

883. Ibid.

884. Ibid.

885. Ibid.

886. Alex Newman, "The Great Reset: Deep State Globalists Taking Over the World and You!," Op cit.

887. Ibid.

888. Ibid.

889. Ibid.

890. Ibid.

891. Ibid.

892. Ibid.

893. Ibid.

894. Ibid.

895. Byas, Op cit.

896. Ibid.

897. Ibid.

898. Ibid.

899. Ibid.

900. Ibid.

901. Ibid.

902. Stacey Rudin, "What's Behind the WHO's Lockdown Mixed

Messaging," In: American Institute for Economic Research (AIER) as cited in https://www. aier.org/article/whats-behind-the-whos-lockdownmixed-messaging/ (14.10.2020).

903. Aya Velazquez, "China and the 'Great Reset,'" Medium, December 18, 2020, https://ayavela.medium.com/ china-and-the-great-reset-f111d297853c.

904. Ibid.

905. Vanessa Molter & Renee Diresta, "Pandemics & Propaganda: How Chinese State Media Creates and Propagates CCP Coronavirus Narratives." In: Misinformation Review. As cited in https:// misinforeview.hks.harvard.edu/article/ pandemics-propaganda-how-chinese-state-mediacreates-and-propaga- tes-ccp-coronavirus-narratives/ (08.06.2020).

906. Isaac Stone Fish, "A Communist Party Man at Davos," *Atlantic*, January 18, 2017, https://www.theatlantic.com/international/ archive/2017/01/china-davos-xi-jinping-trump-globalization/513521/.

907. Ibid.

908. Editorial Team, *The Specter of Communism*, Chapter 18, Part I, "The Chinese Communist Party's Global Ambitions," *Epoch Times*, June 3, 2018, https://www.theepochtimes.com/chapter-eighteen-the-chinese-communist-partys-global-ambitions-part-i_2814398.html.

909. Ibid.

910. Ibid.

911. Vladimir Lenin, "The Third, Communist International," in *Lenin's Collected Works,* 4th English edition, vol. 29 (Moscow: Progress Publishers, 1972), 240–241, Marxists Internet Archive, accessed on May 4, 2020, https://www.marxists.org/archive/lenin/works/1919/mar/ x04.htm.

912. G. Edward Griffin, *Fearful Master: A Second Look at the United Nations* (Appleton, WI: Western Islands, 1964), chap. 7.

913. William Z. Foster, *Toward Soviet America* (New York: Coward-McCann, 1932), chap. 5, Marxists Internet Archive, accessed on May 4, 2020, https://www.marxists.org/archive/foster/1932/toward/06.htm.

914. James Gorrie, "China's New World Order," Epoch Times, April 26, 2019, https://www.theepochtimes.com/chinas-new-world-order_2895934.html.

915. Editorial Team, *The Specter of Communism*, Chapter 18, Part I, "The Chinese Communist Party's Global Ambitions," Op cit.

916. "Commentary Two: On the Beginnings of the Chinese Communist Party," in *Nine Commentaries on the Communist Party* (New York: Broad Press Inc., 2004), http://www.ninecommentaries.com/english-2.

917. Ibid.

918. Qiao Liang 乔良 and Wang Xiangsui 王湘穗, *Chao xian zhan* 超限战 (*Unrestricted Warfare*), (Beijing: People's Liberation Army Literature and Art Press, 1999), 1, 62. (In Chinese), as cited in Editorial Team, *The Specter of Communism*, Chapter 18, Part I, "The Chinese Communist Party's Global Ambitions," Op Cit.

919. Editorial Team, *The Specter of Communism*, Chapter 18, Part I, "The Chinese Communist Party's Global Ambitions," Op Cit.

920. Annual Report to Congress: Military and Security Developments Involving the People's Republic of China, Office of the Secretary of Defense, September 2020, https://media.defense.gov/2020/Sep/01/2002488689/-1/-1/1/2020-DOD-CHINA-MILITARY-POWER-REPORT-FINAL.PDF.

921. Ibid.

922. Ibid.

923. Robert Knight, "America's Ever-Tightening Cancel Culture Makes Communists Happy," *Washington, Times*, January 17, 2021, https://www.washingtontimes.com/news/2021/jan/17/americas-ever-tightening-cancel-culture-makes-comm/.

924. Robert Spencer, "The Left Is Enjoying Its Reichstag Fire Moment," PJ Media, January 9, 2021, https://pjmedia.com/news-and-politics/robert-spencer/2021/01/09/the-left-is-enjoying-its-reichstag-fire-moment-n1327058.

925. David Rutz, "Liberal media, Big Tech increase calls to 'deprogram,' deplatform Trump supporters," Fox News, January 18, 2021, https://www.foxnews.com/media/liberal-media-members-deprogramming-deplatforming-trump-supporters.

926. Tom Ozimek and Jan Jekielek, "Dennis Prager: Capitol Siege Was 'Vile' but Left's Suppression of Free Speech Is Worse 'The left in the United States is totalitarian,'" *Epoch Times*, January 13, 2021, https://

www.theepochtimes.com/dennis-prager-capitol-siege-was-vile-but-lefts-suppression-of-free-speech-is-worse_3655365.html.

927. Ibid.

928. Talia Kaplan, "Parler Announces It's Back Online with New Hosting Service," Fox Business, February 15, 2021, https://www.foxbusiness.com/media/parler-back-online-on-new-platform.

929. Lia Eustachewich, "What Is QAnon? What We Know About the Conspiracy Theory," *New York Post*, October 16, 2020, https://nypost.com/article/what-is-qanon-conspiracy-theory/.

930. "Coup d'etat," Cambridge Dictionary, accessed January 28, 2021, https://dictionary.cambridge.org/ja/dictionary/english/coup-d-etat.

931. Jesse Greenspan, "Starting with Napoleon, Meet Five Leaders Who Initiated Coups d'état to Rise to the Top," History, March 14, 2016, https://www.history.com/news/5-famous-coups.

932. Ibid.

933. Roger Barrier, "Is Coronavirus Ushering in the Antichrist's One-World Government?," Crosswalk, August 12, 2020, https://www.crosswalk.com/special-coverage/end-times/is-one-world-government-foreshadowing-the-rise-of-the-antichrist.html#:~:text=The%20bible%20says%20that%20the%20horned%20goat%20%28Daniel,The%20pieces%20are%20being%20put%20in%20place%20today.

934. Davey Alba, "The Baseless 'Great Reset' Conspiracy Theory Rises Again," *New York Times*, November 17, 2020, https://www.nytimes.com/live/2020/11/17/world/covid-19-coronavirus.

935. "Conspire," Webster Dictionary, accessed January 28, 2021, http://webstersdictionary1828.com/Dictionary/Conspire.

936. "When Demons Conspire to Take Over a Nation…There's Only One Option," Leohohmann.com, December 22, 2020, https://leohohmann.com/2020/12/22/when-demons-conspire-to-take-over-a-nation-theres-only-one-option/#more-5328.

937. Ibid.

938. Ibid.

939. Robert Gearty, "Fighter Pilot Says UFO He Chased in 2004 Committed 'Act of War,'" Fox News, September 14, 2020, https://www.foxnews.com/science/

fighter-pilot-says-ufo-he-chased-in-2004-committed-act-of-war.

940. Ibid.

941. Ibid.

942. Luis Elizondo, "Luis Elizondo: Why Is the Government Finally Admitting UFOs Are Real, and Why Should We Pay Attention?" Fox News, June 15, 2019, https://www.foxnews.com/opinion/luis-elizondo-admitting-ufos-real.

943. Ibid.

944. Ibid.

945. Ibid.

946. Ibid.

947. Ibid.

948. "Psychological Warfare," Fandom, accessed January 31, 2021, https://mind-control.fandom.com/en/wiki/Psychological_warfare.

949. Chad Ripperger, "Demons and the Great Reset, United States Grace Force," December 16, 2020, https://choosing-him.blogspot.com/2020/12/demons-and-great-reset.html.

950. Ibid.

951. Ibid.

952. Ibid.

953. Ibid.

954. Ibid.

955. Ibid.

956. Ibid.

957. Ibid.

958. Ibid.

959. Ibid.

960. Charles E. Bryce, "Why History Repeats Itself," StraightForward, accessed January 28, 2021, http://straightforward.org/article/why-history-repeats-itself.

961. Ibid.

962. Victor Davis Hanson, "Crazy 2020 Is Dead! Long Live Crazier 2021!," American Greatness, January 10, 2021, https://amgreatness.com/2021/01/10/crazy-2020-is-dead-long-live-crazier-2021/?utm_campaign=Newsletter&utm_medium=email&_hsmi=107418845&_hsenc=p2ANqtz--tKcdesdihL32--Nh75__OYpTqvj2rDt6vjIV64frpA

XZ1H1r12jiIT7rUmBqqqNnblsUke3Y4oe8qAuS45_9nAbqwmg&
utm_content=107418299&utm_source=hs_email.

963. A.L.L., "Life under Communism: Hell on Earth," Pro-Life
Activist's Encyclopedia, American Life League, accessed
January 28, 2021, https://www.ewtn.com/catholicism/library/
life-under-communism-hell-on-earth-9633.

964. Ibid.

965. Lenin: Selected Works. 3 volumes, 2,225 pages. Distributed in English
by Progress Publishers, 21, Zubovsky Boulevard, Moscow, as cited in
A.L.L., "Life under Communism: Hell on Earth," *Pro-Life Activist's
Encyclopedia*, American Life League, accessed January 28, 2021, Op
Cit.

966. Revolutionary Communist Party's New Programme, "The Proletariat,
Upon Seizing Power, Will Immediately Take Up the Transformation
of Society," page 78, A.L.L., "Life under Communism: Hell on Earth,"
*Pro-Life Activist's Encyclopedi*a, American Life League, accessed
January 28, 2021, Op Cit.

967. "Vladimir Ilich Lenin: 1923; to the Commissars of Education," Politics
Forum, accessed January 28, 2021, https://www.politicsforum.org/
forum/viewtopic.php?t=37557.

968. Zuzana Janosova-Den Boer, "I Survived Communism. Now,
It's Back, Veiled as 'Environmentalism,'" Stopping Socialism,
January 28, 2020, https://stoppingsocialism.com/2020/01/scientific-
communism/#:~:text=This%20almost%20always%20starts%20
with%20education%3A%20Vladimir%20Lenin,to%20impose%20
their%20ideology%20and%20promote%20socialistic%20values.

969. Spencer Fernando, "I Survived Communism—Are You Ready for Your
Turn?," spencerfernando.com, January 3, 2019, https://spencerfernando.
com/2019/01/03/i-survived-communism-are-you-ready-for-your-turn/.

970. Ibid.

971. A.L.L., "Life under Communism: Hell on Earth," Op Cit.

972. "Short Endings," *Fidelity* Magazine, June 2990, p. 23.
A.L.L., "Life under Communism: Hell on Earth," Op cit.

973. Ibid.

974. Vladimir Lenin's August 22, 1922, letter to the Politburo. Quoted in

Keston News Service, *National Catholic Register*, July 1, 1990, page 8. As cited in A.L.L., "Life under Communism: Hell on Earth," Op cit.

975. Rich Buhler, "What Has America Become by Ken Huber—Authorship Confirmed!," TruthorFiction, March 24, 2016, https://www. truthorfiction.com/america-become-ken-huber/.

976. "What Christians from Communist Countries Say about the US Today," LifeSite News, October 7, 2020, https://www.lifesitenews.com/ news/societal-changes-that-created-nazi-germany-are-already-in-place-in-america.

977. Ibid.

978. Ibid.

979. Ibid.

980. A.L.L., "Life under Communism: Hell on Earth," Op cit.

981. Ibid.

982. Fernando, Op cit.

983. Ibid.

984. "Ronald Reagan," AZQuotes, accessed January 28, 2021, https://www. azquotes.com/quote/523574.

985. Judith Acosta, "How to Prepare for a Communist Coup," *American Thinker*, July 25, 2020, https://www.americanthinker. com/articles/2020/07/how_to_prepare_for_a_communist_coup. html#ixzz6kBJrc9Kj.

986. German Lopez, "The Democratic Convention Highlighted Gun Violence. Here's What Biden Plans to Do about It," Vox, August 20, 2020, https://www.vox.com/2020/8/20/21377041/ joe-biden-gun-violence-plan-dnc-democratic-convention.

987. Caleb Parke, "Chinese Christians Jailed for Faith Memorize Bible Because Guards 'Can't Take What's Hidden in Your Heart,'" Fox News, June 17, 2019, https://www.foxnews.com/faith-values/chinese-christians-imprisoned-for-faith-memorize-bible-guards-cant-take-whats-hidden-in-your-heart.

988. Hugh Whelchel, "What Obedience Looks Like 'In the World,'" November 6, 2017, https://tifwe.org/obedience-in-the-world/.

989. R. C. Sproul, *What Is the Relationship Between Church and State?* (Reformation Trust Publishing, 2014), pp. 39–56.

990. Ibid.

991. Ibid.

992. Francis Schaeffer, "Summary of 'A Christian Manifesto,'"
Answers2ToughQuestions, November 20, 2017,
https://answers2toughquestions.com/2017/11/20/
summary-of-a-christian-manifesto-by-francis-schaeffer/.

993. "Albert Camus," Goodreads.com, accessed
January 28, 2021, https://www.goodreads.com/
quotes/51889-fiction-is-the-lie-through-which-we-tell-the-truth.